A HISTORY OF
THE UNITED STATES

A HISTORY

OF

THE UNITED STATES

BY

EDWARD CHANNING

VOLUME I

THE PLANTING OF A NATION IN THE NEW WORLD

1000–1660

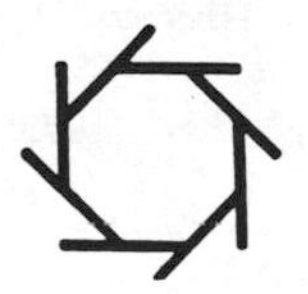

OCTAGON BOOKS

A DIVISION OF FARRAR, STRAUS AND GIROUX

New York 1977

Reprinted 1977
by arrangement with Macmillan Publishing Co., Inc.

OCTAGON BOOKS
A DIVISION OF FARRAR, STRAUS & GIROUX, INC.
19 Union Square West
New York, N.Y. 10003

Library of Congress Cataloging in Publication Data

Channing, Edward, 1856-1931.
A history of the United States.

Reprint of the ed. published by the Macmillan Co., New York.
CONTENTS: v. 1. The planting of a nation in the New World, 1000-1660.—v. 2. A century of colonial history, 1660-1760.—v. 3. The American Revolution, 1761-1789. [etc.]
1. United States—History—Colonial period, ca. 1600-1775. 2. United States—History—Revolution, 1775-1783. 3. United States—History—1783-1865. I. Title.
E188.C445 1977 973 77-8395
ISBN 0-374-91414-1

Manufactured by Braun-Brumfield, Inc.
Ann Arbor, Michigan
Printed in the United States of America

PREFACE

I HAVE undertaken a new study of the history of the United States from the discovery of America to the close of the nineteenth century. In treating the subject, the word "history" is understood in its larger sense as denoting not merely the annals of the past, but as describing the development of the American people from the inception of the colonizing enterprises which resulted in the founding of the thirteen original states and the formation of the Federal Union. The growth of the nation will, therefore, be treated as one continuous development from the political, military, institutional, industrial, and social points of view.

Writers on American history have usually regarded the colonists as living a life somewhat apart from the rest of mankind. Moreover, they have been apt to treat the founding of each colony and state as if it had been unlike the founding of other colonies and states; and they have generally traced the story of each isolated political unit from the point of view of the antiquarian. The outlook of the present work is different. I have considered the colonies as parts of the English empire, as having sprung from that political fabric, and as having simply pursued a course of institutional evolution unlike that of the branch of the English race which remained behind in the old homeland across the Atlantic. I have also thought that the most important single fact in our development has been the victory of the forces of union over those of particularism. It is essential that the forces and institutions which have made for disunion should be treated at length and in a sympathetic spirit; but it is even more necessary that the forces and institutions which have made for union should be constantly borne in mind and brought to the attention of the reader, for it is the triumph of these which has determined the fate of the nation.

The guiding idea in the present work is to view the subject as the record of an evolution, and to trace the growth of the nation from the standpoint of that which preceded rather than from that which followed. In other words, I have tried to see in the annals of the past the story of living forces, always struggling onward and upward toward that which is better and higher in human conception. It is only in this way that justice can be done to the memories of those who have gone before and have left for us a splendid heritage. They treated the problems which arose in their time by the light of the age in which they lived. To estimate them by the conditions and ideas of the present day is to give a false picture to the reader and the student.

In carrying out this purpose I have studied the original records and have also made use of the results of the researches of others; material has been drawn from the original sources for purpose of illustration. This will be found sometimes embedded in the text and at other times in the footnotes to the pages or in the longer "notes" appended to the several chapters. In these notes and footnotes will also be found the names of the leading sources and the titles of the more important secondary works. No effort has here been made to duplicate all of the information given in Justin Winsor's monumental *Narrative and Critical History of America.* The analysis and criticism contained in the present work is in the nature of the opening of the door of knowledge rather than the exhaustive exploitation of bibliography.

The task of handling the enormous mass of the material of American history is great; the time and place of one's birth and breeding affect the judgment, and the opportunity for error is frequent. It falls out, therefore, when sending this book forth to win its place, that one is irresistibly reminded of the words written by Foulkes Robartes nearly four hundred years ago: "Who faulteth not, liveth not; who mendeth faults is commended: The Printer hath faulted a little: it may be the author oversighted more. Thy pain (Reader) is the least; then err not thou most by misconstruing or sharp censuring; lest thou be more uncharitable, than either of them hath been heedless: God amend and guide us all."

CAMBRIDGE, MASSACHUSETTS,
March, 1905.

CONTENTS

MAPS

A HISTORY OF THE UNITED STATES

CHAPTER I

THE DISCOVERY OF THE NEW WORLD

RELIGIOUS enthusiasm, human affection, the pursuit of gain — these three motives account for the peopling of America by men of European stock and Christian faith. The heroism of white missionaries to the yellow races of Asia is fresh in every one's recollection; but they are only the latest of a long line of magnanimous men and women. In the nineteenth century David Livingstone, and other English Protestants, sought the scorching plains of South Africa to convert to Christianity the black men of those arid regions; in the seventeenth century Isaac Jogues, Andrew White, and other Jesuit fathers, both French and English, crossed the Atlantic to rescue the souls of North American redmen, — many of them met torture and death at the hands of those whom they came to save. In the last year of the tenth century Leif Ericsson, the Northman, sailed from Norway for Greenland to carry the blessings of Christianity to his father and his father's friends and neighbors. Falling to the southward of Cape Farewell, he came to a strange land which he named Vinland; he then turned the prow of his ship northward and gained Greenland in safety.

The first writer to mention Vinland, whose work has survived to our time, was Adam of Bremen. He wrote before 1076, and describes, in a well-known and oft-quoted passage, a conversation which he had with Svend Estridsson, King of Denmark. He says that the king spoke of an island in the ocean "which is called Vinland, for the reason that vines grow wild there which yield the best of wine. Moreover, that grain unsown grows there abundantly is not a fabulous fancy."[1] How this information came to King Svend — whether he had heard it from sagamen, or whether it was even then reduced to writing — is not now known.

The original manuscript of Adam of Bremen's book is gone. Probably the oldest account of Leif's voyage that students now can read in the original parchment is the *Codex Frisianus*, or "Friis' Book," which frequently is called the "Book of Kings." It was put together between 1260 and 1300 by a compiler who was merely placing in permanent form things that were perfectly well known at the time of the writing. This is what he says concerning Leif and his Vinland voyage: —

> "Leif, a son of Eric the Red, passed this same winter, in good repute, with King Olaf, and accepted Christianity. And that summer, when Gizur went to Iceland, King Olaf sent Leif to Greenland to proclaim Christianity there. He sailed that summer to Greenland. He found men upon a wreck at sea and succored them. Then likewise he discovered Vinland the Good, and arrived in Greenland in the autumn."[2]

The unknown writer of these lines had three things so clearly in mind that it did not seem necessary to explain them. The first of these was that Leif was sent on his

[1] Reeves's *Wineland*, 92.

[2] *Ibid.*, 14. Vinland is mentioned in earlier Icelandic writings than the *Codex Frisianus*; but the original manuscripts of these older sagas have not been found. These are the "Islendingabók," "Landnámabók," and "Kristni-saga." Extracts from these are given in Reeves's *Wineland*, 7–12.

missionary voyage by Olaf Tryggvason, King of Norway, at whose court he had accepted Christianity. Olaf was killed at the battle of Svoldr in September, 1000; Leif's voyage, therefore, must have been begun in the summer of that year at the latest. The second fact which seemed to be unquestionable to this compiler was that Leif sailed for Greenland in the same summer that Gizur sailed for Iceland — the latter voyage, other documents tell us, was made in the year 1000. From these statements it seems to be tolerably certain that Leif's expedition was in the year 1000. The third fact, which seemed to our chronicler to be beyond dispute, was that Leif visited an unknown land which he named Vinland. To this ancient author, and to many others, the existence of Leif Ericsson and of Vinland were well-established facts which needed neither description nor defense. For us this voyage rests on as good evidence as many facts of early European history which are regarded as incontestable; and we may well regard Leif Ericsson as an historic personage, and Vinland as an ascertained land.

Granting the existence of Vinland, the land which Leif visited must have been some part of America, because the voyager from Norway, missing Greenland, could have fallen in with no land except America. As to the precise whereabouts of Vinland, there has been much controversy, which is not yet closed. The arguments in this debate are based on statements contained in three Icelandic writings of a later time than the *Codex Frisianus.* These manuscripts are the "Book of Hauk," which is so called, from its maker, Hauk Erlendsson; an "Unnamed Manuscript," in the great Arna-Magnæan collection at Copenhagen, containing what is called "Eric the Red's Saga"; and the compilation that is known as the *Codex Flatoensis* or more familiarly in English as "Flatey Book."[1] These three manuscripts were all written between 1299 and 1400; but the dates which are attributed to them are of no real importance, because the statements contained in them are clearly based on earlier manuscripts which have disappeared. This is particularly true of the "Book of Hauk" and the "Unnamed Manuscript," for they are both plainly derived from the same unknown original. The story as given in these two documents is usually referred to as "Eric the Red's Saga"; the narrative of the discovery of Vinland in the *Codex Flatoensis* is generally called the "Flatey Book story." When these three accounts tell us the same thing and that story agrees with what is contained in the earlier manuscripts it seems reasonable to believe them. They are in substantial accord as to the general location of Vinland.[2]

The "Book of Hauk" and the "Unnamed Manuscript" assert that in Vinland there were fields of self-sown wheat and that grapes grew wild there in great profusion. To this description the Flatey Book story adds that in Vinland "on the shortest day of winter the sun was up between eyktarstad and dagmalastad."[3] Interpreting these statements independently and by different processes of reasoning, Arthur Middleton Reeves and Professor Gustav Storm reached almost identical conclusions. The self-sown wheat they declare to be Indian wild-rice and not Indian corn or maize with which it formerly was identified. This seems reasonable, for, when one thinks a moment, it is difficult to

[1] The Vinland portion of this codex is reproduced by photography with printed text and English and Danish translations in *Flateyjarbok, published by the Royal Danish General Staff, Topographical Department*, Copenhagen, 1893.

[2] Critical students, like Storm, Reeves, and Fischer refuse to build any theory on what they regard as the sandy foundation of Flatey Book. John Fiske and E. McK. Avery, on the other hand, accept it as good material. The account of the Vinland voyages in this codex appears to be interpolated, and, unlike other Icelandic writings, it attributes the finding of Vinland to Biarni, son of Heriulf, instead of to Leif, son of Eric.

[3] Reeves's *Wineland*, 66.

understand how a European explorer could have referred to the Indian corn of North America as wheat. Examining the accounts of Cartier's voyage and of other early explorers, and also seeking information as to present-day conditions from reputable persons, Professor Storm determined that Indian wild-rice grew and grows as far north as the fiftieth parallel. Wild grapes, on the other hand, are not found in profusion north of Nova Scotia and the Island of Orleans, which lies in the St. Lawrence River below Quebec; to it, indeed, Cartier gave the name of Island of Bacchus, because in his time it was covered with grapevines.[1] The word "dagmalastad" in the Flatey Book story Professor Storm abandoned in despair. "Eykt,"[2] however, yielded to his researches, and gave him a point between forty-nine and fifty degrees of north latitude as the extreme northern limit for Vinland. To some writers, the descriptions of this land seem to point to a more southern region, as New England; but there is a good deal of the conjectural in their arguments. Whether Nova Scotia or New England best fits the accounts in the sagas, it seems to be thoroughly established that Vinland was a part of America. To Leif, the son of Eric the Red, therefore, belongs the honor of having discovered the New World. Colonies may have been planted in Vinland by the Northmen; but if so, they proved to be only temporary. Before long, voyaging to Vinland ceased, but the memory of the land was preserved by the sagamen and their successors

[1] See below, 93. The parallelism between the accounts of Cartier's second voyage and those of the Northmen is certainly suggestive.

[2] On the meaning of "eykt," see Reeves's *Wineland*, 181–185 and Storm's *Studies*, 1–6. On self-sown wheat, see Reeves, 174, Storm, 48–50, and Fiske, i, 182. On the farthest north of the wild grape, see Storm, 43–48. Bishop Howley (Royal Society of Canada's *Transactions*, second series, iv, section ii, 77–99) places Leif's Vinland in the region of the Gulf of St. Lawrence.

who wrote the documents which we have just been studying.

The whole matter of the Vinland voyages is one of those curious academic puzzles which are chiefly interesting on account of the absurd theories that have clustered around them. The history of America would have been precisely what it has been if Leif Ericsson had never been born and if no Northman had ever steered his knǫrr[1] west of Iceland. In saying this, it is well also to add that in 1492 the Pope knew of the existence of Greenland; and that at some anterior date Christopher Columbus had visited Iceland, where he possibly heard of Greenland, and perhaps even of Vinland. It is probable that fishermen of Western Europe returning from their adventurous cruises sometimes reported that they had seen western lands. These rumors and these stories must have been known to as wide awake and inquisitive a man as Christopher Columbus. Moreover the agreement which he made with the monarchs of Spain and under which he sailed out into the west expressly states that one object of his voyage was to discover and to acquire islands and mainlands in the Ocean Sea. One land, however, we may be sure, had little interest for him, and that was Vinland, for his further task was to find a new and easy route to Cipango and the lands of the Grand Khan, — the bears and barbarians of Greenland, the grapes and skrellings of Vinland were

[1] There were two types of Norwegian boats: one was the long-ship or fighting vessel, like the boat dug up at Gokstad; the other was the round-ship or knǫrr used for carrying cargo. Leif's missionary bark was undoubtedly of the second kind. The long-ship, like the Mediterranean galley, was a coasting vessel and never willingly ventured far from land. The knǫrr, on the other hand, was propelled by sails, was partly decked at least, and had a sea endurance limited only by the skill of her commander and the amount and variety of provisions and supplies stowed in her hold. See Reeves's *Wineland*, 162, Note 12, and Corbett's *Drake and the Tudor Navy*.

not for him. He was seeking kingdoms and empires rich in silks and in spices, in gold and in silver.

The process by which the idea of a voyage to Cipango and Cathay grew in Columbus's[1] mind, until it finally took possession of his entire being, is traced in the *History of the Life and Actions* of his father, by Ferdinand Columbus, from whom Las Casas, in his *Historia*, is supposed to have borrowed the greater part of what he says on the same subject. Until within a few years, scholars were accustomed to rely implicitly on Ferdinand's work, or rather on that which goes under his name. Recently, however, Henry Harrisse has shown with a strong degree of probability that the accounts of both Ferdinand and Las Casas were derived from some common source which is now lost, and the authority of which is not now known. At the present time it is customary to state the inception of Columbus's plan somewhat as follows; those who wish to read the earlier account will find it admirably elucidated in Washington Irving's *Columbus*.

In ancient days the popular and literary conception of the shape of the earth was that it was formed on the general model of a solid wheel, with a peripheral Ocean Sea.[2] Beyond lay Mythland. Men of science, however, even in those early times, advanced very different theories. Aristotle, for instance, held that the earth was spherical[3] in form. He had observed the unvarying circularity of the earth's shadow on the moon in eclipses; he had also noted the fact that stars which are seen in Egypt are not visible in places situated farther north. Reasoning something in this wise, Aristotle felt free to write that "those who apprehend that the place about the pillars of Hercules

[1] The leading works on Columbus are enumerated in Note III, at the end of the chapter.

[2] See Note IV.

[3] Aristotle's *De Cœlo*, ch. xiv (Taylor's translation, v, 253, 257).

connects that which is about India, and thus, that there is one sea, do not appear to think very absurdly." These words were written in the fourth century before Christ.

In the next century, Eratosthenes, librarian at Alexandria, whom Bunbury calls "the parent of scientific geography," estimated the earth to be about fourteen per cent larger than it really is — a most astonishing result when one considers his data and his tools. Some idea of the credit to be attached to the making of this estimate may be derived from the fact that in 1668 the best maps then in use had an error in excess of nearly thirty-three per cent.[1] Like Aristotle, Eratosthenes, and, after him, Strabo, had no doubt of the globularity of the earth. To Eratosthenes, indeed, it was the magnitude of the Atlantic, alone, which stood in the way of a western passage from Iberia to India.[2]

This scientific theory of the shape of the earth was handed down from one scientific man to another, especially among Arabian scholars, who actively studied the old Greek philosophy when it was almost unknown in Christian lands. In the thirteenth century of our era, Roger Bacon, in his *Opus Majus*, repeated Aristotle's ideas of the proximity of Spain and India, and reënforced them by reference to Seneca's *Naturalium Quaestionem*. This paragraph of Bacon was repeated almost entire in the eighth chapter of Pierre d'Ailly's *Imago Mundi*.[3]

While Bacon was finishing his great work, Nicolo and Maffeo Polo, Venetian merchants, were returning homeward from a long and interesting visit to the redoubtable Kublai Khan of far-off Cathay. They soon left Venice

[1] Bunbury's *Ancient Geography*, i, 625, 635.

[2] Strabo's *Geography*, Introduction, ch. iv, section 6. See Note V.

[3] Purchas's *Pilgrimes* (ed. 1625), iii, 23. See Note VI.

again for the East, and this time took with them Nicolo's son, the ever memorable Marco Polo,—then a youngster of seventeen. Once in Cathay, the younger man, by his administrative capacity, won the regard of the Grand Khan, and gained for himself a place in the Chinese annals. In 1295 the three Polos were back again in Venice, busily disentangling from the seams of their tattered garments diamonds and rubies and other precious stones which they had gathered in their wanderings. Another three years went by, and Marco Polo, then a prisoner of war, dictated an account of the wondrous lands which he had visited. This work is still regarded as the greatest contribution made by any one man to the geographical knowledge of the Middle Ages. The book was first printed in 1477. In the Columbian Library at Seville there is a copy of the 1485 edition, with manuscript notes, which were probably made by Christopher Columbus; but this does not prove that in 1492 he had even seen this work, which certainly would have stirred his adventurous soul had he read it.

In *The Book of Ser Marco Polo* the Venetian traveler tells of Quinsai with its twelve thousand bridges of stone and three thousand baths of hot and cold water. Of more interest in the present discussion is the fact that Marco Polo, unlike the earlier writers, describes the eastern edge of Asia as being washed by the waters of the Ocean Sea, instead of being fringed by stupendous marshes, as was the older idea. In other words, the Golden East was accessible to sea-going ships, and not inaccessible, as had formerly been supposed. In the Ocean Sea, at some distance from the mainland, was the island kingdom of Cipango, or Chippanghu, which we call Japan.[1] Marco Polo did not

[1] *The Book of Ser Marco Polo, the Venetian, concerning the Kingdoms and Marvels of the East.* Translated and edited with notes by Colonel Henry Yule,

visit Cipango, for the Cipangoans discouraged visitors, but he relates at second hand stories of its white inhabitants, who possessed endless gold and were partly civilized. The palace of the king of this treasure island was described as roofed with gold, as churches in Europe were covered with lead, and its public rooms and chambers were paved with slabs of gold two fingers thick.[1] The floor of one of its reception rooms might well have comprised treasure enough to ransom half the kings of Christendom, — and it could be reached by sea! The Polos were not the only travelers to visit eastern Asia. Many others, missionaries and merchants, journeyed to India and Cathay. Returning safely home, they recounted their goings and comings in the cloisters of the lonely monasteries and on the quays of the busy seaports.[2] In this way the idea of rich eastern lands became the common property of Mediterranean scholars and seamen, and were repeated by thousands of persons who had never heard of Marco Polo and had never seen his book. It is perfectly possible that in some such way, and not by the perusal of Marco Polo's book, knowledge of the eastern lands may have come to Columbus.[3]

From early times, the silks and spices of the Far East had found their way to Europe. Some of them had come by caravan across central Asia; others had pursued a more roundabout course through the Indian Ocean and the Persian Gulf. As the traffic grew in volume, more articles were added to the list, until it included not only silks and spices, but also cottons, brocades, and cashmere shawls,

2 vols., London, 1871. The third edition was revised and edited by Henri Cordier, 2 vols., London, 1903. For the description of Japan, see the original edition, ii, 199.

[1] Yule's *Marco Polo*, ii, 199.

[2] See Colonel Henry Yule's *Cathay and the Way Thither; being a Collection of Mediæval Notices of China* (Hakluyt Society Series). London, 1866.

[3] It should be noted, however, that E. G. Bourne in his *Spain in America*, 10–15, states without qualification the influence of Marco Polo.

drugs and indigo, amber, pearls, diamonds, and other precious stones. This commerce was at its highest point in the fourteenth century. Then came the fall of the Mogul dynasty of Cathay. Their successors closed China to the outside world for centuries. In 1453 the Turks conquered Constantinople and put an end to such trade as still existed. The finding a new route to India then became a commercial necessity.

Portuguese navigators were the earliest to seek an all-sea route to the Far East.[1] Captains drawn from the maritime races of Europe and trained under the scientific methods of Prince Henry of Portugal sailed down the western shores of Africa. In 1484 Diogo Cam passed the equator; two years later he proceeded a thousand miles farther south, and set up a stone cross on the borders of Hottentot land, which is said to be still standing. In 1486, Bartholomew Diaz, driven by a furious northerly gale, lost all trace of the African continent. When he again sighted land, it was to the west of him, in the neighborhood of Algoa Bay. Sailing southward and westward, he passed the southern end of the Dark Continent, calling that point the Cape of Storms. King John of Portugal, with a truer insight — and less personal recollection — renamed it the Cape of Good Hope. Twelve years later, in 1498, Vasco da Gama, again passing this landmark reached Calicut in India. These early Portuguese voyages[2] were none of them to American shores; but they may well be regarded in the light of a school of navigation for American voyagers. Bartholomew Columbus, the discov-

[1] Major's *Prince Henry the Navigator*; Beazley's *Prince Henry*. Vignaud (*La Lettre et la Carte de Toscanelli*, also published in English as *The Letter and Chart of Toscanelli*) maintains that the early Portuguese voyages were for general exploration and to kidnap negro slaves.

[2] Ravenstein's *Vasco da Gama*, in Hakluyt Society Series.

erer's brother, sailed with Diaz on his great voyage, and the Admiral himself may have shared the hazard and glory of one or more of these ventures, although the particular expedition in which he took part cannot be identified.[1]

With Diogo Cam on his first voyage was Martin Behaim[2] of Nuremberg. He had been a pupil of Regiomontanus, a German mathematician, whose "Ephemerides" form the earliest approach to a nautical almanac. Behaim assisted in adapting the astrolabe to the needs of the navigator. In the summer of 1492, while Columbus was sailing westward across the Sea of Darkness, Behaim in Germany completed a globe to illustrate the shape of the earth. This globe has been preserved and is one of the very few spheres which certainly date back to the period before the discovery of America.[3] Of course Columbus could not have seen this globe before he left Palos in August, 1492, nor is there the slightest reason to suppose that he ever saw it. Indeed, there is no evidence to show that Columbus and Behaim ever met. It is pleasant to think of them as making globes and charts together and talking about the various routes to India, but these thoughts are conjectures, pure and simple. This globe, nevertheless, is interesting because it represents the ideas which Columbus doubtless held as to the size of the earth and the general distribution of the land and water.

[1] In an interesting and stimulating paper Mr. C. F. Adams maintains the thesis that America would have been discovered without Columbus, as, for example, it actually was seen by Cabral in 1500; and that the Columbian discovery, coming when it did, was a curse to humanity (Massachusetts Historical Society's *Proceedings*, second series, viii, 24). It is well, perhaps, to set adverse estimates over against popular opinions as formulated by the popularizers; but both are largely speculative.

[2] There is a good article on Behaim, although now necessarily somewhat out of date, by J. G. Morris in Maryland Historical Society's *Publications* for 1855.

[3] Winsor's *Columbus*, 185–190. Behaim's globe has been often figured. The best representations are in Ghillany's *Behaim* and Ruge's *Christoph Columbus*. Less satisfactory reproductions are in Winsor's *Columbus* and Fiske's *Discovery*.

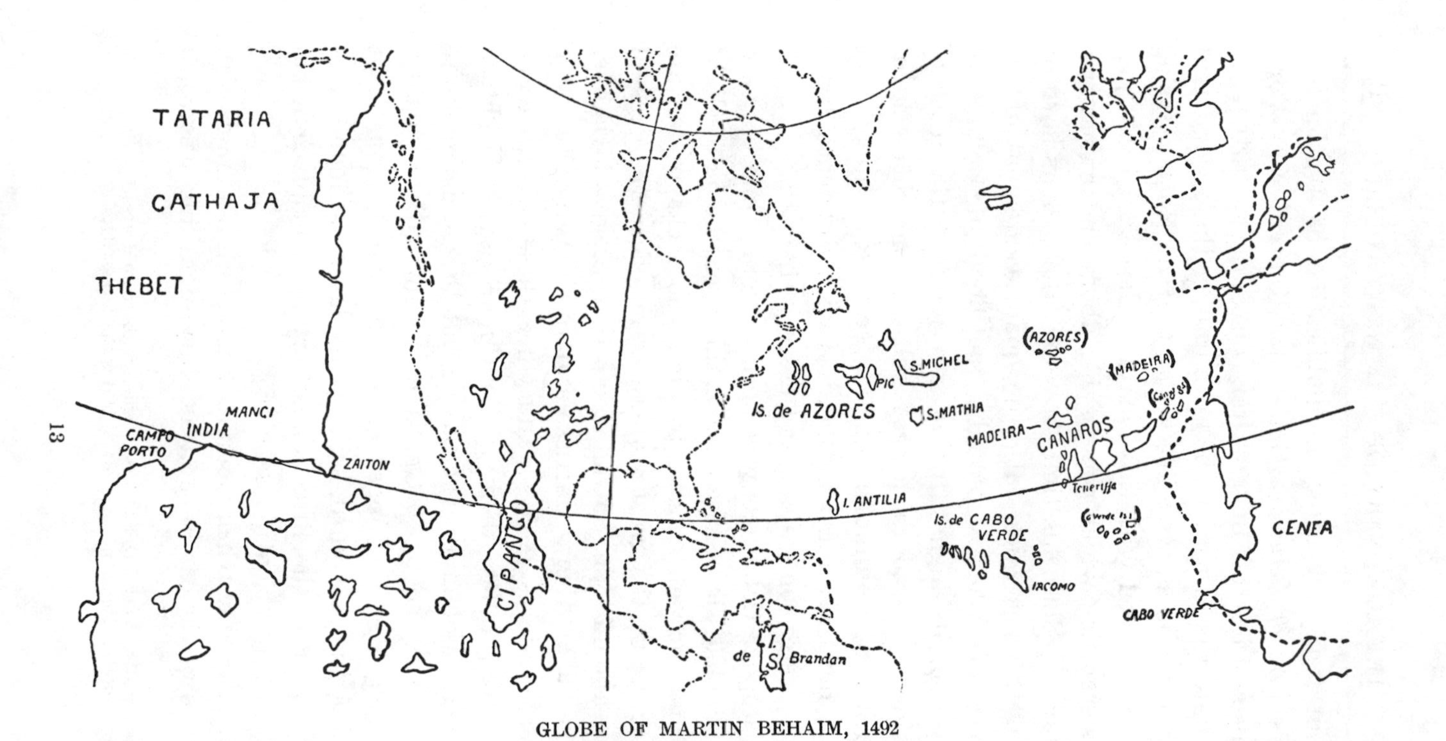

GLOBE OF MARTIN BEHAIM, 1492

(Sketched from Ruge's *Christoph Columbus.* The dotted line on right-hand side of the sketch shows the actual coast line of Europe and Africa; the dotted line in the center shows America in relation to the actual Europe; the true position of the Atlantic Islands is indicated by the names in parentheses.)

About ten years after the publication of Washington Irving's *Life of Columbus* Chancellor Kent of New York, a great admirer of that writer, discouraged further research into the career of the Admiral on the ground that his history was as well known as that of Noah. Irving thoroughly agreed with this idea and deprecated that pernicious erudition which goes prying about under the name of research. Since his time, however, the seekers have redoubled their energies, until the quadri-centennial of the discovery of America brought the flood of Columbian literature to its highest point and reduced the mass of ascertained facts to its lowest ebb. From this general dissolution of Columbian knowledge a few things still remain; but these must be handled with diffidence, lest a new discoverer come along and destroy them also.

Christopher Columbus was born at some time between 1430 and 1456, the precise date of this event being of slight importance nowadays, save to him who seeks to conjure up a picture of the great seaman as he paced the deck of his flagship off San Salvador on that pregnant October night in 1492. Henry Harrisse and Justin Winsor unite in giving the date as 1446–47, and when these two agree one may as well follow them without more ado.[1] Eighteen places claim Columbus as a native, but these scholars unite in giving that honor to Genoa or its immediate vicinity. At an early age he shipped on his first voyage, and kept on sailing the seas until, some years later, he found himself in Portugal, the fifteenth-century meeting-place of adventurous and scientific seamen.

Exactly how or when Columbus made up his mind as to the shape of the earth, the feasibility of sailing westward

[1] More recently Henry Vignaud (*The Real Birth-Date of Columbus*) has argued with some degree of success that 1451 is the correct date.

to India, and determined to do it, is not at all clear. Ferdinand Columbus, for instance, tells us that the Admiral was influenced by the works of Arab astronomers and by Ptolemy and the ancients; but whether this should be taken in more than a general sense may be doubted. Another theory is that Columbus, studying the *Imago Mundi* of Pierre d'Ailly, Bishop of Cambray, came across the old ideas which that compiler had borrowed from Roger Bacon. The first printed copy of the *Imago Mundi* was made at Louvain not before 1480; but Columbus thought that the earth was round, before that time, and there is no evidence that he ever read the Bishop of Cambray's work in manuscript. It is true that in the report of his third voyage (1498) he quoted a sentence from this book, and there still exists a copy of it with marginal notes in his handwriting, or in that of his brother, Bartholomew, for the writing of the two was much alike. But none of these things proves that he had read the work in manuscript, nor is there reason to suppose that the theories of the ancients had much, if any, direct influence upon him. If he had known of the Bishop of Cambray's book before 1492, it is most probable that he would have used it as an authority to reënforce his ideas; but there is no evidence that he did this. Another way to account for Columbus's opinions is to attribute great influence to the letters of Paolo dal Pozzo Toscanelli of Florence. Sir Clements R. Markham even goes so far as to print them as "the sailing directions of Columbus."[1] A more recent writer, Henry Vignaud, has gone to the other extreme and has denied that such letters ever existed.[2]

[1] Markham's *Journal of Columbus*, 1-11.

[2] Vignaud's *La Lettre et la Carte de Toscanelli*. An English edition, revised and enlarged, bears the title *Toscanelli and Columbus. The Letter and Chart of*

There seems no good reason to deny that Columbus received letters and a map[1] from Toscanelli, for Las Casas says that he had had them in his hand.[2] The honesty of the good bishop is beyond dispute; and there was no reason why he should prevaricate on this point. There certainly is confusion in the texts of the letters, but the main outlines are reasonably clear.[3] The Florentine astronomer repeats the stock stories of the Grand Khan and Cathay; he tells of two hundred cities with marble bridges everywhere adorned with columns. He mentions the spherical shape of the earth and writes thus as to its size: "From the City of Lisbon due west there are twenty-six spaces marked on the map, each of which has two hundred and fifty miles, as far as the most noble and very great city of Quinsay. . . . This space is almost a third part of the whole sphere. . . . But for the island Antilia, known to you, to the most noble island of Cipango there are ten spaces. . . . Thus the spaces of the sea to be crossed in the unknown parts are not great." If we knew what kind of miles Toscanelli had in mind and what he meant by the qualifying word "almost," and had confidence in the text of the letter, it would be easy to get at his idea of the size of the earth. The general opinion of those who have carefully studied the matter is that Toscanelli

Toscanelli. For an excellent notice by E. G. Bourne see *American Historical Review*, viii.

[1] The maps which Toscanelli sent to Columbus and Martinez have never been seen by recent scholars. Las Casas borrowed the Columbian replica from its custodians, which Winsor thinks may account for its disappearance. There is no map of Toscanelli's known; the only sketch that can be attributed to him is merely a projection (*Raccolta*, pt. v, vol. i, tav. viiii). The most interesting attempts to reproduce Toscanelli's ideas are in the same volume, tav. x, and in *ibid.*, pt. iv, vol. i, 116. Writers, generally, repeat the sketch made for *Das Ausland*. The reproductions merely show what their makers thought that Toscanelli probably drew. The "Ausland map" is repeated in Fiske's *Discovery*, i, 357; the second "Raccolta" sketch is in Channing's *Student's History*, 27.

[2] See Note VII.

[3] Humboldt's *Examen Critique*, i, 206 and fol.

estimated the size of the earth at about three fourths its true value.[1]

There is nothing in Toscanelli's letters which Columbus could not have obtained from other sources and doubtless already knew. What impression these communications produced on his mind at the moment of their reception cannot be stated. However great or however small that impression may have been at the time, it seems likely that Columbus, instead of carrying the letters with him in the guise of sailing directions, had forgotten all about them in the years which had elapsed between their reception and 1492; for he sailed over the place where Antilia should have been and never thought it worth while to make any mention of the fact.

Oviedo, in his *Historia General*, relates the story of a ship which was driven from her course along European coasts, visited unknown lands to the west, and returned to Europe. The pilot, or navigator, of this vessel is said to have died in Columbus's house and to have told him of the existence of the lands which he and his comrades had discovered.[2] This story, with some variations, is repeated by Las Casas and by other writers. There seems to be no reason to doubt that the idea embodied in this tale was held rather widely in the sixteenth century, and it may be true, although this is not proved. Even if Columbus had never heard such a tale, he had every reason to believe *a priori* that there were other lands between the coasts of Europe and Africa and the shores of Cipango besides the groups of islands already known and colonized, and he

[1] Winsor's *Columbus*, 123; Winsor's *America*, i, 51. There is a prolonged and learned discussion of this and kindred subjects in Vignaud's *Letter and Chart of Toscanelli.*

[2] Oviedo's *Historia General*, i, 13 (ed. 1851). See also Las Casas's *Historia*, i, 103–106 (ch. xiv). The text of this passage, with a translation, is in Thacher's *Columbus*, i, 332–335.

secured such authority to discover and conquer them as the Spanish monarchs could give.[1] Furthermore, there can be little doubt that Columbus really was in search of Cipango, Cathay, and India. In the first place, he secured letters from the Spanish monarchs to the potentates of the East. In the second place, when he reached Cuba, he dispatched messengers to seek out the Grand Khan or other Eastern princes and make known his coming. It is inconceivable that he should have taken all these pains unless he were in earnest in the announced purpose of his search.

His own mind made up, howsoever that was done, Columbus set about to secure the necessary political authorization and financial assistance. Pertinaciously his suit was pressed upon the sovereigns of Spain, France, England, and Portugal. Dissenting in all else, these monarchs were united as to the impracticability of his scheme. Finally, however, the proposed enterprise attracted the notice of four powerful personages at the court of Ferdinand and Isabella; these were the Count of Medina-Celi, a great Spanish grandee, Luis de Sant Angel, treasurer of Aragon, Father Juan Perez, once the Queen's confessor, and the Marquesa de Moya, at the moment her confidential friend. Somewhat by accident, all four suddenly united to induce Isabella to listen favorably to the Genoese adventurer.[2]

[1] These words of the commission are taken from *Christopher Columbus: his own Book of Privileges*, 42 (the Spanish and English texts are also given in Thacher's *Columbus*, i, 441): —

"Primera mente que Vuestras Altezas como Señores que son delas dichas mares oçeanas fazen dende agora al dicho Don Christoval Colon su Almirante en todas aquellas yslas e tierras firmes que por su mano e yndustria se descubriran o ganaran enlas dichas mares oçeanas."

"Firstly, that Your Highnesses, as actual Lords of the said oceans, appoint from this date the said Don Christopher Columbus to be your Admiral in all those islands and mainlands which by his activity and industry shall be discovered and acquired in the said oceans."

[2] Woodbury Lowery (*Spanish Settlements in the United States*, ch. iv) has an excellent brief description of the condition of Spain at the close of the

Irving and Prescott have painted Isabella as little removed from the angels; the German Bergenroth, and other students of the critical school, have described her in colors fitted to a fiend in the guise of a talented woman. In bigotry and duplicity she outran the standard of her time; but the student must be prepared to see and not to be misled by what is unpleasant if he wishes to penetrate deeply into the doings of the men and women of the fifteenth and sixteenth centuries. It is impossible to study Isabella's career at all carefully and not be impressed with her great capacity as a ruler of men — including Ferdinand. Probably it was her business ability which gave Columbus his opportunity. The plan accepted, the Spanish rulers proved amiable: they at once made Columbus a grandee and created him and his heirs Admiral in all the lands and islands which he or they might discover or gain in the Ocean Sea. Furthermore, he and his heirs could reserve one tenth of all the gold and silver found in these wide domains; they might contribute one eighth part of the cost of fitting out any expedition to this region and receive one eighth part of the profits from the voyage. In making this arrangement, Ferdinand and Isabella probably had slight confidence in Columbus's dreams turning into facts.

It used to be said that Isabella sacrificed her jewels to fit out the fleet; but there is no good reason to suppose that she did this. Whatever jewels she had once possessed had probably been pawned long before to provide funds for the Moorish wars.[1] The best idea is that Luis de

fifteenth century. Jean H. Mariejol's *L'Espagne sous Ferdinand et Isabelle* gives in brief form a picture of Spain at the epoch of the discovery. Kayserling's *Columbus* touches on special phases of Spanish life and gives an Hebraic cast thereto. Prescott's *Ferdinand and Isabella* retains its place as a popular recital.

[1] Duro, in *Las Joyas de Isabel la Católica* (Madrid, 1882), says all that can be said on the subject; see also Harrisse's *Christophe Colomb*, vol. i, and Kayserling's *Columbus*.

Sant Angel provided the money out of his own pocket in the form of a loan to the Castilian treasury. Of the total cost of the expedition (four million maravedis[1]) Isabella provided one million one hundred and forty thousand, Columbus five hundred thousand. This latter figure is interesting as serving to bear out Harrisse's contention that Columbus was not so poverty-stricken as sometimes has been supposed. Another way to account for it, however, may be that it represented the contributions of powerful friends. The story of the fitting out of the fleet is equally vague; probably the safest as well as the easiest thing to do is to abandon all further effort to unravel it.[2]

There were three vessels in the fleet — that, happily, is certain. Two of them, the *Pinta* and the *Nina*, were caravels; the third was larger, of the carrack class. Columbus never names her, but always calls her the *Capitana* or flagship, and other writers refer to her as *La Gallega.* Ferdinand Columbus, or whoever wrote the *History of the Life and Actions* of the Admiral, alone of contemporary writers calls her *Santa Maria;* the name certainly was appropriate, as one object of the expedition was to carry Christianity to the people of the Indies. Alone of the fleet, she was decked. On the three ships were ninety persons; among them were an Englishman and an Irishman.[3] Friday, August 3, 1492, in the early morning, the fleet sailed from Palos and steered southwestwardly for the Canary Islands. There the rigs of the caravels were changed, necessary repairs were made, and wood, water,

[1] J. B. Thacher (*Christopher Columbus*, i, 490) has made some careful calculations as to what this sum represents in modern money. His conclusion is that it stands for something under $100,000 in our own conception, but the scale of living has so changed in four hundred and odd years that computations of this kind convey little meaning.

[2] See, however, Harrisse's *Christophe Colomb*, i, 364, 388.

[3] Duro's *Colón y Pinzón, Informe relativo á los pormenores de descubrimiento del Nuevo Mundo*, Madrid, 1883, 164, 165.

and fresh provisions were taken on board. The fleet then sailed forth, steering westward for Cipango, Cathay, and India: —

> "What if wise men as far back as Ptolemy,
> Judged that the earth like an orange was round,
> None of them ever said, 'Come along, follow me,
> Sail to the West and the East will be found.'"

The story of that wonderful voyage is a tale of hope long deferred. The vessels sailed from Gomera in the Canaries on September 6. At first the wind was very light; but on the 9th the breeze freshened and the vessels drove westwardly with increasing speed. At this, the "Journal" tells us "The Admiral arranged to reckon less than the number of miles run, because if the voyage was of long duration, the people would not be so terrified and disheartened." It is difficult to say what this phrase means, for the best calculations that Columbus and the pilots could make were strangely at variance with each other and with the fact. On September 19, for instance, the pilot of the *Nina* made the distance run four hundred and forty leagues; the pilot of the *Pinta* estimated it at four hundred and twenty; the pilot of the flagship, no less a man than Juan de la Cosa, "the most celebrated pilot and cartographer[1] of the time," acting under Columbus's eye, calculated the distance at four hundred leagues. On the way home from San Domingo, Columbus and the pilots were at a loss as to the identity of the first land sighted, whether it was the Azores or the coast of Portugal.[2] When the officers were so thoroughly puzzled as to their true position, what use was there in seeking to deceive the

[1] This phrase is from Harrisse's *Discovery of America*, 13 note.

[2] Thirty years later Magellan's chief pilot, the celebrated Alvo, on reaching the Philippines, was nearly fifty degrees in error as to his longitude, although he had an arrangement of "a chain at the poop" to give him the distance run.

crew? Moreover, the seamen had nearly as good means of observation as the Admiral, for he had neither log nor chronometer. He guessed the speed of the ship by watching the bubbles and the sea-wrack as they floated by. In place of a chronometer, he used a sand-glass to tell the time and complains that the seamen were often negligent in turning it when the sand had run out. One night, when the wind was contrary, Columbus found the flagship headed northeastwardly, in the direction of Spain instead of that of Cipango — for which he reprimanded the helmsman. Bearing in mind all these chances of error, the distances and courses given in the "Journal" need to be handled with great caution.

September 14, when the voyagers were eight days out from Gomera, they saw the first signs of land; after that time for nearly a month scarcely a day passed without other signs of land appearing — but the land itself was elusive. At length, on the evening of October 11, 1492, Columbus, peering into the darkness, saw a light suddenly appear and then go out, again flare up and again go out. Next morning, at two A.M., the lookout of the *Pinta* saw the gleam of a sandy beach beneath the rays of an eastern moon. The vessels at once "lay to under storm-square sails,"[1] waiting for the dawn. When daylight came the land turned out to be an island. At one place in the "Journal" it is described as "very large"; in another place it is termed "small." Columbus further states that it is "very level with very green trees and many streams of water and a very large lagoon in the middle without any mountain." He named it San Salvador, the natives

[1] This phrase is repeated from Professor Montaldo's admirable translation of the entries of the "Journal," relating to the landfall, in Murdock's *Cruise of Columbus*, 151-153. It is to be wished that the entire document might be translated with equal care.

called it Guanahani, or Guanaham, as one follows the "Journal" or Columbus's "Letter to Sant Angel." Irving, relying on a tradition which goes back only to the seventeenth century, identified San Salvador with the Cat Island of the modern map; but this identification is plainly impossible, because Cat Island has no lagoon and is the loftiest of the Bahamas. The best opinion of the present day inclines to Watling's as the island of the landfall. Harrisse dissents from this verdict and Winsor gives it no warm approval.[1] Our difficulty in identifying San Salvador with any known island, however, is small when compared with Columbus's difficulty in identifying it with any land described by Marco Polo and the other narrators of the wonders of the East.

Columbus was seeking Cipango, Mangi, Zayton, Quinsay, and the lands of the Grand Khan. The earmarks of these regions were gold, silver, silks, spices, splendid palaces, and gorgeously attired people. The Cathayans were said to be yellow and the Cipangoans were described as somewhat whiter; but the people of the new island were neither yellow nor white, but the color of the Canarians. "Nor," says Columbus, "should anything else be expected, as this island is in a line east and west from the island of Hierro in the Canaries." Instead of wearing gold-embroidered, silken robes, they were "as naked as when their mothers bore them," save where grease and paint concealed the true color of their skins. Some of them had nose-pieces

[1] Up to the present time it has been impossible to interpret the so-called "Journal" without doing violence to the text or disregarding the geography of the Bahamas and Cuba. Winsor, in his *Columbus* (214) and his *America* (ii, 52) summarizes the controversy, as does Thacher in his *Columbus* (ch. lviii). The leading extended works on the subject are Becher's *Landfall of Columbus*; G. V. Fox's "First Landing Place of Columbus" (United States Coast and Geodetic Survey's *Reports*, 1880, Appendix 18), or, in a popular form, in *Magazine of American History*, ix, 240; J. B. Murdock's "Cruise of Columbus in the Bahamas, 1492" (United States Naval Institute's *Proceedings*, No. 30, 449–486).

of gold, but there were no signs of spices anywhere. Ferdinand Columbus tells us that his father had determined beforehand to call whatever land he might discover India, because that was a name to suggest riches. The name, however, seems to have arisen naturally from the circumstances of the voyage, which was to the "region of the Indies," and was in part, at least, for the christianization of "the Indian inhabitants of the said Indies."[1] It is interesting to note, nevertheless, that Columbus dubbed these savages Indians and not Cathayans or Cipangoans.

From San Salvador, Columbus sailed by way of many smaller islands to Cuba and San Domingo. Soon after reaching the Cuban coast he felt certain that the territory of the Grand Khan could not be far away and sent two messengers to seek out the king of the land and tell him that the monarch of Castile had sent him to inquire after his health. One of the envoys was a converted Jew who knew Hebrew, Chaldee, and even some Arabic, besides the language of Spain, — there must be learned men at the courts of the kings of Zayton and Quinsay, who, he argued, could communicate in one or more of these languages. In fine, Columbus saw in the simple natives of the Antilles and their tropical surroundings, rich monarchs, countless hamlets with numberless inhabitants, great store of gold, islands "of a thousand different shapes," birds "of a thousand different kinds," and trees "so high that they seemed to touch the sky."[2] It is pitiable to compare the lands as he thought he saw them with the islands of the Antilles as we know them, and as others, to their grief, were to know them in a few short months. The expectations which he had aroused could be satisfied only by the fortunes and villainies

[1] Stevens's *Columbus's Book of Privileges*, 45.

[2] These expressions are taken from his "Letter to Sant Angel," describing the first voyage, and from the "Journal," under date of November 1 and 2, 1492.

of Cortez and Pizarro. The remainder of his own life he spent in a melancholy struggle against the fate which remorselessly overtakes the visionary who mixes the real and the wished-for in the actual everyday affairs of the world. For years all things were evil with him; his colonists rebelled; gold was won only in small quantities and with great difficulty; and island after island, peopled with naked savages, appeared where Cipango with its silken-clad princes should have been. Nature itself seemed to fight against him. On his third voyage he sailed into the estuary of the Orinoco. A seaman drawing a bucket of water over the side found it fresh, to his and the Admiral's astonishment. Here was another world and a mighty river; but whence came this great body of water? For south of India on a spherical earth in the geography known to him there was no room for a continent of size sufficient to feed so mighty a stream. Either Cuba was not an Asiatic land, or the earth was not spheroidal in shape; to Columbus it seemed easier to change the shape of the earth than to acknowledge the failure of his life-work. So he declared that the earth was not round, as Ptolemy and others had thought, but was in "the form of a pear, which is very round except where the stalk grows, at which part it is most prominent"; upon the top of the stalk he placed the earthly paradise!

Death mercifully came to him in 1506, before he realized how utter was the wreck of his hopes and his ambitions. And yet it is true to-day, as it was when Charles Kingsley wrote, that since the day when Alaric showed the road to the spoil of imperial Rome, no man has done more to change the course of human history than Christopher Columbus.

NOTES

I. General Bibliographical Note. — Justin Winsor's *Narrative and Critical History of America* is a monument of assiduous and intelligent labor. The value of the work consists mainly in the minute bibliographical information which is contained in the "Critical Essays" that are appended to the several chapters. The great mass of this information was supplied by Mr. Winsor himself; but some of his collaborators, as Mr. Charles Deane in his remarkable essay on the Cabots, strongly seconded the editor in his endeavor to open the sources of information to serious students. Only those who have themselves attempted to explore these sources, in connection with the study of any considerable number of topics, can form a just idea of the boon Mr. Winsor and his co-workers have conferred. The narrative chapters are as good as can be expected in a coöperative work. J. N. Larned's *Literature of American History* is a bibliography pure and simple. It consists of selected titles appraised with more or less care by some student of the subject treated in the book under notice, or by extracts from the better critical reviews, as the *Nation* and the *Dial*. Most of the entries relating to the subject matter of this chapter were admirably appraised by Professor E. G. Bourne. The selection of books, the arrangement of the appraisements, and the index leave much to be desired. On the whole, however, it serves its purpose of guiding librarians as to the purchase of books; but students seeking to go to the bottom of things will find Winsor's *America* a more useful guide.

Of the general works covering the field of discovery and exploration four stand somewhat apart from the rest: Humboldt's *Examen Critique*,[1] Harrisse's *Discovery of North America*, Kretschmer's *Die Entdeckung Amerikas*, and John Fiske's *Discovery of America*. Humboldt's work may almost be said to have begun the critical

[1] Alexander von Humboldt, *Examen Critique de l'histoire de la géographie du Nouveau Continent et des progrès de l'Astronomie Nautique aux quinzième et seizième siècles*. This great work was first published in folio form at Paris in 1834, as a part of a proposed series of volumes on the "Voyage aux regions Equinoxiales du Noveau Continent par Humboldt et Bonpland." An edition of the *Examen Critique* in five vols. was printed at Paris in 1836–39. A German translation by J. L. Ideler, in three vols., was published at Berlin in 1852 with the following title: *Kritische Untersuchungen . . . der geographischen Kenntnisse von der Neuen Welt*. This edition has a full index — which is entirely lacking in the French editions. The work has never been translated into English — except in parts.

study of the period of discovery; even now, after a lapse of sixty years, it is a useful and stimulating book. Harrisse, in his *Discovery of America,* brings together in one large volume the results of a lifetime of discriminating study and places them before the student in an attractive dress with many illustrations in the form of facsimiles of early maps. The cost of the volume ($27.50) greatly limits its field of usefulness. Kretschmer's book is primarily a work on the history of geography, and the early voyages are studied in that relation; but the work is so sound in its judgments and so admirably illustrated with facsimiles of maps, large and small, that no earnest student can approach this topic without frequently consulting it. Fiske's *Discovery of America* is a brilliant setting forth of the results reached by scholars at the time of its writing; but he sometimes states these results with less reserve than seemed good to those who first set them forth. The leading special works and sources will be mentioned under the several topics. The student who desires to go farther will find the way smoothed for him in Winsor's *America,* i, ii, and in Larned's *Literature,* 50–68.

II. The Northmen. — Arthur Middleton Reeves's *Finding of Wineland the Good* (London, 1890) is an indispensable work for all students of the Norse discovery of America who do not enjoy the advantage of reading the sagas in the original. This work consists of facsimiles of the documents themselves, with a printed text on the opposite page. Preceding this is a translation of practically all the sagas relating to America. The book opens with a luminous introduction and closes with an admirable series of notes. Altogether it is a remarkable piece of work and reflects great credit upon an American student whose untimely death at the threshold of his career all students of these themes must deplore. In general agreement with Reeves is Gustav Storm, in his *Studies on the Vinland Voyages* (translated from "Mémoires de la Société Royale des Antiquaires du Nord," Copenhagen, 1889). This is one of the best examples of the application of the scientific spirit to the elucidation of historical controversies. J. Fischer's *Discoveries of the Norsemen* deals especially with those discoveries in their early cartographical representation. As to the Vinland voyages, his conclusions agree with those reached by Storm and Reeves. The material which has lately been found in the Vatican archives relates, with scarcely a possible exception, to Greenland, and not to Vinland. Fischer's general conclusion is worth noting (*Dis-*

coveries, 55): "Every theory in support of a lasting colonization of Wineland has proved untenable, and most important of all, no amount of research has brought to light any Norse remains or Norse ruins."[1]

Professor Sophus Bugge of the University of Christiania has interpreted a runic inscription which was found in Norway in 1817. According to him the inscription commemorated the death of one or more persons while on a voyage to Vinland. The character of the runes takes the inscription back to an early period before 1050 and perhaps as early as 1010. Unfortunately the characters which are supposed to represent the first part of the word Vinland are obliterated in the copy of the inscription upon which Professor Bugge based his research, and the original inscription is lost. The paper[2] is in Norwegian, but a summary in French, which is appended to the original work, is reprinted in the *Proceedings* of the Massachusetts Historical Society, Second Series, xvi, 272.

III. Christopher Columbus. — The intrinsic interest of the theme and the controversies which have centered about it have resulted in a mass of matter relating to Columbus and his career. First of all in value is the great *Raccolta di Documenti e Studi,*[3] which contains the writings of Columbus, documents necessary to an understanding of his life, and admirable dissertations on interesting points and persons. These sources, with the writings of Peter Martyr,[4] the *History of the Life and Actions*[5] of Columbus which is associated with the name of

[1] Joseph Fischer, *Die Entdeckungen der Normannen in America.* Freiburg in Breisgau, 1902. An English translation by B. H. Soulsby was published at London in 1903 (*The Discoveries of the Norsemen in America*). The Bibliography of the Norse discoveries prefixed to the English edition of this work (xi–xxiv) is the most complete in existence.

[2] The full title of this brochure is *Norges Indskrifter med de yngre Runer, udgivne for det norske Kildeskriftfond; Hoenen-Runerne fra Ringerike.* Kristiania, 1902.

[3] *Raccolta di Documenti e Studi; pubblicati dalla Reale Commissione Colombiana pel quarto centenario dalla scoperta dell' America.* 14 vols. Rome, 1892–96.

[4] Peter Martyr's "Letters" give us the impression of the hour. Later he placed in finished form the more complete information, which he had then collected, in a work known as *De Orbe Novo.* The bibliography is fully set forth in Winsor's *America,* ii. The three letters written at the time of Columbus's return from his first voyage are translated in Harrisse's *Notes on Columbus,* 130–134. The first three "Decades" of the *Orbe Novo* were translated into English by Richard Eden and printed in London in 1555, and have often been reprinted.

[5] The *History of the Life and Actions of Admiral Christopher Columbus* is translated in Churchill's *Voyages,* ii, 557–688; also in Kerr's *Voyages,* ii. As to the authorship of this work, see Harrisse's *Fernand Colomb,* or his *Christophe Colomb,* or Winsor's *Columbus,* 43, where Harrisse's ideas are summarized.

Ferdinand, his son, Las Casas's *Historia de las Indias,*[1] and the matter on this subject in Oviedo[2] and Herrera,[3] will serve all except the most exacting students. It may be noted in passing that Ferdinand Columbus and Las Casas accompanied the Admiral on his fourth voyage, and that Peter Martyr gives us oftentimes the words of the explorer as he remembered to have heard them.

Henry Harrisse, in his *Christophe Colomb,*[4] has summarized the existing knowledge on the subject. He is severely critical, sometimes too much so; but the scholarly marshaling of facts compels the student's admiration. Winsor's *Columbus* reflects Harrisse's opinions, and is even more severe in dealing with the sources and with Columbus. Of the older books, Navarrete's *Coleccion*[5] is by far the most valuable. Irving's *Columbus*[6] is founded mainly upon it, and it furnished Humboldt with much of the documentary basis of his remarkable *Examen Critique.* Many and important papers have been discovered since Navarrete and Irving wrote; in their day their works were remarkable productions. The inflated rhetoric with which Irving clothed his ideas has prejudiced modern students against his book; it is only fair, therefore, to say that Irving read with care the documents known in his day, and transferred them to English prose with a degree of faithfulness which was unusual at the time. The "Critical Essay" in the second volume of Winsor's *America* is an admirable presentation of the bibliography of the subject, although now somewhat out of date.[7] Of the smaller books,

[1] Bartolomé de las Casas, *Historia de las Indias.* 5 vols. Madrid, 1875. It is stated that this work, written in the sixteenth century, could not be published sooner, owing to its sweeping condemnation of Spanish rule in the Indies.

[2] The only complete edition of Oviedo's *Historia General y Natural de las Indias* is that published by the Royal Academy of History at Madrid, 1851–55, 4 vols. It has never been translated into English.

[3] Herrera's *Historia General de las Indias* exists in several editions, the best being that of 1728. The portion relating to Columbus is little more than a repetition of what is in Las Casas. A poor English translation was printed at London in 1725.

[4] Henry Harrisse, *Christophe Colomb, son origine, sa vie, ses voyages, sa famille & ses descendants; d'après des documents inédits tirés des Archives de Gênes, de Savone, de Séville et de Madrid: études d'histoire critique.* 2 vols. Paris, 1884–85. It forms one number of Schefer and Cordier's *Recueil de Voyages et de Documents,* but may be obtained separately for about $25.

[5] Martin Fernandez de Navarrete, *Coleccion de los viages y déscubrimientos, que hicieron por mar los Españoles desde fines del siglo xv.* 5 vols. Madrid, 1825–37.

[6] Washington Irving, *Life and Voyages of Christopher Columbus.* 4 vols. New York, 1828. Fiske's one-volume edition is in many respects an improvement on the original, but most persons will prefer to use the book as Irving wrote it.

[7] Columbus's "Letter" describing his first voyage exists in more than one form;

Sir Clements R. Markham's brief biography is the best; indeed it is one of the best books on Columbus, large or small. How Columbus appears to a modern Spaniard is seen in Emilio Castelar's articles in the *Century Magazine* (New Series, xxii).

IV. Geography and Navigation before Columbus. — On the geographical knowledge of ancient days, see H. F. Tozer's *Selections from Strabo, with an Introduction on Strabo's Life and Works*, and E. H. Bunbury's *History of Ancient Geography . . . till the Fall of the Roman Empire* (2 vols., London, 1879). C. Raymond Beazeley's *Dawn of Modern Geography* (2 vols., London, 1897-1901) and the earlier portions of his *Prince Henry* (Heroes of the Nations Series) bring the story of the development of geography down to Columbian times. Kretschmer (*Die Entdeckung Amerika's*, chs. i, ii) gives an admirable summary; in *Geographische Zeitschrift*, v, 7-19, he has an article on *Die Entdeckung des Seeweges nach Ostindien.* Octave Noël, in his *Histoire du Commerce du Monde* (ii, chs. i, ii), presents some interesting matter on the art of navigation in the fifteenth century. W. H. Tillinghast's chapter in Winsor's *America* (vol. i) will satisfy most readers.

V. Strabo's Statement. — Professor Morris H. Morgan has kindly translated the passage from Strabo's *Geography* (I, 64, 65) which is referred to in the text: —

Urging still further that it is in accordance with Nature to say that the distance from the Orient to the Occident is greater,[1] he [Eratosthenes] says that it is in accordance with Nature that the inhabited Earth should be, as we have said, longer[2] from the East

but there is no vital difference between the several early editions. What is known as the "Journal" is really an abstract made by Las Casas. This writer and Ferdinand Columbus, or some one from whom they drew, used the "Journal" in a more extended form. Their books, therefore, contain some matter which is not in the "Journal" as we have it; but those who have carefully compared them all report that the abstract contains all the essential matter. Both the "Journal" and the "Letter" are printed in J. B. Thacher's *Columbus*, in the original texts and in translation. The "Letter" is also found in Major's *Select Letters* (Hakluyt Society Series), 2d ed., 1870, in the "Quaritch Reprints," and elsewhere. The "Journal" is translated in full in Samuel Kettell's *Personal Narrative of the First Voyage of Columbus to America*, Boston, 1827, and in Markham's Hakluyt Society volume entitled *Journal of Christopher Columbus during his First Voyage; and Documents relating to the Voyages of John Cabot and Gaspar Corte Real.* London, 1893. Columbian bibliography is set forth by Harrisse in his *Christophe Colomb* and by Winsor in his *America* (vol. ii), and in his *Columbus*.

[1] Greater; *i.e.* than from north to south, as the preceding chapter shows.

[2] Longer; used like greater above.

to the West;[1] . . . to use the mathematicians'[2] phrase, makes a continuous circle by uniting with itself, so that if the great size of the Atlantic Sea did not prevent, we might sail from Spain to India on the same parallel, although the remaining portion, besides the distance mentioned[3] is more than one third of the entire circle; since the parallel of Athens, on which we made in stadia the above mentioned calculation[4] of the distance from India to Spain, is less than 200,000 stadia in length. He [Eratosthenes] is therefore wrong on this point also; for this phrase about "the temperate zone wherein we are" and to which the inhabited portion of the Earth belongs, may well be used in the mathematicians' sense, but with respect to the inhabited Earth . . . ; for by this we mean the portion which we ourselves inhabit and of which we have knowledge. But it is possible that within the same temperate zone there may be two or even more inhabited earths, and particularly in the neighborhood of the circle drawn through Athens and the Atlantic Sea.

VI. Bacon's Statement.—Following are the words used by Roger Bacon (Bridges's *Opus Majus of Roger Bacon*, i, 290): "Dicit Aristoteles quod mare parvum est inter finem Hispaniae a parte occidentis et inter principium Indiae a parte orientis. Et Seneca libro quinto Naturalium dicit quod mare hoc est navigabile in paucissimis diebus, si ventus sit conveniens." It appears that Bacon must have been quoting from memory, since the passage to which he evidently referred is in the First Book and not the Fifth Book of Seneca's *Naturalium Quaestionem* as follows (Note to the above page of Bridges's *Bacon*): "Quantum enim est, quod ab ultimis litoribus Hispaniae usque ad Indos jacet? Paucissimorum dierum spatium, si navem suus ferat ventus implebit." Professor Bourne (*Essays in Historical Criticism*, 221) thinks that Seneca had no reference to a passage across the Atlantic, but had in mind an eastern way to Asia. It seems certain, however, that Columbus understood Seneca in the same sense that Bacon did, whether this was right or wrong.

VII. Toscanelli's Letter.—Following are the words of Las Casas from his *Historia*, i, 92 (edition of 1875):—

[1] In this *lacuna* there probably was the phrase meaning: the temperate zone wherein we are.

[2] This word as used here denotes scientific men.

[3] Probably the distance by land from India in the East to Spain in the West, which was treated of in the preceding chapter.

[4] In section V preceding.

Rescibida la carta de Cristóbal Colon, el dicho maestre Paulo, respondióle una carta en latin, encorporando la que habia escripto al Hernando Martinez, canónigo, la cual yo vide y tuve en mi mano vuelta de latin en romance, que decia desta manera.

Having received the letter from Christopher Columbus, the said Master Paul [Toscanelli] replied with a letter in Latin, incorporating therewith one which he had written to Hernando Martinez, Canon, which I have seen and held in my hand translated from Latin to Romance, which followeth in this form.

Then comes the Las Casas version of the Toscanelli Letter. In the passage above quoted the final clause clearly refers to the whole letter. See also p. 95 of the same volume. The sentences which are quoted above, excepting the final clause, are given in English in Thacher's *Columbus*, i, 301. Henry Vignaud, *Letters and Chart of Toscanelli* (London, 1902), p. 158, states that Las Casas lent himself to a deceit, "devised for the purpose of exalting the merit of Columbus." In the appendices to Vignaud's work and in Thacher's *Columbus* (vol. i, p. 302) will be found the Toscanelli Letters in the original texts and in translation.

CHAPTER II

THE ISOLATION OF THE NEW WORLD

THE idea of obligation to one's fatherland is of modern growth. At the end of the fifteenth century and the beginning of the sixteenth century and for years thereafter, men of skill and daring served those masters who paid them best or gave them the chance to do that which ambition stirred within them. The Genoese Columbus and the Genoese Cabot served Spain and England; the Florentine Americus Vespucius and the Portuguese Magellan served Spain; and the German Behaim sailed in the employ of the king of Portugal. Of these, John Cabot[1] was born in Genoa, was naturalized in Venice, and did the work which gave him a place in history under letters patent from Henry VII of England.

The impelling reasons for John Cabot's western voyage toward Cathay have never been satisfactorily explained. He may have talked over the project of finding an all-sea route to India with Christopher Columbus or with Bartholomew, his brother; he may have conversed with Martin Behaim when the latter was in the Portuguese service, for Cabot at one time visited Portugal; or he may, independently, have come to the conclusion that the shores of Cathay were not far distant from England, beyond Ireland. There are shadowy hints of a Cabot voyage toward the territory of the Grand Khan as early as 1490; but the usual statement is that the expedition of 1497 was the direct

[1] For the leading works on Cabot, see Note I.

outcome of the Columbian discovery. The connecting links, however, are hard to find. At all events, in May, 1497, John Cabot sailed from Bristol on his perilous quest. Small as were the resources of Columbus, the available means of the Bristol mariner were even more slender. Columbus had three vessels, Cabot had one; Columbus had ninety men, Cabot had eighteen. Yet the latter essayed to cross the Atlantic in the stormy northern latitudes, beside which the passage from the Canaries to the Antilles was child's play. Passing around the southern end of Ireland, John Cabot steered north and west and then west, until, sometime in June, 1497, he anchored his little ship off the coasts of "the territory of the Grand Khan." He saw no inhabitants; but notched trees, snares for game, and needles for making nets showed that the land was occupied by human beings. Early in the following August, he was again in Bristol. It seems to be reasonably certain that in the next year (1498) he sailed from England for the newly found land and that he never returned.[1] These few words tell almost everything that is known of John Cabot. Such as they are, these statements are based on letters written by Italians, the cosmopolitans of that age, who were then residing in England, to their friends and employers in Italy. These letters[2] being contemporaneous and "unconscious" are the best of all evidence and cannot be gainsaid.

Lost in the gloom of the Western Ocean, John Cabot almost at once passed out of the ken of mankind. As his disappearance became more and more complete, the figure

[1] Harrisse (*American Historical Review*, iii, 449) asserts that there is good reason to think that Cabot returned to England, but the evidence is scanty; see *The Cabot Roll, The Customs Roll of the Port of Bristol*, A.D. 1496–99. This shows that money was paid to the credit of John Cabot in 1499; it does not show that money was paid to him in person.

[2] They are printed more or less extensively in nearly every modern account of the Cabots.

of Sebastian, his son, loomed larger and more large. The younger Cabot became Piloto Mayor, or Chief Hydrographer to the king of Spain. After thirty-six years passed in that service, Sebastian returned to England and served as adviser to the Lords of the Admiralty. In 1557, full of years and honor, he died. At the end, he was the Nestor of seamen, uniting the age of Columbus and Vespucius with that of Willoughby and Chancellor. It was natural that sixteenth-century compilers should associate with Sebastian[1] whatever was worthy of remark clinging to the Cabot name.

Only two bits of evidence as to the Cabot voyages can be traced directly to Sebastian. In both of these statements John Cabot is said to have been the discoverer; in both Sebastian's name is coupled with that of his father. George Parker Winship most truly and justly remarks that there exists no ground upon which to base an absolute denial of the truth of these statements. The first of these bits of evidence is the inscription[2] on the portrait of Sebastian Cabot: —

> Effigies · Sebastiani Caboti
> Angli · Filii · Johānis · Caboti Vene
> Ti · Militis · Avrati · Primi · invēt
> oris · Terrae novae sub Herico VII. Angl
> lae Rege.

There is slight doubt of the authenticity of the portrait, and the inscription is generally regarded as of the same age as the painting. The original portrait once belonged

[1] Gossip told at second hand by Ramusio is largely responsible for the idea that Sebastian claimed to be the discoverer. See Ramusio's *Primo Volume, & Terza editione delle Navigationi et Viaggi* (Venice, 1563), p. 374 E. Translated in Eden's *Decades of the Newe Worlde* (London, 1555), p. 255; and often reprinted thence, as in Hakluyt's *Voyages*, ed. 1600, iii, 6.

[2] Winsor's *America*, iii, 31.

to the royal gallery at Whitehall. After adorning the breakfast room of a Scottish lord, it indirectly came into the possession of Richard Biddle of Pittsburg, Pennsylvania, and, with his library, was burned in 1845. Fortunately, he had already described it, and two copies of it had been made which are still in existence.[1] The inscription was unquestionably on the picture when Biddle acquired it; but there is no evidence that Sebastian Cabot authorized it or ever saw it. It certainly is inaccurate in that it describes Sebastian as a knight.

The second bit of evidence connecting Sebastian with the discovery is the so-called Cabot Map[2] which is preserved at Paris. On the face of this map is the declaration that "Sebastian Cabot . . . made this figure in the year . . . 1544." On the sides of the map and on the map itself are printed legends describing the countries therein depicted. On the land north of the St. Lawrence is a reference to Legend No. 8, which has been thus translated: —

> No. 8. This land was discovered by Juan Cabot, a Venetian, and by Sebastian Cabot, his son, in the year of the birth of our Saviour Jesus Christ 1494, on the 24th of June, in the morning, to which they gave the name of "first land seen" (*prima tierra vista*); and to a large island which is situated along the said land they gave the name San Juan, because it had been discovered the same day. The people of it are dressed in the skins of animals. They use in their wars bows and arrows, lances and darts, and certain clubs of wood, and slings. It is a very sterile land. There are in it many white bears, and very large stags *like horses*, and many other animals; and likewise there is infinite fish, — sturgeons, salmon, very large soles a yard in length, and many other kinds of fish, — and the greatest quantity of them is called (*baccallaos*) codfish; and likewise there are in the same land hawks black as crows, eagles, partridges, *linnets*, and many other kinds of birds of different species.

[1] Biddle's *Sebastian Cabot*, Appendix F. [2] See Note I.

It will be noticed that the date of the discovery as given in the preceding extract[1] is 1494 instead of 1497, which is the date given in the contemporaneous letters. Students are united in thinking that the 1494 was a misprint for 1497.[2] The original map, which is preserved at Paris, has only recently been fully accessible to scholars; but now the art of photography has made it possible to study with care the dubious lines and the legends which accompany it.

The landfall of the 1497 voyage has been the subject of vigorous and sometimes acrimonious controversy. Charles Deane, usually the safest of guides, thought that it was at Cape Breton Island. He based this conclusion on the fact that on the Cabot Map, stretching across the Gulf of St. Lawrence from the northerly end of that island to the southern coast of Labrador, are the words *Prima tierra vista* (first land seen). One objection to this view is the fact that the reference on the map to Legend No. 8, a translation of which has just been given, is clearly placed on Labrador and not on Nova Scotia or Cape Breton Island. Henry Harrisse, on other grounds, strenuously argues for the eastern Labrador coast; but Winship points out that the descriptions in the legends and in the contemporaneous letters forbid so high a latitude. In view of this uncertainty, it seems to be useless to seek a definite point for the landfall; it surely was north of Halifax and south of Hudson Strait.

The Cabot Map bears the date of 1544; but there are several maps which were made soon after the Cabot voyages that delineate, among other things, the English dis-

[1] Massachusetts Historical Society's *Proceedings*, Second Series, vi, 333.

[2] The date is given in Roman numerals and the conjecture has been made that the copyist in writing MDXCVII failed to join the lower angle of the V, so that it resembled two I's and was printed MDXCIIII.

coveries. The first of these maps was made by Juan de la Cosa in 1500.[1] It was painted in brilliant colors on an ox-hide and now hangs in the Arsenal at Madrid. It is the oldest map since the discovery of America which is now known. La Cosa depicted Cuba as an island. To the northward and stretching northeastwardly is a long line of seacoast, to the middle portion of which the cartographer attached English flags and stated that this region was discovered by the English. Farther to the northeast in the ocean is a land to which a Portuguese flag is affixed which records the explorations of the Corte-Reals.[2] Moreover, the coast to the south and west of the English portion is continued westward and is removed a considerable distance from Cuba; but whether this mainland represents La Cosa's attempt to combine Asiatic and Columbian coasts or states knowledge of the shores of what is now called North America cannot be determined. Another map was made a year or two later for Alberto Cantino, envoy of the Duke of Ferrara at the court of Portugal. It is a very large map, and is still in good preservation except that some portions of the edges have been sheared away. This map shows a land near Cuba and northwest of that island, which is generally recognized as the peninsula of Florida, and thence continues the coast line northward. Out in the ocean is the end of a peninsula, which seems to be Greenland, and south and west of this is the fragment of a coast line which is labelled

[1] See Note III.

[2] Harrisse in his *Les Corte-Real et leurs Voyages au Nouveau-Monde* ("Recueil de Voyages et de Documents") has treated this subject with his accustomed care and good judgment. He gives many of the documents in this work, and also in his *Jean et Sébastien Cabot*. The papers in the original Portuguese are in Bettencourt's *Descobrimentos . . . dos Portugueses* and in Do Canto's *Memoria Historica* and his *Os Corte-Reaes*. These last books were printed at St. Miguel in 1883. All these works deal generally with Portuguese expeditions to America. Dr. J. G. Kohl's account of the *Discovery of Maine*, forming volume one of the "Documentary History of the State of Maine," is still the best narrative in English. Other works, both original and secondary, are enumerated in Winsor's *America*, iv, 12–16.

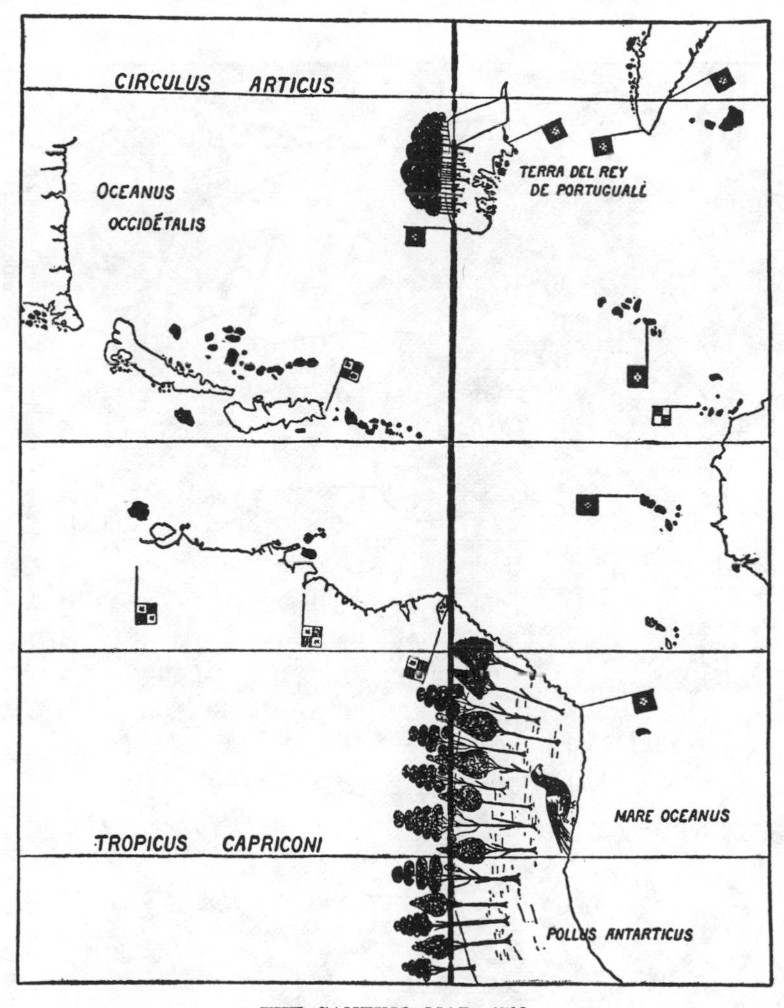

THE CANTINO MAP, 1502

(This sketch of the American part of the Cantino Map is made from the colored facsimile in Harrisse's *Corte-Reals*. Only enough of the ornamentation is shown to indicate its character; most of the names are also omitted.)

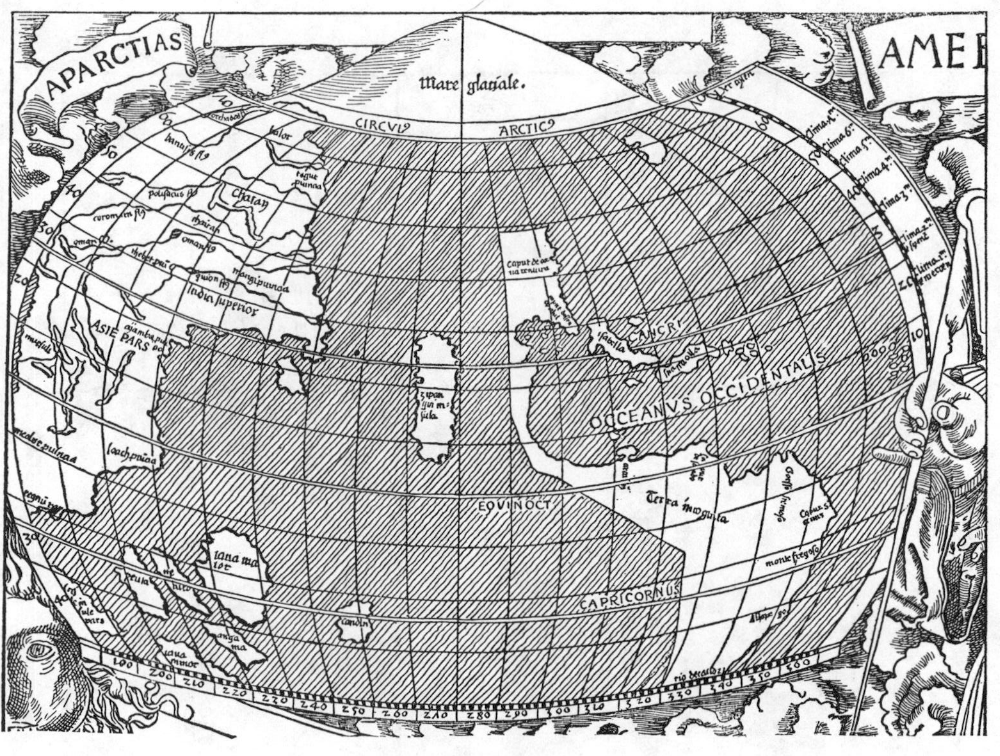

WALDSEEMÜLLER MAP, 1507

(On the main map a water space separates North and South America. This inset is one of the earliest attempts to combine the ideas embodied in maps of the Cantino type with the Ptolemaic conception of Asia.)

"Terra del Rey de Portugall." A third map was made by Martin Waldseemüller in 1507, or perhaps a little earlier. It is constructed on a peculiar projection which is known as the elongated cordiform, and which distorts the lands on the right and left borders. The map also contains the two hemispheres in the form of insets. On the main map the American lands occupy the extreme western portion; but on the inset America is shown in the center of one of the hemispheres. The maker of this map, taking the main map and the inset together, seems to have been uncertain as to whether America, which is so called here for the first time,[1] was a part of Asia or was independent. In the inset a considerable body of water lies to the west of the American continent, but the western limit of that land is so shown that this may well indicate only uncertainty in the mind of the draughtsman.[2] If the main map is tilted around so as to get Florida and Cuba in their proper positions, the delineation corresponds very closely to that of the Cantino Map. These maps are important because their makers seem to have possessed information far beyond that which any documents that have been preserved tell modern students. It has been suggested that the cartographers put in these coast lines from imagination, but it seems unlikely that they could have invented so accurate a shore, or that merely to gratify their fancy

[1] B. H. Soulsby (*Geographical Journal*, xix, 201) describes a map in the John Carter Brown Library, which shows the word "America," and is supposed to antedate by a year or so the map described above. The map of 1507 is reproduced in Fischer and Wieser's *Die Älteste Karte mit dem Namen Amerika aus dem Jahre 1507* (printed in German and in English).

[2] On the other hand an anonymous map of 1502–04, which is sometimes called the "Munich-Portuguese Map," apparently shows Cuba as a peninsula extending from Asia, and a map attributed to Bartholomew Columbus, and supposed to have been made in 1502, seems to connect "Mondo Novo" or South America with Asia. These examples of uncertainty might easily be continued, but enough has been said to show the danger of dogmatizing from these early maps. For the Columbus map, see F. R. v. Wieser's *Die Karte des Bartolomeo Colombo*.

they would have placed so many names on the principal points along these coasts.

The delineation of Cuba as an island and of Florida as a peninsula on these maps make it extremely probable that some navigator or navigators had sailed around Cuba seven years at least before Ocampo, and had visited Florida twelve years or more before Ponce de Leon; but who this navigator was is not known. The Brazilian antiquarian, Francisco Adolpho de Varnhagen,[1] asserts that the unknown visitor to the shores of what is now the United States was no less a person than Americus Vespucius. It may have been so, for no more incomprehensible and inscrutable character waylays the modern historical student than he in whose honor the New World is named. His career has been studied assiduously and interpreted variously and vigorously. On the one hand, Sir Clements R. Markham, President of the Royal Geographical Society, brands him as an impostor who fraudulently filched from Columbus the honor so richly his due. On the other hand, Varnhagen, with a childlike confidence, believes nearly everything that Americus Vespucius ever wrote or that any one has ever claimed was written by him.

Whether John Cabot shall still be regarded as the discoverer of North America, or whether that distinction should be given to Americus Vespucius, may be a matter for debate. Certain it is that it is extremely difficult to find any middle course of safety in treating the latter's career. A few things, however, may be stated with some degree of security. There certainly was a man whom we call Americus Vespucius, although in his own day he was known by names ranging from "Albericus" to "Morigo."[2]

[1] See Note IV.

[2] Winsor gives the various forms in his *America*, ii, 129, note; 179, note.

He was a Florentine who had drifted to Spain as did so many men in that century. At one period he was a merchant and may have been a "beef contractor," as Markham seeks to stigmatize him. Suddenly, in middle life, he abandoned his business career and went to sea. He made voyages of unknown number. Only one of these has been identified with any degree of certainty by scholars from the time of Columbus's friend, Las Casas, to the day of Harrisse and Markham. Probably he was with Alonso de Ojeda in 1499, because Ojeda, under oath, stated that La Cosa, Morigo Vespuche, and other pilots went with him on an expedition in that year to the northern coasts of South America.[1] The fact that Ojeda groups Morigo Vespuche with La Cosa in this statement seems to imply either that Morigo Vespuche was not the Florentine merchant and seaman or that Americus Vespucius had followed the sea for a much longer time than any one hitherto has suggested. There is no question that Americus Vespucius wrote accounts of voyages and that accounts bearing his name led directly to the christening of the New World. It is very doubtful, however, if the precise text in which Americus appears to claim the honor of being the discoverer of the *Novus Orbis* represents faithfully anything ever written by him. The last ten years of his life were passed in the service of Spain as Piloto Mayor, — another fact which tends to show that Americus Vespucius was a trained navigator. He died in 1512, full of years and fame and unmindful of the immortality which ignorance and euphony were to attach to his name.

It is useless to attempt to follow the controversies which have been fought over the career of Americus Vespucius.

[1] Navarrete's *Coleccion*, iii, 544.

There is no original manuscript of his in existence describing the voyage of 1497; and the Latin and Italian versions of some long-lost original abound in errors. Moreover, in the records of that time, so far as we know them, there is not the vaguest hint of any Spanish voyage in 1497, and Americus Vespucius, as a navigator, is almost entirely ignored. Las Casas[1] mentions him indeed, but only to hold him up to scorn. Nevertheless, it is only right to say that the lack of mention of the 1497 voyage is no proof that it was not made. Desire for the New World was on men, but only the subjects of Castile were officially permitted to gather its riches. Whoever else went there had every possible reason to conceal the fact of his going, for confiscation of his cargo and severe punishment for himself awaited such transgressions. Finally, it should be noted that the careful student of the maritime history of the years 1493 to 1512 repeatedly finds unexpected mention of authorized voyages of which he previously had no knowledge.[2]

The story of the naming of America offers less difficulty to the seeker, although it is not entirely free from thorny questions. The letters of Columbus and the news of his discovery aroused comparatively little attention, as any one can see by studying the records of that time. Those who heard of him and his doings thought of him as a seaman who had found a new route to India and had stumbled upon some islands off the Asiatic coast. Americus Vespucius appeared in an entirely different guise, for the Latin version of his third letter made him say, "I have found a

[1] Las Casas's *Historia de las Indias.* The portions commenting on Vespucius are translated by Markham in his *Letters of Amerigo Vespucci*, 68–108.

[2] For instance, Peter Martyr, writing about 1501, declares that "Cuba may be an island, for many affirm that they have sailed around it;" but the first recorded circumnavigation of Cuba is that by Ocampo in 1508. See Harrisse's *Discovery of America*, 101.

continent in that southern part; more populous and more full of animals than our Europe, or Asia, or Africa, and even more temperate and pleasant than any other region known to us." The title itself of this edition aroused expectation, for it was a New World, "Mundus Novus," that was described therein and not merely a new route to an old land, as was the burden of the Columbian song.[1] The letter in this form was printed in many editions and was widely circulated. It chanced that at St. Dié in the Vosges Mountains there was a little collegiate establishment which at one time had sheltered Pierre d'Ailly, the compiler of the "Imago Mundi." This institution had recently acquired a printing press and plans of publication were pertinaciously pushed. Among others, Mathias Ringmann, Professor of Latin, and Martin Waldseemüller, teacher of geography, had in hand a new edition of Ptolemy's Geography. While that scheme was taking shape they printed a little essay on the constitution of the universe. It was entitled *Cosmographiæ Introductio* and purported to be the work of "Hylacomylus," which was the pen name of Waldseemüller. With this essay, possibly to make the performance more sizable, were printed the Vespucian letters in the Latin version, prefaced by commendatory verses of Ringmann's. Not to be outdone by the poetical linguist, or, possibly, at his instigation, Waldseemüller suggested that the New World having been found by Americus should be named, in his honor, America. The islands which Columbus had discovered in the neighborhood of Cipango and Cathay would con-

[1] It is true that Columbus stated that on his third voyage in 1498 he had found another world, but this letter was not printed until 1508, while the Vespucian letter was widely known from 1503 on. See an admirable and brief article on "The Naming of America" by Edward G. Bourne in *American Historical Review*, x, 41.

tinue to bear the names he had given to them, while the "Mundus Novus" would properly be named for its discoverer, Americus Vespucius. More than one edition of this conglomerate work was printed in 1507, and the Vespucian-Ringmann part was also printed separately, to the subsequent delight of bibliographers. From this slight beginning the idea of naming the New World America developed, at first slowly, then more rapidly. When it became evident that not only the "Mundus Novus" was a land by itself, but that all the lands discovered by Columbus and Cabot and their contemporaries were likewise isolated from the Old World, the name America spread until it was applied to all the mainland; but the islands continued to be spoken of, for many years, as if they formed part of the Indies.[1]

Before dismissing this subject from our minds, it should in fairness be stated that no evidence has ever been brought forward to prove that Americus Vespucius instigated or acquiesced in the claim that he had discovered the New World. The Latin text of the "Third Letter" is so unlike the Italian text of the same document that we may absolve Americus from this charge until some proof of his complicity is submitted. Editors, even in our day, take strange liberties with their texts. It is possible, therefore, that the lines in the Latin text are the work of the French editor, Jean Bassin, or of some unknown translator from whose work he compiled the Latin text.

It was with Alonso de Ojeda that Americus Vespucius visited South America in 1499. With them was Juan de la Cosa, who first sailed to the Indies with Columbus in

[1] America was applied to both continents for the first time in 1541 on the Mercator Map published in that year.

1492 as master or mate of the flagship, of which he was the owner. He was chief navigator of the Admiral's fleet in 1493.[1] For years Ojeda and La Cosa together or singly explored the northern shore of South America. At length, bitten with the colonizing fever, they set forth to found a settlement in that region. Their ending was most unhappy; La Cosa, killed by a poisoned arrow, was found suspended from a limb of a tree, his body swollen to double its size in life. Poisoned arrows, indeed, made dealings with the natives of that region so dangerous that the settlers found it impossible to steal the scanty stores of food which the Indians had laid by. The provisions which the settlers had brought with them from Española soon gave out, and Ojeda sailed for the older settlements to procure fresh supplies. Shipwreck and hardships overtook him, and he disappears from history in the guise of a wandering beggar.

Aiding La Cosa and Ojeda in their enterprise was a lawyer of San Domingo named Enciso. Sailing from that island with food and recruits for the perishing settlement, he had got well away from land, when from the bunt of a rolled-up sail or from a cask — for the accounts differ — there suddenly appeared a bankrupt farmer of Española. His name was Vasco Nuñez de Balboa,[2] whom our English ancestors frequently call Blasco Nunnez, and whom we generally dignify with the name of Balboa. He had adopted this mode of escape from his creditors, for in that time even those indebted to the condemned of the

[1] Harrisse's *Discovery of America*, 711.

[2] The best account of Balboa and his doings is in Irving's *Companions of Columbus* (103, 117, 138–146), which is hardly more than a free rendering of the third volume of Navarrete's *Coleccion*. H. H. Bancroft's *Central America* (i, 289–308 and 336 note) and Arthur Helps's *Spanish Conquest in America* (i, 303–317) are excellent accounts. The sources are enumerated in Winsor's *America*, ii, 209–213.

Inquisition were hunted out and forced to pay their debts.[1] Enciso had half a mind to maroon the absconder on the first desert island that loomed above the horizon, but the supplications of the bankrupt were too much even for the lawyer's stony heart; and, unhappily for himself, Enciso took the stowaway with him. Arrived at the settlement, and cognizant of the state of affairs which prevailed in that vicinity, Balboa suggested a removal to a region farther west, to a place where the Indians did not use poisoned arrows. Enciso fell in with this plan, although it carried him outside the limits which had been assigned to him and his partners. Once arrived at the new location, which was on the Isthmus of Darien, Balboa refused obedience to Enciso and sent him to Spain to lay his complaints before the far-off Spanish monarch,[2] and requested the king to allow no more "bachillers of law" to come to the Indies, "for no bachiller has ever come here who was not a devil and who led the life of a devil." Then appeared Nicuesa, who had a regular appointment as governor of that region; him Balboa caused to be so thoroughly frightened that he sailed away in a small boat and was never heard from more. Whether Nicuesa went down in a hurricane, or starved to death, or furnished a scanty meal to some devouring Carib is one of the puzzles of the history of the time. At all events he disappeared, and Balboa expressed his opinion of these incapable rulers in a letter to the king of Spain. "They imagined," he says, "that they could rule the land and do all that was necessary from their beds. . . . But the

[1] Letter of Ferdinand to Diego Columbus, 1510, in *American Historical Review*, iii, 83.

[2] Navarrete's *Coleccion*, iii, 374. Enciso later returned to "Tierra Firme" in a minor capacity. Besides giving Balboa his opportunity, Enciso is chiefly remembered as the author of the first book relating to America printed in the Spanish language: *Suma de geografía que trata de las Indias*. Sevilla, 1519.

nature of the land is such that, if he, who has charge of the government, sleeps, he cannot awake when he wishes; for it is a land that obliges him who governs it to be very watchful,"[1] — a statement which is as true to-day as it was at the time of its writing. By incessant explorings, by firm treatment of his unruly companions, and by shrewd kindness to the natives Balboa made good his place, and procured food, gold, and information.

The most important bit of intelligence that came to Balboa was from the son of an Indian chief. Seeing the Spaniards squabbling over the scanty pickings of gold which they had gathered, he told them not to dispute over such trifles. Beyond the southward mountains was a great water whose waves washed the shores of the golden land whence this treasure had come; there, indeed, gold was so plentiful that the commonest utensils were made of it. This was not the first time that Europeans had heard rumors of the existence of a great ocean to the west. Columbus on his fourth voyage had heard them; but he had no wish to find more water, — the lands of Asia were his goal. Balboa, on the contrary, had every reason to desire by some great achievement to atone for his misdeeds and, possibly, to secure thereby the means to satisfy his creditors.

With less than two hundred men Balboa set out on his hard adventure. Strange as it may seem, the route by which he crossed the Isthmus of Darien is one of the few bits of the earth's surface now absolutely forbidden to civilized man. For two centuries and more, almost since the days of the buccaneers, the Indians of that fever-stricken and densely wooded country have refused to admit any outsider to its recesses. With Balboa it fell

[1] Translated in Markham's *Andagoya*, 5, note.

out otherwise, for after only one serious combat, the Spaniards encamped on the side of a mountain from whose crest could be seen the water of the new sea, — at least so their guide stated. The next morning with a picked band Vasco Nuñez de Balboa began the last ascent. With dramatic instinct characteristic of the man, while yet a few feet below the top of the last ridge, he halted his men. Alone on a peak of Darien, at ten o'clock in the morning of September 25, 1513, gazing southwards he saw the waters of the new sea. He named it Mar del Sur or South Sea. Of this sea, of all the islands in it, of all firm lands on its borders, he took possession for his master, the king of Spain. The water seemed to be near at hand; but the tropical wilderness between it and the mountain baffled the explorers. After four days of effort they reached the salt water. It turned out that what they had seen was not the ocean, but a large gulf which they named San Miguel, — for the patron saint of the day. Wading into the water, with banner in one hand and drawn sword in the other, Balboa again took possession of the new sea and its attendant lands. Later on the discoverers gained the shore of the ocean itself; and, that there might be no mistake, Balboa for the third time went through the ceremony of taking possession, — on each occasion the fact was properly recorded and attested by all the Christians present.

There is no hint in the old narratives that the Spanish explorers in the New World or the geographers in Europe had any conception of the true meaning of this discovery; it conveyed to them no suggestion of the continental character of America or of the tremendous expanse of water which separated America from India and Cathay. These truths were first demonstrated by Fernam Magalhaes, who exchanged his Portuguese sovereign for a Spanish one and his Portuguese name for the Spanish form of Fernan, or Fernando, Magallanes. He is known to English speakers as Magellan.[1]

It cannot be definitely stated that Magellan had any authentic information of the existence of a waterway through South America. There are the usual shadowy accounts of previous voyages to or through such a strait. Pigafetta, who was with Magellan, quotes that commander as saying that he had seen a map on which Martin Behaim had depicted such a passage.[2] Moreover there are hints of earlier voyages to Antarctic lands. Whatever these may amount to, it is reasonably certain that Magellan was the first commander to lead an expedition with the conscious design of penetrating through the American continent in southern latitudes, and thence reaching the islands off the southeastern shores of Asia.

In his earlier days and in the Portuguese service Magellan had visited the Spice Islands, and had made up his mind that some at least of them lay within the Spanish sphere of influence. Writers on this period have oftentimes ridiculed the line of demarcation which Pope Alexander authorized to be drawn. Possibly this has resulted from a misconception of what the Pope really tried to do. In those days European monarchs, all of whom still owed allegiance to the ecclesiastical organization of which the Pope was the head, acknowledged that he had some peculiar authority with regard to the distribution of land. When Columbus returned from his first voyage, therefore,

[1] See Note IV.

[2] After 1494 until his death in 1507 Behaim lived for the most part at Lisbon or Fayal ; there is nothing impossible in the suggestions which have been made of a southern voyage by him to or through Magellan Strait. Except for the statement of Pigafetta, noted above, there is no evidence to show that Behaim had exceptional knowledge of the geography of this region. See Harrisse's *Discovery of America*, 438.

the Pope authorized Ferdinand and Isabella to send out expeditions to lands "situate westwards towards the ocean," and afterwards, owing perhaps to the insistence of the king of Portugal, laid down a definite line to mark the regions beyond which the Spaniards might make voyages of discovery. It does not seem likely that he had any thought of cutting the earth in halves and assigning one half to Spain. What he wanted to do was to prevent fighting. If the earth should turn out to be round and conflicting claims should be set up on the other side, succeeding pontiffs could determine in each case as it arose which party had the better right. As a matter of fact the line was never drawn and the whole question became of little importance, as Spain absorbed Portugal in the time of Philip II. Magellan seems to have been the first man to extend this line around the world and to have argued that lands in the Antipodes belonged to the Spanish sphere of influence.[1]

Born in Portugal and bred to the maritime service, Magellan denaturalized himself and entered the service of Charles I of Spain, who figures more prominently in history as Charles V, Emperor of the Holy Roman Empire. At the moment, Spain was overflowing with Portuguese seamen, who were then playing the part which a few decades earlier had been taken by Italian navigators. No one has ever found it necessary to assail Columbus as a traitor to Genoa, nor in all the vituperation of Americus Vespucius has treason ever been attributed to him. Ma-

[1] See Henry Harrisse's *Diplomatic History of America, its first Chapter*. Professor Bourne, in his *Essays in Historical Criticism* and in the "Historical Introduction" to Blair and Robertson's *Philippine Islands*, has gone into the matter with care, and he has reviewed Harrisse's book in the *American Historical Review*, iii, 709. The bulls, treaty of Tordesillas, etc., are in the first volume of Blair and Robertson's work and in Thacher's *Columbus*, ii, pt. vi.

gellan, on the other hand, has been dubbed a traitor and reproached in the harshest language.

The story of Magellan's search for a patron and a fleet is as unlike that of Columbus as it could well be. Fonseca, Bishop of Burgos and the Admiral's old enemy, espoused the cause of the new adventurer, and Charles I himself took a personal interest in the preparations for the great voyage. Magellan sailed from Spain in the autumn of 1519. His five ships were old and rotten, and his crews were of many nationalities and varying degrees of rascality; but such seems to have been the general equipment of fifteenth-century explorers. Magellan was small in stature, and insignificant in appearance. Besides, he was a Portuguese by birth, while his chief officers were Spaniards. Before the fleet had been many months away from Spain, it was found necessary to put the men on short rations. In addition there was a feeling among both officers and men that Magellan was taking them to destruction. One result of all this was a mutiny at Port St. Julian, which Magellan put down with cold-blooded cunning and cruelty that made an end to open opposition. But the crew of one of his vessels later seized the opportunity of the absence of the flagship to return to Spain, — and they were led in their mutiny by Estevan Gomez, like Magellan, a native of Portugal. October 31, 1520, one year and one month from Spain, Magellan came to the Cape of the Eleven Thousand Virgins, which guarded the opening of the salt-water passage that still bears his name.

Proceeding cautiously westward, the strait suddenly widened out into a boundless, stormless sea, — the Mar Pacifico. Magellan steered first northward and then north-westward, boldly away from land. Day after day, week after week, month after month, ever the same monotonous progress and hunger. The food supply ran lower and lower. Soon the rats which infested the ships became a luxury fit only for the table of the rich, as they fetched half a ducat apiece. The poorer sort contented themselves with the leather which kept the spars from chafing against the masts. This they soaked in the waters of the ocean by towing it over the side, and then roasted it over the embers of a fire. Pigafetta wrote that they ate biscuit, but in truth it was biscuit no longer, but a powder full of worms, for the worms had devoured its whole substance. Had it not been for the lucky chance which led the ships to the island of Guam the explorers would scarcely have reached the Philippines. In April, 1521, Magellan lost his life in an encounter with the natives. Two of the three remaining ships never left the Pacific; in the third — the *Vittoria* or *Victoria*, as English writers translate the name — Sebastian del Cano, one of the mutineers of Port St. Julian, found his way through the Spice Islands, across the Indian Ocean, around the Cape of Good Hope, and so back to Spain. The earth had been circumnavigated, its globularity put to the test, and the theories of the ancient philosophers justified. America stood apart — between it and the Old World were two great oceans. For centuries its life was to develop on lines of its own, influenced indeed by the older civilizations but dominated by its aloofness and by its own peculiar industrial conditions.

NOTES

I. The Cabots. — Harrisse in the appendix to his *Jean et Sébastien Cabot* ("Recueil de Voyages et de Documents") prints nearly all the important evidence regarding the Cabot voyages; in his *John Cabot the Discoverer of North America* he gives a "Syllabus of the original contemporary documents"; in the second chapter of his *Découverte et Évolution Cartographique de Terre-Neuve* he summarizes the facts. Winship's *Cabot Bibliography* is a most satisfactory book because he prints abstracts or essential extracts from the documents, gives an admirable summary of the whole subject, and tells where one may go for unlimited matter. Of less scope, but of almost equal value, is Charles Deane's chapter on the Cabots in Winsor's *America,* iii. Markham prints the documents relating to the 1497 voyage in his *Journal of Columbus* (Hakluyt Society). Winsor summarized the "Cabot Controversies" in the *Proceedings* of the Massachusetts Historical Society for 1896. S. E. Dawson's *The Voyages of the Cabots* and other papers, C. R. Beazeley's *John and Sebastian Cabot,* and G. E. Weare's *Cabot's Discovery of North America* weave most of the evidence into their narratives. These are reviewed at length by Winship in the *American Historical Review,* iv, 559. H. P. Biggar (*Revue Hispanique,* vol. x) has shed some light on a few obscure details.

Charles Deane secured thirteen photographs of the Cabot Map in the size of the original. One of these was given to the custodians of the map; the others were distributed among the leading libraries and collectors of Americana. Smaller representations of it abound: that in Brymner's *Dominion Archives* (for 1897) is large enough for most purposes. Harrisse (*Jean et Sébastian Cabot*) reproduces the colors of the original.

The legends for a long time puzzled scholars. That relating to America is at the lower left-hand corner of the map. Until the map was photographed it had to be studied on one's knees by the light of a candle. The legends are now accessible and have been often printed in the original and in translation, the first time in the *Proceedings* of the Massachusetts Historical Society (1891, 312–339), whence they are copied in the *Dominion Archives,* as above.

II. Americus Vespucius. — Sir Clements R. Markham in his *Letters of Amerigo Vespucci* (Hakluyt Society, 1894) prints translations of the Vespucian letters and the condemnatory passages from Las Casas's *Historia.* More satisfactory texts are to be found in Quaritch's *The First Four Voyages of Amerigo Vespucci,* which contains the Florentine text of 1505–6 in facsimile besides translations. F. A. de Varnhagen, in his *Amerigo Vespucci, son caractère, ses écrits (même les moins authentiques), sa vie, et ses navigations,* Lima, 1865 (for a list of Varnhagen's writings, see Winsor's *America,* ii, 156, note), argues strongly for Vespucius; his views are set forth in English by Fiske (*Discovery of America,* i) and J. B. Thacher in his *Continent of America, its discovery and its baptism.* The other side of the matter is elucidated by Santarem (*Recherches sur Améric Vespuce,* Paris, 1842) whose work has been translated by E. V. Childe as *Researches respecting Americus Vespucius, and his Voyages.* Henry Harrisse in a volume entitled *Americus Vespucius: a Critical and Documentary Review of Two recent English Books,* — of which the first is Markham's edition of the Vespucian letters, — adopts a judicial tone which is in wide contrast with that of the other writers on the subject. H. H. Bancroft (*Central America,* i, 99–107) and Winsor (*America,* ii, 153 and fol.) summarize the evidence. There is an extended bibliography appended to the latest edition of Bandini's *Vita di Amerigo Vespucci* (Florence, 1898).

III. **La Cosa and Cantino Maps.** — A facsimile in colors of the La Cosa Map was made by Cánovas Vallejo and Traynor (Madrid, 1892). Vascáno's *Ensayo Biográfico del Juan de la Cosa* (printed in Spanish, French, and English) was compiled to accompany and explain this facsimile. Thirty years previously Jomard had printed a facsimile in his *Monuments de la Geographie.* Facsimiles and sketches in black and white, often accompanied by explanatory text, are in many places: Harrisse's *Découverte et Évolution Cartographique de Terre-Neuve,* 18–25; Harrisse's *Discovery of America;* Ghillany's *Behaim;* Humboldt's *Examen Critique;* Stevens's *Historical and Geographical Notes,* etc. Winsor's *America* (iii, 8) contains a small facsimile of the American portion with valuable notes.

The American part of the Cantino Map is reproduced in colors and size of the original in Harrisse's *Les Corte-Real et leurs Voyages au Nouveau Monde.* The whole map is given by Stevenson in his *Maps illustrating early discovery and exploration in America, 1502–1530, reproduced by photography from the original manuscripts,* No. 1. Harrisse, in his *Discovery* and his *Terre-Neuve* (chs. vi, vii), discusses the various points of interest.

This is a good place to call attention to the great value of Parts iii, iv, and v of Harrisse's *Discovery*. These are entitled respectively "Cartographia America Vetustissima" (366–648), "Chronology of Maritime Voyages Westward, Projected, Attempted, or Accomplished" (651–700), "Biographical Notes concerning Portuguese and Spanish Pilot-Majors, Pilots, and Cartographers of the First Half of the Sixteenth Century" (704–746). If Mr. Harrisse had never done anything else for students of early American history, his name would be always kept in grateful remembrance by them.

IV. The Naming of America. — Winsor, in his *America* and his *Columbus*, has treated this subject at considerable length with abundant references. J. B. Thacher (*Continent of America*) provides nearly all that can be asked for in the way of facsimiles both of maps and of texts. Major, in his *Prince Henry the Navigator*, and his *Discoveries of Prince Henry*, traces the story somewhat fully but with a good deal of the conjectural. More or less space is given to this topic in every book on the period of discovery and in the many works on Columbus.

V. Magellan. — Pigafetta's narrative of the voyage and other papers relating thereto are printed in translation in the Hakluyt Society volume, which is inexactly entitled *First Voyage Round the World by Magellan* (London, 1874); the documents are preceded by a pompous and out-of-date introduction. Las Casas,[1] Oviedo,[2] and Herrera[3] used material which is not now accessible; but the works of the first two have not yet been translated into English. The best biography[4] of Magellan is that by F. B. G. Guillemard[5] (London, 1890).

The most interesting controversy which has arisen over Magellan is as to a previous discovery of the strait which bears his name and Magellan's knowledge thereof. The materials upon which a decision must be based — if one is given — are of the poorest. Such arguments

[1] Las Casas's *Historia de las Indias*, v, ch. cliv (also in *Documentos Inēditos para la Historia de España*, lxv).

[2] G. F. de Oviedo y Valdés's *Historia General y Natural de las Indias* (Madrid, 1851), vol. ii, 7 and fol.

[3] Antonio de Herrera's *Historia General de las Indias Occidentales*, decada ii, libro ix, chs. x–xv; decada iii, libro i, chs. iv, ix–xi.

[4] Navarrete printed a biographical sketch of Magellan in his *Opúsculos*, vol. i.

[5] Schöner's Globe of 1523, on which Magellan's track is traced, is in Henry Stevens's *Johann Schöner*; in Wieser's article in the *Sitzungsbericht* of the Vienna Academy; and on a very reduced scale in Guillemard's *Magellan*. The latter volume also contains other interesting cartographical matter relating to the voyage.

as can be made are set forth by Harrisse (*Discovery*, 484, etc.) and by Dr. F. Wieser (*Magalhâes-Strasse und Austral-Continent auf den globen des Johannes Schöner*), and see also a paper entitled "Der verschollene Globus des Johannes Schöner von 1523" in *Sitzungsberichte der Philosophisch-Historischen Classe der Kaiserlichen Akademie der Wissenschaften*, Wien, 1889 (vol. cxvii). E. S. Balch, in his *Antarctica* (Philadelphia, 1902), necessarily has something to say on the matter.

CHAPTER III

FLORIDA AND NEW MEXICO

The eastern coast of the mainland of what is now the United States had probably been seen and traced before 1502, but the first voyage to that region of which we have specific information was made by Juan Ponce de Leon in 1513. This intrepid warrior first came to the Indies with Columbus in 1493. Twenty years he passed in San Domingo and Porto Rico, kidnapping or killing Indians and gathering gold and silver. Indian tradition, assisted perchance by a desire to induce the Spaniards to seek other lands, pointed to the existence of a wonderful country to the north. Its name was Bimini. Gold abounded there, and a fountain restored to the drinker of its waters youth, more to be desired than gold and precious stones.

On Easter Sunday, 1513, Ponce de Leon [1] sighted land to the west, and running northward anchored off the site of the later town of St. Augustine. In honor of the day he called the new land Florida. Sailing southwardly along the coast, he doubled the end of the peninsula, voyaged up its western side for some distance, and returned to Porto Rico. Wherever he landed he found

[1] Modern knowledge of Ponce de Leon's voyages to Florida rests on the papers printed in the *Documentos Inéditos* and Herrera's *Historia General* (they are enumerated in Winsor's *America*, ii, 283, 284). The only satisfactory account in English is by J. G. Shea in the same volume, 232–236. On the date of the voyage, see *ibid.*, 284, note 1. William Roberts's *Account of the First Discovery . . . of Florida* (London, 1763) contains interesting maps and plans.

the natives hostile, — a fact which points irresistibly to the presence of earlier European explorers in that region. At the time Florida was supposed to be an island. When it was definitely shown that it was part of a continent, the name was extended northward and westward. For centuries it served to designate the Spanish possessions and the lands claimed by Spain north of the Gulf of Mexico and east of the Great Plains.

Three years later, in 1516, Diego Miruelo made a trading voyage along the Florida shore and Hernandez de Cordova in 1517 visited the coasts of Yucatan and Florida. In the next few years Diego Velasquez de Cuellar, Governor of Cuba, and Francisco de Garay, Governor of Jamaica, dispatched formidable expeditions to the northern and western shores of the Gulf of Mexico. The leader of one of these, Hernan Cortez, threw off obedience to his chief and conquered Mexico for himself.[1] Another, Alonzo Alvarez de Pineda, sailing along the northern edge of the Gulf of Mexico (1519), discovered a river of great size, which he called the Rio del Espiritu Santo.[2] Students usually have regarded it as the Mississippi, but recently attempts have been made to identify it with Mobile Bay.

In 1521 Ponce de Leon again sought the Florida coast. This time he had settlement in view and took with him colonists, cattle, sheep, and horses. He landed at some undefined spot; but the natives fell upon the settlers, killed and wounded many of them, including their commander, and drove them away. Ponce de Leon lived only a few weeks after reaching Havana — the second leader to whom

[1] The student of United States history will gain a sufficient knowledge of the conquest of Mexico from Prescott's brilliant work or, better, from Bernal Diaz del Castillo's *Historia Verdadera*, of which there are several translations — that by Lockhart best preserving the rugged strength of the original.

[2] See Note I.

Florida had proved fatal, for Cordova also had perished from wounds inflicted by the natives of that coast.[1]

Among the higher Spanish officials in the Indies was Lucas Vasquez de Ayllon.[2] Bitten with the desire to explore and conquer for himself, he sent Francisco Gordillo to examine the eastern Florida coast (1521). Accompanied by one of the Indian kidnapping expeditions, Gordillo reached the shore of the mainland in the neighborhood of Cape Fear (33° 30′ north latitude). Near at hand was a large river, which the explorers piously named St. John the Baptist, and then set to work capturing Indians. With ill-gotten cargoes they returned to San Domingo. Ayllon, to his honor, refused to profit by the evil deeds of his lieutenant, and ordered the Indians returned to their native shores, but whether they ever reached them is doubtful.

In 1526 Ayllon himself sailed with six hundred colonists to the northern main; among these were women, negro slaves, and one hundred horses. A settlement named San Miguel was made to the north of Cape Hatteras or Cape Trafalgar, as they called it. Eighty-three years later a Spanish navigator, who was familiar with the early charts, identified the San Miguel of Ayllon with the English Jamestown. It may have been the identical spot, for the stories of the two settlements are much alike: miasmatic fevers, sudden nipping cold, savage Indian attacks, and domestic strife were common to both. The Spaniards had the further disadvantage of having to combat an insurrection of the blacks, as well as mutiny among the whites and attacks by the natives. Within a few months Ayllon

[1] The authorities for this voyage are enumerated in Winsor's *America*, ii, 214, 284.

[2] The sources are printed in *Documentos Inéditos* (xxxiv and xxxv). See also Oviēdo's *Historia General* (libro xxxvii, ed. of 1851, vol. iii, 624–632).

was dead of fever and the expedition was a failure. Eventually some one hundred and fifty of his companions found their way back to San Domingo; the others lie in unnamed graves in our soil, or perished on the homeward voyage.

Meantime, in 1524 or 1525, Estevan Gomez,[1] that Portuguese traitor whose desertion of Magellan has already been alluded to, took it upon himself to discover a northern passage to India through the American barrier. It is certain that he made a northern voyage and found no strait; but there is nothing else about the voyage that can be stated with confidence. On what is known as the Ribero Map, Gomez is credited with having explored a considerable extent of seacoast, stretching from Delaware at least as far north as Nova Scotia. The voyage is best known, however, from the story of the "clavos" and "esclavos" first told by Peter Martyr: Gomez had sailed to India for a cargo of spices (clavos); he returned with a lot of slaves (esclavos). Some busybody, misled by his Portuguese accent, rushed off to court with the great "news" of the discovery of the northern strait. When the truth and the slaves appeared, a laugh was raised which has not yet ceased.

While Ayllon and his colonists were fighting pestilence, cold, and human depravity on the banks of the James River, Panfilo de Narvaez was busily engaged in organizing a great expedition to conquer and colonize the northern borders of the Gulf of Mexico. On learning of the rebellion of Cortez, Velasquez had sent Narvaez to Mexico to compel obedience, with the result that the unfortunate Panfilo had

[1] The evidence for this voyage is a passage in Herrera (*Historia General*, ii, 241) and the inscription on the Ribero Map. See Winsor's *America*, iv, 29. The fullest account in English is in Murphy's *Verrazzano*. But this work must be read with caution as Mr. Murphy believed that the "Verrazano Letter" was an adaptation of information derived from Gomez.

passed two years in a Mexican prison, while his men had formed a most welcome addition to Cortez' victorious army. Now, well supplied with soldiers, horses, mechanics, laborers, and priests, Narvaez set forth to conquer for himself a virgin land to which Hernan Cortez could advance no claim. In June, 1527, with five vessels and six hundred souls, he sailed from Spain for Florida.

In those days the people of Europe were united in holding that the whole earth belonged to the followers of Christ; no non-Christians had any rights to the soil or to their own bodies. As between themselves, Christian nations and kings furthermore held that the Pope could partition the non-Christian portion of the earth among the colonizing nations. A part of the earth he had assigned to the Spanish king and that monarch had parceled it out among his followers. The Spaniards were great sticklers for the appearance of legality; to make sure that everything was properly done, a document called a "Requerimiento" was drawn up and supplied to would-be conquerors. A translation of the Requerimiento issued to Narvaez is printed in Buckingham Smith's *Cabeça de Vaca*[1] and will repay a moment's examination. It recites that in behalf of Charles V and of Doña Juana, his mother, Narvaez is to make known to the natives that God had created Adam and Eve and through them the nations of the earth. All these God had placed in charge of one person, Saint Peter, who was commanded to place his seat in Rome. One of the successors of Saint Peter had given the American lands to the Spanish sovereigns. In this way Charles and Juana are the rulers of the natives of those countries. Turning to such of these as were in attendance, the reciter of this docu-

[1] Appendix III, 215. It is also in French's *Historical Collections of Louisiana and Florida*, ii, 153.

ment should say that these rulers command you to recognize the Church as mistress of the universe and to listen to what the religious men shall preach to you. "If you do this, you shall retain your women, children, and estates and shall not be required to become Christians except, when informed of the truth, you desire to be converted. If, however, you do not do this, I will subject you to obedience to the Church and their Majesties. And I will take the persons of yourselves, your wives, and your children to make slaves of, and your goods, doing you all the evil and injury that I may be able. . . . And I declare to you that the deaths and damages that arise therefrom will be your fault and not that of his Majesty, nor mine, nor these cavaliers who accompany me." The Spanish conquest of America had in it certain of the elements of the crusades, the Spaniards sincerely desiring to convert the natives to Christianity. Such of them as became converted were treated with a consideration which was somewhat foreign to the Indian policy of later settlers of the United States.

Almost from the beginning Narvaez[1] was unfortunate: at San Domingo one hundred and forty men deserted him, and in the harbor of Trinidad, Cuba, two vessels with sixty men and twenty horses went to the bottom during a fearful hurricane. At length, in the spring of 1528, Narvaez, driving before a southerly storm, made a harbor on the northern side of the Gulf of Mexico. Thinking that he was not far from the Rio Grande, the southern boundary of the present state of Texas, he landed a part of his men and set out to seek that river. In reality his port of debarkation was at the northeastern corner of the Gulf of Mexico on the coast of the modern Florida. One vessel was sent to Havana for recruits and supplies; the

[1] On the Narvaez expedition and the adventures of Cabeza de Vaca, see Note II.

other vessels he directed to sail along the shore, while the army marched on the land. This was the last that was seen of Narvaez. Years after four of his companions reached the Spanish settlements on the Pacific shore of Mexico. Their story was most interesting. From their account it appears that Narvaez, once on shore, had altered his plan. Allured by Indian stories of the wealth of the neighboring province of Apalache, he had set out to conquer an empire, with two pounds of biscuit and one half pound of bacon for each of his three hundred Spaniards. Through swamps and tangled forests the adventurers pressed on until they came to Apalache, which they conquered without trouble, as the fighting men of the place chanced to be away. Here they found some food, but no gold. For nearly a month the Spaniards remained in the village, fighting for their lives, for the warriors returned and attacked them again and again.

At length the Spaniards abandoned Apalache and sought to regain the seacoast and their fleet. Nine days of marching and fighting brought them to a place called Aute. Thence Alvar Nuñez Cabeza de Vaca, treasurer of the expedition, with horse and foot, went on in advance, and after one day's march reached salt water in the vicinity of Pensacola Bay, where the main body soon joined him. The Spaniards called the place Bahia de Caballos,[1] because there they killed and ate their horses while they were building five boats or brigantines. Iron was lacking, but they beat their stirrups and spurs into spikes. The seams of their crazy craft they caulked with palmetto fibers and resin. The rigging was made from their horses' manes and tails, and their horses' hides, with por-

[1] T. H. Lewis (*American Antiquarian*, xxii, 357) identifies Bahia de Caballos with the modern Bay Ocklockonee.

tions of their own clothing, served for sails. The skins of the horses' legs they tanned as well as they could, and used as water vessels until they rotted. With provisions, water, and men on board, the boats swam scarcely a hand's breadth above the tide. On one of the last days of September, 1528, they set sail from the Bahia de Caballos, and steered westwardly for the Rio Grande. Soon their food began to give out, and such water as remained grew putrid. At one point they passed the mouth of a great river, whose strong current poured far out into the sea; it was the Mississippi. And so in their sinking boats, starving and thirsting, they kept on toward the west.

Eight years later one of their number saw on the neck of an Indian the buckle of a sword belt, and stitched to it the nail of a horseshoe. When asked what these things were, the Indian said that they had come from heaven; that certain men with beards had come from heaven, had lanced two Indians, and had left these objects behind.[1] This was on the western Mexican seaboard. Not long afterwards the Spanish slave catchers themselves appeared and were amazed at the naked white man who spoke Spanish. He was Cabeza de Vaca. With three companions, two of them white, the third a negro from Azamor, he formed the sole remnant of Narvaez's band. The tale these men had to tell was a strange and curious one. For years they had wandered over the country between the Mississippi and the Gulf of California, from the land of the cactus on the south to the ranges of the buffalo on the north. At first they were cruelly treated, beaten, and starved by the natives. Finally they became great "medicine men," followed and obeyed by hundreds and even by thousands. They told of hunchback cows, and rumors of

[1] Smith's *Cabeza de Vaca*, 173, 236.

populous towns, with very large houses. These last were far away to the north and near lofty mountains, whence came emeralds and other precious stones,[1] as the Indians had told them. The whole story of their hardships and triumphs, as it was written out by Cabeza de Vaca, remains to this day one of the most thrilling of the Spanish narratives.

Hernando de Soto[2] is the most dramatic figure in the story of Florida. He had served his apprenticeship with the conquerors of Peru, and among that murdering, money-getting gang none was more respectable than he, and for that reason, possibly, the companionship of Francisco Pizarro and Diego Almagro was offensive. Instead of remaining in Peru and fighting for his fair share of the riches of the Incas, De Soto returned to Spain with a paltry hundred thousand ducats, and looked about for new adventures. Of the available fields for exploit, none offered greater attractions than Florida. De Soto easily obtained the necessary license to conquer and colonize that land. At this moment Cabeza de Vaca reached Spain, too late to secure the grant for himself, but in ample time to arouse curiosity by what he said and by what he forebore to say. Six hundred men were easily gathered,—the most distinguished company of would-be Indian killers and robbers that had come together on Spanish soil since 1493. Nor were the comforts of life forgotten. De Soto had with him "a steward, a gentleman usher, pages, a gentleman of the horse, a chamberlain, lackeys, and all other officers that the house of a nobleman requireth."

In May, 1539, one year after its departure from Spain, the expedition landed on the shores of Tampa Bay or the

[1] In his account Cabeza is careful to state that the Indians gave him this information. Smith's *Cabeza de Vaca*, 167.

[2] See Note III.

neighboring Charlotte Harbor.[1] Once on shore the fighting and marching began. It proved to be wearisome work, because the country was cumbered with woods and bogs, where the horses often stuck fast and fell with their riders. Soon the adventurers came upon a white man who was naked as an Indian and had almost forgotten his Spanish speech, but he managed to cry out "Sevilla" and make the sign of the cross in time to prevent their killing him. He was Juan Ortiz, who had originally come to Florida with the unlucky Narvaez, but had returned to Cuba with the fleet. Again seeking Florida, on one of the Narvaez search expeditions, he had fallen into the hands of the Indians, and for twelve years had lived amongst them as a slave. He proved to be a most useful interpreter to De Soto. Exploring, killing, and kidnaping now began in earnest and continued with scanty interruption until September, 1543, when the survivors of the expedition reached a Spanish settlement in Mexico.

In the beginning the natives bore the duplicity and brutality of the Spaniards with comparative complacency. But at the town of the "Evil Peace" the Indian slaves set upon their masters with great suddenness and vigor. Their leader knocked De Soto senseless and injured his teeth so effectively that he had to eat hash for twenty days, — so Garcilaso de la Vega, the least reliable of the chroniclers, relates. When order was restored De Soto gave some of the youngest of the vanquished rebels to those who had good chains; the others were tied to stakes and shot. From this time on the slaves were led in chains with iron collars on their necks. These equipments had been brought from Spain. Sometimes, ironed as they were, the slaves killed their guards and made for the forest, chains and all:

[1] This is T. H. Lewis's identification (*American Antiquarian*, xxii, 356).

"Those that were perceived paid for themselves, and for the rest!" Even those who smashed their chains with stones did not always escape, for De Soto had dogs with him that were early "fleshed"[1] on the Indians and were keen for their capture.

Onward the Spaniards marched at least as far as the Savannah River. They then turned westward and southward to the fortified Indian town of Mauvila on or near the bank of the Alabama River. In the early morning De Soto, with the advanced guard and the baggage, entered the village to secure porters. Suddenly an Indian chief whom they had with them as a sort of hostage slipped away. It soon became evident that thousands of armed men were concealed in the town. The Spaniards who were in the village sought immediate safety in flight, their leader falling twice or thrice before he gained a place of refuge.

Collecting his entire force, most of which had remained outside of the town, De Soto attacked in his turn. The Spaniards crushed in the gates, set fire to the houses, killed thousands of Indians, and destroyed their own baggage, which had been abandoned in the village by the carriers on the first sign of danger. On the Spanish side a score or two were killed and many were wounded.[2] Another fire and another battle at Chicaca completed the destruction of their military equipment and clothing. In the latter disaster they also lost fifty horses and four hundred hogs. The survivors set to work to make new swords and lances, and they even reclothed themselves

[1] This word is from the *Gentleman of Elvas*.

[2] The number of Indians slain is given by the *Gentleman of Elvas* at 2500, by Garcilaso de la Vega at nearly 11,000. These figures show how the story grew by lapse of time and also how little reliance can be placed on the last named author's *Historia del Adelantado, Hernando de Soto*.

with skins. When they reached the banks of the Father of Waters, De Soto and his men must have looked like a band of Robinson Crusoes.

In April, 1541, De Soto came to a great river which he named the Rio Grande, but which we know by its Indian name, Mississippi. At that point it was so wide that if a man stood still on the further bank, he could not be distinguished from a tree stump. The river was of great depth, and its rapidly flowing muddy waters bore trees and masses of timber. Crossing to the western bank, the Spaniards marched northwestward into Arkansas and then southward again. But go where they would, there was always the same unyielding country — no gold, no silver. Copper, indeed, was found in small quantities. Cloth made from the bark of trees, robes from the hides of buffaloes, and corn completed the list of commodities; but what were these to the seeker of gold?

The winter of 1541–42 seems to have been unusually severe, and the Spaniards, encamped thirty miles from the site of the present Fort Smith, suffered greatly from cold. At one time, indeed, the snow inclosed them so that they could not travel. Had not the horsemen, with their steeds, tramped out a path to the nearest forest and procured fuel, they all would have frozen to death. In the early spring of 1542 the wanderers again reached the Mississippi. De Soto, worn out with fever and disappointed hopes, took to his bed. Before he died he sent a force to the town of Nilco[1] with orders to spare no male Indian, for the chief of that place had treated him rather cavalierly. Nuño de Tovar led the soldiers; he attacked so suddenly that not

[1] Professor Lewis thinks that Nilco was not far from the site of the present Arkansas Post; in the next year he carries the wanderers to about latitude 33° and longitude 101°. See Mississippi Historical Society's *Publications*, vi, 449.

an arrow was shot at the Christians. A hundred Indians, more or less, were slain outright; many more were wounded with great wounds and suffered to escape, that the sight of them might strike terror into the rest. Some of the Spaniards, brutal and butcherlike, killed all they met, old and young alike, though they made no resistance.

With this slaughter soothing his dying hours, Hernando de Soto passed away. Furtively they buried him in a wet ditch, trampling the freshly turned earth under their horses' hoofs. When the Indians inquired for him they said that De Soto had gone to heaven for a few days and would shortly return. All was to no purpose, however, for the Indians, on passing the grave, pointed to it. In secret, therefore, the Spaniards dug up the body, heaped sand into the mantle which served as a winding sheet, carried the corpse to the middle of the river, and lowered it into the muddy waters — all with the greatest secrecy. They then held an auction of the defunct Adelantado's effects: two men slaves, two women slaves, three horses, and seven hundred hogs.

Luis de Moscoso was now joyfully acclaimed as leader, for he declared that he wished to see himself in a place where he might sleep his full sleep rather than govern a country like Florida. At first the daunted adventurers tried to march overland to Mexico, or New Spain, as it was then called. They went as far as the plains of western Texas or of Oklahoma, when Indian settlements became scanty and little food was found. Back they turned and regained the Mississippi.

In the winter of 1542–43 they built seven brigantines and rowed, drifted, or sailed down the great river for seventeen days. At first the Indians attacked them again and again. But the Spaniards soon left the thickly settled regions behind them and enjoyed their first peaceful days and nights since they had landed in Florida four years before. Leaving the mouth of the Mississippi, they steered westward and southward, and, fifty-two days later (September, 1543), entered the Panuco River. Sailing up that stream, in four days more they reached the Spanish settlement of Panuco. Presently they went to church and gave thanks to God for their miraculous escape; of the original six hundred, three hundred and eleven were still alive. When one considers all the circumstances of their journey — the dangers from malarial fevers, hostile Indians, and wild beasts, and the perils of land and sea — surely one must award to these men, cruel and merciless though they were, a meed of praise for their constancy, courage, and devotion.

Cabeza de Vaca brought to the world of civilized men the first actual information of the hunchback cows and the first reliable reports of the cities of stone to the north of New Spain, as Mexico was then called. Before his time the Spaniards had heard rumors of the existence of these cities from the Indians, and had built these stories into the fabric of European folklore. One of the most interesting of the European tales was of the flight of Seven Bishops to Antilia, where they either found or built a city each for himself.[1] These Seven Cities slowly moved westward and northward until at length they became mixed with the Seven Caves, whence the ancestors of the Mexican Indians were said to have emerged. Another story was that off the northwestern Mexican shore was the island of Ciguatan, which was inhabited by Amazons who were abundantly supplied with pearls and gold.

[1] Bandelier, in his *Contributions to Southwestern History* (1-23), has summarized available information. For older forms of these stories he refers to W. H. Tillinghast's remarkable chapter in the first volume of Winsor's *America*.

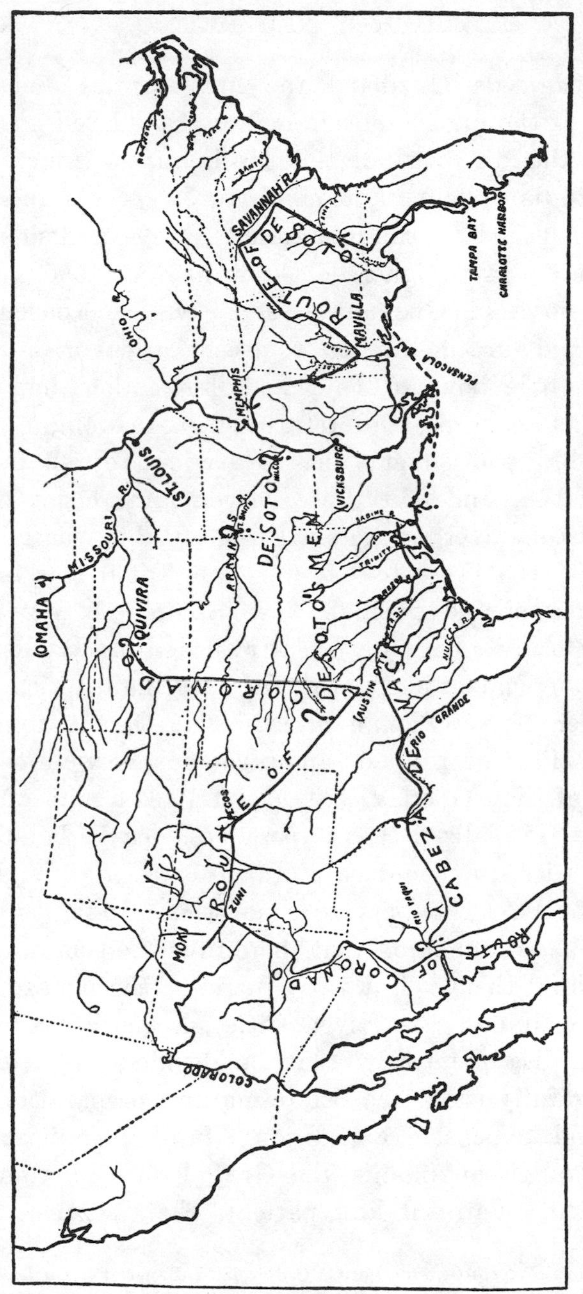

ROUTES OF SPANISH EXPLORERS

Nuño Beltran de Guzman,[1] the most brutal and least deserving of the higher officers in New Spain, led an expedition to the discovery of this land, but he found only ordinary Indian women and children, for at his approach the men had fled to the mountains. He established the settlement of San Miguel de Culiacan. In 1530 a slave named Tejo told Guzman a story which roused his cupidity and urged him on to fresh endeavor. When he was a little boy, so Tejo said, his father had gone to the back country, and returning had brought great store of gold and silver; once or twice Tejo had gone with his father and had visited seven large cities which had streets of silver workers. Probably this was not the actual story that Tejo told to Guzman, but it was in this form that it spread through New Spain. A few years passed by and Cabeza de Vaca returned to civilization with an independent account of the stone-built cities.

The ruler of New Spain in 1536 was Don Antonio de Mendoza. Patient, prudent, and sagacious, he well merited the name of the "Good Viceroy." He was a man of skill in affairs. He realized that Cabeza de Vaca had not seen the Seven Cities, but had only heard of them through the Indian reports. The persistence of these Indian stories, however, made him think that there must be something of reality behind them. But the pursuit of the Amazons, of El Dorado, and of the Seven Cities, hitherto, had been so full of disappointment that he decided to have the ground carefully examined before making preparations for a large and expensive expedition. For this mission he selected Franciscan monks, the Gray Friars, as they are often called. Faithful and patient, their services were

[1] See Oviedo's *Historia General*, libro xxxiv, ch. viii, edition of 1851, vol. iii, p. 576; H. H. Bancroft's *North Mexican States*, vol. i, ch. ii.

inexpensive and they would not kidnap Indians. How many friars started on the quest is not clear; only one, Fray Marcos de Niza, saw the first of the Seven Cities and returned to tell the tale.

Fray Marcos de Niza,[1] the Savoyard, or the Frenchman, as he is often called in the early writings, left behind him no other name; but he was a remarkable man. In Peru he had been present at the murder of Atahualpa; in Central America he had walked barefooted from Guatemala to the City of Mexico; in New Spain he had labored successfully in the conversion of the northern Indians. Before his journey to Cibola he was Vice Commissary of the Franciscans and soon after his return he became Provincial of the Order.

In the spring of 1539 Fray Marcos left the northernmost Spanish settlement on the western coast and entered the unknown regions beyond. He had with him a lay brother, who did not get very far, Cabeza de Vaca's black companion named Estevan, and an unknown number of Indians. A month later, grown weary of the negro, he ordered him to proceed in advance for fifty or sixty leagues and to report the probability of success by sending back wooden crosses. If the news which the negro gathered was of moderate importance only, he was to send back a cross the size of the palm of his hand; if the news were better, the cross might be larger. Four days later an Indian came into camp with a cross as tall as a man. With him was another Indian, who told the friar of seven large cities with houses of stone and lime, some of them four stories in height. The portals of the principal houses, he said, were ornamented with designs in turquoise. Other crosses greeted Fray Marcos as he journeyed onward. Instead of awaiting the

[1] See Note IV.

coming of his chief at the appointed distance, Estevan pushed on to the wonderful city, where he was at once murdered. Indian traditions still tell of his coming and his going; of how he related to those in the city that he was the messenger of two white men, one of whom was skilled in things of the heavens. The Indians at once made up their minds that he was a liar, for it was incredible that a black man should be the agent of two white men. They set him down for a deceiver and also found that he was greedy, without morals, and a coward. Seeking to escape, they fell upon him and killed him; if they had got hold of the white men and the attendant Indians, they would doubtless have massacred them also, — a curious slaughter of red, white, and black. At other times the prospect of death would not have deterred the Vice Commissary of the Mexican Gray Friars from fulfilling his mission to the utmost. In this case, however, his demise would have utterly defeated the purposes of his coming. He contented himself, therefore, with viewing the city from afar; and then, with more fright than food, as he himself expressed it, he took to his heels. The city that he saw in the clear light of a southwestern day had, he said, "a very fine appearance for a village, the best that I have seen in these parts. The houses, as the Indians had told me, are all of stone, built in stories, and with flat roofs. Judging by what I could see from the height, where I placed myself to observe it, the settlement is larger than the City of Mexico."

On reading the extract which has just been given, care should be taken to separate what Fray Marcos states of his own knowledge and what he says the Indians told him. He stated, for instance, that the city in the distance had a very fine appearance for a village and was larger than the City of Mexico. This was undoubtedly true; but the City of Mexico to which he referred was the Spanish village that had taken the place of the old capital of Montezuma, and preceded the modern city of the name. The explorer's report referred to gold and precious stones, but always as coming from native descriptions. It could hardly be expected that the people at the time who had no opportunity to read his report would differentiate carefully between what he had said of his own knowledge and what he narrated at second hand. At all events, they did nothing of the sort. In a short time the rumor ran throughout Mexico that Fray Marcos had discovered a city which was large enough to hold two Sevilles with room to spare. Moreover, under oath, one man declared that his son-in-law, who was a barber, had heard Fray Marcos say that "the cities [beyond the mountains] were surrounded by walls, with their gates guarded, and were very rich, having silversmiths, and that the women wore strings of gold beads and the men girdles of gold and white woolen dresses; and that they had sheep and cows and partridges and slaughterhouses and iron forges." Undoubtedly, Fray Marcos never said anything of the kind; but one of the saddest convictions that sooner or later comes to the historical student is the knowledge that men and women seldom, if ever, view events as they really are, but color them to suit the fancies of the hour. So it fell out that Fray Marcos de Niza stood in people's minds for what they wished him to have said and not for what he actually did say.[1]

[1] For more than three hundred and thirty years this man's reputation for veracity was a by-word and reproach among historians and ethnologists. Cortez declared him to be a liar, and the chroniclers of the Coronado expedition vigorously seconded the efforts of the Conqueror of Mexico to blast the monk's good name. In recent years Adolph Bandelier and Frank H. Cushing have done something to clear his reputation. But it must be said that even if the good

Mendoza at once set to work to fit out an expedition for the conquest of the Seven Cities of Cibola, and of whatever else might be worth conquering in that northern region. Every one wished to go. It soon became a question whether enough would stay behind to protect the villages and ranches of Mexico. As finally organized, the expedition numbered some three hundred horsemen and seventy foot soldiers, with a varying body of Indian allies, estimated at from three hundred to one thousand. The white soldiers were splendidly armed and the expedition was attended by a thousand horses, an immense herd of cattle and mules, and a great flock of sheep. Among the implements of war were half a dozen light swivel guns, — but there is no record of their use.

The commander of this band of cavaliers was Francisco Vasquez de Coronado,[1] governor of the northwest province of New Spain. A month's march from Compostella to Culiacan convinced him that the expedition must be divided in order to make better progress. Accordingly, with a picked band he left Culiacan for the Seven Cities early in April, 1540. The bulk of the troops and attendants would follow at a slower pace. Rough roads, scanty food for man and beast, and finally lack of water retarded the advance. Horses and Indian carriers dropped down and died, and the soldiers and servants were poisoned by eating unfamiliar herbs and fruits. But the survivors pressed on and came out of the mountainous wilderness on to the plains of southern Arizona where they were met by four Indian scouts. Coronado bid them return to their city and tell the people to remain quietly in their houses. The soldiers were now in dire need. Urging them on — for he knew

father spoke the truth himself, he did not offer all the opposition he might have made to the exaggerations spread by others and attributed to him.

[1] See Note V.

the necessity — Coronado reached the first city. Before its walls stood some of the defenders massed behind lines of meal drawn on the ground. Soldier and priest summoned them to surrender. In reply they shot an arrow through Fray Luis's robe, and grew so bold as to come up almost to the heels of the horses. At length, the priest approving, Coronado ordered the onset, and the Indians fled to their housetops. It proved to be difficult to dislodge them, for the crossbowmen and musketeers were so weak that they were scarcely able to stand on their feet — much less properly to discharge their weapons. The Indians defended their homes valiantly and well. They shot arrows at the attackers. They hurled stones down upon them. Especially they singled out Coronado, not, he tells us, because he went in advance, but because his armor was gilded and glittered. They knocked him down twice, and would have killed him but for the excellence of his headpiece. To no avail was this stout defense. The invaders gained a lodgment on the roofs and drove the defenders out. At last the Spaniards held as their own one of the Seven Cities of Cibola. The mystery was solved, the illusions were gone. And yet Fray Marcos had spoken truth. The pueblos from afar resembled a city. The storied houses were the communal dwellings of the Zuñi Indians. The jeweled portals were the hatchways, decorated with gemstones, which led from the flat roofs to the rooms below. Nowhere was there gold, nowhere was there silver.

Soon the other villages of the Zuñi valley were visited, with the same sense of disillusionment. But westward and eastward wonders of the natural world were found which astonished even the Spaniards. It was in the autumn of 1540 that Don Garcia Lopez de Cardenas and a dozen comrades gained the banks of a river which seemed to be a mile or so below them. The natives described the water course as half a league wide. From their elevated positions it appeared to be about six feet in width. For three days Don Garcia Lopez and his men sought a way to the water. At one point three of the most agile of them started to go down by a favorable-looking path. They soon disappeared. Returning, they reported that they had been down about one third way. From that point the river seemed to be very large. Rocks on the side of the chasm which from above looked nearly as high as a man, when reached by the climbers proved to be "bigger than the great tower of Seville." The Grand Cañon of the Colorado has never been more graphically described than by these first European visitors. As they could not reach the river — to say nothing of crossing it — and as water was scant on the upland, Don Garcia Lopez returned to headquarters.

Hernando de Alvarado led the eastern exploring party. He returned with no tales of yawning chasms, but he found what was even more remarkable — vast plains in which there was no chasm great or small. Alvarado also came across other cities on his way to the plains. One of these was the pueblo of Acuco (Acoma), perched on top of a rock so high that only a very good musket could throw a ball to the summit. Still another pueblo, Tiguex (Tiguesh), was much better than Cibola, and Alvarado advised the removal of the army to that place.

These things were all interesting; but Alvarado had found something much more satisfactory, for he had picked up an Indian from Florida who told him great stories of the abundance of gold and silver in that country. They called this loquacious native "The Turk" because he looked like one. With these tales in their ears they "did not care about looking for cows," but hastened back to report the welcome tidings to Coronado. Meantime the main army had pushed on from Culiacan. By the beginning of December the whole force was comfortably housed at Tiguex, one of the best of the pueblos. They were well supplied with food — both from what the natives had abandoned and from the live stock driven from New Spain.

In the winter came a serious Indian insurrection. The causes of the rebellion have been set forth by the Spanish chroniclers in exculpatory terms. The Indian version has never been told, and never will be known. But the Spanish narratives give us causes sufficient to account for many revolts. They seized the Indians' dwellings with their stores of food; they seized the natives' clothing off their very backs. Castañeda describes the scene in his rough, simple way: "Thus these people could do nothing except take off their own cloaks and give them to make up the number demanded of them. And some of the soldiers who were in these parties, when the collectors gave them blankets or cloaks which were not such as they wanted, if they saw an Indian with a better one on, they exchanged with him without more ado, not stopping to find out the rank of the man they were stripping, which caused not a little hard feeling." When the natives complained to Coronado, the offenders were not punished and the Indians rebelled.

The surrender of the first of the "rebels" was followed by a breach of faith which exasperated the natives, but with which Coronado himself had nothing to do. Some two hundred prisoners had been taken. Don Garcia Lopez, not knowing that they had surrendered on condition that their lives should be spared, ordered them to be burnt. No one cognizant of the truth told him of the conditions, "not thinking that it was any of their business," so Castañeda writes. Don Garcia ordered two hundred stakes to be made ready. But these were not all used, for when the prisoners saw the Spaniards beginning to roast their comrades, they made a wild rush for freedom. A few escaped and spread the news that the invaders did not respect the peace that they had made. The next pueblo beat off the besiegers for sixty-five days.

Meantime, while this fighting had been going on, "The Turk" had been cheering the Spaniards with stories of riches far away toward the north and east. Whenever Spanish explorers or English explorers or French explorers report Indian stories which turn out to be false, it is generally assumed that the Indian lied. But this assumption is not necessary. In the case of the southwestern Indians it is likely that they confounded gold, with which they were not familiar, with copper with which they were familiar, or with pyrites. Early English settlers made strange blunders in this regard, although they were acquainted with all three. Furthermore, the Spaniards frequently did not understand the Indians; and, finally, we have the accounts of what the natives said generally at second or third hand. Castañeda, for instance, in old age wrote down the camp gossip of 1540–41. Probably he never knew what "The Turk" really said. In the case of this particular romancer another element comes in. Just before "The Turk" was garroted and when death was plainly in sight, he confessed that he purposely had led the Spaniards to the pathless plains to perish there or to grow so weak that on their return to the pueblos they would be easily overcome.

In April, 1541, Coronado set out from Tiguex for the rich land of Quivira. For a month and more he and his men journeyed on and found plains, hunchback cows, and

Indians. The natives at first interested them; they were unlike the pueblo dwellers and lived like Arabs in skin tents. As the Spaniards marched along, one of their number was directed to count his steps. After going two hundred and fifty leagues according to this reckoning, Coronado and the leading men decided that it would be impossible for the whole force to reach Quivira — in that season, at all events. With two score picked men, he pressed on while the others marched back to Tiguex. Fifty-two days of riding northward by the compass brought them to Quivira — in central Kansas. The long-sought city turned out to be a village, or a series of villages, of the Indians of the plains. One piece of gold was found, but Coronado suspected that this had been given to the Indian who possessed it by one of his own men.

Heart-broken, Coronado returned to Tiguex and, after another winter, to New Spain. Don Antonio de Mendoza received him coldly, although he had done all that human endeavor could have accomplished. But he had found neither cities nor treasure. Through no fault of his he had failed; and Coronado disappears thenceforth as completely as if he had not solved the age-long mystery of the Seven Cities.

While Coronado was leading his men northward from Culiacan, Hernando de Alarcon was sailing up the Gulf of California to give succor to the land force, if there should be need. Passing the shoals at the northern end of the gulf, he entered the estuary of a great river, the Colorado. Before he returned south again he made two boat expeditions up its waters — gaining a point not far from the beginning of the Grand Cañon, about eighty-five leagues from the sea. The natives told him of a city thirty or forty days' march away. Recently, they said, white men with "things which shot fire" had come to this city. Alarcon, unable to communicate with Coronado, left letters, as he had been instructed to do, and returned southward. One of these letters was recovered by Melchior Diaz, whom Coronado had placed in command of one of the garrisons on the line of advance. In the years 1540–41, therefore, the Colorado was reached by three parties of Spaniards. But beyond the wonders of the Grand Cañon it had nothing to reward its discoverers.

With unquenchable zeal Mendoza in 1542 dispatched another sea expedition — this time for the exploration of the western shore of Lower California which Alarcon had shown to be a peninsula. Juan Rodriguez Cabrillo went in command, with Bartolomé Ferrelo as navigator. Cabrillo died before much had been done, and Ferrelo steered northward along the California coast to 44° north latitude. The amount of driftwood indicated the nearness of a great river; but a storm drove him off the coast before he saw the mouth of the Columbia. It is interesting to note, however, that the natives of the Pacific coast told Ferrelo of the presence in the interior of men like himself with beards and swords. And the Indians by pantomime tried — so Ferrelo thought — to signify to him men on horseback with lances.[1] With the return of this expedition Spanish interest in the region west of the Mississippi fades away. Missionaries offered themselves as sacrifices, and a trader or two now and then may have visited the pueblos. But the colonization of the Southwest and of California was reserved for a later time.

To the friars a better harvest seemed to lie in the region explored by De Soto. In 1549 a missionary ship approached the Florida coast, south of Tampa Bay. But

[1] For Alarcon's and Cabrillo's voyages, see Winship's *Coronado*, 403 and fol.

the Indians killed the missionaries as fast as they ventured on shore. The last to die was the leader, Fray Luis Cancer de Barbastro. Ten years elapsed and another expedition approached the same fatal Florida land (1559). Tristan de Luna y Arellano was the commander, and he had under his orders fifteen hundred soldiers and settlers. With provisions for one year he landed not far from the modern Pensacola. Immediately a terrific hurricane destroyed seven of the fleet and ruined large quantities of supplies. Then came fever and hunger — the latter slightly appeased by food sent from Mexico and corn looted from the natives — and the colony was abandoned. The last of these ineffectual Spanish attempts at colonization was made in 1561 by Angel de Villafañe. The scene of his projected settlement was Santa Eleña — now Port Royal Sound — on the South Carolina coast. But the soil of that region did not suit the Spaniards. They sailed northward as far as the Santee and, despairing of success, returned to San Domingo. On the 1st of January, 1562, there was not a Spaniard — there was not a white man of any race — on the soil of the mainland of what is now the United States.

NOTES

I. Discovery of the Mississippi. — The main sources of information for the voyage of Pineda are the official papers in Navarrete's *Coleccion*, iii, 147, and the *Documentos Inéditos*, ii, 558. The chroniclers, especially Herrera, mention the voyage but give little information. As to the identification of the Espiritu Santo with the Mississippi there is still a good deal of dispute, see Dr. Shea in Winsor's *America* (ii, 237). Rye in the Introduction to the Hakluyt Society's edition of the *Narrative of the Gentleman of Elvas* (p. xxiii) quotes Greenhow with apparent approval as assigning the honor to Pineda. Winsor, in a note on p. 292 of vol. ii of his *America*, appears to be in doubt; but in his *Cartier to Frontenac*, 5, and his *Mississippi Basin*, 6, he shows no doubt as to Pineda's being the discoverer of the Mississippi. The most strenuous opponents of this identification are Walter B. Scaife (*America, its Geographical History*, Supplement) and Peter J. Hamilton (*Colonial Mobile*, 10). These students identify the Espiritu Santo with Mobile Bay. It is perhaps needless to point out that, even if Pineda's claims are discarded, Cabeza de Vaca and other comrades of Narvaez clearly saw the mouth of the Mississippi and perhaps crossed its lower course. In any event, therefore, De Soto cannot be regarded as the discoverer of the "Father of Waters."

II. Narvaez and Cabeza de Vaca. — For Narvaez and the fortunes of his companions we are necessarily forced to rely on *La Relacion que dio Alvar Nuñez Cabeza de Vaca de lo acaescido en las Indias en la Armada donde yua por governador Páphilo de Narvaez*, 1542. In the third issue (1749) the title appears as *Naufragios de Alvar Nuñez Cabeza de Vaca; y Relacion de la Jornada, que hizo á la Florida con el Adelantado Pánfilo de Narváez.* This has been admirably translated by Buckingham Smith as the *Relation of Alvar Nuñez Cabeça de Vaca* (New York, 1871). This volume also contains other matter on the same theme. The "Relacion" was not written until many details had become dim in Cabeza's memory. Oviedo (*Historia General*, ed. of 1851, libro xxxv, vol. iii, pp. 579–618) gives the substance of a letter or report made by Cabeza and one of his companions.

There has been a good deal of controversy as to Cabeza's line of march from the Gulf of Mexico to that of California.[1] The best

[1] On the question of the route the best recent discussions are three papers in the Texas State Historical Association's *Quarterly*, especially one by Judge Coopwood (iii, 108–140, 177–208; iv, 1–32). Preceding these should be mentioned Bande-

opinion nowadays favors an extreme southern route, but as to the exact localities visited no two students agree. One point may be urged against this conclusion: Cabeza understood the Indian language perfectly; it is difficult, therefore, to see how he could have gone so near the Spanish settlement at Panuco and not have heard of it. It is generally admitted that Cabeza did not go far enough north to see a pueblo. Apart from this the question of the route has mainly a local interest.[1]

III. De Soto. — There is no satisfactory account at first hand of De Soto's expedition. Probably the best narrative is the *Relaçam verdadeira . . . Agora novamēte feita per hũ fidalgo Delvas.* This was translated into English by Hakluyt and is usually cited as the "Narrative of the Portuguese Gentleman of Elvas." A much briefer statement is that made by Biedma in a *Relacion del suceso de la jornada que hizo Hernando de Soto.* Biedma was an officer of the expedition, and his narrative was written at about the time of his return; who the "Gentleman of Elvas" may have been, or when he wrote, or what his sources of information were, are not known. The longest account is Garcilaso de la Vega's *La Florida del Inca. Historia del Adelantado, Hernando de Soto.* This was based upon the narratives of three survivors and was written some forty years after the return of those veterans to civilization. A fourth account is given in Oviedo's *Historia General* (ed. of 1851, i, 544–577). This is founded on a report which Rodrigo Ranjel, De Soto's secretary, compiled soon after the arrival in Mexico. It was based on a diary which was kept probably from day to day. Oviedo gives only an abstract of the report, which becomes briefer and briefer as the journey proceeded. For exactness of statement the attenuated Ranjel seems to give the greatest satisfaction. Then comes Biedma, the "Gentleman of Elvas," and Garcilaso de la Vega in the order named.[2] For fanciful pictures of battles and suffering the order should be exactly reversed.

lier's statement in his *Contributions to the History of the Southwestern Portion of the United States* and H. H. Bancroft's *North Mexican States*, i, 63 note.

[1] Bandelier's narrative in his *Contributions* referred to above is the best account for the serious student. In briefer form his views are set forth in *Magazine of Western History*, iv, 327. References to other accounts are in Winsor's *America*, ii, 288.

[2] As to the value of these narratives, see an extract from a note written by Dr. J. G. Shea in Mississippi Historical Society's *Publications*, vi, 450. See also Shea's article in the second volume of Winsor's *America*.

The relations of the "Gentleman of Elvas" and of Biedma are translated in W. B. Rye's *Discovery and Conquest of Florida* (Hakluyt Society, 1851) and by Buckingham Smith in his *Narratives of the Career of Hernando de Soto* (New York, 1866, 125 copies).[1] An "abridged translation" of Ranjel's report as given by Oviedo, containing the ethnology, topography, and itinerary of the narrative by Professor T. H. Lewis, is in the *American Antiquarian*, xxii, 351–357; xxiii, 107–111, 242–247. Garcilaso de la Vega's *Florida del Inca* has been translated into English by Barnard Shipp[2] and has been made the foundation for the more popular accounts of this part of De Soto's career.[3] The accounts, except that of Garcilaso de la Vega, are in Bourne's *Narratives of Hernando de Soto* (he uses Smith's translations of the Elvas and Biedma accounts).

IV. Fray Marcos. — Bandelier's *Contributions*[4] contains nearly all that can be said as to Fray Marcos and his journey. At times, in his desire to clear the friar's reputation, Mr. Bandelier has somewhat exaggerated the points in his favor; but the chapter as a whole is of the highest importance. Winship, in a paper entitled *Why Coronado went to New Mexico in 1540*[5] and in his *Coronado* (353–370), has stated the facts clearly and well. The surviving report of Fray Marcos is in *Documentos Inéditos* (iii, 325). Winship in the introduction to his *Coronado* notes all other references.

V. Coronado. — In his *Coronado Expedition*[6] George Parker Winship has brought together in one volume everything that can be regarded as "sources" of information, has translated these with abundant

[1] Buckingham Smith also brought together many documents relating to the Florida expeditions in *Coleccion de varios documentos para la historia de la Florida y tierras adyacentes*, London, 1857 (vol. i all ever issued). See also his *Letter of Hernando de Escalante Fontaneda.*

[2] Barnard Shipp's *History of Hernando de Soto and Florida.* Theodore Irving's *Conquest of Florida*, Cunningham-Graham's *Hernando de Soto*, and Grace King's *De Soto and the Land of Florida* are among the best of the popular accounts.

[3] Harrisse (*Discovery of America*, 644) gives a map which was made after the return of Moscoso and before 1559. It gives a detailed topography of the Gulf region with many names which resemble those of the narratives. It is poorly reproduced in Mississippi Historical Society's *Publications*, vi, 449, where an attempt is made to identify localities. Jones's *Georgia*, Pickett's *Alabama*, and Hamilton's *Colonial Mobile* also attempt identifications. Rye, in the Hakluyt Society volume noted above, brings together material as to the western part of the journey.

[4] *Contributions to the History of the Southwestern Portion of the United States*, 106–178.

[5] American Historical Association's *Report* for 1894, 83–92.

[6] *Fourteenth Annual Report of the Bureau of Ethnology;* also issued separately.

notes, and has prefixed to the work a luminous and invaluable Introduction. The document around which this admirable work has been built up is Pedro de Castañeda de Naçera's *Relacion de la Jornada de Cibola.* It is a wonderfully graphic description, but it was written years after the events which it portrays. In an earlier publication, in the *American History Leaflets,* No. 13, Mr. Winship printed translations of several papers which were later included in his large work. The documents in Ternaux-Compans's "Cibola volume" are so poorly edited as to be of little assistance. The best brief account of this expedition is in C. F. Lummis's *Spanish Pioneers.* Henry W. Haynes's chapter in Winsor's *America,* ii, was written before the Castañeda became accessible except through Ternaux's French version.

CHAPTER IV

FRENCH COLONISTS AND EXPLORERS, 1500–1660

FISH and furs, and the hope of silks and spices, drew men to the barren shores of northeastern America. To their hopeful imaginations it also seemed that the passage to Cipango and India might there be found. In 1497 John Cabot thought that he had come near the goal, and the next year (1498) he lost his life in the further prosecution of the search. Within five years of his disappearance Gaspar and Miguel Cortereal perished in the same quest; the precise mode of their dying still forms one of the most attractive mysteries for the searcher of the unknown in American history. French fishermen frequented the banks of Newfoundland from a very early day; they may have been there as early as 1500. With them were fishermen from other maritime nations of Western Europe; and there is no evidence that the Frenchmen were the first to come.[1] Fur traders from France anchored off the shores of Newfoundland and Labrador before 1534. The most peculiar thing about these fishing and trading voyages is their failure to contribute anything to the world's stock of geographical knowledge. In the fifteenth and sixteenth centuries, voyages for the purpose of making money by peaceful means and expeditions for discovery and exploration were widely different enterprises and demanded dis-

[1] Parkman (*Pioneers*, 189–194) gives the traditions and stories of the French fishermen. D. W. Prowse, in his *History of Newfoundland* (pp. 1–50), brings together a mass of material which proves little more than the presence of many fishermen on the American fishing grounds in the sixteenth century.

similar capacities. The explorer often was more akin to the buccaneer and the corsair than to the dealer in furs or the salter of fish.

The first corsair and explorer to sail under the French flag in American waters was Giovanni da Verrazano,[1] a native of Florence. It was in 1524 that he crossed the Atlantic with the favor of Francis I, King of France. Seeking a western waterway to China, he first saw the American coast somewhere near Cape Fear. Before long he came across a party of natives who appeared to him to be as black as negroes and quite unlike the Indians of Eastern Asia ; but the Indies were doubtless near at hand. Perhaps for this reason, he thought that the color of the New Jersey and Delaware sands denoted the presence of gold. Sailing northward, the navigators followed the coast and entered New York harbor ; but they made no long stay there because their anchorage just inside of Sandy Hook was exposed to the winds from the sea. At Newport they made a longer visit and were greatly impressed by the natives of that region, whose mild and pleasant expression, to their delighted eyes, closely resembled that of the folk of antiquity. From this aboriginal paradise the explorers followed the shore northeastward and thence returned to France. Soon after, Verrazano disappeared from historic scene, almost as suddenly as he had entered it, — where, or how, no one knows.

Probably no single event in our history has aroused sharper controversy than the voyage which has been described in the preceding paragraph. Three able and subtle disputants have argued the case so learnedly and so lengthily as thoroughly to befog the points at issue. These debaters were Henry C. Murphy, J. Carson Brevoort, and

[1] See Note I at end of the present chapter.

Benjamin Franklin De Costa, representing three distinct racial origins. Mr. George Dexter, of a fourth stock, has shown how obstacles which seemed formidable to the enthusiastic controversialist yield to the touch of common sense. Mr. Murphy, for example, seeks to discredit the Verrazano voyage because no original manuscript of the "Verrazano Letter" is in existence.[1] In reply it might be said that if we were to follow him in this, we should throw out the voyages of Christopher Columbus and Magellan, of Jacques Cartier and Francis Drake, to say nothing of the plays of Shakespeare and Johnson, and of all that went before them. We may safely accept the Verrazano voyage in its broad outlines and leave the settlement of the details to posterity.

Ten years passed away before another explorer crossed the western Atlantic under the ensign of France. It was in 1534 that Jacques Cartier[2] of St. Malo passed the Strait of Belle Isle and coasted the southern shores of Labrador. At one place he found a fur trader of La Rochelle peacefully lying at anchor. The stones and rocks of the neighboring land were bare of soil and vegetation; the country, it seemed to him, must be that assigned to Cain.[3] Turning his prow southward, Cartier sought more congenial shores. After touching at various points, he entered a bay which promised at first sight to be the hoped-for passage to China, for he, too, was seeking the Northwest Passage. The shores of this bay were delightful; wheat, with an ear like that of rye, grew wild;[4] the climate was warmer than that of Spain, for Cartier was there in summer,—he named it the Baye de Chaleur,

[1] Murphy's *Voyage of Verrazzano*, 10.

[2] See Note II.

[3] *Relation Originale* (edition of 1867), 11.

[4] *Relation Originale* (edition of 1867), 34.

which it is still called. He coasted northward to Gaspé, where he planted a cross and kidnaped two Indians. He then sailed to Anticosti. The water passage between that island and the Labrador coast especially interested him; but for some unknown reason[1] he abandoned further exploration for the time being. On September 5 he was once more at St. Malo and immediately began preparations for a new expedition.

By August of the next year, 1535, Cartier was again at Anticosti. Passing between that island and Labrador, he successfully braved the dangers of the lower St. Lawrence and reached the wondrous gloomy mouth of the Saguenay. Proceeding upward, the voyagers came to the vine-clad Isle of Bacchus[2] which Cartier later named Isle d'Orleans. Just beyond its upper end the frowning cliff of Quebec narrowed the waterway to more river-like proportions. The inhabitants of this region were Indians like those whom Cartier had seen on his first voyage. In the interior, however, he understood the natives to say, was the kingdom of Saguenay, where there were white people who wore woolen clothing and in the country of Picquemyans there were men with only one leg apiece.[3]

In his smallest vessel and then in rowboats, Cartier proceeded onward and upward beyond Quebec[4] until the La Chine rapids barred further progress. Near this barrier was the Indian village of Hochelaga, — the capital city of the kings of that region. Escorted by a troop of savages.

[1] Parkman (*Pioneers*, 203) appears to attribute this early return to "gathering autumnal storms." As it was then early in August, this seems an insufficient explanation. De Costa (Winsor's *America*, iv, 50) speaks of "supplies running low," but there is no hint of this in the original accounts.

[2] *Brief Recit* (edition of 1863), 14.

[3] *Ibid.*, 40.

[4] Quebec is probably the phonetic French spelling of the Indian word signifying strait. Cf. Parkman's *Pioneers*, 336 note.

Cartier ascended a steep hill that stood hard by the stream; he named it Mont Royal and it is so called now. As he looked about him, his dream of a Northwest Passage faded away; forest-clad mountains and an impetuous river greeted his eyes.[1] Returning to Quebec, he wintered in its neighborhood and twenty-five of his men perished from scurvy. All the Frenchmen might have died had not the Indians told them of a marvelous medicine. As a requital for this saving draught, Cartier kidnaped the friendly Indian chief and carried him to France, where he speedily died.

Two more voyages to the St. Lawrence and one more winter of death and hardship completed Cartier's American experience. Other Frenchmen came to these northern regions to trade for furs or to draw fish from the seas; but, until 1604, nothing was done that can be called colonization. The French turned to a kindlier clime, where was enacted a more cruel tragedy than the scurvy-ridden regions of the North or the depths of the Iroquois forests ever witnessed, — the murder of Christians by their fellow-Christians in the name of Christ and Philip the Second, King of Spain.

Jean Ribaut of Dieppe was a seaman of renown in his day; but in the cold light of history he appears lacking in those decisive qualities which make a successful sea fighter and prosperous pioneer.[2] In 1562 he led an exploring expedition to the American coast and made land not far from the site of the later St. Augustine. Coasting slowly northward, he entered the estuary of what promised to be a great river. It was May Day, and accordingly he called the stream the River of May; but it is now known

[1] *Brief Recit* (edition of 1863), 27.

[2] The more important of the books on the French in Florida are enumerated in Note III.

by its Spanish name of St. Johns. Going ashore, the Frenchmen were joyously received by the natives, to whom they seemed to be "Children of the Sun," bringing an Indian millennium! To Ribaut the land appeared to be "the fairest, fruitfulest, and pleasantest of all the world." The Frenchmen thought that gold and silver and pearls abounded there, and best of all that only twenty days' journey away was Cibola with its Seven Cities. Whatever one may think of the Spaniards and their doings in America, one cannot help admiring the skill with which they concealed their geographical knowledge. A score of years after Coronado's return and De Soto's burial the Seven Cities seemed desirable to Frenchmen, and to be within a short distance of the Atlantic coast.

Without waiting to test the truth of these stories, Ribaut sailed northward and came to river after river, which he named for those other rivers, dear to every Frenchman, — Seine, Somme, Loire, Charente, Garonne. He determined to leave a garrison to hold the land. Calling for volunteers, the greater part of his men wished to remain. Thirty only were chosen to remain behind. The settlers built a fort on Port Royal Sound, not far from the Beaufort of the modern maps, and named it Charlesfort for that soulless monarch, Charles IX of France. Then began the everlasting story which was to mark settlement after settlement on the Atlantic shore: hunger, mutiny, bloodshed. Killing their leaders, the mutineers built a rude boat and sailed for France. At first the wind blew them gayly onward, then it died away. The daily allowance of food was reduced to twelve grains of corn and then to nothing. For a time their shoes and leathern jackets afforded a meagre subsistence. When that was gone, they drew lots to see which of their emaciated bodies should sustain the lives of the rest. As the flesh of the first victim gave out, the coast of France came into sight. Unfortunate to the end, between them and their beloved land was an hostile English vessel.

A year and more passed away before, in June, 1564, another French fleet sailed into the River of May. The commander of the new expedition was René de Laudonnière, a Huguenot. His men were mainly French Protestants, and they had come to found a colony in the New World. On the southern bank of the river, about five miles from the sea, they began a fort of generous proportions which they named Fort Caroline. A year's winds and rains made huge breaches in its ill-constructed ramparts, which the occupants were too feeble or too lazy to repair. At the beginning the neighboring natives were friendly; they gave the settlers food and a wedge of silver, which latter proved to be a fatal gift. For, instead of cultivating the soil, the settlers searched for treasure and allied themselves with one tribe of Indians against other Indians, their enemies. Hungry and disheartened, they began to quarrel among themselves. Too cowardly to stab Laudonnière, the conspirators sought to poison him with arsenic or to blow him up with gunpowder placed under his bed of sickness. Some of the discontented colonists stole away in boats to plunder the towns of the Cuban coasts. Hunger forced them to surrender to the Spaniards, who thus gained information of the existence of the French colony on the Florida seashore. Still another band of mutineers wrung from Laudonnière a commission to fight the Spaniards; in no long time they returned unsuccessful and starving; but these attacks, coupled with those of earlier French corsairs, convinced the Spanish government that the French settlement must be broken up or it would become a nest for marauders.[1]

The aspect of affairs on the River of May was pitiful. For a year no supplies had come from France, and the colonists had not planted a single seed. The country round about them teemed with game and the river at their door held myriads of fish, but in the midst of plenty, they starved. They sustained an existence by roots grubbed up in the forest and fish bones dug from the heaps of refuse. "Return to France" was now the cry. August 3, 1565, the lookout at the river's mouth saw a great ship standing toward the land. Soon three others came into view. These were the *Jesus*, *Solomon*, *Tiger*, and *Swallow*, commanded by the redoubtable John Hawkins, who was returning home from his second slave-trading voyage. Needing water, he bethought himself of the French Protestants on the River of May. Seeing their sorry plight, he offered to take them all to France free of cost. But this plan savored too much of national humiliation to be acceptable. Laudonnière was willing, however, to buy one of Hawkins's vessels, for which he gave his heavy guns, and to receive supplies of food, for which he never paid. Favoring winds blew Hawkins off the coast. The French colonists were still awaiting another favorable wind when Jean Ribaut, with recruits and supplies, anchored in the river's mouth. There was a sudden revulsion of feeling; everything seemed favorable to success. "But, lo," wrote Laudonnière, "how oftentimes misfortune doth search or pursue us, even when we think to be at rest." In the night of September 4, 1565, a Spanish fleet sailed into the midst of the French vessels swinging lazily at their moorings.

[1] On this subject, see Ruidíaz y Caravia's *La Florida: su Conquista y Colonización*.

The commander of the Spanish expedition was Pedro Menendez de Aviles, the bloodiest Spaniard who ever cursed American soil — and one of the ablest. Moreover, he was one of the few practical seamen who commanded fleets for Spain, and neither private griefs nor two years' imprisonment in the dungeons of the Spanish Council for the Indies had daunted his fierce spirit or lowered his masterful courage.

The sea route from the treasure ports of Mexico and Central America was through the channel between Florida and the Bahamas. This region was within the sweep of the West India hurricanes, and shipwrecks were not infrequent. Menendez's son had disappeared one stormy day, and the father was fitting out an expedition to search for him when news reached Spain from Cuba of the French settlement in Florida. At almost the same moment reports came from France of the fitting out of Ribaut's fleet. Menendez was placed at the head of a large expedition of nineteen vessels and fifteen hundred men and ordered to destroy the French colony. Storms dispersed his fleet, and with three ships only he reached the Florida coast.

When the Spanish vessels unexpectedly ranged alongside the French ships lying at anchor off the mouth of the River of May, the crews of the latter were mostly on shore; the ship-keepers exchanged insults with the Spaniards, cut their cables, and stood out to sea, firing as they went. The Spaniards pursued, but the French ships were too fast to be overtaken. Menendez returned to the river to find that Ribaut was prepared to dispute the entrance with his smaller vessels. The Spaniards then sailed southward. Fifty miles away they made a landing and began the settlement of St. Augustine (September 5, 1565). Gathering his scattered ships and taking with him nearly all the able-bodied men at Fort Caroline, Ribaut followed the Spaniards. He came upon them in confusion — some on shipboard, others on shore. Now was a leader's opportunity; but Ribaut turned his ships offshore. A few days later a hurricane drove the whole French fleet on the sandy beach some miles to the southward of St. Augustine.

No hesitant was Menendez; besides, unlike Ribaut, he had definite orders to attack and to destroy. Conceiving intuitively the Frenchman's plight, and certain of his absence from Fort Caroline, Menendez forced his men through storms, forests, and swamps to the French settlement. September 19 found him and his soldiers at the gates of the fort, weak with hunger, drenched to the skin, and in water up to their knees. La Vigne, the officer of the watch on the ruined ramparts, had dismissed his men to their quarters, and himself had gone to bed; but a trumpeter, who had not yet deserted his post, sounded the alarm. The Spaniards poured into the fort through the unguarded opening. Laudonnière and fifty more Frenchmen jumped from the walls, deserting the women, the children, and the sick. After terrible suffering most of them gained a few small vessels which still remained in the river. The commander of one of these ships, Jacques Ribaut, son of the admiral, with unparalleled cowardice sailed for France, leaving his father to his fate.

Ribaut and his shipwrecked crews struggling northward over the sands of the coast, one after another, fell into Menendez's power; with their hands tied behind them they were put to the knife.[1] Such of them as refused to

[1] Letter of Menendez in Massachusetts Historical Society's *Proceedings*, Second Series, viii, 429; Ruidíaz y Caravia's, *La Florida: su Conquista y Colonización*, ii, 89.

surrender except on conditions, four carpenters whose services were desirable, and a few who declared themselves Roman Catholics were saved from the slaughter, as were about fifty women and the younger children. The dead were all Protestants, and it appeared to Menendez that "to chastise them in this way would serve God our Lord, as well as your Majesty, and that we should thus be left more free from this wicked sect to plant the Gospel in these parts." On the margin of this dispatch in the handwriting of Philip II are the words: "Say to him that as to those he has killed he has done well: and as to those he has saved they shall be sent to the galleys." [1]

The story now turns again to the frozen North, for there lay the hope of French colonization in America. Of the earlier French explorers, fur traders, and colonists none showed more indomitable perseverance than Samuel de Champlain. Born in 1567, he first saw the coast of America in command of a ship bearing recruits to the Spanish garrisons in the West Indies. Visiting Panama he advocated the cutting of a canal through the isthmus; a project which had already been advanced, and had been met with the objection that the expense would be so great as to empty the treasure-houses of Charles the Fifth.

In 1603 Champlain [2] made his first voyage to the scene of his future labors. He came to the St. Lawrence with Pont Gravé, a fur trader who had already made several expeditions to Canada. While their vessel was completing her cargo, Pont Gravé and Champlain voyaged up the

[1] Massachusetts Historical Society's *Proceedings*, New Series, viii, 429 and 459. The latter quotation in a somewhat free rendering is in Parkman's *Pioneers*, 151. For a literal translation, see Note IV.

There is no account of the retaliatory expedition of Dominic de Gourges in the text because the expedition, if it was made, produced no permanent results and because the sources of information are meagre and do not seem to be authentic.

[2] The books on Champlain are mentioned in Note V.

river to the falls near Mont Royal. The villages, which had been thronged with Indian life in 1535, were now deserted. Champlain essayed to ascend the rapids; but after a trial gave over the attempt and made his way down the river. On his return to France, he presented to the king a map and a report, the first of a long series of papers from his pen.

Pierre de Guast, Sieur de Monts, now conceived the project of a combined fur-trading and colonizing enterprise,[1] the profits of the business to defray the expenses of the colony and possibly leave a balance. With influence at court, he secured from Henry IV a commission authorizing him to colonize and govern the region between the fortieth and forty-sixth parallels of latitude, stretching from Philadelphia to northern Nova Scotia, under the name of La Cadie or Acadia, as the English called it. At the same time De Monts secured a grant of a monopoly of the fur trade of this region and of the St. Lawrence Gulf and River.

In 1604 with Champlain and other gentlemen, mechanics, and criminals De Monts sailed for Acadia. After a brief exploration he began to build houses on an island which he called St. Croix. This island was in the estuary of one of those rivers which give an amphibious character to the country around Passamaquoddy Bay. In later years, when the St. Croix River came to mark the eastern end of the boundary between the United States and British America, the identity of the island became a matter of lively interest. All doubt was finally set at rest by the discovery of the ruins of De Monts's houses.[2]

[1] The story of this enterprise is well set forth by H. P. Biggar in his *Early Trading Companies of New France*, ch. iv.

[2] See on this point the Report of the Joint Commission of 1798 and American Antiquarian Society's *Proceedings* for October, 1896, pp. 160 and 188. In one

St. Croix Island was well fitted to mark a boundary. It proved to be unsuitable as the site of a settlement. Its wind-swept surface was cold and dreary; it was too small for cultivation; and the soil was poor. There was little firewood on the island, and the winter ice in the river made it difficult to bring fuel from the mainland. The season was severe; scurvy and other diseases attacked the colonists; and when the warm weather came again nearly one half of them were dead. Abandoning this inhospitable spot, the survivors crossed the Bay of Fundy and settled on the shores of Annapolis Basin, which they called Port Royal.

Champlain, abounding in energy, could not remain quietly at St. Croix. In the autumn of 1604 he sailed along the coast as far west as the Penobscot River, and in the spring of 1605 accompanied De Monts as far south as the heel of Cape Cod. The ill-fortune that dogged Champlain and French explorers and colonists generally, led the voyagers past the harbors of Portland and Boston without seeing their entrances. Had they entered either of these ports, they could hardly have failed to recognize their possibilities, and had a settlement been made on the shores of Boston Harbor, it might very well have turned out that New England would have been New France, and the whole history of North America would have been unlike the actuality. As it was, the explorers entered Plymouth Harbor, and Champlain made an interesting map of it, calling it Port St. Louis.[1] In 1606 he rounded Cape Cod and sailed to Vineyard Sound, but failed

of these articles it is stated that the stones on Douchet Island or St. Croix, which were regarded as those of De Monts's foundations, were later used in "building the lighthouse and the keeper's cottage" on the island. There is now no trace of the foundations.

[1] The English Martin Pring had visited the spot in the preceding year, and had named it Whitson Haven.

to push his discoveries as far as Newport, Long Island Sound, or New York. In 1607 De Monts abandoned his share in the enterprise, and Champlain returned to France.

For a century and more the Acadian settlement led a lingering existence — the climate, the soil, and the racial peculiarities of the settlers made against success. One episode in the dreary story deserves fuller mention — the attempt of French Jesuits to found a mission on the coast of what is now New England. It was in 1613 that four priests, well supplied with food and workingmen, landed on the shore of Soames's Sound, a deep indentation in the picturesque island of Mt. Desert. The colonists had scarcely disembarked when Samuel Argall, sailing northward from Jamestown on a fishing cruise, learned of the existence of the embryonic settlement. What legal right or instructions he had to attack the Frenchmen is not perfectly clear, but Argall was not a man to stickle at technicalities.[1] He set upon the colonists, captured some of them, drove the remainder away, and returned to Virginia with his prisoners. A few months later he again came north, and this time he had definite orders to kill and destroy. Visiting Port Royal he burned the settlement, but the settlers fled to the woods and could not be captured. As soon as he was gone they rebuilt their ruined huts, and continued to keep up a semblance of civilized life; but Acadia never prospered under French rule.[2] In 1671 there were not four hundred white people[3] in the vast region east of the Kennebec.

In 1608 Champlain returned to America in the three-

[1] On Argall's doings on the Maine coast, see Alexander Brown's *Genesis of the United States*, ii, 664, 700, and *First Republic in America*, 191–195, and Massachusetts Historical Society's *Proceedings*, Second Series, i, 187.

[2] Besides the works of Murdoch and Hannay on Nova Scotia, or Acadia, may be mentioned Moreau's *Histoire de l'Acadie Françoise* (Paris, 1873).

[3] Rameau's *La France aux Colonies*, 23.

fold guise of fur trader, explorer, and colonist, which he was to maintain for the rest of his life. Ascending the St. Lawrence to Quebec, he built a fort or garrison house, which may be looked upon as the beginning of the present town of that name. In the autumn Champlain, with twenty-seven men, remained to hold the post for France. When spring came, in 1609, and the ice in the river broke up, eight only of the twenty-eight were alive, and four of the eight were ill.[1]

In the long idleness of the winter Champlain had formed a plan which was as bold as it proved to be disastrous. Briefly, his scheme was to enter into an alliance with the Indians of the northern bank of the St. Lawrence and with them make war on their enemies, the Iroquois. His reward would be the opportunity to explore the heart of the land. For France, the conquest of the Iroquois might mean much. They were the implacable enemies of the northern Indians. Their conversion to the Christian faith might follow their conquest and would give France the mastery of lands which perhaps would prove to hold the road to China and the golden East. Champlain may have reasoned in some such wise; but he had not the means to reach a definite conclusion, for the might and cohesive force of the Iroquois confederacy were unknown. Had the Iroquois been an ordinary Indian tribe, the plan might have succeeded; but so far from being an ordinary tribe, the League of the Iroquois was unlike all other Indian tribes, — it was the strongest and most formidable organization in North America.

Champlain, with two white men and an Indian war party, plunged into the wilderness by way of the River of the Iroquois, now known as the Richelieu. He soon

[1] Slafter's *Champlain*, ii, 199.

came to where the river widened into a charming lake which still bears its finder's name. Somewhere on its western edge, probably not far from the site of the later Ticonderoga, an Iroquois war party was descried. The hostiles barricaded themselves, and the invaders spent the night in their canoes. In the morning the two bands came together, the Iroquois leaving their fort and advancing across open ground; suddenly Champlain, armor-clad, with a plumed headpiece, stepped out from the throng of the invaders and discharged his gun. Two Indians dropped dead and a third was borne away wounded. A timely shot from one of his men on the flank killed a third Iroquois, when the others turned and fled. This unexpected attack aroused in the Iroquois a fierce hatred of Frenchmen and things French. A few weeks later a Dutch ship, the *Half-Moon*, commanded by an English sailor, Henry Hudson, encountered another band of Iroquois — members of the Mohawk tribe — in the mid-reaches of the Hudson River. He entertained the native chiefs most royally with biscuit and grog. Ever afterward the Iroquois clave to the Dutch and the English, who bought their furs and supplied them with fire-water and firearms. On the other hand, they killed or tortured very nearly every Frenchman, whether he were missionary or explorer, who fell into their hands. Holding the routes leading from the St. Lawrence southward and living on the flank of the most feasible route from the Upper Lakes to Montreal, their hostility closed a large part of the continent to the French and at the same time protected the English colonies from French attack. Had the case been reversed, it is difficult to see how the northern English colonies could have maintained themselves.

Champlain's assault at Ticonderoga was not an isolated

instance of French aggression. In 1610 the northern Indians, aided by French guns, inflicted a severe defeat upon the Iroquois. In 1613 Champlain and a dozen white comrades accompanied a great Indian war party to what is now western New York. Ascending the Ottawa River and making several portages, the expedition reached Lake Huron.[1] Proceeding thence, the party crossed the eastern end of Lake Ontario and attacked an Iroquois stronghold which was situated not far from Lake Oneida. This fort was well designed and constructed, and the Iroquois remained behind their defenses. Against an ordinary Indian attack, it was impregnable; but Champlain caused a movable platform to be built, lofty enough to overlook the palisade. From this fortified perch the French gunners drove the defenders from the walls, but this was the limit of Champlain's success; for his Indian allies, mad with excitement, rushed promiscuously and prematurely to the attack and failed. They then retreated, carrying Champlain in a basket for part of the way on account of a wound which he had received. His prestige was gone; this was the end of his exploring and fighting. The rest of his life he passed in voyaging between France and Canada and in trying to infuse vigor into the barren and inert post at Quebec.

French interest in Canada was bound up with the fur trade, and Quebec was merely a permanent trading post. Commerce in those days was greatly hampered by royal grants of exclusive privileges, and French commerce in particular was closely bound. Owing to the eccentricities of the French government, monopolies which were dependent upon it were apt to be temporary in their nature.

[1] Cf. Parkman's *Pioneers*, 394 and fol.; C. W. Butterfield's *History of Brulé's Discoveries and Explorations* (Cleveland, 1898); Winsor's *Cartier to Frontenac*, Index, under Brulé.

No one, who held for a brief and indefinite time the exclusive right to the Canadian fur trade, could be expected to invest much money in making a permanent settlement at Quebec. The capitalists kept the garrison supplied with food, but steadily refused to lay out money for enlargements or for repairs, except such as were absolutely necessary. In 1627 Richelieu was the ruling power in France. He put an end to the existing monopoly and formed a new company, with himself at its head and Champlain as his leading assistant. This new body was called The Hundred Associates. As long as Richelieu lived and maintained his place, it held the monopoly firmly in its grasp. The new enterprise was exclusively Roman Catholic; in the future not a Huguenot was to visit New France.

The year 1628 marked the beginning of a war between England and France. English privateers thought that the French fur traders and their belongings would be valuable spoil. In their capture Gervaise Kirke and his three sons were especially active.[1] In 1629 they sailed to the St. Lawrence, plundered the trading station of Tadoussac at the mouth of the Saguenay River, captured or destroyed the vessels bearing the year's supplies to the garrison at Quebec, and returned rich with booty to England. The Englishmen had made a happy voyage; but the following winter was marked by fearful suffering at Quebec. Only one family at the post had cultivated enough soil to supply food for its own necessities. The rest of the people were fed from France and this year the food did not arrive. The inhabitants managed to exist on acorns and

[1] Original material on Kirke's voyages is in Royal Historical Manuscripts Commission's *Reports*, xii, Appendix, pt. i, 374, 376, 377, and in *Calendar of State Papers, America and West Indies, 1574–1674*. See H. P. Biggar's *Early Trading Companies of New France*, chs. viii and ix.

roots and such game and fish as they could procure. When the returning Englishmen arrived off Quebec in 1629 they were cordially welcomed, and New France passed into the power of Charles I. The English king did not appreciate the opportunity this conquest gave him, and returned Canada and Acadia to France.[1] The consideration for this was an installment of Henrietta-Maria's dowry, which Mr. Parkman estimated as worth about a quarter of a million dollars in our money. Few events in English history led to more disastrous consequence than the marriage of Charles I to the daughter of Henry IV. It was even more disastrous to America; for this restoration of the French possessions made possible the series of wars and massacres which form the most dreary and heartrending tale of woe in our annals.

New France next became a Jesuit colony. The conception of the French Jesuits was a grand one. It was no less than the conversion to Christianity of the North American Indians and their rescue from the torments of hell. It was an heroic task and had heroes commensurate with its greatness; in martyrology, few names stand more conspicuous than those of Brebeuf, Garnier, and Jogues.[2] But Christianity and Indian strength did not thrive together. Conversion saved the aboriginal soul in the next world; it weakened mind and body in this. Burning with fierce, savage enmity, not counting the numbers of their enemy, their resources, or their allies, the Iroquois

[1] The text of the treaty of St. Germain-en-Laye of 1632 is in *Mémoires de Commissarires*, 12mo edition, 1755, ii, 5; important papers relating to the negotiations are in Nicolas Denys' *Description Geographique et Historique des Costes de l'Amerique Septentrionale*, i, 238; Ganong's article on "Boundaries of New Brunswick" (Royal Society of Canada's *Transactions*, Second Series, vii, 174); Murdoch's *Nova Scotia*, i, 88, and many other places. Dr. Ganong's article is especially valuable for its topographical discussions.

[2] An interesting paper on the "Scenes of the Huron Missions," by James J. Dunn, is in *American Catholic Researches*, v, 105.

waged relentless war on the French Indians and the missionaries. They drove the Hurons from their home by the Great Lakes, they followed them in their flight and attacked the scanty remnant of that once great tribe in its place of refuge, the Island of Orleans, within sight of Quebec. They even pursued their quarry into the streets of the seat of government of New France, and killed them wheresoever they caught them. As the supply of Huron victims grew scanty, they took to torturing, roasting, and killing the white missionaries, settlers, and soldiers.

In 1660, at the end of this period, there were not more than three thousand white settlers in New France and Acadia put together. A new chapter in the history of French colonization began when Louis XIV interested himself in the fortunes of New France. Soldiers were sent to Canada, and the Iroquois were forced to accept peace. The soldiers were then disbanded, turned into semipeaceful settlers, and tied to the soil with wives provided by the paternal care of the king and Colbert, his minister.

Frenchmen occupied the cold and barren country of the North, barren in colonial days except for animals wearing valuable skins. Spaniards seized upon the subtropical land of Florida as a guardhouse for a trade route and not as a colony. Between Port Royal on the north and St. Augustine on the south were thousands of miles of rocky and sandy shore. Extending from the thirtieth to the forty-fifth parallels of latitude, this region had various climates and was suited to the production of many commodities, from the rice of the low-lying tracts adjoining Florida to the ice of northern New England. Throughout its length, Indian corn, or maize — the settler's best crop — throve with marvelous return for the care bestowed upon it. Everywhere superb harbors, splendid rivers, and extensive sounds, welcomed the ocean-going emigrant sailing ship. Nowhere on the surface of the earth was there a region better fitted for European colonization. Frenchmen and Spaniards passed it by, as it offered slight hope of present gain. A higher power reserved it for the slower, more patient Englishman and his kinsfolk from Northern Europe. These came with their wives, their children, and their simple household belongings. They were a homely people. About them lingers none of the romance of the forest which distinguishes the French missionary and the *coureur de bois.* About them there is none of the bloody splendor of De Soto or the Spanish *conquistadores.* They were plain English, Dutch, or Swedish folk. Their mission was to plant a nation in the New World.

NOTES

I. Verrazano. — Our knowledge of the Verrazano voyage rests on two documents which are known respectively as the Verrazano Letter and the Verrazano Map. The letter purports to have been written on July 8, 1524, by the navigator himself, and exists in two versions, both in Italian. The map was made by the navigator's brother, Hieronimo, about 1529. On this map the coast line between Florida and Labrador is traced, not very accurately, and it bears an inscription stating that it was discovered "by Giovanni di Verrazano, of Florence, by the order and command of the Most Christian King of France." The Maiollo Map of 1527 has much the same general outline, and labels the coast "Francesca."

The first serious attack on the Verrazano voyage was made by Buckingham Smith at a meeting of the New York Historical Society in October, 1864. Smith's chief follower was Henry C. Murphy, whose *Voyage of Verrazzano* was published in 1875. On behalf of Verrazano the most effective works are B. F. de Costa's *Verrazano the Explorer*, and Signor Desimoni's essay in the publications of the Socièta Ligure di Storia Patria. The letter is printed in nearly all the Verrazano books, and in the New York Historical Society's *Collections*, Second Series, i, and Asher's *Henry Hudson.* The map has been often reproduced; the facsimile in De Costa's *Verrazano* is the best for students, and Winsor (*America,* iv) gives reproductions of this and other maps of the same period which are large enough for ordinary use. The most interesting feature of the Verrazano Map is what is known as the Sea of Verrazano, a great bay of the Pacific, which almost reaches the Atlantic coast in the vicinity of Chesapeake and Delaware bays. John Fiske, in his good-natured way, makes out the best case he can for Verrazano, and even suggests the exact spot where that navigator may have seen the sea which bears his name (*Dutch and Quaker Colonies,* i, 58).

George Dexter has summarized the arguments for and against this voyage, with abundant references and critical comment, in Winsor's *America,* iv, 19–28. In a note to his *Pioneers* (i, 231 note), Parkman gives the titles of the more important works on the subject, and says, "A careful examination of these various writings convinces me that the evidence in favor of the voyage of Verrazzano is far stronger than the evidence against it," — a statement with which the best modern students agree.

II. Jacques Cartier. — Our knowledge of the First Voyage rests mainly on the *Relation Originale du Voyage de Jacques Cartier au Canada en 1534.* This exists in several forms which are substantially similar. The Second Voyage is described in a document generally cited as the *Brief Recit, & succincte narration, de la navigation faicte es ysles de Canada, Hochelage & Saguenay,* etc. For the other voyages our knowledge is based on what is given in Hakluyt. In 1843, the Société Littéraire et Historique de Québec published a volume entitled *Voyages de Decouverte au Canada, 1534–42,* which contains the Cartier narratives in French in convenient form. For translations Hakluyt gives the earliest English rendering. Hiram B. Stephens, in a book entitled *Jacques Cartier and his Four Voyages to Canada,* gives modern English translations, and Joseph Pope (*Jacques Cartier, His Life and Voyages*) embodies in the text important extracts. In French, the memoirs of Cartier by Longrais and N. E. Dionne deserve mention. The two narratives mentioned above are sometimes ascribed to Cartier, especially the first one, but there is no direct proof that they are his work, or, indeed, that they were written by one of his companions. Further references in great abundance will be found in Winsor's *America,* iv, 62–68, and in his *Cartier to Frontenac;* see also H. P. Biggar's *Early Trading Companies of New France,* Appendix.

Much interest has been aroused over the question of Cartier's route. This has been treated at great length by W. F. Ganong in the Royal Society of Canada's *Transactions,* v, section ii, 121, and *ibid.,* vii, 17–58, and by Bishop Howley of West Newfoundland in *ibid.,* xii, section ii, 151. Harrisse also has something to say on the subject in his *Terre-Neuve,* 136 and fol.

III. The French in Florida. — Francis Parkman, in his *Pioneers of France in the New World,* has placed in enduring English prose the leading facts regarding this ill-fated venture, — the general reader need go no farther. The French view is set forth in Paul Gaffarel's *Histoire de la Floride Française* (Paris, 1875), which also contains a valuable appendix of documents. In a Prefatory Note to his later editions, Parkman has enumerated the sources; they are also given by Dr. Shea in Winsor's *America,* ii, 292–298. Only the most accessible will be mentioned here. The exploring expedition of Ribaut in 1562 is narrated in Hakluyt's *Divers Voyages* (reprinted by the Hakluyt Society, and by French in his *Historical Collections of Louisiana and Florida,* ii). Basanier's *L'Histoire Notable de la Floride* (Paris, 1586) includes narratives of the years 1562, 1564, 1565. This was translated by Hakluyt as the *Notable History,* and was also included in the third volume of his *Principal Navigations* (reprinted by French in his *Historical Collections of Louisiana and Florida,* i). Nicolas le Challeux, one of those who escaped, wrote a *Discours de l'histoire de la Floride* (Dieppe, 1566, and other editions) which is included in Ternaux-Compans's Florida volume. The above are from the standpoint of the French colonists; the Spanish side is set forth in Eugenio Ruidíaz y Caravia's *La Florida: su Conquista y Colonización por Pedro Menéndez de Avilés* (Madrid, 1893). This contains Gonzalo Solis de Merás's *Jornadas de Pedro Menéndez de Avilés* (vol. i, the author was the conqueror's brother-in-law), the *Relacion hecha por el Capellán de armada Francisco Lopez de Mendoza,* and other narratives. More important than these are the letters or dispatches to the king written by Menendez at the time and printed in volume ii; many of these are in English in the *Proceedings* of the Massachusetts Historical Society, Second Series, viii, 416–468. See also Andres Gonzales Barcia's *Ensayo Cronologico para la historia general de la Florida.* Dr. Gilmary Shea's account in the second volume of Winsor's *America* is also noteworthy as coming from a Roman Catholic and a scholar who was deeply versed in the Spanish sources; he has also treated this subject in his *Catholic Church in America,* i, 133–141. Ruidíaz y Caravia's *La Florida: su Conquista y Colonización* (appendix to vol. ii) contains a list of papers and manuscripts on ancient Florida.

IV. The Words of Philip II. — These words are copied from a manuscript volume in the Cabinet of the Massachusetts Historical Society: —

Decreto del Rey. } **Esto serà bien escribir luego à este Gobernador, y à Pero Menendez lo que serà bien que haga de los que ha tomado vivos trayendolos alli al Vemo*[1] *si tubiere en qué, y le pareciere saguro ; ò enviandolos para que aca lo anden en las Galeras ; y esto à los que ofreció la vida, que de los demas muy bien hace en hacer justicia.*

On the margin the first transcriber has written: —

* Todo lo rayado està en el origin[1] de letra del mismo Rey Ph^e. 2°.

[1] This word the translator has read "Remo."

The following literal translation of the king's words is taken from the Massachusetts Historical Society's *Proceedings,* Second Series, viii, 459: —

"The King's Order.

"It will be well to write immediately to this Governor and to Pero Menendez, that it will be well that he shall put those whom he has taken alive to the oar, if he can, and it seems to him to be safe; or else send them here to go to the gallies. This as regards those to whom he offered their lives; as to the rest he does very well in executing justice upon them."

V. Champlain. — The best edition of Champlain's writings is that by Laverdière (6 vols., 4to, second edition, Quebec, 1870; the first edition was destroyed by fire); the most complete translation into English is that published by the Prince Society, the translation by C. P. Otis and the editorial work by Edmund F. Slafter. Gabriel Gravier's *Vie de Samuel Champlain* (Paris, 1900) is based on the best material. The Memoir prefixed to Slafter's *Champlain* is very full and the volumes contain facsimiles of Champlain's original drawings. Most readers, however, will be content with the lively and scholarly account by Parkman in his *Pioneers of France.* Slafter, in Winsor's *America,* iv, 130–134, gives the bibliography of the several pieces which go to make up the collective edition of Champlain's works. Attempts have been made to identify Champlain's route in 1615 by Laverdière in his monumental edition of Champlain's *Œuvres* and by O. H. Marshall in the first number of the *Magazine of the American History.*

CHAPTER V

THE ENGLISH SEAMEN

JOHN CABOT'S discovery[1] gave Englishmen the right to occupy large portions of North America; but it stimulated them to no great effort like that which Spain saw in the years following the return of Columbus. In 1497 Englishmen were setting their affairs to rights after the long Wars of the Roses; before this task was accomplished the Reformation gave them other things to think about than arduous and doubtful voyages to unknown lands, — there was excitement enough at home. From this condition of inactivity Hawkins and Drake rudely aroused their countrymen; they prepared their minds for great enterprises and wrested sea power from Spain. To English sixteenth-century seamen Great Britain owes her colonial empire and the United States its existence.

Three Hawkinses appear in the history of English maritime enterprise. Of these the first was William Hawkins of Plymouth in Devonshire. He made three voyages to the coasts of Guinea and Brazil, and served Plymouth as its mayor and its representative in the House of Commons. He is generally regarded as the beginner of England's commercial expansion. His son, John Hawkins, early learned the lore of the sea and studied the commercial habits and needs of the Spaniards and Portuguese. It occurred to

[1] For a discussion of the general subject, see B. A. Hinsdale's "Right of Discovery" in *Ohio Archæological and Historical Quarterly*, December, 1888.

the younger man that money might be made from the acquisition of negroes on the African coasts, their transport to America, and their sale to the Spanish planters, who were always eager for laborers, whether they were white, red, or black.

The enslavement of the negro dates back to remote antiquity. American slavery began with Columbus, possibly because he was the first European who had a chance to introduce it; and negroes were brought to the New World at the suggestion of the saintly Las Casas to alleviate the lot of the unhappy and fast disappearing red man. Hawkins was in no sense the father of the slave trade, and it is not at all likely that he was the first illegal slave trader to Spanish America. We happen to know so much about Hawkins and his doings simply because his later career induced people to note down and preserve everything concerning him who became one of the greatest seamen of his day.

Of all the contradictions of history one that impresses the student is the constant and sincere religious fervor of the men with whom he comes into contact whose actions otherwise are often not commendable according to present day rules of conduct. The Spanish Menendez honestly believed that when he slaughtered fettered captives it was "for the glory of God." The English Hawkins was equally pious; on his second slave-trading voyage his flagship was *The Jesus.* He ordered his crews "to serve God daily" and "to love one another." Francis Drake, the greatest sea fighter and plunderer of his day, commended his lieutenant to "the tuition of Him that with His blood redeemed us." Nor were these expressions of piety confined to the leaders of great undertakings; the humble chronicler of Hawkins's second and most profitable slave-trading voyage concludes his tale with: "His name therefore be praised for evermore. Amen."[1] The standards of those days were not the standards of our day, and the standards of three hundred years hence will doubtless be unlike those of our time.

In the sixteenth century and the first part of the seventeenth one code of morals prevailed in Europe, and a very different one held sway "beyond the line." The explanation is that the Spaniards and the Portuguese had grasped the whole New World without consulting their fellow-Christians. Englishmen and Frenchmen and, a little later, Dutchmen denied this preposterous claim. They paid no attention to Spanish regulations in America; they hesitated not at all to attack Spaniards in America in time of full peace in Europe. On their side, the Spaniards assailed the French and English colonists, and killed them whenever they had the power. It is no hard matter to stigmatize as a pirate a man who died three hundred years ago. Drake's great voyage to the Pacific has been termed a piratical cruise, partly on the ground that he had no commission, which may or may not have been the case. One thing, however, is certain, his voyage was approved of by a great nation and by one of the greatest monarchs who ever occupied a throne. Elizabeth may not have given Drake a regular commission; she certainly was directly and financially interested in the success of the voyage, and protected its leader after his return to England. In this connection one further point may be made. In Elizabeth's time the word "pirate" had no such deep significance as it has at the present day.[2] He was a pirate who attacked in European waters a vessel of a power with which England was at peace. The duty of the government to stop that

[1] Hakluyt's *Voyages*, iii, 521.

[2] *Acts of the Privy Council*, April 29, 1576.

practice was fully recognized; the investigation and punishment of piracies formed one of the regular duties of the Council. The question as to what should be done in the case of voyages like those of Hawkins and Drake was always one of expediency and not of legality; a deed which would have met with condign punishment if perpetrated in European waters was looked upon as meritorious if it took place on the Spanish Main and did not bring on war with Spain.

John Hawkins[1] sailed for Africa on his first slave-trading voyage in October, 1562. Partly by purchase from the natives of the coast and partly by other means he secured about three hundred negroes, whom he exchanged in Hispaniola for pearls, hides, and other products of the Indies. With these he filled his own vessels and two cargo ships, or "hulks," as they were called. With a childlike confidence in his own innocence and in the justice of the Spaniards, he sent the hulks to Spain. The Spanish authorities confiscated them and their cargoes, and began that conflict with John Hawkins and his comrades which in the end terminated in the destruction of the "felicisima Armada."

Hawkins's second voyage occupied portions of the years 1564–65. His traffic in the Indies did not proceed as smoothly as it had before, because the authorities had received stringent orders from Spain to prohibit trade with foreigners. They would not permit Hawkins to sell even his lean and hungry slaves unless he first paid an impost of thirty ducats. This sum he thought was too high; he sent one hundred armed men to the market-place, and all things were speedily arranged "to his content." From this time on his voyage proceeded pros-

[1] Note I.

perously. In September, 1565, his fleet sailed into the harbor of Padstow in Cornwall, laden with valuable commodities, among which were "gold, silver, pearls, and other jewels great store."[1]

The third voyage (1567–68) was disastrous in its ending; for Philip II sent a strong fleet across the Atlantic to make sure that Spanish officials and English slave traders obeyed the laws of Spain. Hawkins was found "sheltering himself" in the port of Vera Cruz on the Mexican coast. He could have kept the Spaniards out, because he had taken the precaution to occupy the defenses of the harbor; but for the last time in his life he trusted the word of a Spaniard. Regardless of their pledges they set upon the English and killed hundreds of them and destroyed or captured all but two of their vessels. In one of these, Hawkins made his escape out of the harbor; in the other, his young kinsman, Francis Drake, followed on.

Hawkins and Drake appear to have regarded this attack in the light of a personal affront; they devoted the remainder of their lives largely to revenge. On his part, Hawkins made ready the royal navy to dispute the supremacy of the sea with the armadas of Spain; while Drake, by his onslaughts on the Spanish colonies, diminished the resources of Philip II and at the same time repaid himself for the losses at Vera Cruz. Before long, the West Indies and the Spanish Main came to be so securely guarded that an English expedition could not with impunity put a town to ransom. A bold design came into Drake's mind, — to sail through Magellan Strait and sweep up all the loose treasure on the west coast of America.

With one hundred and fifty men and boys in five vessels,

[1] *Hawkins' Voyages*, 64.

Francis Drake sailed forth to attack an empire and to sail over seas that no English keel had ever known.[1] Disaffection, mutiny, hardship, and cowardice deprived him of men and ships until (1578) he found himself in the Pacific Ocean with a single vessel, the *Pelican*, which he himself commanded. Gales drove him southward until he reached "the utmost island of Terra Incognita," where the Atlantic Ocean and the South Sea "meet in a most large and free scope." From this stormy region, with much difficulty and danger, the *Pelican* made her way northward, searching vainly for her consorts.

Valparaiso was the first port which rewarded the adventurers for the sufferings and dangers they had undergone; for at that place they seized "a certain quantity" — in reality a most uncertain quantity — of fine gold of Baldivia. Farther north, at Tarapaca, going ashore for water, they "lighted on a Spaniard who lay asleep, and had lying by him thirteen bars of silver." "We took the silver and left the man," so wrote the chronicler of the voyage. Proceeding profitably northward, the adventurers learned that the *Cacafuego*, the treasure ship of the Mar del Sur, had sailed from Lima for Panama only fourteen days earlier, — but what was fourteen days' start to an Elizabethan ship! Now the *Pelican* spread her wings in earnest and in due season ranged alongside of the Spaniard. In a moment, the galleon's mizzenmast went overboard, and Francis Drake had a Spanish treasure ship at his mercy; but what she contained will never be known. We read of "a certain quantity of jewels and precious stones, thirteen chests of ryals of plate, eighty pound weight of gold, twenty-six tons of uncoined silver, etc." Her cargo was large enough to require a week for its transfer from the

[1] See Note II.

Cacafuego to the English ship. Drake gave the Spanish master the latest European news, a safe-conduct to protect him from the missing English ships, a little linen and some food, and let him go. Thinking himself now "sufficiently satisfied and revenged, and supposing that Her Majesty, at his return, would rest satisfied with this service," the Englishman sailed for home.

Drake first steered northward along the coast to the forty-eighth parallel, searching for a passage to the east through America. At the farthest northern point, the cold was keen, even in the month of June, and no opening appeared. So he retraced his course and came to anchor in a harbor in latitude 38° 30′ according to his observations. At this port the ship was careened and refitted for her long voyage to distant England. What harbor this was, has long been a matter of controversy. Many writers have argued that it was San Francisco Bay; but this is impossible, for there is not the slightest hint in the narratives that have come down to us of the wonderful scenery of that region. The general opinion among students is that Drake's anchorage was in a small harbor not far from the entrance to the Golden Gate.[1] Drake called the country New Albion "for two causes; the one in respect of the white banks and cliffs, which lie toward the sea; the other that it might have some affinity even in name also, with our own country, which was sometimes so called."

With a clean hull and new rigging the *Pelican* sped westward from New Albion to Plymouth, England, by way of the Cape of Good Hope. Stopping at the Spice Islands, she took on board tons of pepper, much of which was soon jettisoned to float the ship off a reef. At this point in his

[1] Cf. American Antiquarian Society's *Proceedings*, April, 1889, pp. 13 and 78.

account, Mr. Fletcher, the chaplain of the expedition, grows piously eloquent: "it was therefore motioned," he tells us, "and by general voice determined, to commend our case to God alone, . . . And that our faith might be better strengthened and the comfortable apprehension of God's mercy in Christ be more clearly felt, we had a sermon." The ship thereupon slid from her rocky perch, assisted by a sudden change of wind. Fletcher's prominence on this occasion, or something which he had said, seems to have angered Drake, for he took an early opportunity to excommunicate the chaplain, consigning him "to the divell and all his angels" — having first carefully chained the parson by one leg to the fore hatch.

The amount of Drake's spoil was known only to the queen and himself, and probably not to them with accuracy. The booty was immense, and so was the wrath of the Spaniards. With feminine grace Elizabeth yielded to the storm and directed the treasure to be fetched overland to the Tower. She furthermore ordered that Drake, for a brief space, should have sole and unwatched possession of the *Pelican* and that his estimate of the amount of the treasure should be accepted without question. Drake and his men were doubtless well rewarded for their hardships, and Elizabeth was also recompensed for her protection of them, as she never paid over to the Spaniards the bulk of that which went into the Tower, except in the form of powder and cannon balls. As if further to show her approbation of Drake and his doings, she visited the *Pelican* and knighted him on his quarter-deck.

While Drake was tracing his dangerous homeward course, Sir Humphrey Gilbert was sailing westward [1] to explore

[1] On the date of Gilbert's first voyage, see George Dexter in Massachusetts Historical Society's *Proceedings* for October, 1881.

the northeastern shore of America for that waterway whose western end Drake had sought in vain. Gilbert was the leader of a group of Devonshire men who were actively interested in projects of exploration and colonization. In 1578 Elizabeth, by patent, authorized him and his heirs and assigns for "inhabiting and planting" to discover such remote, heathen, and barbarous lands as were not possessed by any Christian prince and "to have, hold, occupy and enjoy [such lands] with all commodities, jurisdictions and royalties, both by sea and land."[1] From this wording and from other writings it is evident that Gilbert and his associates intended to occupy eligible positions on the line of the northwest passage to the Pacific, should they be so fortunate as to find it. Gilbert sailed in 1578, but soon returned to port with "the loss of a tall ship; and more to his grief, of a valiant gentleman named Miles Morgan." On a subsequent voyage, in 1583, he gained the western side of the Atlantic and "took possession of Newfoundland for Elizabeth by right of the discovery of John Cabot." He then sailed southward, seeking a site for his settlement. Two of his four vessels were speedily lost; with the remaining two he set his course for England and himself sailed in the smaller. One night her light went out, and Sir Humphrey Gilbert[2] was never heard from more: —

[1] Hakluyt's *Voyages* (edition of 1810), iii, 174.

The Prince Society has issued a volume entitled *Sir Humphrey Gylberte and his enterprise of colonization in America*, edited by Carlos Slafter. It contains the patent, the "Hakluyt Narratives," many letters never before printed, and a memoir by the editor.

The Rev. George Patterson (Royal Society of Canada's *Transactions*, Second Series, iii, section ii, 113) maintains that the scene of the shipwreck of the *Delight*, which led to Gilbert's disastrous return, was Cape Breton Island, on or near the shores of Louisburg harbor, and not Sable Island as has usually been supposed.

[2] This famous incident was related by Edward Hayes, one of the survivors on the larger vessel, to Hakluyt, and by him printed (*Voyages*, ed. 1600, iii, 159); it will be noticed that Hakluyt's informant said "a book" not "the book" as Longfellow described him: —

"Monday the ninth of September, in

"He sat upon the deck,
The Book was in his hand;
'Do not fear! Heaven is as near,'
He said, 'by water as by land!'"

Adrian Gilbert, brother of Sir Humphrey, and their half-brother, Walter Ralegh, succeeded to the dead explorer's rights. Walter Ralegh's astounding rise[1] in the favor of Elizabeth is no less certain than its history is doubtful; it assumed the tangible form of grants of estates seized from the Church and from so-called Irish rebels. In 1584 Elizabeth granted him a charter which confirmed to him, without limit of time, the powers that Gilbert had had.[2]

In May, 1584, two vessels sailed from England for America. They were fitted out by Ralegh, and were commanded by Philip Amadas and Arthur Barlowe.[3] Steering by way of the Canary Islands and the West Indies, it was July before they reached the mainland. Proceeding northward, they entered Pamlico Sound, "took possession" of the country, explored the neighborhood, and discovered Roanoke Island. They met many Indians — kings and brothers of kings, as well as those of humbler

the afternoon, the frigate [the *Swallow*, on which was Gilbert] was near cast away, oppressed by waves, yet at that time recovered: and giving forth signs of joy, the General [Gilbert] sitting abaft with a book in his hand, cried out unto us in the *Hind* (so oft as we did approach within hearing) *We are as near to heaven by sea as by land.* Reiterating the same speech, well beseeming a soldier, resolute in Jesus Christ, as I can testify he was."

[1] It is told from Fuller's *Worthies* (ed. 1662, 261), in Scott's *Kenilworth*, which is fully as reliable as many of the biographies of Ralegh, and vastly more interesting.

[2] It is sometimes stated that Ralegh's charter was confirmed by Act of Parliament, but no evidence of this has been adduced. A draught of a bill for this purpose is calendared in Royal Historical Manuscripts Commission's *Reports*, iii, p. 5. The "Journals" of the Lords and of the Commons show that the bill passed the lower House, and was lost in the Lords owing to a sudden adjournment (*Journals of the Lords*, ii, 76a). Mr. Hugh E. Egerton writes me that no act for this purpose is mentioned in the list of the unprinted statutes. It is possible that it was passed, and that all reference to it was excised from the records at the time of Ralegh's attainder.

[3] On the Ralegh expeditions, see Note III.

clay. The king's brother had on his head a broad plate of gold or copper; but which it was they could not tell, as, with a modesty unusual in Elizabethan seamen, they did not seize the savage and make a closer investigation. Perhaps it was on account of this excessive modesty on their part that the natives seemed to them to be "most gentle, loving, and faithful, void of all guile and treason, and such as live after the manner of the golden age." The sandy soil of the seashore of North Carolina appeared to the explorers to be fully up to the standard of its inhabitants, as it was "the most plentiful, sweet, fruitful, and wholesome of all the world." After a brief stay of two months, the expedition returned to England.

The explorers' glowing reports aroused great enthusiasm in England. Elizabeth permitted the new land to be named Virginia in her honor, and she knighted Ralegh for what Amadas and Barlowe had written — which probably had been carefully edited by the would-be knight. On his part, Ralegh had a new seal cut, on which he was denominated "Lord and Governor of Virginia," and set on foot a new expedition for a more careful exploration.

The commander of this second fleet was Sir Richard Grenville. Years later he won imperishable renown in command of the *Revenge* in her fight with fifty-three Spanish ships. He was a thoroughgoing Elizabethan seaman of the most ungovernable type, and possessed of "intolerable pride and insatiable ambition," according to one who had served with him. He had already been before the Council on charges of piracy, and the purpose of the present expedition was mainly plunder, with exploration distinctly of secondary importance. With Grenville went Cavendish, the third circumnavigator of the globe, who died at the early age of twenty-nine, after a career of plundering and sailing which was surpassed only by that of Sir Francis Drake. The party which was to explore Virginia was commanded by Ralph Lane, a man of reputation, but not of the stuff from which pioneers are made.

The fleet reached Porto Rico in May, 1585, and anchored in an unoccupied harbor. Going ashore, the adventurers erected a fort and began the construction of a pinnace from timber which they cut in the neighboring forest. Spanish horsemen appeared erelong. They viewed these proceedings from a safe distance and made off, when a party of footmen was sent against them. Later on, a stronger band of Spaniards ventured to expostulate with the newcomers about their "fortifying in their country" and refused to sell them supplies. In reply, the Englishmen set fire to the woods which surrounded the harbor and sailed away. Grenville next proceeded to Hispaniola. On the passage, he captured a couple of Spanish vessels laden with goods and "divers Spaniards of account." The latter bought their freedom with generous ransoms, and the captured articles were exchanged for supplies at San Domingo, somewhat against the will of the inhabitants of that town, who may have recognized the goods. Meantime, Lane with one of the vessels visited a port on the southern side of the island and seized a cargo of salt, while the Spanish owners stood helplessly by.

On June 20 the English fleet reached the coast of Florida and three days later nearly ran ashore in the vicinity of Cape Fear. Leaving Lane with one hundred men on Roanoke Island, Grenville sailed for home, capturing on the way a rich prize which probably paid the expenses of the voyage. The exploring party planted a few seeds and made sundry expeditions into the amphibious coastal region of North Carolina. On one of these they narrowly missed finding Chesapeake Bay.[1] Most of the time, however, seems to have been passed in a hopeless search for food. Grenville could spare scant store of provisions, and Lane wrote on the eve of the former's departure that provisions already were short, but that God "will command even the ravens to feed us."[2] He did not await this somewhat precarious mode of supply, but ordered the Indians to feed himself and his men. The natives at once forgot the "manners of the golden age"; they stole from the whites and prepared for a general massacre. Lane forestalled them in this, and by killing a number of the savages averted danger for the time.

Eight days after this event, Sir Francis Drake, fresh from the ransom of Cartagena, anchored off the coast. On his way north he had visited St. Augustine, destroyed the settlement at that place, and seized coin to the value of two thousand pounds sterling; but the Spaniards made off to the woods with such speed that none of them were captured.[3] Seeing the explorers' plight, he offered to take them back to England or to leave with them a vessel fully provisioned for the return voyage. A sudden storm sent the relief ship to the bottom. Drake had no other ship of suitable size, but said that, if Lane insisted on remaining,

[1] For a learned attempt to identify localities, see Hawks's *North Carolina*, i, 72.

[2] *Calendars of State Papers, America and West Indies, 1514–1660*, p. 3, also in *Archæologia Americana*, iv, 12. There are other letters from Lane in the same volume which are written in a tone of complaint against Grenville.

[3] See "A Summarie and true discourse of Sir Francis Drakes West Indian Voyage begun in the year 1585, wherein were taken the cities of Saint Jago, Santo Domingo, Cartagena, and the town of Saint Augustine in Florida. 1589. Publ. by Mr. Thomas Cates." This is now very rare; Hakluyt has included the substance of it in his *Voyages* (ed. 1600, iii, 534–548). The account of the destruction of St. Augustine is on pp. 546-548. A Spanish version of the Florida part of the story is in Barcia's *Ensayo Cronologico* (Madrid, 1723), under date of 1586.

one of his larger vessels should cruise off the coast until the explorers were ready to depart and then carry them home. But there was so much that was uncertain in this plan that Lane and his men embarked on Drake's fleet and reached England after a speedy passage of little more than a month.

The low shore of Virginia had hardly faded from the eyes of Lane and his men when a supply ship anchored off the coast, followed a fortnight later by Sir Richard Grenville himself, with provisions and recruits. Leaving fifteen men at the deserted post on Roanoke Island, he sailed for the West Indies where he extracted from the Spaniards the expenses of the expedition with added interest. A company of "Associates" was now formed, but under Ralegh's charter. Some of these associates were English capitalists who supplied the needed money; others came to Virginia as colonists. The story of their expedition is one of the tragedies of American history. Unfortunately, our knowledge of it rests almost entirely upon the testimony of its leader, John White;[1] what credence can be given to his evidence can best be gathered from the following summary of the narrative which has come down to us.

It was in May, 1587, that three vessels with men, women, and children sailed from Plymouth, England, for Virginia. No seaman was in chief command, and White was a landsman. It fell out, therefore, that he necessarily trusted the good faith and knowledge of the navigator, a Portuguese sailor, Simon Ferdinando, who had acted in that capacity for Grenville. The plan seems to have been

[1] John White was with Lane and drew the well-known pictures of native life. The original drawings are in the British Museum; nearly seventy-five of them have never been reproduced. See E. E. Hale in *Archæologia Americana*, iv, 21.

to seek out Chesapeake Bay, of which Lane had heard, although he had not seen it. On the way thither the expedition first visited Roanoke Island, to take on board the men whom Grenville had left there. These could not be found, but Simon Ferdinando, if we may believe White, induced the sailors to refuse to reëmbark those of the colonists who had already landed at Roanoke. The result was that all the settlers were set ashore at that place. White, the governor, went back to England with the home-going vessels to hurry forward supplies, for the colonists already seem to have been short of food. He left his daughter, his infant granddaughter, and his household effects at Roanoke as an earnest of his early return, and carried with him a certificate signed by the leading men to the effect that his going to England was necessary.

When White reached home Ralegh, even in the face of the coming Spanish Armada,[1] secured permission for two ships to sail for Virginia; but these vessels were so roughly handled by pirates at Madeira that they returned to England. In 1589 Ralegh made another assignment of his rights to a band of associates which included the colonists already in Virginia, through their attorneys in England, and merchants living in the home land. The history of Virginia in the years 1589–1605 is still vague and uncertain; but among the stockholders in this company of 1589, whether they were interested in the earlier enterprise or not, were several men who became prominent in the history of the later Virginia Company. Of these Richard Hakluyt was one, and it is not unlikely that the Thomas Smythe of 1589 and the treasurer of the later Virginia Company were one and the same person,

[1] Hume's *Ralegh*, 94.

although it is possible that one was the father, the other the son.[1]

It was 1591 before John White again visited Roanoke Island. The houses in which he had left his colonists were still standing, but they were tenantless. On the bark of a tree was cut the word "Croatoan." This was the name of an Indian tribe which lived at the other extremity of Pamlico Sound and was friendly, possibly because of the distance from Roanoke Island. White could not visit Croatoan because the commanders of the fleet which had brought him to Virginia were eager to get at the Spaniards. From that time to this the fate of "the lost colony" has been a fruitful theme for conjecture. The Jamestown settlers understood the Indians to say that the Roanoke people had been slaughtered by order of Powhatan. The more probable story is that they were befriended and assimilated by the Indians of Croatoan.[2] Even now it is not impossible that some of their descendants may be living in the Carolina mountains.

The year 1588, which was so eventful in the case of the first English colonists in America, was one of the most memorable years in the history of the English race. For the United States, it was more than memorable, it was vital. The defeat of the Spanish Armada accomplished the destruction of the morale of Spanish seamen; and that made possible the founding of Virginia, New England, New Netherland, and New Sweden on the Atlantic seashore of North America; from these in course of time developed the American Nation.

The people of the sixteenth century had different ideas from those which now prevail on commercial and colonial

[1] The statement in Brown's *Genesis* (i, 19) as to the "Associates" differs materially from that in Hawks's *North Carolina*, i, 195.

[2] See Note III.

matters. For Spain, colonists and colonies existed solely for the benefit of the mother country and its people. Colonists should buy from the mother country alone, paying such prices as the monopolizing home-dwellers saw fit to charge; they should also sell only to the home government and home merchants at prices which were regulated by the purchasers. The natural result of this policy was that the Spanish planters in the Indies cordially welcomed Hawkins and other illicit traders. Indeed, many of the reported captures and ransomings of towns by Drake and other Englishmen were possibly nothing more than carefully veiled illegal trade. Owing to their remoteness, it was equally difficult for the Spanish government to protect its colonists or to compel them to obey the commercial laws of Spain. The only way to check the growing commercial activity of Englishmen, therefore, was to attack it at its source, and to add England to the Spanish empire. This would at once and for all time put an end to these assaults on the Spanish colonial system. Such was the principal cause of the sending the Invincible Armada[1] to England. The religious difference between the two peoples was entirely secondary. The Spaniards seem to have been willing to do what they could to meet the religious prejudices of the English, with whom they had been close friends for generations.[2] On the English side, however, there was not the slightest thought of conciliation. A third cause which contributed to the sending of the Armada was the execution of Mary of Scotland, which left Philip II with a good claim to the

[1] The books on the Armada are enumerated in Note IV.

[2] See J. R. Seeley's *British Policy*, pt. i, and Laughton's masterly Introduction to the "Armada Papers" (Navy Records Society's *Publications*). The wild work Froude sometimes made with the records is noted on p. xxi of Laughton's Introduction. On a preceding page (xviii) Laughton makes the suggestion that writers have sometimes forgotten that "*Inquisicion* means equally the Inquisition and a judicial inquiry: *inquisidor* might be an inquisitor, or a magistrate, or, in the armada, the provost-marshal."

English throne, provided the Protestant holder and the Protestant heir apparent were passed over.[1] So we may say that Philip declared war mainly because the commercial situation had become intolerable and that to this both his religious prejudices and his dynastic hopes prompted him. War once begun, like a wise ruler he used to their utmost the religious and racial prejudices of his people. Before closing this part of the subject, it may be well to remember that the estrangement between the Spanish and English peoples was only a matter of less than half a century; and it should also be borne in mind that Philip II in his earlier years had expressed great admiration for Elizabeth Tudor and would gladly have made her his wife. On their part, Englishmen had come to view Spaniards and Spanish interests and desires with a savage contempt that by itself would almost have made war inevitable.[2]

Fortunately for England, in this last half century of growing estrangement and hatred, the Spaniards had not progressed in the art of maritime warfare, while Englishmen had broken loose from the traditions of the past and had evolved a new art of war applicable in the rough waters which washed the coasts of the British Isles. They invented a broadside fighting ship, placed on board of her the heaviest and best ordnance then known, and supplied her with crews drawn almost entirely from the seafaring population of the coast.[3] A fleet of fifty

[1] See Edwards's *Ralegh* (i, 290) for a genealogy which is there reprinted from a "Book against the King's title," alleged to have been circulated by Ralegh.

[2] Charles Kingsley's *Westward Ho!* gives an admirable lifelike picture of this religio-political fervor complicated with business and war. There is nothing resembling it in English history again until we come to the period of the Glorious Revolution of 1688.

[3] The defeat of the Armada was the "triumph of advanced organization and science over a maritime system that was dead and service traditions that had sunk into senility," Julian Corbett's *Drake and the Tudor Navy*, i, 365. For details of ships, see *ibid.*, i, ch. xii; ii, ch. vi, and

ships of this kind encountered a fleet of sixty-two Spanish vessels built on the lines of the Mediterranean sea fighter and designed for hand-to-hand conflict in still water. There could be only one result, and the failure of the Spanish Armada was scarcely doubtful after the fleets had been one day in contact. Led by Drake in the *Revenge*, the English line of battle swept to windward by the end of the Armada, sending broadsides into the windwardmost Spanish ships, to which no effective reply could be made. So went on the merry dance up Channel until the neighboring shore of France prevented the English from keeping the weather gauge. Fire ships, heavy winds, and strong currents drove the Spaniards through the Straits of Dover in grave disorder. Then came the seaman's opportunity. Round and round the disordered fleet the English vessels sailed, pouring broadside after broadside into the helpless Armada until the gunners on the Spanish ships fled from their pieces and groveled on the decks.[1] Only a sudden squall prevented Gravelines from being an earlier Santiago. Northward, the Invincible Armada fled and returned to Spain by way of Scotland and Ireland, every now and then dropping a vessel in the hungry sea or on the desolate shore. In all the Spaniards lost sixty-three vessels[2] and eight thousand men, but of the vessels lost only eleven were fighting ships, the remainder being supply vessels, dispatch boats, and the like.

This loss in fighting ships could be easily repaired with

Oppenheim's *Administration of the Royal Navy*. On the general question of the size of vessels of this period, see Massachusetts Historical Society's *Proceedings* for 1864, p. 464.

[1] The English *Vanguard* fired five hundred rounds from her great guns on this occasion. The English government had bought up the visible supply of gunpowder; all of it was weak and some of it was very poor. Had it been otherwise, no sudden change of wind could have saved the Armada.

[2] In all one hundred and twenty Spanish ships entered the Channel, but of these only sixty-two were fighting ships.

the resources at the command of Philip II; a new armada was speedily built, the individual vessels of which were greatly superior as fighting machines to those which had entered the English Channel under the command of the gallant Medina-Sidonia. The morale of the Spanish seamen, which had been destroyed in this unequal encounter, has never been restored. Occasionally, when two or more Spanish vessels came across a lonely English ship, they attacked her, as was the case with the *Margaret and John*, while on her way to Virginia in 1620 with colonists and supplies.[1] On this occasion, after five or six hours of cannonading, the Spaniards, who had certainly three guns to the Englishman's one, made off with their scuppers running with blood. Usually, however, the Virginia emigrant ships were allowed to sail unmolested among the islands of the Indies.

Once in a while, as for instance in 1609, the Spanish government sought to retaliate upon the Englishmen. In that year Captain Francisco Fernandez de Ecija in the *Asuncion de Christo* was ordered to sail to the James River, to investigate the English colony there, and to attack such English ships as he might fall in with. On July 24, at five o'clock in the afternoon, the Spaniards entered Chesapeake Bay and the lookout man reported a vessel — presumably an English ship — at anchor. Captain Ecija and his officers held a council of war and declared themselves to be most anxious to serve "God our Lord and his Majesty, the King." In the night, however, the other ship grew in size, and the next morning appeared to be "long and high." Captain Ecija now dis-

[1] Brown's *First Republic*, 415. More detailed accounts are in Purchas's *Pilgrimes* and Captain John Smith's *General History*, and an account was printed separately at Amsterdam in the same year.

covered that his mast was injured, and, again counseling with his officers, decided that "God and his Majesty would be best served by our going back," and so back he went.[1]

In writing of the destruction of the Armada, Julian Corbett compares the English and Spanish ships to rifle and blunderbuss. If the Elizabethan Age had produced nothing more, its reformation of the offshore sailing ship would in itself mark an era. Sir John Hawkins and those who worked with him in the reorganization of the royal navy had first of all sheared off one or two stories from the castles or cageworks which then oppressed the ends of the fighting ship. Over the low, middle portion of the ship, or the waist, as it is termed, Hawkins placed a deck. The result of this process was a high-sided, double-decked ship with low ends compared with the vessels of the preceding fifty years. The Elizabethan ship was cut away underneath at the ends, leaving long overhangs fore and aft, something after the manner of the racing yachts of our time.[2] On this hull were placed tall masts and a large sail area. Vessels of this type could keep the sea and work to windward as long as they could carry sail. In the whole course of Elizabeth's reign not one ship of the royal navy was lost by misadventure, and one only was lost in battle, and that through the rashness of the redoubtable Sir Richard Grenville in fighting single-handed a Spanish fleet. The Elizabethan ship was held up to her

[1] The only ship in the James at that time was Argall's small vessel, which had entered the river a few days earlier. At the moment Argall and his men were probably engaged in succoring Captain John Smith and his starving comrades; possibly the Spanish imagination formed a vessel from the trees and vines on shore. Brown's *First Republic*, 87-91.

[2] The *Vanguard*, Hawkins's latest ship, was 108 ft. keel and 145 ft. "overall." She was 32 ft. wide and 13 ft. deep. She was rated at 561 tons and belonged to the same class as the *Revenge* and the *Nonpareil*. See Oppenheim's *Administration of the Royal Navy*, 124.

work by a great quantity of sand or gravel, which was shoveled into her hold when she was launched and remained in place during her life. This large amount of ballast occupied the space which might otherwise have been given to supplies of food, drink, and clothing. One vessel, to make a long voyage, required two or three attendant storeships to keep her supplied with the necessaries for her crew — as was the case, for example, on Drake's great voyage to the Pacific. It also made it impossible for a vessel to carry more than enough food to an American colony to feed her passengers on the way over and see her crew safely home to England. The lot of the passengers, indeed, was anything but an enviable one. On the sand ballast under the main hatch was built a brick fireplace, its chimney extending through the hatchway. On the same ballast, at varying distances from this center of food and heat, were the emigrant's quarters. The condition of one of these interiors during a five months' voyage from the Thames to the James River through the tropics baffles description; the captain who reached port with the loss of only ten per cent of his passengers might consider himself fortunate.

To the modern reader the armament of an Elizabethan ship seems nearly as bewildering as it did to the unfortunate Spaniard: cannon, demicannon, culverin, and demiculverin vie with harquebus-a-croc, murtherers, and fowlers to drive all understanding from one's head. The matter is not difficult of comprehension, however, if we divide the guns on these old ships into main and secondary battery, as the guns on a modern war vessel are divided. The three pieces last named were small guns mounted on the non-recoil principle and were breechloaders. In the breech was cast a "stirrup-piece." The ball was placed in the bore of the gun and wrapped in hemp or grass to keep it from rolling out with the surge of the sea; into the slot of the stirrup was placed a "chamber," which was filled with powder and was wedged into its place. When firing, the gunner was careful not to stand on one side of the gun, lest the wedge should fly out and kill him. Some of these guns could be discharged as often as once in every two minutes. They were the "quick firers" of their time and when the supply of iron ran low, as it did in 1588, arrows were fired from them.[1]

The cannon and demicannon, the culverin and demiculverin and the sakers formed the main battery. The demicannon were short guns similar to the thirty-two-pound carronade of the War of 1812; the culverin was not unlike a long seventeen-pounder of the same epoch, while the demiculverin answered very well to the long nine-pounder with which the American privateers of that time were often supplied. These guns in the time of Hawkins and Drake were light because the powder used in them was poor. English ships in the reigns of Elizabeth and James I were heavily armed with long guns, mostly of the demiculverin type, with a small secondary battery; the Spaniards, on the other hand, carried guns of the demicannon type, with a large secondary battery. In this way may be explained the fact that the *Margaret and John* of eight guns for five hours kept up a running combat with two Spanish ships of sixteen and twelve guns respectively.

The reigns of Elizabeth Tudor and of James Stuart, her immediate successor, mark in English history the transition from mediæval to modern times, which is shown not only

[1] For details as to ordnance, see Oppenheim and Corbett and W. W. Greene's *The Gun and Its Development*.

in the remodeling of the fighting ship, but in other ways as well. The Tudor monarchy was essentially feudal, while the England of Charles I was as essentially modern. The world was rapidly changing; this silent revolution took place in England earlier than elsewhere. The causes were many: the keen religious excitement of the preceding half century, the wave of imperialism which swept over the English race, and the reorganization of domestic economy which the religious disturbances and the intercourse with Eastern countries brought about. To this revolution Elizabeth and James powerfully contributed through the defects of their qualities: Elizabeth by her strength prevented reform; James by his foolish cunning made certain that the process of reorganization which was inevitable would, nevertheless, not be easy.

Elizabeth was a typical Tudor. Lacking in the finer qualities of humanity, she possessed unerring political foresight and indomitable will; no modern politician has ever gauged the people's wish more accurately than she. Whenever it was clearly safe to do so, she domineered over her subjects like an Eastern despot; when it was time to yield, she gave way with a smiling graciousness of demeanor that completely hid the constitutional point involved.[1] For example, on one occasion she sought to give pecuniary advancement to a favorite in a way which was clearly illegal. When the judges declared her order to be against the law of the land, against their oaths as judges, against her coronation oath, and in contempt of God, Elizabeth "well accepted" the rebuff and looked about for some safer way to reward a friend.[2] Frequently she raised

[1] See Simonds D'Ewes's *Journal of the Parliaments of Elizabeth*, 460, 478.

[2] The "Matter of Cavendish." Anderson's *Reports*, i, 152 (in English in Thayer's *Cases in Constitutional Law*, i, 12).

money in an unconstitutional manner; when the victim of a forced levy appeared before her, she smiled graciously, held out her hand to be kissed, and, if convenient, rewarded him with the grant of a monopoly or of lands filched from the Church or seized from the Irish. Two things, however, she would not allow to be discussed; these were reforms in religion and in politics. On one occasion she directed the Speaker of the House of Commons to bring to her a bill which that House had under consideration. When he came with it, she took it and tore it up. The English nation bore with these actions of its aged ruler, because, in the first place, they respected her, and in the second place, it was quite certain that she could not live forever. After her would come the deluge.

In the first year of the seventeenth century the flood of desire for change rose to such a height that for a moment it seemed as if the deluge were come. This was the movement which is known as the Essex Affair, and was an attempt to force Elizabeth's consent to radical measures. It cost Essex his life, Elizabeth keen sorrow, and several founders of Virginia their liberty for the remainder of her reign. For instance, Sir Thomas Smythe, the first treasurer of the Virginia Company, was committed to the Tower and stayed there until the accession of James; the Earl of Southampton, the third treasurer of the Virginia Company, was convicted of treason and barely escaped the block; and Lord de la Warr, long the mainstay of the Virginia enterprise, was involved in the scheme. Sir Edwin Sandys, the second treasurer of the Virginia Company, was out of England at the moment, or he would, doubtless, have kept Sir Thomas Smythe and the Earl of Southampton company. As it was, he was one of the first Englishmen to reach the court of the Stuart king. Had her successor been the wisest and bravest ruler who ever lived, changes were certain to follow Elizabeth's decease. He turned out to be one of those curiosities whom the laws of inheritance occasionally bring to the notice of mankind.

Shrewd and wary, well educated, and trained in the school of adversity, James Stuart lacked personal dignity and political wisdom; in spite of his cunning, he sometimes said things which years of gravity and success would not cause men to forget. Take, for example, the story of two speeches[1] to the assembled members of Parliament. In the one he said that he and Buckingham were "like a cow's tail." In the other he described himself as an old and experienced king, and declared that "kings are not only God's lieutenants upon earth and sit on God's throne, but even by God Himself are called gods." Without thought, he involved himself in dispute after dispute with the various religious and civil elements which were pressing forward for changes in Church and State. Once entangled in an argument on any subject, James I never knew when he was beaten. He found himself obliged to submit to many humiliations; he solidified against his son the most active and aggressive elements in the English population.

[1] The first of these speeches is described by Gardiner in his *History of England*, iv, 49; the second is taken from the *Works of King James* (ed. 1616), 529; it is also given in Prothero's *Statutes*, 293. These examples might be largely multiplied as, for instance, James's First Speech to Parliament, *ibid.*, 485.

NOTES

I. The Hawkins Voyages. — The Hawkins expeditions are narrated by Hakluyt in his *Voyages*[1] (ed. 1600, iii, 500–525). These accounts are accessible to the ordinary reader in the Hakluyt Society's volume entitled *The Hawkins' Voyages.* Turned into the clearest English prose, they are in Southey's *British Admirals,* vol. iii. An excellent reprint of this portion of Southey's work is *English Seamen by Robert Southey,* one volume, edited by David Hannay. Arber's *English Garner* (vol. v) contains the best modern reprint of the Hakluyt narrative; but the notes are of uneven value. E. J. Payne's *Elizabethan Seamen* is full and useful on the matters treated in this chapter. Julian Corbett, in his *Drake and the Tudor Navy* (i, 414), has a valuable bibliographical note on the Third Voyage. Froude's *English Seamen in the Sixteenth Century* is interesting and painfully inaccurate.

II. Drake's Voyage. — The best life of Drake is Julian Corbett's *Drake and the Tudor Navy;* this part of the great seaman's life is treated in the first volume. The main source of information concerning the voyage to the Pacific is *The World Encompassed by Sir Francis Drake, collected out of the Notes of Master Francis Fletcher* (London, 1628). This account, with nearly all other known material, is printed in the Hakluyt Society's volume with the above title; the notes to this edition are of little value. Markham's *Sarmiento's Voyages* (Hakluyt Society) gives the Spanish view. A few other papers are noted in Corbett's *Drake and the Tudor Navy,* i, 423. The poor proofreading of Markham's chapter on "Voyages and Discoveries, 1485–1603" in Laird Clowes's *History of the Royal Navy* greatly detracts from the value of what would otherwise be a convenient summary.

III. The Ralegh Expeditions. — On these expeditions, see the narratives in Hakluyt's *Voyages* (ed. 1600, iii, 243–295). These are reprinted in Hawks's *North Carolina* and in the Prince Society's volume entitled *Sir Walter Ralegh.* The Ralegh patent is in *Charters and Constitutions of the United States,* ii, 1379.

As to the "lost colonists" and their fate, see Brown's *Genesis,* i, 189; S. B. Weeks in *Magazine of American History,* xxv, 127, and

[1] The most convenient edition is the MacLehose reprint of 1903–05, which has the pagination of the 1600 edition on the margin.

American Historical Association's *Papers*, v, pt. 4; "Loungings in the Footprints of the Pioneers," by E. C. Bruce in *Harper's Magazine*, xx, 730; "The Surroundings of Ralegh's Colony," by Talcott Williams in American Historical Association's *Papers*, 1895, 17; and Hamilton McMillan's *Sir Walter Ralegh's Lost Colony*.

IV. The Armada.—Few subjects have undergone such a thorough reconstruction within the last few years as has this. Oppenheim, Laughton, and Corbett, to use the last named's homely phrase, "have disinterred the truth" and set it where he who cares to may read. The original records are in the *Calendars of State Papers*,[1] in the first two volumes issued by the Navy Records Society under the editorship of Professor Laughton and entitled "Armada Papers" and the corresponding Spanish publication edited by Captain Duro as "L'Armada Invincible." Of the secondary books may be mentioned Oppenheim's *Administration of the Royal Navy*, which is an excellent book with an extremely misleading title, and Julian Corbett's *Drake and the Tudor Navy*. Of the older accounts that by Southey in his *British Admirals* remains decidedly the best. Froude's description in his *History of England* is woefully misleading. There are some good illustrations in Clowes's *History of the Royal Navy;* but like all coöperative works it is disappointing and sometimes irritating. There is no good modern account in brief compass; that by W. F. Tilton in *The Century* best represents the facts.

[1] *Domestic, 1581–1590; Spanish, 1587–1603.* See also *Acts of the Council, 1588.* The *Calendars* are reviewed by W. F. Tilton in *American Historical Review*, v, 754.

CHAPTER VI

THE GENESIS OF THE UNITED STATES

In one hundred years before 1600 the stock of gold and silver in Western Europe increased threefold.[1] In this statement may be read the misery and death of the native races of America and the dislocation of the social organization of European countries, notably of England, from which in turn flowed the first great wave of English colonial and commercial expansion. The effects of this increase in the circulating medium were earliest felt in Spain; it was the middle of the century before their results were especially noticeable in England. Then, as Elizabeth's reign progressed, there were seen an ever increasing display of luxury in the mansions of the rich and an increasing amount of misery in the homes of the poor, — which seem to be significant of rapid changes in the supply of the standard of exchange.

The opening years of the seventeenth century found landowners in receipt of the largest income from their acres that they have ever received. The *Verney Memoirs*, for example, tell us that one estate in Buckinghamshire let for more pounds sterling in 1630 than it did in 1870, although the purchasing power of the pound sterling in 1630 was about four times what it was in 1870.[2] Yet it may well be doubted if the landowners were as prosperous in the reign of James as they had been in the last

[1] See Lexis in *Handwörterbuch der Staatswissenschaften* (ed. 1899), iv, 751, 762; vi, 732, and Wiebe's *Preisrevolution*, 272.

[2] *Verney Memoirs*, i, 130.

years of Henry VIII. Their returns in money were greater, it is true; but the prices of those commodities which might be described as the necessaries of the rich had largely increased, and at the same time the scale of living had undergone so great a change that the mode of life of their grandfathers and grandmothers seemed to savor of the days of barbarism. Castles hoary with age, which had sheltered a manorial family for centuries, gave place to Elizabethan mansions, which were provided with such new-fangled conveniences as chimneys and glass windows. Rugs and carpets, linen sheets, and silken doublets were becoming fashionable and were very expensive. Lady Verney gives the price of her "best sheets" in 1640 as eight pounds, at a time when ten pounds would purchase a good horse.[1] The growing oceanic commerce brought wealth to the merchants and the shopmen; it caused ever increasing expenditures on the part of the aristocracy. The last years of Elizabeth saw an outburst of splendor and luxury which even now, after three hundred years have passed away, fairly staggers belief. The problem of clothing and housing younger sons and giving them a start in life was becoming more difficult every year.

While the war with Spain continued "gentlemen volunteers" found fame and fortune on the decks of the privateer or of the more regular war ship. Elizabeth's successor stopped that outlet for energy by making peace with Spain. There was nothing remarkable in this change of policy, for Spain was tired of war and James had no cause of enmity against the Spaniards. The son of

[1] *Verney Memoirs*, i, 10. In 1598 the churchwardens of St. Michaels in Bedwardine in Worcester paid 1*s*. 8*d*. for one pound of sugar. Ale and wine were still the staple beverages; chocolate seems to have been "quite new" in 1650, at which time coffee begins to be mentioned, and tea comes in with the second Charles in 1660. See *Verney Memoirs*, i, 13, and Pepys's *Diary* under 1660.

Mary Stuart, the Catholic Queen of Scots, had no dislike for those who obeyed the Pope; some writers maintain, indeed, that Robert Cecil urged on the Gunpowder Plot[1] for the express purpose of rousing James's anger against the Roman Catholics. Furthermore, with his ideas of the divine right of kings to do as they pleased with the lives and property of their subjects, James had no sympathy with the Dutch, who were striving to wring their independence from Spain. On the contrary, he regarded the gallant men of Holland as no better than so many rebels. In 1604, by treaty between the representatives of England and of Spain, it was agreed that the war between the two powers should come to an end.[2] Undoubtedly it never occurred to Philip III of Spain that the gentlemen volunteers, deprived of their old occupation, would throng the decks of the English emigrant ships bound to the Indies. Yet so it was, for among the early comers to Virginia we find George Percy, the younger brother of the Duke of Northumberland, and Francis, John, and Nathaniel West, ninth, twelfth, and thirteenth children of the second Lord de la Warr. Penelope West, their sister, married Herbert Pelham; and among her sixteen children were the first treasurer of Harvard College and the second wife of John Bellingham, governor of Massachusetts.[3]

[1] Among the recent books on this subject may be mentioned Gerard's *What was the Gunpowder Plot?* and Gardiner's *What Gunpowder Plot was*. Gerard (p. 279) gives an interesting table showing amounts received as "Recusants' Fines."

[2] The treaty is in Dumont's *Corpus Universal Diplomatique du Droit des Gens*, v, pt. ii, 32, and in Rymer's *Fœdera*, xvi, 617. Gardiner gives extracts from an English translation in the Harleian Mss. in his *History of England*, i, 208–213.

[3] Historical writers have been altogether too prone to draw a hard and fast line of demarcation between the settlers of the Southern colonies and those who founded colonies north of the fortieth parallel. For instance, it is sometimes said that the Northern colonists came to the New World for conscience' sake, and the Southern planters sought wealth alone; but no such generalization can truthfully be made. Moreover, it is oftentimes the custom to point out some mysterious difference between the Virginian and the New Englander, which

The rise in prices and increase in the scale of living, which made it difficult for the well-to-do to make the two ends meet, produced a far more disastrous effect upon those in the community who depended for their food upon the earnings of their hands; the prices of food rose out of proportion to the rise in wages; while landowners and tenant farmers found it necessary to make every acre produce its utmost, with slight regard for the well-being of the laboring classes. It is true that prices increased less in those things that the poorer people used than they did in those things which the richer sort now demanded. At the same time, however, wages rose slightly if at all.[1] Nowadays, if the workingman does not obtain the return in money which he deems fitting, he stops working until his employer is worn out and settles the dispute, or until the laborer acknowledges himself to be beaten. In the days of which we are now speaking, the landed gentry of each neighborhood, in the guise of justices of the peace, fixed the wages which should be paid. If a laborer regarded these wages as insufficient and declined to work for them, the law provided that these same justices could have him arrested as a vagabond, a valiant rogue, or a sturdy beggar, send him to the whip-

can be expressed by the words "cavalier" and "Puritan," the latter term, when thus used, signifying a social condition below that of the cavalier. No such characterization is possible. If there was one person in England who possessed those distinctions of blood which no king could give, that man was John Hampden. His cousin, Oliver Cromwell, was nephew of Sir Oliver Cromwell, one of the members of the Virginia Company, and was closely related to Sir Thomas Smythe, the head of that enterprise. Isaac Johnson, son-in-law of the Earl of Lincoln, was one of the first victims of the inhospitable climate of Boston, and Sir George Yeardley, governor of Virginia, was the son of a merchant tailor and first cousin to John Harvard's stepfather.

[1] On the general subject of prices and wages, see Thorold Rogers's *History of Agriculture and Prices*. The following Magistrates' Assessment for wages in Rutlandshire is taken from Traill's *Social England*, iii, 544: —

		1564	1610
Artisans	Summer	9*d.*	9 or 10*d.*
	Winter	8	8
Agricultural laborers	Summer	7	7
	Winter	6	6

ping post, bind him out to a master, or put him in jail. The century under review witnessed, in the midland counties, that change from agriculture to sheep raising [1] which has been often described, and the results of which have been sometimes overestimated. However great or small the change may have been, undoubtedly there was some change, and each holding diverted from agriculture and turned into sheep walks meant the employment of fewer persons on the land. The dissolution of the monasteries, in the time of Henry VIII, threw upon the charitable people of England many helpless men and women; the story of the dispossessed monks and nuns is not a pleasant one to turn back to. Still less pleasant is the story of the tenants and laborers on the monastic properties; those establishments seem to have been easy landlords and masters, which the new owners certainly were not. With the closing of the monasteries, also, one source of help for the poor and friendless had dried up, and new sources of aid were slowly provided. New avenues of employment opened to the industrious working people in the demand for homespun yarn and for hands to operate the looms which were now marking the beginning of the manufacture of cloth in England. But these conditions did not exist for the poorest of the poor. For them there was little besides the constable's lash,[2] the deck of the war ship, or the hold of the emigrant vessel.

One further way of relieving the land of its surplus inhabitants remains to be noticed, and that was the plague. This was endemic in England in the reigns of Elizabeth

[1] See map prepared by E. F. Gay to illustrate his article on "Inclosures in England in the Sixteenth Century" in *The Quarterly Journal of Economics* for August, 1903.

[2] In the little parish of Bromsgrove, in Worcestershire, in the first year of James's reign, eleven men and six women were punished with the stocks and whipping (Worcester County *Records*, i, 70). See also *Records of the North Riding* (Yorkshire).

and James. Every few years a peculiarly violent visitation of the plague sheared off a portion of the submerged tenth of the population, and left the survivors poorer and more helpless than they were before. Scurvy, also, was a common disease on shore as well as at sea; for the winter's meats were necessarily salted, and fresh vegetables, as the potato, were not yet available. From 1607 to 1625 the plague and the scurvy[1] claimed only a tithe of their usual victims, and left the balance free to die of malaria and starvation on the banks of the James River.

While the poor were thus growing poorer, the upper and middle classes were increasing in wealth. For the first time in English history capital was abundant; the use of credit in commercial affairs became extended, and new avenues for investment were eagerly sought. One significant change of the time is the turning of the shops of the goldsmiths of London into banking rooms, and the legalization of usury; in the future, the effort of legislators is to restrain the exacting of exorbitant interest, it is no longer to prohibit money lending on interest. Capitalists were beginning to seek new modes of investment as, for example, in manufacturing enterprises, many of which were now being set on foot, especially by artisans who had fled from the devastations of the religious wars of the continent. Above all, moneyed men sought investments in commercial ventures to far-off seas and foreign shores. In 1599 thirty thousand pounds were subscribed for an expedition to the East Indies; among the subscribers were sixty persons who afterward became

[1] There is a great mass of interesting information on these somewhat lugubrious topics in Charles Creighton's *History of Epidemics in Britain*, vol. i, and in the same author's chapters in Traill's *Social England*, vols. iii and iv. The weak part of Dr. Creighton's work is his description of epidemics in the colonies.

interested in the Virginia Company.[1] Fourteen years later four hundred thousand pounds, the equivalent of eight million dollars in our time, were raised in a fortnight to equip an expedition to the Far East.

Sir Thomas Smythe,[2] the first treasurer of the Virginia Company and the manager of that enterprise in its most critical years, did more than any other merchant of his day to open the world to English commerce. He was the son of Mr. "Customer" Smythe, collector of the subsidy of Tonnage and Poundage, and second cousin "once removed" of Oliver Cromwell. At an early age the younger Smythe began to be interested in schemes of exploration and colonization, and by his connections and business ability rapidly accumulated wealth. Probably he was one of the assignees of Ralegh's patent in 1589. When the East India Company was formed, in October, 1600, he was appointed its first governor. He was believed to be complicated in the Essex Affair, was dismissed from the shrievalty, and was sent to the Tower. He also resigned the governorship of the company. Three years later, on the accession of James, he was released from prison, was knighted, and again took his place at the head of the East India Company. With the exception of one year he remained in charge of that great enterprise until 1621, when he requested the shareholders to relieve him of the burden. It is not going too far to say that he was the founder of the British empire in India.[3] He was also governor of the

[1] Brown's *Genesis*, i, 25.

[2] Cf. Wadmore's "Sir Thomas Smythe" (*Archæologia Cantiana*, also printed separately); Professor Laughton's article in *Dictionary of National Biography*; Brown's *Genesis*, ii, 1012 (portrait on p. 900); and Markham's *Baffin's Voyages* (Hakluyt Society's *Publications*, with portrait).

[3] On this part of Smythe's career, see books on the East India Company, especially Birdwood and Foster's *Register of Letters*. Besides Smythe and Sandys, about one hundred other members of the East India Company were interested in Virginia at one time or another.

Muscovy Company,[1] which traded to Russia, and in 1604 went on a special embassy to the court of the Czar. He was interested in the Levant Company and in other enterprises, and was the constant patron of explorers. For instance, he was one of those who sent Hudson to Hudson Bay, Thomas Poole to Greenland, Thomas Button to discover the Northwest Passage, and William Baffin to the Arctic. His name was attached by grateful commanders to headlands, bays, islands, and capes the world over; among others to Smith Sound in the Arctic, and to Smith Island at the entrance of Chesapeake Bay. In 1618 he was appointed one of the commissioners of the royal navy, and in 1622 was elected to Parliament. His house in Philpot Lane must have been of generous proportions, as it lodged at one time the Marquis Tremouille, ambassador from France, and his retinue of one hundred and twenty persons. For years it was the headquarters of the Virginia Company, and in its rooms were doubtless held the consultations which resulted in the formation of that corporation and the founding of Jamestown. Owing to its convenient situation it may also have witnessed the meetings which led to the settlement of Boston, as it later belonged to Increase Nowell, secretary of the Massachusetts Bay Company.

Sir Thomas Smythe's interests and those of his partners in the first expeditions to Virginia were of a twofold character, but both of a purely business nature: they hoped that the long-sought-for passage to India and Cathay led through the American continent at that point, and they had no unreasonable expectations that gold and silver would be found there in such quantities as to pay the costs of the expeditions and possibly bring in fortunes

[1] The Muscovy Company was founded by Smythe's grandfather, Sir Andrew Judd.

to all concerned.[1] With our present knowledge of that region those expectations appear chimerical. To do justice to Sir Thomas Smythe and his advisers, we must put ourselves in their places and view things as they knew them. Thus seen, there is nothing fanciful in their expectations. America was then deemed to be the land of gold and silver. Wealth untold had poured into the coffers of Spain from Mexico and from Peru; why not into those of England from Virginia? The explorers of that region, time and again, had reported signs of gold; Ralegh's men had even seen ornaments of gold or of copper, but exactly which, they could not definitely determine. The old tales which had lured Spaniards to New Mexico now enticed Englishmen to Virginia. The best known of the latter type is Seagull's description in *Eastward Hoe* which was partly written by no less a person than Ben Jonson. In this play Virginia is pictured as a land "Where gold and silver is more plentiful than copper is with us;"[2] one ton of the latter metal could be exchanged for three tons of the former in that land of enchantment where even the prisoners' fetters were made of fine gold. These expectations at first seemed to be well founded, for Newport, returning home in the summer of 1607, brought with him a small bit of real gold and a barrel of pyrites or "fool's gold."[3] The particles which glistened in the sand had deceived Captain Martin, whose father was Master of the Royal Mint and whose brother-in-law, Sir Julius Cæsar, was later Chancellor of the Exchequer or Minister of Finance. It was not until two assays had been made in England that

[1] Chapter i of Bruce's *Economic History of Virginia* summarizes the more important information on this topic.

[2] This well-known passage is printed in full in Brown's *Genesis* (i, 30) and in many other places.

[3] Brown's *First Republic*, 32.

Captain Martin's belief was proved to be unfounded; and it is not impossible but that he was right and the assayers were wrong, for, curiously enough, free gold often exists in Virginia in close association with pyrites. When Newport returned to Virginia, he carried over with him two goldsmiths upon whose recommendation a whole shipload of pyrites was taken to England. When this was also proved by assay to be "fool's gold," the search in Virginia was extended toward the mountains. One Faldo, "an Helvetian," actually discovered a mine, but died before he could find it again. When the son of the Master of the Mint, expert goldsmiths of London, and professional prospectors like the "Helvetian" go wrong, why heap ridicule on plain business men whose occupation forces them to rely on expert opinion? As a matter of fact there was gold in that region, for in the fifty years from 1804 to 1853 the states of Virginia and North Carolina produced nine and one quarter million dollars' worth of gold, and even as late as the year 1899 forty-two thousand dollars' worth of gold and silver were produced in those states.[1] With the history of California, of Australia, of South Africa, and of the Klondike in one's mind, it is easy to imagine what would have happened in Virginia had gold in paying quantities been found there in the first part of the seventeenth century instead of two hundred years later.

Next to greed of gold, the controlling motive which inspired the partners in the Virginia venture was the probability that a sea route to China was awaiting some happy explorer in the vicinity of the fortieth parallel. No living

[1] See J. D. Whitney's *Metallic Wealth of the United States*, 145; Williams's "Mineral Resources of the United States" (*Geological Survey Reports*, 1882, p. 180); Day's *Report on Mineral Resources* (1902), 120, 122.

person had then the slightest conception of the size of North America, and the natives who ought to have known constantly affirmed that only a few days' march from the seaboard there was a "great water." One form of this story, which seems to have impressed even so scientific a man as Thomas Hariot,[1] was that the waves of this supposed western sea sometimes washed into the heads of rivers which emptied into the Atlantic. At different places along the coast, the natives told what amounted to the same story; and it was true. But the "great water" which the whites interpreted to be the South Sea, in the Indians' minds stood for Lake Champlain, or the Great Lakes, or the Mississippi River. Furthermore, no one can voyage through Chesapeake Bay or Delaware Bay with the story of the early explorers in his mind without seeing how entirely justified they were in their expectation that they were on the long-sought passage to the South Sea. And, finally, until every inlet of those bays and of the Hudson River had been explored by water or environed by land, no one could say definitely that the next returning ship would not bring news of the discovery of the western waterway. At all events, it is quite certain that without some such material inducements, as those just noted, to spur them on, Sir Thomas Smythe and his partners would not have sent the *Susan Constant* across the Atlantic in the winter and spring of 1607.

Even if the hoped-for treasure should fail to be found

[1] Thomas Hariot's *Brief and True Report of the new found land of Virginia*. This was first issued in 1588-89 and has been many times reprinted, as, for instance, in facsimile, by Henry Stevens, with an admirable biography (reviewed by Charles S. Peirce in *American Historical Review*, vi, 557), in the *Bibliographer*, i. With White's drawings it was printed by De Bry at Frankfort in 1590, and has been reprinted, in facsimile, by the Holbein Society from that edition. Quaritch in 1893 reprinted the text of the 1590 edition with the pictures in reduced facsimile, but large enough for ordinary use.

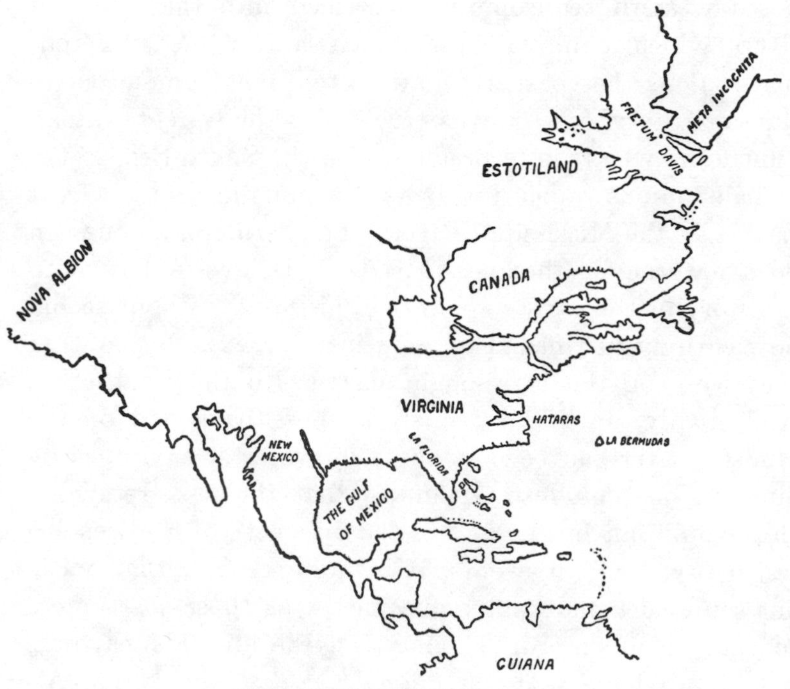

THE "MOLINEAUX" MAP, 1600

(This sketch of the outlines of the Molineaux Map of 1600 shows the geographical knowledge of North America at the disposal of Sir Thomas Smythe in forming his plans for the Virginia voyage of 1607.)

and an easy route to the East Indies should continue to prove elusive, there still was hope that the holders of Virginia stock might receive some slight return from the money which they invested in the enterprise. Ralph Lane, Ralegh's chosen explorer, had reported the soil of Virginia to be the "goodliest under the cope of heaven," and "very well peopled and towned." Besides the deposits of gold and silver, Hariot, "the Huxley of his time,"[1] reported the existence of mines of copper and of iron. In those days, when iron was smelted with charcoal, the latter discovery was of great importance because the forests of England were limited, while those of Virginia were illimitable. Not only would these forests provide charcoal, they would also furnish lumber of all shapes and sizes, from clapboards to ships' masts. Virginia grapes were reported to be larger and finer than those of Europe, which gave good promise for the production of wine.

The considerations which have been adverted to in the preceding paragraphs were all of a material kind, but the first expeditions to Virginia were purely business ventures. With the last years of the old century and the first years of the new there was a widespread revival of English maritime enterprise. Trading voyages to the East Indies turned out to be profitable, and plundering expeditions were constantly harassing the Spaniards in the West Indies, while fishing vessels crossed the North Atlantic to Newfoundland, and fur traders began to frequent the shores of New England. Many of these voyages are known to us only from scattered hints, but a few of them are better chronicled and deserve some slight attention in this place.

[1] G. Brown Goode gave Hariot this designation (*Beginnings of Natural History in America*, 2).

Sir Walter Ralegh's patent still interfered to hamper expeditions to North America. Once in a while he himself fitted out an expedition to plunder the Spaniards and incidentally to look up "the lost colonists," or to secure valuable cargoes by purchase or by honest labor. Among these was the voyage of Samuel Mace[1] in 1602, and of Bartholomew Gilbert in 1603 — the latter was murdered by the Indians somewhere between the capes of the Chesapeake and Sandy Hook. The preceding year, 1602, besides the expedition of Samuel Mace, two other voyages were made across the Atlantic. One of these was sent out by the East India Company, under the command of George Weymouth, to seek a waterway to the Pacific; he reached Greenland, or possibly Labrador, and returned home.[2] The other expedition was commanded by Bartholomew Gosnold and was fitted out, in part at least, by the Earl of Southampton. Gosnold coasted the shore of what are now the states of New Hampshire and Massachusetts, built a rude hut on one of the islands which lie off the southern coast of the latter, filled his vessel's hold with sassafras, and returned to England in safety. The proceeds of the trip were at once confiscated by Ralegh, but this exercise of power was one of his last acts in connection with North America, as his attainder caused the forfeiture of his patent.

In 1603, the same year that Bartholomew Gilbert sailed in Ralegh's service, John Whitson and other Bristol merchants dispatched Martin Pring with two vessels to the

[1] For this paragraph and those immediately following I am indebted to Mr. G. P. Winship for a sight of his "Introductions" to Stevens's reprint of the accounts of Archer, Brereton, and Rosier. These may conveniently be used in Massachusetts Historical Society's *Collections*, Third Series, viii. Brereton's *Briefe and True Relation* (London, 1602) is reprinted in the *Bibliographer*, i. See also Purchas's *Pilgrimes*, pt. iv, bk. viii, chs. 9–13.

[2] Stevens's *Dawn of English Trade to the East Indies.*

New England coast. In 1604 George Weymouth again crossed the Atlantic. Arundel of Wardour and the Earl of Southampton were those whose names figure most prominently as the promoters of this expedition; for this reason, it has sometimes been surmised to have been a Roman Catholic enterprise. At all events, Weymouth, falling short of the Northwest Passage, "happened into a river on the coast of America called Pemaquid," which accident, according to Sir Ferdinando Gorges, "must be acknowledged the means under God of putting on foot and giving life to all our plantations."[1] In point of fact, Weymouth's glowing report of the climate and resources of the country in the neighborhood of the Kennebec River was the one thing necessary to stimulate persons of influence and capital to exploit more thoroughly than had yet been done the resources and possibilities of the Atlantic seashore of North America. In 1606 James I issued a patent under the great seal, which is generally cited as the first Virginia Charter.[2]

This document is a landmark in the history of territorial boundaries and of the constitutional rights of English colonists in America. In it the English king definitely claimed the right to colonize American lands between the thirty-fourth and forty-fifth parallels of latitude,[3] or from Cape Fear River to Halifax — the northern and southern limits of "Virginia." The grantees under this patent were divided into two groups, each of which was denominated a colony or company. The idea of the king seems to have been to establish two plantations on plots of ground each

[1] See Brown's *Genesis*, i, 50, for the passage in full.

[2] The charter is in *Charters and Constitutions of the United States*, ii, and in Brown's *Genesis*, i.

[3] On the northern boundary, see W. F. Ganong's "Boundaries of New Brunswick" in Royal Society of Canada's *Transactions*, Second Series, vii, section ii, p. 139 and fol.

extending one hundred miles along the seacoast and one hundred miles inland. That group of grantees having its headquarters in London was given the exclusive right to plant the first settlement between thirty-four and thirty-eight degrees of north latitude.[1] Similarly, those patentees who lived in the west of England were to have the exclusive right to plant the first colony between forty-one and forty-five degrees of north latitude. The intervening degrees of latitude (thirty-eight to forty-one) were to be open to colonization by either company, but the first body to make a settlement should have one hundred miles of seacoast — fifty miles north and fifty miles south of the site of its first settlement — whether made within its own peculiar territory or within the region common to both colonies.[2] This curious arrangement is doubtless an example of that silly cunning which earned for James the title of "the wisest fool in Christendom." At all events, neither group of grantees sought to appropriate the region common to both; each took good care to plant its first colony on land to which the other had no right.

The most extraordinary thing about the Virginia Patent is the bald and barefaced claim which James Stuart made to a large part of the New World only two years after the signing of the treaty of London. The only circumstance parallel to it is the further fact that, notwithstanding his

[1] The thirty-eighth parallel marks the mouth of the Potomac River; the forty-first parallel crosses the Hudson River just north of Manhattan Island.

[2] In other words, Virginia stretched from Cape Fear to the middle part of Nova Scotia. The London partners had the exclusive right to plant the first settlement between Cape Fear and the mouth of the Potomac River. Similarly, the Plymouth partners had the exclusive right to make the first settlement between Manhattan Island and Halifax. Either company, instead of making its settlement within its own peculiar territory, might plant a colony between the mouth of the Potomac and Manhattan Island. Wherever planted, the fact of settlement gave the group making it the right to one hundred miles along the seacoast, fifty miles north and fifty miles south of its settlement, and one hundred miles inland. There is a good map of the colonial bounds of Virginia in the Society of Colonial Wars in the District of Columbia's *Publications*, No. I.

truckling to the Spanish power in other matters, he would not order back to England the settlers on the James River. This is more to be wondered at since the project of a matrimonial alliance with the royal family of Spain occupied much of his time and attention for the greater portion of his reign. The affair of the "Spanish Marriage" brought him greatly under the control of successive Spanish ambassadors, one of whom went so far as to request the king to punish the seditious insolence of the members of the House of Commons, since he had, so he wrote, "no army here at present" with which to punish them himself;[1] but no Spanish ambassador, by word or deed, could induce James to interfere with the Virginia enterprise.

It was in October, 1607, that Don Pedro de Zuñiga, Spanish ambassador in London, complained to James that Englishmen were going to Virginia, which was a part of the Spanish Indies. James replied to him that he did not know the king of Spain had any claim to Virginia; moreover, seeing that the Spaniards had discovered many new regions, it seemed only right that Englishmen should have the like liberty. He promised, however, that the Council should look into the matter and if it was found that Englishmen were going to prohibited places, they might be punished. Nothing further was done, however, and the reason may have been that there was no provision in the treaty of 1604 forbidding Englishmen to visit and occupy those parts of the New World which were not actually held by the Spaniards. At the time of the negotiation of that treaty the Spaniards had been very anxious to secure the insertion of words prohibiting Englishmen from going to the Indies. But the English negotiators, among whom were Lord Howard of Armada fame and Robert Cecil,

[1] Gardiner's *History of England*, i (iv, 249), from the "Simancas Mss."

refused to insert any provision as to the country beyond the line of demarcation, unless the Spaniards would acknowledge the right of Englishmen to the unoccupied shores of the New World.[1] Under these circumstances, reference to the Council, where Cecil was supreme, implied that nothing would be done, and nothing was done. For years Lord Burleigh's son, Robert Cecil, soon to become Earl of Salisbury, was the strongest man in England, a constant patron of the Virginia venture, and an equally constant sponsor of an anti-Spanish policy, which some writers have thought strange, since he was in receipt of a pension from Spain and complained vigorously when the quarterly payments were not promptly made.[2] When it was seen that nothing could be gained from the English government, Zuñiga sought to stir to activity his master in Spain. In 1609, for example, he implored Philip III to "give orders to have these insolent people [the Virginians] quickly annihilated." His activity was not entirely in vain, for the *Asuncion de Christo* was dispatched from St. Augustine for the Chesapeake to spy out the land, as has already been described, and recoiled from the apparition of an English ship. In 1611, however, a Spanish caravel entered the James River, landed three men who were immediately seized, and sailed away with the English pilot who had boarded her with the intention of taking her under the guns of the fort.[3] For years an active correspondence between the English and Spanish governments over this matter continued. One of the three Spaniards was a "grandee." He remained at Jamestown for some

[1] Minutes of the Commissioners to negotiate the treaty of 1604 in Earl of Jersey Mss. (Royal Historical Manuscripts Commission's *Reports*, viii, Appendix, 95 and fol.).

[2] Gardiner's *History of England*, i, 214 and Brown's *Genesis*, ii, 951. Sir Edward Monson, in command of the Channel fleet, was also a pensioner of Spain.

[3] Dale to Salisbury in Brown's *Genesis*, i, 507.

five years and from time to time sent home reports of the condition of affairs at that place. These were carried in the boots of faithless English sailors or were hid in coils of rope. His letters have lately been unearthed from the Spanish archives and give us an interesting picture of life on the James River.[1] Probably the Spaniards were set on shore for the precise object of sending these reports. In connection with this subject it is also worth noting that in 1611, and in 1612, Sir John Digby (afterwards Earl of Bristol), the English ambassador at Madrid, on three separate occasions called the attention of the English government to rumors which prevailed at Madrid. "They bite the lip again at Virginia and the Northwest Passage," he wrote on one occasion, and intend, so he said at another time, to "serve us as they did the Frenchmen in Florida."[2] Nothing came of any of these attempts and the Spanish king waited with exemplary patience, but in vain, for the enterprise on the James River to die a natural death.

The Virginia Charter was even more memorable for its constitutional declarations than it was for its assertion of England's claim to a share of the New World. The clause is worth reading; it provides that the English colonists and their posterity "shall have and enjoy all liberties, franchises, and immunities within any of our other dominions, to all intents and purposes as if they had been abiding and born within this our realm of England or any other of our said dominions." This famous clause repeats in substance the guarantee which was in the Ralegh patent which again repeated in substance what was in the Gilbert charter.[3] In all three the English monarch declared

[1] They are printed in Brown's *Genesis*, and are given in briefer form in his *First Republic*.

[2] Royal Historical Manuscripts Commission's *Reports*, x, Appendix i, 558, 576, 583, 600, 608. Some of them are summarized in *Calendar of State Papers, East Indies, 1513–1616*, 238.

[3] Gilbert's charter is in Hakluyt's *Voyages* (ed. 1600), iii, 135.

to the world that English colonization was to be unlike that of Spain, France, and the nations of antiquity. It was the fate of pre-English colonists and of contemporary settlers of other nations to be looked upon as beings who were outside the laws and privileges of the dwellers in the home-land; English colonists, on the other hand, were to enjoy the protection of the Common Law equally with the inhabitants of England.[1] As a declaration of a new colonial policy, this statement is interesting; but as maintaining, in the smallest essential, the rights of English subjects, it was of slight importance. The rights of Englishmen were not subject to the king's fancy; for, as Bracton said, "the king is under no man, but is under God and the law." Go where he would, so long as he settled on land claimed by England and acknowledged allegiance to the English crown, the Englishman carried with him as much of the Common Law of England as was applicable to his situation and was not repugnant to his other rights and privileges. Nevertheless, this enunciation, now the third time repeated, marked an epoch in colonization. Permanent settlements, which in time were to grow into a great nation, were to be made under its guarantees. The success of the new movement was to depend largely on the proposition that colonists had the same rights as home-dwellers — a fact that marks off English colonization from all other colonization, ancient and modern.

The Virginia Charter provided a cumbrous form of government in which there was no one-man power, but everything was confided to councils. These were five in number. First and over all, there was to be in England a Council for Virginia composed of leading men who might or might

[1] See Note III.

not have pecuniary interest in the affairs of the company. Then, each "colony," or "company," should have its council in England and each plantation should have its council in America. All the members of these councils were to be appointed by the king in the first instance, and later on the plantation council should be appointed as the king by written instructions might determine. When one considers the extreme feebleness of the plantations in America during the life of this charter, this paraphernalia of government appears absurd. It should be remembered in James's favor, however, that he and those who worked under him were breaking out a new path. This form of government which confided the supreme oversight of the colonies to an appointive body was soon abandoned, because it was felt that those who invested money in colonial enterprises should have the management of them.[1] In the end, however, the English government has been obliged to revert to James's original plan and to assume the government of every chartered colonizing company. In the charter of 1606 James merely anticipated by some one hundred and seventy years the principles of the act for "regulating" the East India Company.

The charter granted, James soon appointed the first Council for Virginia. Among its members were Sir Thomas Smythe, Sir Francis Popham, son and heir of

[1] See, for example, a letter from Gorges to Cecil (Baxter's *Gorges*, iii, 125). It is dated May 10, exactly one month after the charter was issued. In it Gorges asks to have the Plymouth partners in the undertaking "exempted from having to do with those citizens and townsmen nominated in his Majesty's grant." The names of the Virginia councilors are given in the "Articles and Instructions" which were issued by the king in the same year. These are printed in Hening's *Statutes* and in Brown's *Genesis* (i, 65). There is some question as to the date, whether it should be April 12 or November 20; this letter of Gorges would seem to confirm the earlier time which is given in Purchas (*Pilgrimes*, iv, 1667). Alexander Brown states that he is "quite sure" that the councilors named were members of the two companies. He gives no proof and the above quoted letter of Gorges would seem to imply the opposite.

the chief justice, and Sir Ferdinando Gorges. In the next year the council was tripled in size and among the new members was Sir Edwin Sandys. These preliminaries settled, preparations were earnestly begun to send out the first expeditions to seek gold and silver and the Northwest Passage, and to fortify a post in some convenient place on its borders. December 20, 1606, three vessels sailed from the Thames for the southern part of Virginia.[1] These were the *Susan Constant*, the *Godspeed*, and the *Discovery*; they belonged to the Muscovy Company and their commander was Sir Christopher Newport, a seaman of discretion and proved ability, who later commanded a fleet for the East India Company and died at Bantam in 1618. For weeks the vessels lay at anchor in the Downs and in various Channel ports awaiting favorable winds to blow them out to sea and across the Bay of Biscay. At length they cleared the Channel and steered for the Canary Islands, which they reached in March. In pursuing this extreme southern course Sir Christopher Newport was only following the track of previous mariners. From the Canaries the fleet sailed across the Atlantic Ocean and in April reached Dominica in the West Indies. Passing northward by Marigalante, Guadalupe, Monserrat, Nevis, St. Kitts, and the southern shore of Porto Rico, the expedition reached the island of Mona. At Nevis the explorers spent six days in cleansing themselves and their belongings; at Mona they again went on shore and filled their water casks. At the latter place the gentlemen of the expedition went hunting. It was now April, and the heat of the sun was great; it so oppressed Edward Brooks that "his fat melted within him" and killed him — at

[1] This account of the voyage is based on Percy's "Discourse," which is printed in Purchas's *Pilgrimes*, iv, 1684, and in Brown's *Genesis*, i, 152.

least so Percy tells us. Of the sufferings of those whom this noble chronicler would have termed the "common people" he is silent; but the voyage was fatal to some of them, for of the one hundred and twenty who embarked in England only one hundred and four landed in Virginia.

On May 6, 1607, at daylight, the capes of the Chesapeake were above the horizon. The ships stood into the bay, and charmed with the sight and smell of the land, some of the chief men sought the shore. Among them was George Percy, who "was almost ravished at the first sight" of the fair meadows and tall trees of Virginia. Later in the day the savages, "creeping on all fours from the hills, like bears, with their bows in their mouths," attacked the white invaders. They wounded Captain Gabriel Archer and a sailor and were themselves unharmed.

That night the sealed commission and instructions which the explorers had brought with them were opened and the names of the land commanders were for the first time made known. During the voyage Newport had exercised supreme control, and the concealment of the names of the land rulers had been in conformity with the custom of the East India Company. The "Articles and Instructions for the Government of Virginia,"[1] which James had issued, were in reality a constitution of government. So much ridicule has been heaped on them and their royal author that it will be well to examine them with some care to see whether these jeers are well deserved. The supreme governing body was a council which exercised executive, legislative, and judiciary functions. It possessed despotic authority, which seemed to be necessary, as the expedition was in the nature of a "forlorn hope" sent out to attack the American soil and savages.

[1] Hening's *Statutes at Large of Virginia*, i, 67, and Brown's *Genesis*, i, 65.

The attempt proved to be full of difficulty and danger, owing partly to the ignorance which then beset all Englishmen, of how large expeditions should be conducted, and more especially to the climatic and human environment of Virginia. To these formidable obstacles, rather than to defects in the governmental framework, must be attributed the tragedy of Jamestown.

The Articles, furthermore, contain a good deal of legislative matter which provided reforms in the mode of dealing with crime to which England did not attain for centuries. For example, in Virginia the death penalty was reserved for some six offences. The exclusions and inclusions, in comparison with contemporary English practice, are not uninteresting. On the one hand, petty larceny and consorting with gypsies would not bring death in Virginia, as they did in England. On the other hand, this brief list included adultery, to which the common and statute law then attached no penalty whatever. Moreover, James also provided that a person refusing to plead to his indictment should be adjudged guilty and should not be pressed to death, as was the practice in England.

The instructions[1] which the Virginia Council had prepared for the president and council in Virginia were admirable. They ordered their agents to seek out a river that should be navigable for a long distance inland — if one could be found with a northwestern bend, so much the better, "for in that way you shall soonest find the other sea." In such a river they were to select an island, or other strong place, a hundred miles from the sea, if possible, where a vessel of fifty tons could lie at anchor near the shore. No site should be chosen which was overburdened with trees, "for all the men you have shall

[1] Brown's *Genesis*, i, 79, and Arber's *Works of Captain John Smith*, p. xxxiii.

not be able to cleanse twenty acres a year, besides that it may serve for a covert for your enemies round about." They also were to avoid a low or moist situation.

In flat contradiction of these instructions, the president and council picked out a low island or peninsula[1] which was bordered on one side by a swamp and was covered with a dense growth of splendid trees. In other respects the site was all that could be desired, for it was distant from the sea, and the water was so deep, close to the shore, that vessels could unload directly on to the land. On the westward end of this peninsula, a triangular fort was marked out, having three bulwarks, one at each corner, in which were placed four or five pieces of artillery.

While the laborers and the seamen were building the fort and unloading the vessels, Newport, with a strong party, ascended the James River until he came to the falls where Richmond now stands. At that point he met Powhatan, the "emperor" of those regions. With true English hospitality, Newport regaled the astonished savage with beer, brandy, and wine, a combination which somewhat staggered that potentate. In the absence of the explorers, the natives attacked the party at the fort; they were beaten off, but not until four of the five councilors present had been wounded and President Edward Maria Wingfield "had an arrow shot clean through his beard."

Returning to England, Newport sailed directly across the Atlantic; he left the James on July 2 and reached Plymouth on August 8 following. His reports were cheerful,[2] but the gold ore which he brought with him

[1] See L. G. Tyler's *Cradle of the Republic*, 29. This volume forms a useful guidebook to the James River. See also C. W. Coleman's "Along the Lower James," in *The Century*, xix, 323; and "The Site of Jamestown" in *Virginia Magazine of History*, 1904.

[2] See his letter dated Plymouth, July 29, 1607. He says that he and his comrades had discovered the country for

turned out badly. He suggested, however, that his samples had been taken from the wrong heap. It was, therefore, determined to send him back at once with recruits and supplies. The recruits were sorely needed, for Newport had hardly sailed from the Chesapeake before malarial fever attacked those whom he had left behind. When he anchored off James Fort,[1] in January, 1608, not one half of those whom he left there six months before were alive. Fever, Indian arrows, and hunger had combined to cut off the English intruders. Indian enmity by good management might have been largely avoided; but malarial fever was certain to kill from fifty to sixty white men out of every hundred who came to the valley of the James, and starvation was almost equally certain to account for twenty-five more. At first sight it might seem that in 1607 one hundred men could have been taken across the Atlantic and set on shore in Virginia with sufficient food to keep them alive for six months; but the experience of these early expeditions shows that such expectation was not likely to be fulfilled. Nor is this to be wondered at. In the first place, the ships of that day, as has already been pointed out, had not sufficient space for passengers and cargo. In the second place, there were no storehouses of food in England from which supplies could be drawn. The story of the sufferings of those who saved England from becoming a province of Spain is to the point. The letters of Burleigh and Walsingham in 1588[2] show what preparations were made on that occasion: how sheep were bought, driven to the seacoast,

near two hundred miles and found it very rich in gold and silver. Northumberland Mss. in Royal Historical Manuscripts Commission's *Reports*, iii, 54.

[1] It is worth noting that Percy, Archer, and Smith called it James Fort not Jamestown. See Arber's *Works of Captain John Smith*, lvi, xli.

[2] See "Armada Papers" in Navy Records Society's *Publications*.

slaughtered, and salted; how wheat was bought, ground into flour, and baked into bread. So it must have been with all the early expeditions; those who had charge of them had to buy the meat on the hoof, the bread in the shock. The early fleets which sailed to Virginia were not even properly provisioned for the long roundabout voyage. Had not one half of the newcomers promptly died of fever or of pneumonia as the season of their arrival dictated, all, both old and new comers, would certainly have perished of starvation. There were fish in the river, oysters in the bay, and game in the forests, but the white invaders were neither fishermen nor sportsmen and the oysters were far away. The forest-clad region of their settlements could be brought under cultivation, but only with great labor. The hoards of the natives were the white man's only chance of life, but the North American Indian seldom had spare food on hand; for that which he possessed he was willing to risk his life.

With men sick and starving, a gloomy river in front of them, a forest and a pestilential swamp at their back, and Indians, intent on killing, behind every convenient bush and tree, there was sore need of a leader, and at the fort on the James River there was none. With Gosnold's death, in September, 1607, all forbearance and sense of human kindness seems to have deserted the unfortunates. When Newport reached the post after his six months' absence, of the council only Ratcliffe and Martin were alive and at liberty. Of the rest Gosnold had died of disease, Kendall had been executed, and Wingfield[1] and Captain

[1] Wingfield was of good stock, if the fact that his cousin married the Earl of Southampton's widow proves anything. Like Southampton, he was believed to be a Roman Catholic; this idea possibly may have helped to rouse against him the hostility of the starving men in the fort on the James River. At all events his harsh treatment by them seems to have been undeserved. See Wingfield's "Discourse" in *Archæologia Americana.*

John Smith were in custody, the latter awaiting execution.[1] At one time Gabriel Archer, the secretary, had suggested that all the surviving members of the expedition should be taken into consultation; but this savored too much of democracy to be favorably received, — the establishment of partial self-government came years later and then from the company in England.[2]

Newport reached James Fort on January 12, 1608. Two days later fire consumed the dwellings and storehouses on the shore. The Englishmen, living in tents and shelters made of boughs, soon sickened in the nipping cold and died. When he sailed for home, in the following April, more than one half of those who were living on January 14 were dead. Since November, 1606, one hundred and ninety-seven persons had embarked in England for Virginia; of these only fifty-three were alive. It is needless to follow in detail the further history of these early years; it is the story of an awful human tragedy in which men, women, and children[3] played their parts and laid down their lives. They were the first heroes of American history.

While these scenes were enacting on the James River, the Plymouth members of the Virginia Company were by no means idle. In August, 1606, they sent Captain Challons across the Atlantic, and two months later dispatched Thomas Hanham and Martin Pring in another ship to act

[1] This bit of Virginia's history is best set forth in Alexander Brown's *First Republic*, 54 and fol.

[2] In connection with his description of this expedition, Gardiner (*History of England*, ii, 253) makes the extraordinary statement that such enterprises needed strong government and not representative institutions, a dictum which is in direct opposition to the teaching of American history, as is evident from a comparison of the history of Virginia and Plymouth. In one there was a council with sufficient power to hang the king's subjects; in the other the majority ruled. Or compare New Netherland under the tyranny of the Dutch régime with the neighboring English colony of Connecticut, where the franchise, in those days, was most liberal.

[3] The first marriage of white persons in Virginia was solemnized at Jamestown, in December, 1608.

with him. Challons pursued the extreme southern course, sailed straight into the midst of a Spanish fleet while it was shrouded in fog, and was captured when the mist cleared away. Hanham and Pring had better fortune and, returning safely home, made "a perfect discovery" of the northern coasts. In consequence of this favorable report, George Popham and Ralegh Gilbert, in two vessels, the *Gift of God* and the *Mary and John*, sailed for the northern part of Virginia in June, 1607. In August they anchored in the estuary of the Kennebec, which was then known as the Sagadahoc. This expedition was well supplied with artisans and laborers who built a fort, which was named St. George, and a pinnace, which was called the *Virginia*. In October and December the vessels returned home, carrying back to England all but forty-four persons. These remained with Popham and Gilbert to hold the post during the winter. One of the home-going ships also carried a letter from George Popham, which is interesting as showing the delusions under which the early comers to North America often labored. He says that "so far as relates to commerce, all the natives constantly affirm that in these parts there are nutmegs, mace, and cinnamon, besides pitch, Brazil wood, cochineal, and ambergris. . . . Besides, they positively assure me that there is a certain sea in the opposite, or western part of this province, distant not more than seven days' journey from our fort of St. George in Sagadahoc; a sea large and wide and deep, of the boundaries of which they are wholly ignorant, which cannot be any other than the Southern Sea, reaching to the regions of China, which unquestionably cannot be far from these parts."[1]

As to the suitability of the country for nutmegs, Pop-

[1] Brown's *Genesis*, i, 146; Baxter's *Gorges*.

ham was undeceived when the cold weather set in. The freezing Englishmen piled the wood into their ill-constructed stoves, and thereby set a fire which consumed their storehouse, with part of their food supply. George Popham, already an old man, and a few others, died; but the mortality was not nearly as great as that which prevailed on the James. In 1608 a relief ship brought supplies and also tidings of the death of Sir John Popham and Sir John Gilbert, who had been the mainstays of the enterprise. Ralegh Gilbert decided to return to England, and his surviving companions either went with him or sought the fishing vessels off Newfoundland. At all events Fort St. George was abandoned, and that, says Strachey, "was the end of that northern colony on the river of Sagadahoc."

The enterprise was a failure in both its branches. For years nothing more was done in the North; in 1620 Sir Ferdinando Gorges, Sir Francis Popham, Ralegh Gilbert, and their associates secured a new charter from the crown under the name of the Council for New England. An outburst of colonizing zeal in England saved the James River enterprise from extinction and gave to it new life.

NOTES

I. General Bibliography. — It is only within recent years that it has been possible to make a scientific study of the early history of Virginia. Now, however, since the publication of numerous extracts from county and parish records in the pages of the *Virginia Magazine of History*, in the *William and Mary Quarterly*, and in the *Lower Norfolk Antiquary*, it is possible for a beginning to be made. As yet Philip Bruce's *Economic History of Virginia* and Alexander Brown's *First Republic in America*, and to some extent the brief narrative by Edward Eggleston in his *Beginners of a Nation*, stand apart from other Virginia books as being the first attempts to correlate this material.

The records and official papers of the Virginia Company for the years covered by chapters vi and vii of this volume are lost. Their place is only filled in part by the documents collected with admirable patience by Alexander Brown[1] and Edward D. Neill.[2] The student of Virginia history will always be grateful to these untiring accumulators of material, although he will not always find it possible to agree with their conclusions. Campbell's *Virginia* is now antiquated and Fiske's *Virginia and her Neighbours* is largely founded on the same classes of material as Campbell. Like all of Fiske's works, it is interesting and stimulating.[3]

[1] Alexander Brown's *Genesis of the United States* (2 vols., Boston, 1890) consists of documents extending to 1616 arranged chronologically. These are of great value, although some of them have been printed in earlier publications. The latter part of the second volume contains biographies of persons who had to do with early Virginia. These are exceedingly valuable. The same author's *First Republic in America* treats of the early years and carries the story forward to 1624. In this single volume Mr. Brown combines his own exposition with quotations from documents, many of which have never been printed. It is a work of reference, not of literature, and often loses in influence because of its intemperate abuse of Captain John Smith, who, after all, accomplished a good deal in the world even if he depreciated the services of others and exaggerated the importance of his own doings. The title *First Republic* is also regrettable inasmuch as it is historically untrue. William Wirt Henry and Alexander Brown have an interesting discussion as to the value of the *First Republic* in the *Virginia Magazine of History*, vol. vi.

[2] E. D. Neill's *History of the Virginia Company of London* (Albany, 1869) and *Virginia Vetusta* (Albany, 1885). These books are really collections of notes and documents for the use of students and are exceedingly valuable. Neill also contributed a series of "Notes" to the *William and Mary Quarterly*.

[3] Lists of the older books will be found in Winsor's *America*, vol. iii, ch. v. This chapter was written by R. A. Brock, at the time Secretary of the Virginia Historical Society; he has also noted the sources in

II. Captain John Smith. — No fiercer controversy has ever raged around any character in American history than has been fought over the credibility of Captain John Smith. Until within recent years the question of his truthfulness was of vital importance. Nowadays, owing to the documents contained in Alexander Brown's *Genesis of the United States* students are no longer obliged to rely on Smith's writings. A careful comparison of the dates and sequence of events as related by Smith and as given in the other original documents shows the utter unreliability of Smith's account entirely apart from the Pocahontas story. The best edition of Smith's writings is that of Edward Arber in the *Scholar's Library*, No. 16. It is noteworthy that Arber thinks the *General History*, which was printed sixteen years after the events therein described, is more reliable than the *True Relation*, which was first printed in 1608. His reason for this opinion is that the *General History* was written for the press and the *True Relation* was not. As to the relative importance of what historians call "conscious" and "unconscious" evidence, Arber disagrees with Henry Adams, Justin Winsor, Charles Deane, and Alexander Brown. Probably the most unfortunate aspect of "The Affair Smith" is that, unmindful of his descent from the revolutionary statesman, Patrick Henry, William Wirt Henry treated the controversy as a sectional matter and used it to stimulate Southern hatred of New England scholars.[1]

III. Extension of the Common Law. — The extension of the Common Law of England to the colonies has been many times affirmed by jurists of eminence. In 1720 Mr. West, legal adviser to the Board of Trade, declared that "the Common Law of England, is the common law of the plantations, and all statutes in affirmance of the common law, passed in England, antecedent to the settlement of a colony, are in force in that colony, unless there is some private act to the contrary, though no statutes, made since those settlements, are there in force, unless the colonies are particularly mentioned.

the *Collections* of the Virginia Historical Society, New Series, vii, Introduction.

[1] The most important contributions on this subject are Charles Deane's edition of the *True Relation* and Henry Adams's notice of it in the *North American Review* for January, 1867, and Alexander Brown's *Genesis* (especially ii, 784 and 1006), his *First Republic* (index under Smith), and his *English Politics in Early Virginia History*. The other side is well represented in John Fiske's *Virginia*.

Smith's falsehood as to several incidents in his early life is adverted to by Lewis L. Kropf in the London *Notes and Queries* for 1890 and *American Historical Review*, iii, 737.

Let an Englishman go where he will, he carries as much of law and liberty with him, as the nature of things will bear." Later, Attorney-general Charles Pratt and Solicitor-general Charles York, both of whom afterwards became lord chancellors, stated that "in respect to such places as have been, or shall be, acquired by treaty, or grant, from any of the Indian princes or government, your majesty's letters patent are not necessary; the property of the soil vesting in the grantees, by the Indian grants, subject only to your majesty's right of sovereignty over the settlements, as English settlements, and over the inhabitants as English subjects, who carry with them your majesty's laws, wherever they form colonies, and receive your majesty's protection by virtue of your royal charters" (Chalmers's *Opinions*, i, 194). See also Chalmers's *Introduction to the History of the Revolt*, i, 308.[1]

In 1815 the question came before the Supreme Court of the United States in the case of the Town of Pawlet *vs.* D. Clark and others (Cranch's *Reports*, ix, 333). The opinion was given by Mr. Justice Story; the portion dealing with this topic is as follows: "Independent of such a provision [requiring the proceedings to be as consonant and agreeable to the laws and statutes of this our realm of England, as the present state and condition of our subjects inhabiting within the limits aforesaid and the circumstances of the place will admit] we take it to be a clear principle that the common law in force at the emigration of our ancestors is deemed the birthright of the colonies, unless so far as it is inapplicable to their situation or repugnant to their other rights and privileges. *A fortiori* the principle applies to the royal provinces."

[1] See also *Ex parte* Anderson, Ellis and Ellis's *Reports*, iii, 204, 490.

CHAPTER VII

THE COLONY OF VIRGINIA

THE disasters on the James and the Sagadahoc damped the enthusiasm of the early investors in the Virginia enterprise; but new men came to the front and with those of the old partners, who were willing to go on, made another trial. Of the new men, some were inspired by political motives, by the desire to establish an English sphere of influence in North America; others were dominated by that missionary spirit which has ever been the precursor or companion of English colonizing endeavors. The attempt to found a colony in Virginia appealed to these people as a national and Christian endeavor.

The king was favorable to the new undertaking, and issued letters patent under the great seal creating a corporation to be known as the Virginia Company, and giving it certain exemptions from export and import duties. In this second Virginia Charter, as it is usually called, the word "Virginia" has a more limited meaning than was given to it in the charter of 1606; but the new bounds of the colony were exceedingly vague. Point Comfort, which is now called Old Point Comfort, was the central point of the grant on the Atlantic shore. North and south "all along the seacoast" Virginia extended two hundred miles, and between the parallels of the ends of those two hundred miles its northern and southern limits ran "west and northwest" to the South Sea. The delightful vagueness of these terminal bounds was of no importance in colonial days, as the Virginia Company was overthrown in 1624, before any dispute had arisen as to its territorial limits. There was never any judicial interpretation of this language; but in 1620, while the Virginia Company was still in active existence, James gave a royal interpretation to it so far as it related to the northern boundary when he assigned the fortieth parallel to the Council for New England as the southern limit of its territory. Under the first charter the subscribers to the common stock had practically nothing to say as to the conduct of the enterprise, and the failure of the earlier schemes had been attributed to this cause. The king now removed this obstacle by placing the whole government of the corporation and its plantation in the hands of the stockholders. Finally, to attract subscriptions, the list of grantees was left open, in order that the names of late subscribers might be inserted therein. Three years later, in 1612, by the third Virginia Charter, James further enlarged these governing powers and provided for the holding of general meetings of the stockholders under the name of The Great and General Courts of the Council and Company of Adventurers for Virginia. The charter of 1609 belongs to a class of commercial letters patent of which the charter of the East India Company is the best example; it is altogether likely that Sir Thomas Smythe and his partners used the latter grant to show what provisions they wished to have inserted in their new patent.[1]

[1] The Virginia patents are in *Charters and Constitutions of the United States*, ii. It is useful to compare them with the charter of the East India Company, which is in Birdwood and Foster's *Register of Letters* [of the East India Company], p. 163, and less perfectly in Purchas's *Pilgrimes*. Relying on a statement of Sir Thomas Smythe's: "This is the article of the letters patents: 2 whereof were drawn by Sir Ed. Sandys himself" (Brown's *Genesis*, i, 47), Alexander Brown has built up a fanciful structure. In this the charter of 1609 is made to appear as a liberal constitution and Sandys as a far-sighted statesman antici-

The new company at once set to work to raise money and recruits. Broadsides,[1] full of allurement and falsehood, were printed and distributed far and wide. When the condition of affairs on the James River is recalled, the assurances of Smythe, Sandys, and the other signers of these documents seem truly appalling.[2] The financial propositions set forth by the promoters of the enterprise are worth examination. In the language of those days, the planters were those who emigrated and staked their lives against the climate and the hardships inseparable from a new colony; the adventurers were those who stayed at home and risked their money in the venture. Each adventurer in the Virginia scheme who contributed twelve pounds ten shillings to the common stock of the corporation should be entitled to one share,[3] and each planter, whether man, woman, or child, above ten years of age, should also be entitled to one share. The humblest planter, even the exiled vagrant, was promised meat, drink, and clothing, with a house, orchard, garden, and one hundred acres of land for himself and each member of his family; while clergymen, knights, and physicians, who could render special service, should receive larger amounts. At the end of seven years the assets of the company in lands, stock, and profits should be divided between the adventurers and the planters, according to the number of shares standing on the books of the com-

pating the constructive work of later times.

[1] Brown (*Genesis*, i, 248, etc.) brings together documents of this kind. See also Massachusetts Historical Society's *Proceedings*, Second Series, ii, 243.

[2] L. D. Scisco (*American Historical Review*, viii, 261) sums up the conditions of failure in what he terms "the Plantation type of colony."

[3] See receipt for twelve pounds ten shillings giving Lionel Cranfield (afterward Lord Treasurer and Earl of Middlesex) proportionate share in gold and silver, etc., found in Virginia. Royal Historical Manuscripts Commission's *Reports*, iv, Appendix, p. 283 (De la Warr Mss.).

pany in their names. Large contributions of money and swarms of proposing emigrants came to the great house in Phillpot Lane. In all, from the subscribers and from the proceeds of lotteries, about two hundred thousand pounds were collected between 1609 and 1624.[1] The money came from many directions, from the London companies, from municipal corporations, and from "Lords, Knights, Gentlemen, Merchants, and others," while all classes in the community were represented on the emigrant ships which sought Chesapeake Bay.[2] To avoid, if possible, the disputations of the earlier time, Gates was appointed "sole and absolute governor."[3]

On June 2, 1609, nine vessels sailed from Plymouth, England, for the James River.[4] Sir Christopher Newport was again in command; with him in the *Sea Adventure* sailed Sir Thomas Gates, Sir Thomas Dale, and John Rolfe, whose energy and skill were to assure the permanency of English colonization in America. As captains of the three largest vessels Ratcliffe, Martin, and Archer returned to the scene of their recent sufferings. The ships

[1] This is the estimate in Wodenoth's letter as given in Brown's *Genesis*, i, 51.

[2] The emigrants of 1609 appear to have included in their number some unsavory characters. In 1610 referring to this expedition (Brown's *Genesis*, i, 355) the company states that "experience hath too dearly taught how much and many ways it hurteth to suffer parents to disburden themselves of lascivious sons, masters of bad servants, and wives of ill husbands, and so to clog the business with such an idle crew, as did thrust themselves in the last voyage." This relates solely to the 1609 voyage; there is nowhere else in the papers of the Virginia Company any confirmation of Captain John Smith's stigma on the first comers that they were "broken down noblemen, decayed serving men, and the like." Indeed, he stands alone in his condemnation of his comrades. Probably the early expeditions to the James River were made up of energetic men whose expectations were adventures and wealth, not too hardly acquired. They were not colonists in any sense of the word, but crossed the Atlantic to discover the Northwest Passage and to pick up gold and silver along the shores; but after 1610 the Virginia emigrants were colonists in the true sense of the word, and represented the several strata of English society.

[3] See Professor Osgood's summary of the Instructions of 1609 in his *American Colonies*, i, 61.

[4] On this voyage, see the account by Archer, which Brown (*Genesis*, i, 328) reprints from Purchas's *Pilgrimes*, iv, 1733.

bore about five hundred emigrants, including, probably, one hundred women and children. Before leaving the Thames the plague broke out on one of the vessels, but it had run its course before the James River was reached. Calenture, or virulent tropical fever, also appeared on one of the ships after the fleet left the Canaries, — thirty-two bodies were thrown overboard from these two vessels. As the fleet neared the end of its long, roundabout course the "taile of a West Indian horacano" struck it, and in forty-four hours sent one ship to the bottom and cast the *Sea Adventure* on the Bermudas. The other seven vessels straggled into the James,[1] and there the newcomers found a condition of woe which contrasted most painfully with the promises that had been made to them in England. Truly "the hand of God," as one writer expressed it, "was heavy on the enterprise." About one hundred white persons were still alive. They were dispersed and starving: some of them were living with the Indians; others were near the oyster beds, twenty miles from Jamestown.[2] The newcomers brought little or no food. Starvation, malaria, and pneumonia soon played their parts. In May of the next year two pinnaces unexpectedly sailed into the river bearing the survivors of the *Sea Adventure.* The tales of misery which were told them by those of the colonists who had outlived their fellows are without parallel in the history of English colonization. The starving

[1] That the Virginia voyage attracted European interest is evident from the note in the *Kölnische Zeitung* for June 18, 1609, announcing the arrival of this expedition in the Chesapeake, after experiencing great misfortune at the hands of the Spaniards. See *Virginia Magazine of History*, v, 221.

[2] Letter of Archer in Brown's *Genesis*, i, 330. One of the leaders of this expedition was Sir George Somers. His absence from England caused remark in the House of Commons, of which he was a member. Probably no new writ was issued on the ground that it was a grace, not a disgrace, to be a governor in Virginia; but the language is not perfectly clear. This is the earliest record in the journals of either house of Parliament referring to the colonies. See *Commons Journals*, February 14, 1609 (i, 392).

settlers, like men on a wreck at sea, dogged the steps of the dying that they might fill their hungry bellies with the flesh of their dead comrades — some of them dug up the bodies of dead Indians and fed on the putrid flesh. Gates wisely decided to abandon the colony, at least for the time being; but as he and the survivors were proceeding down the river they met Lord de la Warr fresh from England with food and recruits. So back they turned, and once more reoccupied the hated Jamestown.

This was the lowest point in Virginia's story. In all, more than nine hundred persons had landed on the banks of the James River — of these about one hundred and fifty were still living in Virginia. These were seasoned to the climate, and formed the nucleus around which the colony developed. In 1611 Sir Thomas Gates, who had returned to England to stir the subscribers to new endeavors, again came to Virginia and remained in control there until 1614, when the permanence of the colony was assured.[1] His principal helpers in this accomplishment were Sir Thomas Dale, John Rolfe, and George Yeardley. De la Warr, in the short time of his stay in Virginia, had published a series of regulations which had been drawn up by the officials of the company in England. Dale had governed under them, and Gates republished the whole set with possibly some additions. This code is always known as Dale's Laws. The reason for giving them his name is not clear, but probably this unhappy distinction was conferred on the best of the early governors of Virginia because, as holding the office of marshal, it was his duty to punish delinquents.

[1] Dale preceded Gates with supplies and recruits. He ruled the colonists from May to August, 1611; then came Gates, who remained until March, 1614, when Dale resumed the command which he held until April, 1616.

The "Articles, Laws and Orders, Divine, Politique, and Martial for the government of Virginia,"[1] to give the code its full title, were based on the military laws of the Netherlands, in which hard school Gates, Dale, and Yeardley had been educated. The first thing which strikes the peruser is the spirit of religious intolerance which pervades them. For this the king must be held primarily responsible, owing to the conditions which were contained in the letters patent, providing that only persons who had taken the Oath of Supremacy could be transported to Virginia. This was designed to exclude Roman Catholics from the colony. The Articles provided that no one should speak against the Trinity under pain of death, and all newly landed emigrants should speedily repair to the minister and satisfy him of their religious soundness or receive a daily flogging until they did so. Religious service should be held daily, at which all the colonists must be present under pain of the loss of their rations for the first offense; for the second, a whipping; and for the third, service in the galleys for six months. Swearing in God's name, or derision of God's holy word, brought death. Profane cursers were treated with greater leniency: the first offense was punished with a whipping;

[1] Force's *Tracts*, iii.

In 1622 Captain John Bargrave presented a petition to the Privy Council reciting many alleged wrongful acts on the part of Sir Thomas Smythe and his associates. Among other things he charged Smythe with having printed "a certain book of tyrannical government in Virginia" by which he meant these Articles. In April, 1624, Smythe replied, denouncing as a "bold slander" the charge that he printed the said book which was done by the direction of the Council for Virginia. For his part, he had disliked the strictness of the code, "fearing it would discourage men from going to the plantation," and had so expressed himself in a letter to Captain John Martin. Probably, in the midst of the multifarious business enterprises in which he took part, Sir Thomas Smythe had slight knowledge of the details of Virginia business; but he was the head of the company and must bear his share of the responsibility. Sandys, also, cannot be dissociated from this chapter in Virginia history, for he expressly lauded the services of Gates and Dale. Brown's *Republic*, 225.

For Bargrave's petition and Smythe's reply, see *Virginia Magazine of History*, vi, 226, 378.

for the second offense, a bodkin should be thrust through the offender's tongue; for the third offense, he should suffer death. Disrespect toward those in authority was equally reprobated and was punished with death for the third offense.

At that time the colony was conducted as a military establishment; whatever the settlers produced went to the common stock, while they were fed and clothed from the company's storehouse. Much of this code relates, therefore, to the stealing of tools, to idleness, to the killing of domestic animals belonging to the company, and to the embezzlement of food by the company's employees. The knife, the lash, the galleys, and the gallows met the offender at every turn. As the times went, there was nothing especially bloody in these enactments, for nose-slitting, ear-cutting, the whipping-post, the pillory, even the *peine forte et dure*, were everyday matters in England.[1] The study of methods of dealing with crime in Shakespeare's day is distressing; but justice to those who drew up the early penal laws for Virginia, Maryland, and New England demands that the reader should have some slight acquaintance with the subject.

Seventeenth-century English county clerks were economical of words, although they might spell pretty much as they chose; but for ten consecutive years in the middle of James's reign a conscientious hand held the pen in Middlesex County sessions, and the results of his efforts have been printed. This court had cognizance of crimes in the country about the city of London, excluding the city itself. Probably the following figures should in each case be

[1] Extreme sentences, involving fine, pillory, whipping, and personal humiliation, were also pronounced by the Court of Star Chamber. See, for instance, Royal Historical Commission's *Reports*, iii, Appendix, 57.

doubled to give an adequate impression of the condition of things in the city of London and its immediate vicinity.[1] In the ten years beginning with 1609 no less than seven hundred and thirty-six persons were hanged or pressed to death in the County of Middlesex, excluding London; of these, seven hundred and four died by the rope, thirty-two of the *peine forte et dure*,[2] of whom three were women. Between 1603 and 1625 ninety-two women were sentenced at the Middlesex sessions alone to be executed by hanging. There are signs, however, that even in the reign of the first Stuart the plain people — from whose good sense reform has usually proceeded — were beginning to have doubts as to the decency and expediency of the public execution of women by hanging. In those days the stealing of goods amounting in value to twelve pence or over was felony, which was punished by death and forfeiture of chattels; juries therefore brought in verdicts in the case of women "guilty of stealing eleven pence half penny," the punishment of which was a fine.

Three cases which occurred at the end of Elizabeth's reign illustrate the growing tenderness of juries and judges toward women and even toward men. In one of these a jury found a woman who was charged with larceny of goods to the value of six shillings guilty of hav-

[1] These figures and cases are taken from the *Middlesex County Records*, edited by J. C. Jeaffreson. The second volume deals with the reign of James I. The statements contained in this sentence are taken from pp. xvii–xxii of the excellent Introduction to that volume; see also Hamilton's *Quarter Sessions*, 30–33.

[2] The accused was placed on his or her back on the dungeon floor, and heavy weights were piled on the chest. The object of this torture was to extort a confession, or failing that, to induce the accused person to plead not guilty. As the law stood, unless a person pleaded either guilty or not guilty he or she could not be convicted and sentenced to death and forfeiture of chattels. By refusing to plead, therefore, even a guilty person could save his or her property for the family by dying in unutterable agony instead of by hanging. With the substitution of the whipcord for the heavy weights this practice continued in England until the American Revolution. See Pike's *History of Crime in England*, i, 210; F. A. Inderwick's *Side-Lights on the Stuarts*, 338–345.

ing stolen eleven pence half penny's worth, and she was dismissed with a fine. At about the same time, two men were charged with stealing a tablecloth and a napkin which were valued together at six shillings; one of them was hanged, the other was pressed to death. Moreover, the judges sometimes sentenced convicted felons to punishments less than death, and acted illegally in so doing. For instance, when three men were convicted of stealing lead to the value of five shillings, they were sentenced to sit in the stocks for three days, with papers signifying their crimes on their heads, be whipped from Newgate to Bridewell, and there be kept at hard labor as long as they lived.

The most brutalizing punishments of the time were the public whippings. Stripped half naked and secured to the cart's tail or to the whipping-post, the culprits — women as well as men — were flogged until the blood streamed from their wounds. In fourteen months' time, in the period under consideration, seventy-one persons were condemned to whipping and branding for vagrancy in Middlesex alone; of whom twenty-one were women. After the whipping the vagabond was given his or her clothes and dismissed, with every chance of a speedy re-arrest and another whipping in a near-by town. Toward the end of James's reign, however, houses of correction were built in many parts of England, — among others in Middlesex. This last was not an attractive place of detention according to present-day ideas; but it was undoubtedly a great improvement over the roadside. According to the rules of the new institution, men and women were to be separated, but all were to work "hardly and incessantly" from six in the morning to seven in the evening, except the time given to praying and eating. The straw upon which they slept was to be changed once a month and they were to have warm pottage thrice weekly. In making these arrangements the justices, no doubt, felt the lenient spirit of the new time. At all events the building was clean when it was opened, which was not the case with any of the older prisons, for these were foul in the extreme. Possibly as many persons perished from jail fever or the "pyning sicknes" as died on the gallows and in the pressing dungeons.

Perhaps the most interesting remnant of mediæval times which one comes across in these records is "benefit of clergy." [1] By this process the convicted felon, when the sentence of death was about to be pronounced, "called for the book," read his neck verse, was branded on the brawn of the thumb with the "Tyburn T," and dismissed a free man. An interesting case of the usefulness of "benefit of clergy" was that of Ben Jonson the playwright, who was charged with having killed Garibel Spencer, an actor, in a duel, with a five-shilling sword. He pleaded guilty, called for the book, read like a clerk, was branded and released. Their sex debarred women from "benefit of clergy," as they could not be clerks. Parliament now

[1] As is the case with most English legal institutions, "benefit of clergy" goes back to mediæval days, when social and political conditions were entirely unlike those which prevailed in later times. In the Middle Ages the Church had courts of its own that dealt with misdeeds of the clergy. When a clergyman, therefore, found himself in a secular court, he proved his profession by reading, which few persons except the clergy could do, and was turned over to the clerical authority. After the Church courts ceased to exercise effective jurisdiction over clerical criminals, and after the ability to read ceased to be peculiar to the clergy, benefit of clergy continued to be allowed in cases of felony, except murder and homicide, and after 1611 manslaughter. Benefit of clergy was allowed in felony for the first offense only; but notwithstanding the fact that the iron was hot in the reigns of Elizabeth and James, it was so easy to disguise the wound and so difficult to prove the identity of the person that practically the well-to-do classes enjoyed considerable immunity. Benefit of clergy continued in the colonies until the Revolution; it was abolished in Virginia, for instance, in 1796. Recorded cases of its invocation are rare, but it was allowed in Virginia in 1670, the convict being burned in the hand. See Virginia *Magazine of History*, ix, 44.

remedied this injustice by providing that the minimum limit of grand larceny, which was felony with the death penalty, in the case of women should be ten shillings, instead of one shilling which continued to be the limit for men.[1]

Sir Thomas Gates, Sir Thomas Dale, and George Yeardley, the new rulers of Virginia, were soldiers hardened to the usages of war, as exemplified in the Dutch school of William of Orange. They compelled the colonists to work as they had never worked before. They protected them from the Indians, they fed them, and punished them when they idled away the company's time. In 1612, while Gates was in active command, some discontented persons seized the two boats belonging to the colony, with the intention of escaping in them. Being captured, they were shot, hanged, or broken on the wheel, according to their forwardness in the plot. Dale at this time was waging war against the Indians, and this execution was probably the work of Gates and George Yeardley, the latter being in command of the garrison at Jamestown. Breaking on the wheel was a punishment which was seldom, if ever, inflicted in England or in the colonies outside of Virginia and New York, in both of which continental influences were strong.

Virginia and the United States owe a great debt of gratitude to Sir Thomas Gates and his co-workers; yet it may well be doubted if the James River colony would have long continued had it not been for the discovery of how

[1] Blackstone's *Commentaries on the Laws of England*, bk. iv, ch. xvii. See Giles Jacob's *Law Dictionary* and Coke's *Third Institute*.

The sum of twelve pence, or one shilling, had been fixed in the reign of Athelstan, when the value of money was inconceivably greater than in 1600. Consorting with an Egyptian, witchcraft, removing the plate from an inn table, forgery, acknowledging bail in the name of another person who is not privy or consenting thereto, horse stealing, embezzling of records, murder, robbery on the highway, burglary, and other offenses also were punished by death.

to grow tobacco with profit. At the time of the Virginia enterprise tobacco sold in England for ten and even twelve shillings a pound, at which rate sixteen pounds of tobacco was the equivalent of a good horse. It was said that each year two hundred thousand pounds sterling went up in tobacco smoke.[1] The tobacco which was thus consumed was of Spanish production; Englishmen, even in Virginia, refused to smoke the tobacco of that region. The reason for this distaste was the bitterness of Virginia tobacco, which was itself due to the crude methods employed by the Indians in its cultivation and preparation. In 1609 John Rolfe left England for Virginia in the *Sea Adventure* and was wrecked on the Bermudas, but later reached the James. He was a man of substance and ability and discovered how Virginia tobacco could be cured for the English market. In 1616 a consignment from his plantation was sold at a good price in London, and the permanence of English colonization in America was assured.

Upon Gates's return to England, in 1614, the management of affairs in Virginia devolved upon Dale, who remained there two years longer. In his time the seven years' period of the common stock came to an end and land was given to such of the old planters as were then living.[2] The production of tobacco demanded the use of considerable tracts of ground, which in turn required immunity

[1] This total is given in a petition for an exclusive patent for inspecting tobacco. The petitioner would not probably have exaggerated the amount. He offered five thousand pounds per annum to a courtier to secure an exclusive patent for him. See Royal Historical Manuscripts Commission's *Reports*, iv, 283. The date of the petition is March 23, 1613.

[2] Brown's *Genesis*, ii, 777. Campbell, in his *Virginia* (ed. 1860, p. 116), referring to Chalmers's *Introduction to the Revolt*, 10, states that this reform was brought about through the influence of Dale, who was "one of the best of the early governors." Dale, however, was only carrying out promises which had been made years before, although possibly not in that precise form.

from Indian attacks. This Dale secured by entering into an arrangement with the natives that upon the yearly payment to the Englishmen of two and one half bushels of corn for each Indian they should be free from further exactions. This arrangement secured peace for eight years, and was, to use Rolfe's words, "the foundation and groundwork of their thrift and happiness."[1]

In 1616 Sir Thomas Dale followed Sir Thomas Gates to England. George Yeardley remained in Virginia in command of the colony, but he was soon succeeded in that position by Sir Thomas Smythe's young kinsman, Samuel Argall. Dale entered the service of the East India Company, fought a successful action in the East Indies with his old employers, the Dutch, and succumbed to an attack of the fever in 1619.[2] Up to the time of his departure from Jamestown, 1650 persons had sailed from England for Virginia, three hundred of whom had probably returned home. There were then living in the colony three hundred and fifty-one white persons, including sixty-five women and children. It follows from this computation that about one thousand persons had perished in Virginia or on the voyage thither. As the world views the acquisition of colonies, this was not an excessive price to pay for the overturn of Spain's title to one of the most valuable bits of land to be found anywhere on the surface of the earth.

Sir Thomas Smythe was no longer young and vigorous. He desired to be relieved of some of his burdens and turned over the management of the Virginia Company to Sir Edwin Sandys,[3] who was chosen treasurer in May, 1619.

[1] Rolfe's description of Virginia in 1616 is in *Virginia Historical Register*, i, 107; *Southern Literary Messenger* for 1839, etc.

[2] On Dale, see Bruce's *Economic History*, i, 215.

[3] There is no good life of Sandys. A. F. Pollard's article in the *Dictionary*

Son of that "obstinate and conscientious Puritan"[1] Edwin Sandys, Archbishop of York, the new treasurer of the Virginia Company was at the head of the reformers in Parliament. Edward Winslow, the Pilgrim, terms the younger Edwin "a religious gentleman." Taken in connection with other facts, this remark makes it seem probable that the new treasurer was a Nonconformist. He certainly was a radical by instinct, and this natural propensity had been fostered by his intercourse with his tutor at Oxford, Richard Hooker, the famous author of *The Ecclesiastical Polity.*[2] This great work was written to justify the existence of the State Church in England; but into it, in one way or another, crept many ideas which savored of republicanism. As Hooker completed the several parts of the manuscript, he submitted them to Sandys and his friend George Cranmer for criticism, and some of the books were completed practically under their editorship. Indeed, it is sometimes difficult to determine whether *The Ecclesiastical Polity* reflects most strongly the views of master or of pupils. The modernity of these ideas may easily be seen by the perusal of the following sentences which were quoted by Locke in his second *Essay on Government,* — a work which powerfully influenced the course of American history.

of National Biography is the best thing yet printed; but Alexander Brown's note in the biographical portion of his *Genesis of the United States* is very good. Other material is enumerated at the close of the first of these articles. A vivid view of Sandys's career can be gained by reading the passages noted under "Sir Edwin Sandys" in the *Index to the Journals of the House of Commons* and all the references to Sandys in Alexander Brown's *First Republic.* S. R. Gardiner, in his *History of England,* necessarily gives a good deal of space to Sandys.

[1] This is Pollard's phrase, in the *Dictionary of National Biography.*

[2] The best edition of Hooker's great book is Church and Paget's *The Works of that Learned and Judicious Divine, Mr. Richard Hooker.* 7th ed., 3 vols., Oxford, Clarendon Press, 1888. This edition contains Sandys's "Notes to the Sixth Book" and a learned dissertation on the authorship of that part of the work. Sidney Lee's article on Hooker in the *Dictionary of National Biography* will meet the needs of most students. At the end of this article is a critical note on the biographical works descriptive of Hooker's life.

To Hooker the natural equality of man was so evident that he scarcely tried to justify it; "seeing those things which are equal must needs all have one measure. . . . My desire, therefore, to be loved of my equals in nature as much as possible may be, imposeth upon me a natural duty of bearing to themward fully the like affection. From which relation of equality between ourselves and them that are as ourselves, what several rules and canons natural reason hath drawn for direction of life, no man is ignorant." Political society was formed to supply those defects which were inherent "in us living singly." Society demanded government and government demanded law. As to the law, it must be obeyed unless "the law of reason, or of God, doth enjoin the contrary." Some years later, in 1614, the *Journals of the House of Commons* attribute to Sandys the assertion that monarchy was elective, for he said, "No successive king, but first elected. Election double of person and care; but both come in by consent of people, and with reciprocal conditions between king and people."[1] In these disjointed notes of the clerk of the Commons, one finds the whole thesis of "government by compact." In truth, Sandys and those nearest to him were the forerunners of the radicals of the New Model Army[2] who demanded a "law paramount," or constitution. In all the parliaments of James there was no more active reformer than he. In his *Survey of Religion in*

[1] *Journals of the Commons*, i, 493; Gardiner's *History of England*, ii, 240. See also ch. viii of the present work, Note IV.

[2] On this whole subject of the political theories of the Puritans, see the *Clarke Papers* in the publications of the Camden Society (now included in those of the Royal Historical Society). Mr. Firth's introduction to that volume is full of instruction. Gardiner's *Civil War*, especially vol. iii, Jenks's *Puritan Experiments*, and Borgeaud's *Rise of Modern Democracy* should be read by all who wish to trace the rise of the modern state. Gardiner's Introduction to his *Constitutional Documents of the Puritan Revolution* shows the points of resemblance between the "law paramount" of the Protectorate and the Constitution of the United States.

the Western Parts of the World he had argued for fairness toward Roman Catholics. He now endeavored to retain the Nonconformists in the Established Church by granting to them the substance of the demands which they had put forward in the "Millenary Petition" and at the Hampton Court Conference. But the bills which he introduced for that purpose were so mutilated in the Lords that he withdrew them. Spurred on possibly by this disappointment, he declared in the House that "matters were carried, by the cunning of lawyers, clean contrary to the meaning of the House in matters ecclesiastical."[1] This statement met with general approval, for the Speaker, when he sought to free the lawyers of this charge, was interrupted and not allowed to speak. Sandys had been a student at the Middle Temple, but he seems to have had a poor opinion of the law, or at least of the way in which it was administered. On one occasion he even had the temerity to suggest in the Commons that all persons accused of crime should be permitted to employ counsel in their defense; but this proposition was rudely brushed aside on the ground that granting it would "shake the corner stone of the law."[2]

Many things in England besides religion were crying aloud for reformation, and to these Sir Edwin also addressed himself. Among them few attract the attention of the modern student more certainly than wardships.[3] Like other relics of feudalism, in their time and place wardships were fitting enough, but in the reign of James

[1] For Sandys as a religious reformer, see *Journals of the Commons*, i, 265, 311, etc., and Spedding's *Life and Letters of Francis Bacon*, iii, 264.

[2] See Gardiner's *History of England*, i, 123–127, 129–132, 339; Pike's *History of Crime*, ii, 89–96; Stephen's *Criminal Law*, i, 324–357; Reeves's *History of English Law*, iii, 806–811.

[3] *Memoirs of the Verney Family*, i, 113. See also Gardiner's *History of England*, i, 171, 174; Spedding's *Bacon*, iii, 176–180, 210; and the *Journals of the House of Commons*.

they were a public and private scandal. To free England from the curse of wardships, feudal tenures, and purveyance was Sir Edwin Sandys's ambition. He failed to effect his object, for James, with his Scottish obstinacy, refused to give way except on terms which could not be accepted. It is noteworthy, however, that these incidents of feudalism scarcely ever prevailed in the colonies.

Sir Edwin Sandys was also interested in the overthrow of monopolies and the introduction of freedom of trade. For years he struggled, and always unsuccessfully, for at every turn the king's prerogative and the royal will appeared and proved insurmountable. Each rebuff drove Sandys farther away from the position of an upholder of monarchical institutions, until it is possible that the form of the Genevan state, as it had been worked out by Calvin and his immediate successors, may have secured some hold on his imagination and desire, but the subject is by no means clear. What is clear now and should have been in 1619 was the unfitness of Sir Edwin Sandys for the position of chief administrator of the Virginia Company. For if there was one position in England which should have been occupied by one who had the confidence of the king, that place was the executive head of the colonizing enterprise whose success depended in very great measure upon the good will of the reigning monarch.

Another man with whom the student of colonial history becomes familiarly acquainted is Robert Rich, who became successively Lord Rich and Earl of Warwick.[1] His mother was Penelope Devereux, sister of Elizabeth's favorite, Walter Devereux, Earl of Essex; his brother,

[1] For an appreciative account of Warwick, see F. E. Greville's (the Countess of Warwick) *Warwick Castle and its Earls*, i. She sums up his career as follows: "He lived in times of transition and confusion, and he played a prominent and, upon the whole, a creditable part in them."

Henry Rich, Earl of Holland, in later years became the favorite of Henrietta Maria, Queen of Charles I, and his kinsman, Nathaniel Rich, played an important part in the founding of Virginia. Warwick's son, moreover, married Sir Thomas Smythe's daughter, without the latter gentleman's knowledge or consent and rather to his dismay. Warwick early became interested in the Virginia Company. Fond of maritime matters, he seems to have set on foot trading expeditions to Virginia in coöperation with prominent members of the corporation, and probably with the consent of that body, although no documents justifying this statement have been preserved to the present time. Warwick, following the example of Ralegh and Drake, also sought to make spoil of the Spaniard. To save himself from charges of piracy, he secured commissions from the Duke of Savoy which authorized his captains to prey on the Spaniards. The operations of his ships interfered with the trade of the East India Company and ended in the seizure of two of them by the company's captains. For this Warwick demanded twenty thousand pounds, a claim which Sir Thomas Smythe regarded as "altogether impertinent."[1] In this way began an estrangement between the two fathers-in-law which was soon complicated by a curious turn in the fortunes of Samuel Argall, "that ingenious and forward" young kinsman of Smythe. For some years Argall had been employed by De la Warr and Warwick and others as commander of the ship *Treasurer*. In 1617 he was sent to Virginia as governor, in succession to George Yeardley, who was administering the government after the retirement of Sir Thomas Dale.

Like all these early governors, Argall found everything in confusion in the colony. The buildings, fortifications,

[1] *Calendars of State Papers, East Indies, 1617–1621*, No. 781 and fol.

and boats belonging to the company he described as "much ruined,"[1] while the colonists appeared to be cheerful, although "many have scarce rags to cover their naked bodies." Similar sights met each succeeding governor, and such travelers as returned to England and recounted their Virginia experiences said the same thing. Probably their eyes, fresh from English trimness, failed to make due allowance for the inevitable rudeness of colonial conditions. "James Citty" was a small collection of hovels, defended by a stockade, and remained so for years, notwithstanding the efforts of company and king.

Argall seems to have come out with some intention of securing repayment of the money which his patrons had put into Virginia by getting possession of whatever public property had a pecuniary value. In this endeavor he had a measure of success, if one can judge from the complaints of the non-participating members of the corporation. Besides doing this, Argall ruled the Virginians as might be expected from an arbitrary and successful naval captain. In 1617, for instance, he sentenced one man to death for stealing a calf and running away to the Indians, and another, a certain John Hudson, to be "exiled and banished, and if he returns to be put to death without further judgment." What John Hudson's offense was is not known, but the moral condition of the colonists certainly needed a strong curb, if one may judge by a perusal of Conway Robinson's notes from the Virginia records. Either his severity or his successful financial dealings or both in combination procured the filing of charges against Argall; but warned in time,[2] he left Vir-

[1] Rolfe to Sandys, *Virginia Magazine of History*, x, 136.

[2] Robert Cushman (*Cushman Genealogy*), writing from London, May 8, 1619, says of Argall's arrival there, "It seemeth he came secretly." On Argall and his career, see *Dictionary of National Biography*, Brown's *Genesis*, ii,

ginia and returned unharmed to England. Once there, he courted the fullest investigation, but nothing was ever proved against him. It is not at all impossible that the evil name which has been given to Argall was due largely to the machinations of the Spanish ambassador and to Yeardley's desire to justify himself for his hasty charges against his rival. In 1620 Argall became a member of the Council for New England, and two years later was knighted by King James. In the first year of Charles's reign he sailed against the French at the head of a fleet of twenty-four vessels, and disappears from recorded history. Warwick at the moment seems to have thought that Sir Thomas Smythe was disposed to sacrifice Argall, and warmly espoused the latter's cause. It was in wranglings like this over personal and pecuniary matters, and not over political theories, that the disputes between the leaders in the Virginia Company originated.[1]

Sir Edwin Sandys and his friends were now in control of the company. Smythe and Warwick had sunk enough money in the enterprise. If Sandys and his friends wished to undertake the impossible, let them do so, — at least, that is the way the case seems to stand in those records which have survived accident and human design. The new rulers of the company breathed fresh life into the venture and conducted it on a new basis. Sandys and Southampton turned to Virginia as a field for

and, above all, Massachusetts Historical Society's *Collections*, Fourth Series, ix, 11–59, notes. It is noteworthy that Sandys thought it necessary to clear himself of the charge of setting the Spanish ambassador against Argall (*Virginia Company Records*, i, 72). The cases of severe punishment given in this paragraph are from Conway Robinson's abstract of the *Court Records*, i, 138, 143 (Ms. in the Virginia Historical Society at Richmond).

[1] Alexander Brown (*First Republic*, 557 note) says, "The parties in the company had originated in disputes over business matters, auditing accounts, the magazine, the tobacco contracts, etc., and not in opposition to the popular charters." It is unfortunate that he uses the word "parties" to describe these factions.

social and philanthropic experiment, in which, perhaps, religion may have had some slight part. It is not unlikely that they expected that groups of colonists in different parts of Virginia would become practically self-governing, each group managing its religious concernments, as well as its civil affairs, in its own way.

The second part of the plan which Sandys and his friends seem to have had in mind was the establishment of landed proprietors in Virginia. The general idea was to give fifty acres of land to every one who should transport one person to the colony. The instructions embodying this provision were issued while Smythe was still treasurer, and this arrangement remained the basis of the Virginia land system throughout the colonial period. In making provision for the future, the company also proposed to do justice to the survivors of the first colonists by giving them larger quantities of land. Finally, in the requital of services rendered or to encourage emigration, the company also granted considerable tracts of land to groups of persons or to individuals. They also gave the holders of these large grants power in the way of government, and made them independent of the company's officers at Jamestown. Cases of this kind, which will be noticed hereafter, were the grants to the Pilgrims, to Captain John Martin, and to John Smith of Nibley[1] and his associates.

The third part of the scheme was the securing a monopoly of the tobacco market of England to the company, or to some of its members. A fourth part of the plan contemplated that the company, or some of its members,

[1] Among other proposed colonists was a body of Walloons. See "Agreement signed at The Hague, 19 July, 1621," in the form of a "Round Robin" (reproduced in facsimile by A. S. Clark). Walloon emigrants later (1623) sought New Netherland, but none came to Virginia.

should enjoy the whole trade of the colony. This was to be done by sending out "magazine ships" from which the settlers could obtain their supplies and to which they could sell their tobacco. The scheme in its entirety possessed great possibilities. Practical freedom of government, practical freedom of religion, and practical monopoly of the English tobacco trade were offset by the necessity of paying a small quit-rent on the land obtained from the company and of confining buying and selling to the magazine ships. The scheme, however, failed. Warwick and Smythe made up their feud; they and their friends turned on the Virginia Company and brought about its overthrow in the hope, perhaps, that from the wreckage they might get back a part of the money which they had sunk in the enterprise.

On one of the last days of April, 1619, Sir George Yeardley landed at Jamestown. Soon after his arrival, in conformity with his instructions, he issued a proclamation[1] directing the inhabitants of each place and plantation to elect two burgesses to a general assembly to be held at Jamestown. On July 30 the assembly[2] met in the wooden church at Jamestown. There were present the governor, the councilors, and twenty-two burgesses, representing eleven places, three of which were denominated cities. The session was opened with prayer, and all the burgesses, "none staggering at it," took the Oath of Supremacy. The House of Commons in England had wrested from the king the right to judge of the quali-

[1] Brown's *First Republic*, 312.

[2] *Colonial Records of Virginia* [edited by T. H. Wynne and W. S. Gilman]. This is sometimes cited as *Senate Document (Extra)*, 1874, as it was printed by the general assembly of Virginia. Bruce, for instance, cites it in this way. The first paper in this volume is "A Report of the Manner of proceeding in the General Assembly convented at James City in Virginia, July 30, 1619." See also Sainsbury in the *Antiquary* for July, 1881.

fications and elections of its own members. So here the assembly at once proceeded to exercise the privileges which in England belonged to the Commons, and questioned the right of the burgesses from Captain Ward's and Captain Martin's plantations to sit in the House. It appeared that Captain Ward had "squatted" on the company's land; on promising to obtain a regular title he and the other burgess from his plantation were permitted to remain.

The case of Captain John Martin was more complicated. He had been one of the first comers to Virginia and a member of the first council, and had powerful connections in England, as his brother-in-law, Sir Julius Cæsar, was Master of the Rolls and a much trusted member of the Privy Council. Although Martin's sister had been dead many years, and Cæsar, in the interval, had had two other wives, he continued to manifest a strong interest in the colonizing captain and his affairs. In its grant to Captain Martin,[1] the Virginia Company had authorized him to govern and command all persons whom he should transport to Virginia or who should be sent to him, free from any control by the colony except it be to assist against any foreign or domestic enemy. The assembly voted that Captain Martin should either give over that part of his patent, or the burgesses from his plantation should withdraw from the assembly. He refused to abandon his peculiar privileges, and his representatives were dismissed. These preliminaries arranged, the assembly proceeded to legislative business. As the laws which they passed were the first to be made by a legislative body in America, it will be well briefly to notice them.

[1] Documents and discussions relating to this case are in *Virginia Magazine of History*, vii, 136, 268.

In general, it may be said that the assembly sought to adapt English practice to Virginian conditions without much regard for "Dale's Laws." As to religion, for example, it was provided that all clergymen should read divine service and perform their ministerial functions according to the laws and orders of the Church of England. Every one in the colony should attend divine service on Sundays, both forenoon and afternoon, or forfeit three shillings for each absence, which should go to the use of the Church; servants, however, in case their absence were due to disobedience of their master's commands, should suffer bodily punishment. Idleness, gambling, drunkenness, and "excess in apparel" were vigorously reprobated. The idler might be bound to serve for wages until he showed signs of amendment; the gambler should pay ten shillings and forfeit his winnings, if any; the drunkard for the first offense should be privately reprimanded by the minister; for the second offense he should lie in the bolts, or bilboes; for the third offense he should undergo such severe punishment as the governor and council might determine. The legislators' attention was directed to excess in apparel by the appearance of a freed servant in a beaver hat with a band of pearls. To curb this tendency to wasteful display, it was enacted that a man should be taxed in the Church for all public contributions; if he be single, according to the appearance of his outer clothing; "if he be married, according to his own and his wife's or either of their apparel."

Among the few reforms which James Stuart allowed to appear on the Statute Book of England was a law directed against profane swearing,[1] which Sandys thought

[1] 21 Jac. i, C. 20. The penalty was a fine of one shilling for use of the poor or the stocks; or if the offender was under twelve years of age, a whipping by the constable or by the parent in his presence.

would not be of great service because the upper classes were the worst offenders, and for them the penalties attached were small.[1] The Virginia assembly, acting possibly on instructions from England, provided that every master of a family who persisted in swearing should give five shillings for the use of the Church, while a servant who cursed should be whipped unless the master "redeemed his back" by paying the fine, or the servant publicly acknowledged his fault in the church. Whether this law was of much value, or, in fact, was ever vigorously enforced, nowhere appears in the scanty records which have been preserved.

The production of tobacco was the one employment in Virginia in the prosecution of which there was certain profit. Nowadays, under these circumstances, every effort would be made to foster such a wealth-producing industry. In those days, however, men thought differently; and the assembly, acting in harmony with the Virginia Company in England and with the English government, sought to restrict the production of tobacco and to stimulate that of silk, flax, and wine, and particularly the growing of sufficient food for the needs of the colonists. For instance, to foster the silk culture every planter each year for seven years should plant and maintain six mulberry trees under penalty of censure by the governor and council.

Besides these legislative acts, the assembly sat as a court of law in two cases. The first of these was that of Thomas Garnett, who by false accusation had sought to bring about his master's downfall. For this he was sentenced to stand in the pillory for four days with his ears nailed to the board, be publicly whipped on each of those days, and make such satisfaction to his master as the gov-

[1] *Commons Journals*, i, 548.

ernor and council should deem appropriate. The other case was that of Captain Henry Spellman, who had spoken slightingly of the new governor; for this he was degraded from his office and sentenced to act as interpreter for one year.

The manner of holding this assembly is described by the secretary of the colony as if the burgesses and the council played somewhat different parts. He says that the governor "being set down in his accustomed place, those of the Council of Estate sat next him on both hands, except only the Secretary, then appointed Speaker, who sat right before him." This information comes to us from John Pory, who describes himself as holding these two important offices. As the assembly, governor, council, and burgesses put together, numbered only some twenty-five or thirty persons, the ceremonies described by the recorder would seem to have been excessive, especially in view of the fact that the governor took an important part in the legislative work of the body. Possibly, from infirmity of memory, Mr. John Pory assigned to himself a somewhat over prominent part. Be this as it may, the assembly of 1619 is of first importance in our annals; it was, indeed, the "mother" of the American representative legislature.

NOTES

I. The Virginia Records. — When the government definitely made up its mind to destroy the Virginia Company, it impounded the records and other papers. These have not yet come to light, but the Historical Commission may any day bring them to notice. Alexander Brown (*English Politics in Early Virginia History*, 68) states that "James I. left no stone unturned in the effort to find and to have destroyed all evidences which were favorable to the popular course of government" in the Virginia Company. He brings forward nothing which can be termed evidence to support this view. In the absence of such evidence it does not seem likely that James would have exhibited in this instance a constancy of purpose which was quite foreign to his character. Probably the papers are still moldering away in some attic or cellar. Before handing over the record book a transcript was made which in a curious way has come into the Library of Congress. This has never been printed in full, but the needs of all save the most exacting are filled by the "Abstract of the Proceedings of the Virginia Company of London, 1619–24" which was printed in the *Collections* of the Virginia Historical Society, New Series, vols. vii, viii.

II. The Great Charter. — The Instructions of 1618 are sometimes called the Great Charter by Virginia writers, notably by Edward Eggleston and Alexander Brown. The term is also said to be used in some of the land grants. It applies probably to the instructions to Yeardley, which were drawn up in England (November 28, 1618) when Sir Thomas Smythe was still treasurer. Brown (*First Republic*, 266, 293) says that similar instructions were given to Lord De la Warr in 1617; but of this he gives no proof. The question of the genesis of the form and matter of the Instructions of 1618 may be doubtful. There can be no doubt whatever as to the great importance of the document itself; although the comparison with Magna Charta may be overdrawn. These instructions contain the provision, as we infer from what was done under them, which authorized Yeardley to summon the assembly of 1619, which was the forerunner in America of all legislative assemblies. The instructions themselves also became the precedents for the later instructions, not merely while the company continued to live, but under the crown as well. In this way the form of government established by Sir Thomas

Smythe, Sir Edwin Sandys, and their co-workers in 1618 became the model on which the constitution of the royal province of the later time was worked out; but this was due largely to the fact that it reproduced in a colony the essential features of the political organization of England itself. The Instructions of 1618, so far as they have been preserved, are printed in *Virginia Magazine of History*, ii, 154. There is no evidence in any contemporaneous document which has so far come to light that the assembly of 1619 was called in response to a demand from Virginia, as stated by John Fiske in *Virginia and her Neighbours.* Its summoning was due to the liberal ideas of the leaders in the company in England and also, perhaps, to the hope that a freer government in the colony might attract settlers.

III. Emigration to Virginia. — The following figures have been compiled from Alexander Brown's *First Republic* : —

1606–1625	5649 emigrants left England for Virginia	1095 colonists were living in Virginia in 1625

Or to go into detail : —

1606–1609	320 emigrants sailed for Virginia	Of these from 80 to 100 were alive in Virginia in July, 1609
1606–1618	1800 emigrants sailed for Virginia	Of these 600 were living in Virginia at end of 1618
1619–1620 (12 months)	1200 emigrants sailed for Virginia	Of these 1000 died on voyage or in the colony before April, 1620

From 1622 to 1623, just twelve months, 347 persons perished in the Indian massacre and nearly 1000 died of disease or starvation on the way to Virginia or in the colony.

CHAPTER VIII

THE OLD DOMINION

DURING the years 1618 to 1624, Sandys, Southampton, and Nicholas Ferrar were supreme in the company's affairs. They made great and successful efforts to send over colonists and supplies; in three years' time no fewer than 3570 emigrants crossed the Atlantic to Virginia. As there were six hundred white persons living in the colony at the beginning of this period, the total number of human beings to be accounted for is 4170. In March, 1622, before the Indian massacre, there were living in Virginia twelve hundred English colonists, showing that in three years nearly three thousand persons had perished from disease and starvation.[1] The "massacre" cost the lives of three hundred and forty-seven more. Instead of carefully searching out the causes of these disasters, the company continued to pour settlers into the colony; but in 1624, when a careful enumeration was made, there were only 1232 colonists alive, including in this number twenty-three negro slaves.[2] The years of the Sandys-Southampton

[1] Brown's *Republic*, 464. Sandys's description of the colony in 1619 is in *Virginia Company Records*, i, 64.

[2] *Virginia Magazine of History and Biography*, vii, 364. The reports upon which this statement is based were taken to England by Captain John Harvey in the spring of 1625; they probably reflect the condition of the colony in the autumn and winter of 1624–25. Brown (*First Republic*, 611–628) gives long abstracts. His figures are slightly different from those given in the *Virginia Magazine*: "Inhabitants. Free, 432 males and 176 females; servants, 441 males and 46 females; total, 1095 emigrants, 107 children, making 1202 English; 2 Indians; 11 negro men, 10 women, and 2 children = 23 negroes. Grand total, 1227." See also Wynne and Gilman, *Colonial Records of Virginia*, 37: "Lists of the Livinge & Dead in Virginia," February 16, 1623 [February 26, 1624, N.S.]. John Fiske's statement that there were at

rule were for the most part a season of hardship and distress in Virginia comparable only to that earlier starving time which has been so graphically described by the Virginia annalist, William Stith.

In writing of Virginia in the earliest years, one is obliged to rely partly on what may be termed hostile testimony, but the following statements as to the condition of Virginia in this later period are derived from members of Sir Edwin's own family, whom he sent to Virginia, partly, no doubt, that he might get at the truth, and partly from that stain of nepotism which is always so apt to become rife in political and business life. These witnesses are George Sandys, Sir Edwin's brother, whom he appointed treasurer in Virginia; his niece, Margaret Sandys, wife of Sir Francis Wyat, whom he had sent over as governor in succession to Yeardley; and Wyat himself.[1] George Sandys, writing in March, 1623, stated that five hundred colonists had recently died and there "were scarcely as many left, so that the living could hardly bury the dead." Everything had failed, shipbuilding and glassmaking included, and a pestilent fever was then raging. Sir Francis Wyat, the governor, wrote that there was an antipathy between the commands of the company and the doings of the colonists; he wished "little Mr. Ferrar" were in Virginia, "that he might add to his zeal a knowledge of the country." Lady Wyat, in a letter to "Sister Sandys," tells her that the ship in which she had voyaged to Virginia had been "so pestered with peo-

least 4000 people in Virginia in 1622 is doubtless a copyist's error (*Virginia and her Neighbours*, i, 189).

[1] Royal Historical Manuscripts Commission's *Eighth Report*, Appendix ii, 39, 40, 41. See also Wyat and the Virginia Council to the company, *Virginia Magazine*, vi, 236, 374. These official letters are less despondent in tone than the others, but contain some energetic remarks on the management of the transportation of supplies and emigrants.

ple and goods . . . so full of infection that after a while they saw but little but throwing folks overboard;" few were left alive when they anchored off Jamestown. Once landed, she found little to encourage her, and asked for the speedy sending of supplies, especially of bacon and cheese, for the cattle as well as the men had perished on the way over. When the wife of the governor fared thus ill, what must have been the lot of the servant!

The twelve hundred or thirteen hundred colonists living in Virginia in 1624 were scattered through nineteen settlements, ranging in size from Wariscoyack, with two houses and eight inhabitants, to Elizabeth City, with sixty-nine houses and two hundred and fifty-seven inhabitants,— James City at that time had thirty-three houses and a total population of one hundred and seventy-five souls. In all there were two hundred and seventy-eight houses in Virginia. The reports further contain many interesting details as to supplies and munitions, from which the following articles have been noted as illustrating the different phases of colonial progress, or lack of it: 2288 barrels of corn, 58,380 pounds of fish, 364 head of cattle, 509 pigs, 220 goats, 1 horse, 775 hens, 40 boats. One silkworm house and a vineyard of two acres were all that remained of twelve years' earnest effort. Of munitions of war there were 1129 pounds of gunpowder, 9657 pounds of lead and shot, 932 "fixt peeces," or guns, 429 swords, 342 suits of armor, 260 coats of mail and headpieces, and various other things. It is well to call to mind the accouterment of a Virginia soldier as he marched through the forests clad in mediæval panoply of war and pursuing an Indian who was clad in nothing at all. The white warrior, indeed, was a species of itinerant fortress, as the

Indian arrows fell harmless from his cuirass and the tomahawk fared little better when it came in contact with the iron pot or headpiece.

The most pressing need of Virginia after 1624, as well as before that date, was to secure the necessary amount of labor to cultivate tobacco to the greatest advantage. The tidewater region of Virginia, which was necessarily the first portion to be settled, had a soil of such extraordinary fertility that the first wheat which was planted at Jamestown grew six feet in not many more weeks. Most of the ground was covered with splendid trees, which had to be cut down to make way for tobacco plants, which soon exhausted the soil. The course of agriculture, therefore, became one interminable round of clearing the land and planting and curing tobacco. The whole life of Virginia turned on the cultivation of tobacco, for that was its staple product in these early days.[1] The production of tobacco was simply a question of the supply of unskilled labor; the demand in Virginia for human beings, other than Indians, was therefore very great and was supplied in several ways.

White women and marriages and family life there had been in Virginia since 1608, when John Laydon married Anne Burrus,[2] who came to the colony in that year as maidservant to Mrs. Forest, and "pressing" maidens to be transported to Virginia was a business as early as 1618. The great mass of Virginia settlers, however, were still

[1] Of course other things were produced in Virginia. Corn was sometimes sent from there to the Northern colonies; but speaking generally and referring to these early days, it is correct to speak of tobacco as the staple product. See, however, L. G. Tyler in *The Century*, xxix, 636.

[2] Virginia Laydon, the first of four daughters to be born to this pair, was probably the first child of English parents to be born in the Old Dominion. In 1636 Laydon received a grant of land in recognition of "the personal adventures of himself and wife." See *Virginia Magazine of History*, v, 93.

without wives to tie them to the soil. To provide them with permanent interests in the colony, Sir Edwin Sandys conceived the shrewd project of sending over "maids for wives," and nearly one hundred young maidens reached the colony in 1619.[1] The company had no expectation of loss in this venture, for the husbands were to pay the entire cost of transporting the brides. This expense was apportioned equally on each of the maids who survived the voyage. It is not clear, however, whether any allowance was made for those of the number who were so unfortunate as not to secure a husband.

Notwithstanding the best that the company could do, women were scarce in the colony in 1623, if one may reach a general conclusion from the following single case.[2] It was in that year that the Rev. Grivell Pooley sought the hand of Mrs. Samuel Jordan of "Jordan's Journey" within "three or four days" of her husband's decease. She, very properly, desired time to mourn her departed spouse, but Mr. Pooley pursued his suit so persistently that erelong the blushing widow permitted him to kiss her in presence of Captain Madison. Presuming on this compliance, Pooley declared to Mrs. Jordan: "I am thine and thou art mine till death us separate." He was oversanguine, however, for the fair Cicely Jordan soon afterwards contracted herself to Mr. William Ferrar in the presence of the governor and council. Thereupon the Rev. Grivell sued her for breach of promise, but the rulers declined

[1] *Virginia Magazine of History*, vi, 228. *Virginia Company Records*, i, 66, states that ninety "young maidens to make wives of for so many of the former tenants" and one hundred "boys to make apprentices" for those tenants were sent over in 1619. The De la Warr Mss. calendared in the Royal Historical Commission's *Reports* (iv, 283) contain a "Note of the shipping, men, and provisions sent to Virginia by the Treasurer in the year 1619. Ships — People — Commodities — Gifts"; see also *Virginia Magazine*, vi, 231.

[2] This case is given at length in Brown's *First Republic*, 563–565; he does not state where the manuscript may be found.

to meddle with the matter and sent the papers to England. The further history of this love affair of Mr. Pooley is unknown, as the company perished before making any decision. The governor and council in Virginia, however, were determined to guard against future trouble of the kind and issued a proclamation denouncing corporal punishment, or fine, for the third offense of using entangling words "tending to the contract of marriage,"—and this they did without the formality of consulting the general assembly.

The earliest comers to the James River were gentlemen volunteers, their personal attendants, and a small number of laboring men to perform the necessary hard work. The first band of colonists which came out in 1609 included many laborers and also many undesirable persons of all classes. On the other hand, the expedition of 1610 was composed of excellent material, consisting largely of artisans and mechanics. When the profitable cultivation of tobacco was made possible, about 1616, the whole mode of settlement underwent a complete alteration. After that time two classes of people mainly came to Virginia, men with capital and those who emigrated under some form of contract of service. The last years of Elizabeth's reign and the first years of James's rule were a critical period in the history of the laboring class in England. The time was one of regulation, when it seemed possible to determine human fate by law, and, especially, to guide human affairs so as to be most beneficial to the class which made the laws. We find, therefore, that the laws provided that all unemployed persons not conversant with some art or mystery, as clothiers, arrowhead makers, or butchers, having no property and not being of gentle birth or students, could be compelled to serve in husbandry for one year, and at the end of that time could not leave the parish where he was employed without a certificate. In the period of harvest, the magistrates could even compel artificers to leave their usual vocations and work in the fields for day wages.

Notwithstanding the efforts just described, the roads of England became exceedingly pestered with vagabonds. In 1572, therefore, Parliament again grappled with the problem, and this time in a sanguinary frame of mind. In the future vagabonds and sturdy beggars, women as well as men, should be grievously whipped, and then burned through the gristle of the right ear with a hot iron one inch in diameter. It behooved a person so marked to secure employment, for if such a one were again apprehended, he or she should suffer death as a felon. Among the classes of persons who were deemed vagabonds in this act, were those who feigned to have knowledge of palmistry, idle persons who were whole and mighty in body, unlicensed jugglers, peddlers, and tinkers, and those scholars of the University who were found begging without a certificate under the University seal. In 1598 Parliament passed the great act for the support of the poor, which is usually associated with the year 1601, when it was made permanent. By this law, each town and parish should take care of its own poor under the oversight of the justices. Vagabonds and beggars, men or women, found wandering on the highway, should be "stripped naked from the middle upwards, and be openly whipped until his or her body be bloody," and then be sent to the parish wherein he or she was born or last employed. If no such place could be discovered, the justice might condemn the wanderer to the house of correction, or, in case the vagabond appeared to be dangerous, the justices might sentence him or her to banishment under pain of death in case of return.[1]

This brief description of the laws for the treatment of idlers of the working classes, taken in connection with what has been said as to the punishment of what are now regarded as minor crimes, will serve to show the powers under which the English magistrates acted in supplying Virginia with laborers, and also some of the inducements which impelled those out of employment in England to seek the New World. One further class of unfortunates remains to be noticed, those waifs and strays of the London streets, whose tender years did not bring them under the sweep of the enactments just mentioned. These the London authorities gathered by the hundreds and turned over to the Virginia Company. Compulsion[2] was sometimes used, and those who declined to go were bound out to hard masters.

Every now and then the doors of English prisons were opened, and batches of convicted felons, the heinousness of whose crimes may be guessed from the laws described above, were handed over to the officers of the company for conveyance to Virginia. The peculiarity of the few entries relating to this subject which have been discovered has called an undue amount of attention to them. The first convicted murderer to be sent to Virginia (1619) was

[1] The first Parliament of James further provided (1 Jac. c. 7) that incorrigible or dangerous rogues should be branded on the left shoulder "with an hot burning iron of the breadth of an English shilling, with a great Roman R upon the iron, and the branding upon the shoulder to be so thoroughly burned and set upon the skin and flesh that the letter R be seen and remain for a perpetual mark upon such rogue during his or her life," and if such rogue be again found wandering or begging, he or she should suffer death as a felon, without benefit of clergy.

[2] In 1620, Sandys applied for a warrant to enforce the transportation of children from London to Virginia, as some of the worse disposed were unwilling to go. *Calendars of State Papers, Domestic, 1619–1623*, p. 118. See also, on this general subject, *ibid.*, *James I.*, viii, 183; *Charles I.*, v, 433; vii, 166, 569; xiii, 270.

Stephen Rogers, a carpenter, whom Sir Thomas Smythe asked the justices to hand over to him for transportation to the James River, on the plea that carpenters were much needed there.[1]

The generic term which came to be employed to describe the white laboring class of Virginia was "servant." The meaning of this term was different in different periods of the Old Dominion's history, and, indeed, its application was not the same in widely separated parts of the colony at any one point of time. The servant was employed according to the terms of an indenture.[2] These varied greatly — some required seven years of service, others only two or three years, some permitted the holder of the indenture to sell the servant's time to any one whom he saw fit, others provided that the servant upon arrival in the colony should seek out his own master and have two weeks' time in which to find one. These facts point to the conclusion that the servants themselves varied greatly — some of them were educated men who served as schoolmasters, others were vagabonds and convicts, who performed severe manual labor. In those cases where no indenture was made, the servant's term and condition of life were regulated by "the custom of the country," which was from time to time changed by law. Generally speaking, the term of service for a person nineteen years of age, or over, was five years — a person under that age

[1] *Middlesex Records*, ii, 224.

Smythe had earlier procured a few felons for transportation to Virginia. See J. D. Butler's "British convicts shipped to American Colonies" (*American Historical Review*, ii, 17); Ballagh's "White Servitude in Virginia" (*Johns Hopkins Studies*); E. D. Neill's *Virginia Vetusta*, and *Virginia Carolorum*, and "Notes" in the *Virginia Magazine of History*; J. D. Lindsay's "Extradition and Rendition of Fugitives and Criminals in the American Colonies" in *National Magazine*, vol. xvi. The general subject of the transportation of criminals to the colonies will be further treated in the second volume of the present work.

[2] One is calendared in Royal Historical Manuscripts Commission's *Reports*, xv, Appendix, pt. 2, p. 323; others are given in Brown's *Genesis*.

should serve until he or she were twenty-four. The term of service of the transported thief or murderer was naturally longer, but in other respects his treatment was the same as that of the ordinary servant.

In general, although the work of clearing the forests was severe, and there were inhuman and cruel masters in Virginia as elsewhere, the agricultural laborer was much better off in Virginia than he was in England. In the colony he was fed, clothed, and lodged on a better scale than the farm hand in England could feed, clothe, and lodge himself. There was no hope that the latter could better his condition — there was every chance that the Virginia servant, if he had anything in him, would rise in the world. At the end of his term of service the freedman received clothing, food, and other articles to the value of ten pounds sterling; land was easily acquired, and the industrious man could soon become a planter and employer of labor — sometimes, indeed, he might vie in prosperity with his late master within a comparatively short number of years. Until the close of the seventeenth century, servants formed the great mass of the laboring population of Virginia; negro slaves, however, were becoming more numerous every year.

Probably the first negroes to land in Virginia after 1606 were twenty in number, who came to the colony in a "Dutch man-of-war" in the year 1619. These unfortunates had been twice captured, first on the African coast and again in the West Indies. The identity of this slave ship is still disputed; it is not impossible that she was one of those irregularly commissioned vessels which the Earl of Warwick and other Englishmen sent to scour the seas.[1]

[1] Whence came these slaves and by whom imported, or were they the first slaves in Virginia? These questions are ably discussed by Brown in his *First*

This introduction of negro slavery into English colonies on the continent, — it already prevailed in the English islands, — was purely accidental. There was no pressing demand for negroes in Virginia, and their number at first increased very slowly. On the other hand those negroes that were brought in seem to have found a ready sale.

Englishmen in the seventeenth century saw no harm in enslaving the negro, and they would doubtless have converted the Indians of Virginia into human chattels, as the Spaniards did those of the West Indies, had not the Northern red men proved untameable. A few of the planters employed the natives as huntsmen, providing them with arms and ammunition. The impolicy of so doing did not at once occur to the whites, and, indeed, Sir George Yeardley is distinctly charged with setting the example. In the rush for available tobacco fields, the planters spread out over the land, leaving, as a rule, several miles between plantations for future enlargement. They not only cleared the primeval forest; they also took possession of the cornfields of the natives, which aroused the latter's resentment. Under the lead of Opechancanough, the new war chief of the James River Indians, the savages fell upon the unsuspecting whites, destroyed some of the outlying plantations, and killed three hundred and forty-seven persons,[1] perhaps one quarter of the whole population of the colony. The blow fell so suddenly and so severely that the settlers generally abandoned their plantations and sought shelter in the few towns then

Republic (325) and *Genesis* (ii, 980), and by Bruce in his *Economic History* (ii, 65–74). Brown says that he has nowhere seen it stated in any contemporaneous document that these were the earliest importation. As slaves were introduced into the Somers Islands as early as 1616, it is by no means impossible that a few may have been brought to Jamestown before 1619.

[1] Alexander Brown (*First Republic*, 467) suggests that this number is an underestimate.

existing. For the time being the survivors postponed retaliation and planted corn and grew tobacco as usual. In the autumn, however, they turned with sudden fury upon the Indians. They killed many, they drove others from their villages, and they destroyed the Indians' food supply for the coming winter.[1] The English sometimes resorted to stratagems which were as treacherous as those of the savages themselves, and it was charged at the time that Dr. John Pott, the physician general of the company, had destroyed numbers of the Indians by poison. At the moment it was supposed that Opechancanough had been killed on one of these expeditions; but he lived long enough to organize another massacre in 1644. That was his last feat, however; for, being captured, he was shot in the back by one of the colonists who had been appointed to guard him.[2]

Among the capitalists and groups of capitalists who sought to exploit the cultivation of Virginia tobacco on a large scale was John Smith of Nibley, in England.[3] In 1619, with three other capitalists, he obtained from the Virginia Company a grant of six thousand acres of land in addition to fifty acres for each person whom they should transport to Virginia within seven years, there to abide for three years, unless death overtook them in the meantime. After six years, the grantees should pay an annual quit-rent of twelve pence per fifty acres, and when the first tract was "planted and peopled" the associates should receive as much more. The Virginia Company also agreed within seven years to grant the adventurers

[1] See Wyat and council to Virginia Company in *Virginia Magazine of History*, vi, 374–378.

[2] L. G. Tyler's *Cradle of the Republic*, 40.

[3] *John Smith of Nibley Papers.* These are calendared in the *Bulletin of the New York Public Library* for July, 1897. The papers used in this chapter are printed at length in *ibid.*, iii, 161, 208, 248, 276.

letters of incorporation, with liberty to make orders for the government of all persons to be settled upon the associates' land. In 1620[1] the Virginia Company made a general rule that captains or leaders of particular plantations, together with some of the gravest and discreetest of their company, should have liberty to make orders for the better directing of their business and servants, provided that such regulations were not repugnant to the laws of England. It was under this vote, or at all events in conformity with the policy indicated by it, that the grant was made to John Smith of Nibley and his associates as well as to other groups of capitalists and colonists, notably the Pilgrim Fathers. John Smith of Nibley and his fellow-adventurers set to work with enthusiasm and speedily fitted out two ships with emigrants and supplies. It occurred to them that it would be a good plan to interest Sir George Yeardley, at the time governor of the colony, in the success of their enterprise. So they proposed to him that he should become one of the partners and be entitled to a share in the profits without the necessity of contributing any money. This earliest attempt at official corruption which is mentioned in our records is interesting for two reasons. First, because Yeardley declined, and secondly, because the very fact that it was made throws light on the conduct of English business concerns at the time of the settlement of the English North American colonies.

In two years' time the adventurers dispatched at least two vessels for Berkeley Hundred, the *Margaret* and the *Supply*. In them, and possibly in other vessels, were embarked over eighty emigrants, of whom only thirteen were living three years later; of the balance forty-one are

[1] *Virginia Company Records*, i, 39.

marked as dead on the margin of the list of their names, while eleven more are marked as slain, which word probably refers to the "massacre." Money was not spared in fitting out these vessels, the total cost being £1436 1*s.* 11*d.* in the money of that time. The list of articles put on board the ships covers seventeen quarto printed pages of forty-seven lines each, and included among other things "three books on the practice of piety," two pounds of brimstone, sixty gallons and one "pottle" of aquæ vitæ, one bushel of mustard seed, three dripping pans, fifteen gross of buttons, one hundred and five pair of "Irish stockins," twenty pounds of soap, two thousand hobnails, and four thousand sparrow bills, or small shoe nails. John Smith of Nibley bore a dauntless soul. When his eighty colonists and his seventeen quarto pages of goods went the way of most things in early Virginia, he provided other men and other supplies, and was still working for success ten years later, in 1632.

Meantime, in England, the company was faring as badly as the colonists were in Virginia; ever recurring disputes in the corporation were combined with controversies between it and the king and his leading ministers. Sir Edwin Sandys in 1603 had hastened to the Scottish court and had been among the first to greet James as king of England; in return, James had knighted him soon after they reached London. Now, however, sixteen years of controversy between the king and the forces of reform, which were led by Sir Edwin, had wrought a radical change in the views of both of them; the king had come to distrust Sandys, and the latter had lost faith in the king.[1] James had good reason for lack of confidence in

[1] The beginning of this estrangement is hard to find; but the statesman's opposition to the "union" with Scotland, which the king had much at heart,

Sir Edwin, for Sandys was touched by the republican spirit of Calvinism, and, as the leading member of the House of Commons, he naturally turned to that body when in difficulty, with the result that the Virginia Company, to all intents and purposes, appealed from the king to Parliament.

The period of the Southampton-Sandys supremacy (1618–25), which ended in the company's downfall, was coincident with the first stage in that great religious conflict which is known in European history as the Thirty Years' War. One of the first events in that war was the ejectment of James's son-in-law, Frederick, and his wife, Elizabeth Stuart, from the throne of Bohemia, which they had ascended without any clear right, and from the Palatinate which Frederick had inherited from his ancestors. James, with his mixed cunning and timidity, could not bring himself to adopt any clear and straightforward line of action. Besides, at the moment, he was involved in one of the last scenes in that seriocomic drama known as the Spanish Marriage. It occurred to him that the easiest way to restore Frederick and his daughter to the former's paternal estate would be to operate through the king of Spain, who was naturally supposed to have a good deal of influence with the German branch of his family. Besides, the dowry of the Spanish Princess, or Infanta, would postpone the necessity of summoning Parliament. As we look back upon it, the Spanish Marriage was never a possibility, because his Most Catholic Majesty, the king of Spain, could not consent to his daughter's going to England except on conditions respecting the religion of the children, and the treatment

had a great deal to do with it. See, for example, *Commons Journals*, i, 952, 954, 955; Spedding's *Life and Letters of Francis Bacon*, iii, 328.

of English Catholics, which James could not grant unless he was prepared to seek safety in speedy flight to Scotland. James either could not or would not see these things, and it was not until Prince Charles and the Duke of Buckingham journeyed to Madrid (1623) that the futility of the scheme was recognized. It may seem a far call from Virginia tobacco to the Infanta of Spain; but in reality it proved to be impossible to encourage the production of tobacco in Virginia without irritating the Spanish government.

The prosperity of Virginia, upon which was contingent the very life of the colony and the hope of pecuniary return for the company and its shareholders,[1] was dependent upon the profitable production of tobacco. This in turn required at least something approaching the monopoly of the English tobacco trade. In early life, and even as late as 1620–21, Sandys strongly opposed the system of monopolies which had come down from Elizabeth; but he saw no harm in proposing legislation to exclude Spanish tobacco from England.[2] He approached the subject in a roundabout way by lamenting the scarcity of coin within the realm. This was due, he maintained, to the fact that Englishmen paid out gold and silver for foreign commodities, while foreigners, especially Spaniards, were able to pay for English goods with commodities in-

[1] In 1620–21 objections were raised to the lotteries, by which the Virginia Company had gained large sums of money. This opposition was due in part to the rising spirit of Puritanism in England. James also expressed his dislike of them and said that he would suspend and suppress them. He further declared that he had given way to the scheme because he had been told that Virginia could not raise money in any other way. At about the same time an act was introduced into the House of Commons for suppressing the odious and loathsome sin of drunkenness, and for the restraint of the excessive price of beer and ale. One third of the penalties to be imposed under the proposed act were to go to the company of Virginia; but the bill did not pass. (*Commons Journals*, i, 528; *Debates of 1620–21*, p. 99; Royal Historical Manuscripts Commission's *Reports*, iii, 18.)

[2] See, for instance, *Commons Journals*, i, 531–564.

stead of with gold and silver. He seems to have thought that Spain necessarily imported a certain fixed amount of goods from England, and that if she was not allowed to pay for these goods in tobacco, she must pay for them in coin. Whether Sir Edwin was sincere in his belief, or whether, as seems more likely, his desires were based upon the necessity of protecting the Virginia tobacco interest, it was perfectly certain that the Spanish tobacco trade would be the principal sufferer. Gondomar, the Spanish ambassador in London, picked up statements that were attributed to Sandys in which he advocated republican ideas. Whether these rumors were true or false, the Spaniard recognized their utility to discredit Sandys[1] with James.

The company was between the upper and nether millstones; it wished to handle the whole tobacco crop, the king wished to make all he could in the way of taxation, the persons who collected the taxes strove to make them as heavy as possible that their profits might be large, and the growers wished to have the freest possible market for their staple. Furthermore, the company tried to monopolize the whole import trade of the colony. The result of the system was that the profits from the production of

[1] In 1621 Sandys was committed to the custody of the Sheriff of London by order of the king for something which he had done or said outside of the House of Commons. What that was is not known; but it may have been in connection with Sandys's opposition to the wishes of James as to the management of the Virginia Company. See *Journals of the Commons*, i, 513, 654; *Debates of 1620–21*, ii, 179, 181, 182, 198, 259, 276, and Appendix. Peckard, in his *Life of Ferrar* (p. 110), states that Sandys's imprisonment was on account of the Virginia business. Southampton was also taken into custody. Among the subjects upon which he was questioned were his intimacy with the "Brownists," and his discontent with the existing order of things (*Calendars of State Papers, Domestic, 1619–1623*, p. 269). The questions asked Sandys, but not his answers, are printed in *Debates of 1620–21*, ii, Appendix (sig. Bbb 2). See Note IV.

For the debate on the want of money and the exclusion of Spanish tobacco, see *Journals of the Commons*, i, 527, 579, 581, and *Debates of 1620–21*, i, 95, 97, 104, 151, 237, 249, 250, 252.

tobacco were not great to the planter, nor to the company, nor to the king, nor to the collector of customs, — the planters and merchants engaged in the Virginia trade complained of the company, the company complained of the collectors, while the king and the collectors felt aggrieved at the action of the company. The whole matter has so many branches and twistings[1] that it cannot be unraveled briefly. At one time the king forbade the importation of Virginia tobacco,[2] and the company sent all their tobacco to the Netherlands, an act which seemed high presumption, to say the least, to the Privy Council.

One way out of the tangle seemed to be for the government and the company jointly to monopolize the handling of the Virginia crop, in which case, of course, the importation of Spanish tobacco would be stopped and the growing of tobacco in England prohibited. A scheme for the carrying out of this plan was drawn up and almost adopted. It failed, however, both with the government and with the company. At the last moment the government demanded things which could not be acceded to, and the announcement of the contract[3] which provided a considerable salary for Sir Edwin Sandys, as director, brought forth open opposition in the company. The leader of the Smythe-

[1] See, for example, Captain Bargrave's charges in *Virginia Magazine of History*, vi, 225.

[2] This was not due to the king's dislike of tobacco-taking; his *Counterblast*, if he wrote it, was printed in 1604, before Virginia tobacco was known in England, except as a curiosity. Probably James looked upon the cultivation of tobacco as likely to increase the revenue of the crown, and therefore to be cherished. The action of the government at this time was in the nature of retaliation.

[3] Rymer's *Fœdera*, xviii, 190, 233; Chalmers's *Annals*, i, 41, 70, contain the royal proclamation and commission for the regulation of tobacco. It is to be noticed that Sir Thomas Roe, one of the members of the company, obtained a patent for garbling or inspecting tobacco. The *Journals of the House of Commons* for 1620–21 contains numerous entries relating to the attempted legislation to give the Virginia Company a monopoly of the English tobacco trade. These are largely reprinted in Brown's *First Republic*. He does not seem to know the much fuller notes contained in a volume entitled *Debates in the House of Commons in 1620–21* (see, for instance, Brown, 400, and *Debates*, i, 238).

Warwick forces was Sir Thomas Wroth, whose most famous act was moving in Parliament, years later, that Charles I should be impeached and the kingdom settled without him. He now objected to the contract, on account of the salaries proposed for the director and the other officials and because Southampton and Sandys and their friends had secured the passage of these measures by underhand means and by browbeating. These accusations were met with denial by the Sandys party and the necessity of proper salaries was vigorously defended. Whichever faction was in the right, the controversy within the company gave the government its opportunity.

It would seem that with the disasters in Virginia, the discontent of the planters there, the ill-humor of Gondomar, and the dissensions within the corporation, the Sandys faction had its hands full. Either Sandys was "riding for a fall," or he had not the statesmanlike qualities which have generally been attributed to him, for at this time the company was actively involved in the dispute with Captain John Martin, and Sandys almost at once became the manager on the part of the Commons of the impeachment of Lord Treasurer Middlesex, who was the negotiator of the tobacco contract on the part of the government. The controversy with Captain Martin had come down from the Smythe period; but there seems to have been complicated with it a good deal of personal resentment on the part of Sir George Yeardley and others. A perusal of the published documents gives one a feeling of respect for Martin and of distrust for Yeardley. Whether this feeling is justified in either case may be a matter for argument; but it must be conceded that the controversy was extremely unfortunate for the Virginia Company. Among the members of the Privy Council who assiduously attended the meetings at which the Virginia business was discussed was Sir Julius Cæsar, the Master of the Rolls, who also had the ear of the king. As the only way to secure justice to Martin, he pushed on the destruction of the Virginia Company.

When it became clear that the king was determined on the downfall of the corporation, an attempt was made to secure protection from the House of Commons by the presentation of a petition to that body. In this paper it was stated that the evil practices on the parts of some members of the company were due to the corrupt influence of Lord Treasurer Middlesex. Three days later the Speaker read a letter from the king concerning the Virginia petition. The contents of this royal epistle are unknown; but it exercised an important influence, as the petition was thereupon "by general resolution withdrawn."[1] So perished the last hope of the Virginia Company, for, in those days, the judges held their office during the pleasure of the king, as James had been careful to make clear to them.[2] When, therefore, the attorney-general moved for judgment against the charter, it was at once given.[3] At the time, it was probably expected that the company would keep up its organization as a trading corporation. It may be that James even intended to confer upon its members a new charter without administrative rights; but the company

[1] On the question of the appeal of the Virginia Company to the House of Commons by petition, see *Journals of the House of Commons*, i, 691, 694; Royal Historical Manuscripts Commission's *Fourth Report*, 122; *Calendars of State Papers, America and the West Indies, 1574–1660*, 220; *Virginia Magazine*, vi, 383. The petition itself is in *Virginia Company Records*, ii, 263. See also Brown's *First Republic*, 595–600.

[2] Technically, the judges held office during good behavior, but since the accession of Elizabeth not a single judge had been dismissed for political reasons (Gardiner's *History*, ii, 8). It was reserved for James to set the pernicious example of removing judges for political reasons by dismissing Sir Edward Coke.

[3] See Massachusetts Historical Society's *Collections*, Fourth Series, ix, 68–72. Egerton (*British Colonial Policy*, 37) states that the charter was resumed by order of the Privy Council.

was bankrupt and moribund. It died an easy death, although the judgment against it was not entered until 1632 and then only at the instance of Lord Baltimore.[1]

As matters turned out, the destruction of the company was beneficial to all concerned; for that corporation was insolvent in 1624 and whatever further exertions it might have made would have been in the nature of recouping its members for past expenditures. James died in 1625, and his son, Charles I, immediately became involved in those financial and religious controversies which led to the Petition of Right, the martyrdom of Sir John Eliot, the meeting of the Long Parliament, the battle of Naseby, and the scaffold in front of Whitehall. Virginia and the other colonies were left to develop in their own way, with slight interference from the king and the royal officials.[2]

As Charles's finances became more and more involved, he and his advisers looked farther afield for possible profits and soon lighted upon the Virginia tobacco crop as a promising subject from which a few thousand pounds might be squeezed. The proposition now was that the government and the planters should go hand in hand to monopolize the industry; the government to make Virginia tobacco

[1] Papers printed in the *Virginia Magazine of History* (vol. viii) serve to show that in 1631–32 Charles had it in mind to restore the commercial rights to the Virginia Company but not the powers of jurisdiction; but as judgment had not been entered against the Virginia Company this would seem to have been unnecessary. It is also interesting to note that the Virginia planters for some years after 1624 "groaned under the oppression of unconscionable and cruel merchants" who monopolized their trade under "unjust contracts, made wholly without their consent." Petition of governor, council, and burgesses to the king in *Virginia Magazine of History*, vii, 260. It is not impossible that the company may have continued to exercise trading rights for some time.

[2] The royal commission of 1624 erecting a Commission to oversee Virginia affairs is in Rymer's *Fœdera;* Hazard's *Historical Collections*, i, 138; and in abstract in *Virginia Magazine*, vii, 40. Other constitutional documents relating to this period are printed in later numbers of the same magazine. Wyat's commission (Hazard's *Historical Collections*, i, 189) authorized him and his council, which was the existing council, to govern as they had been governing under the company's commission until they should receive further instructions from the king.

supreme in England and the planters in Virginia to produce only as much tobacco as the government could advantageously sell. This project necessarily required the assent of the planters, and to gain this an assembly was held at Jamestown in 1627, at which the Virginians refused to enter into partnership with the king except on their own terms, which would have resulted in little profit to the royal exchequer.[1] From this time on, at least until 1635, spasmodic attempts were made to bring about agreement, but the tobacco business always "stuck fast," to use Sir John Harvey's graphic phrase.

The revocation of the charter brought no change to the property owners in Virginia, for it is a principle of English law that where a person has once acquired a legal title to land or other possession he cannot be divested thereof without just cause. The rights of private property were respected by the king, and even the company continued to hold title to bits of land which had been cultivated for it. The undivided land became the property of the crown, and as to that, the royal policy was based directly on that of the company, which had been liberal.

In the ten years following the downfall of the company, the population of Virginia increased fivefold, from about one thousand to about five thousand. In 1635 no less than twenty-one vessels visited the colony, bringing sixteen hundred immigrants, of whom probably twelve hundred were servants. The demand for labor was so great that "no doubt the persons in England who supplied this demand were not at all particular as to the character"[2] of those whom they sent over. One evidence of this fact is found in a letter from the "Customer of

[1] *Virginia Magazine of History*, vii, 258-268.

[2] This phrase is that of the editor of the *Virginia Magazine of History*, ix, 271. For other references to this subject, see Note II.

London," or collector of customs at that port. He declared that he could not enforce, as to Virginia emigrants, the Proclamation of 1637. That proclamation[1] provided that no one could go to the colonies who did not have a certificate from the minister of his parish that he was conformable to the discipline of the Established Church; but the "customer" writes that this is impossible as to Virginia "because most of those that go thither ordinarily have no habitation [*i.e.* are vagabonds] and can bring neither certificate of their conformity nor ability and are better out than within the kingdom."[2] As in the earlier time, these immigrants were so crowded together while on shipboard that they often bred a pestilence in the places where they landed. This statement is based upon contemporary evidence, but it may mean only that great numbers of these newcomers died in the "seasoning" which all the early Virginia immigrants had to undergo. The survivors and their descendants, like their brethren of New England, were a picked stock, for only those of steadfast mind and sound body could sustain the shock of contact with the American wilderness.

The story of Virginia in the fifteen years following the dissolution of the company is one of slowly growing contentment and prosperity. In the course of that time there is but one incident which requires detailed treatment. Among the royal commissioners who had come to Virginia to spy out the misdeeds of the company was Captain John Harvey. He did his work well and was rewarded for his faithfulness by the honors of knighthood and the office of governor of the colony. It was almost uniformly the case that prosperity, instead of making a colonial governor more gentle, worked in pre-

[1] See Note III. [2] *Virginia Magazine of History*, ix, 271, 272.

cisely the opposite direction and contributed greatly to his irascibility, — certainly it was so with Governor Harvey, whose hot temper on one occasion led him to strike out Captain Stevens's teeth with a cudgel.[1] The colonists had two other causes of grievance against him; one was that he tried to induce them to agree with the royal government as to the tobacco contract, which it was his duty to do as representative of the crown; the other was that he smoothed the way for Baltimore's colonists, as the Privy Council directed him to do, instead of quenching the Maryland enterprise by his opposition. The burgesses protested against the tobacco contract and desired to send their remonstrance to England by the hands of agents of their own. To this Harvey objected, and instead, sent the document in an official letter to the Secretary of State. Sir John also seems to have been rather harsh in enforcing the rights of the crown to forfeited and escheated estates and in the collection of the quit-rents; all of which things served to make him unpopular. The occasion which brought on the crisis was an assemblage of Harvey's opponents, that was held to formulate some kind of protest against his actions.[2] Soon afterward, at a session of the council, the governor demanded a

[1] He also caused his immediate predecessor, Dr. John Pott, to be tried on a charge of stealing cattle. Pott was convicted by a jury, which is said to have been the first jury trial in the Old Dominion. Harvey at once seized his goods. The king pardoned Pott on the ground of the superficiality of the trial and because he was the only physician in Virginia. See *Virginia Company Records*, i, 139 note. See also *Virginia Magazine of History*, vii, 368, 384; viii, 33.

[2] "Account of the Mutiny of the Virginians" by Richard Kemp — a most prejudiced narrative — is in *Virginia Magazine of History*, viii, 301–306, and see *ibid.*, viii, 151, 398–407; ix, 34–43. Sir John Zouch was in Virginia in 1634; Harvey calls him a "Puritan" and says that he stirred up strife. Zouch's account is in Neill's *Virginia Carolorum*, 118. There is an interesting letter from Mathews, dated May 25, 1634, in *Maryland Archives* (Council, 1636–67), 33. The best modern account of the "Mutiny" is by Latané in his *Early Relations between Maryland and Virginia*, p. 23. He notes that Burk in his *Virginia* has almost exactly reversed the facts.

statement of the people's grievances, to which Mr. Minifie, one of the council, replied that one of their objections to his rule was his not sending their answer about the tobacco contract to England by the agents whom they had chosen. Thereupon Harvey's temper overcame him; he burst forth with: "Do you say so? I arrest you upon suspicion of treason to his Majesty." In return, "Captain Uty and Captain Mathews, both of the council, laid hands on the governor, using these words: 'And we you upon suspicion of treason to his Majesty.'" After more words Captain Mathews again addressed Harvey, saying: "Sir, the people's fury is up against you and to appease it is beyond our power, unless you please to go for England there to answer their complaints." At the moment Harvey declared that he would rather be cut into a thousand pieces than yield, but softer councils prevailed and he departed for England.

At court Harvey speedily got the better of his enemies, some of whom had crossed the Atlantic with him. These were cast into prison and kept there for eighteen months, more or less, when they were released on giving bonds in the sum of one thousand pounds sterling apiece to come up for trial when summoned. Harvey thought that his return would be more triumphant if he were conveyed back to Virginia in a ship of the royal navy. This was impossible, but the king loaned him a prize ship, the *Black George*, which proved to be so leaky that, after she had sailed twenty leagues beyond the Scilly Isles, she was obliged to return to Portsmouth, and the triumphant governor sailed for Virginia on an ordinary trading ship. William Laud and two other members of the Privy Council signed an order permitting Harvey to repay himself out of the estates of those who had sent him to England, "when they should be convicted for that their insolent presumption."[1] They were never convicted; but Harvey hastily seized their goods, servants, and cattle, while they were still languishing in English prisons. They were powerful men, and in due time he was forced to disgorge a portion, if not all, of his booty. He continued as governor until 1639, when Sir Francis Wyat succeeded him, to give place in 1641 to Sir William Berkeley.

Of those who held office in colonial days, none enjoyed a longer period of rule than Sir William Berkeley, and few governed more absolutely than he — in his later years. He exercised the office of governor from 1641 until 1653, and again from 1658 to 1677, when he finally returned to England. His original appointment was made in August, 1641, when the Long Parliament had already been in being eight months. Soon after the Long Parliament began its fateful session the adventurers and planters of Virginia presented a petition to it, requesting the renewal of the charter. This petition, and one other for the formation of a company for America and Africa, were referred to a committee, at the head of which was Mr. John Pym. The committee never reported.[2] At the time Pym had other things to think about, for it was on May 12, 1641, that Strafford was executed. In November of the same year the Grand Remonstrance was voted and in January, 1642, Charles entered the House of Commons for the purpose of arresting Pym and four other members of that

[1] *Virginia Magazine of History*, ix, 42.

[2] Alexander Brown (*First Republic*, 603) states that "in the beginning of the parliament of 1640, the opponents to Baltimore's patent for Maryland took out the Virginia patent again under the Broad Seal of England"; but he gives no citation. For the petitions referred to above, see *Commons Journals*, ii, 54, 276, 818. The statement that the petitioners asked for a renewal of the charter is based on a letter of the king in *Calendars of State Papers, America and the West Indies, 1574–1660*, 324.

body. This preoccupation, doubtless, explains why Mr. Pym apparently failed to notice that Sir William Berkeley was a man entirely after the heart of King Charles and Archbishop Laud; or, it may be that he let him go because he felt that Virginia was as good a place for cavaliers as Charles is reported to have said that New England was for Nonconformists. Pym did not lack warning of the new governor's character, because the Rev. Anthony Panton or Penton[1] had sought to enlighten the members of both Houses of Parliament on this and other points. Mr. Panton had been minister in the parishes of York and Chiskayack, Virginia. He may have been religiously unsound, as his language implies; he certainly was violently opposed to the existing government in Virginia. Harvey and his council had sentenced Panton to banishment under pain of death in case of return. Mr. Richard Kemp, then secretary of Virginia, and afterwards reappointed as such with Berkeley, had gone beyond Sir John in giving full power to any one to execute Panton in case of his return.[2] In his trial, Harvey and Kemp, following English precedents before the legal reforms of the Puritan time, had denied Panton a copy of the charges against him or time to secure evidence in his behalf or even the right to summon witnesses. As soon as they had convicted him, they seized his goods. The Privy Council in England ordered Harvey's successor to examine the case anew, which proved difficult, because Kemp departed secretly for England with the depositions and other writings. The council in Virginia, neverthe-

[1] B. W. Green's *Word-Book of Virginia Folk-Speech*, Richmond, 1899. There is an able review of this work in the *Virginia Magazine of History*, vii, 218, and an article on the same subject in *William and Mary Quarterly*, iii, 271. See also Latané's *Early Relations between Virginia and Maryland*.

[2] *Virginia Magazine of History*, v, 123–128.

less, ordered that compensation for Panton's losses should be made out of the sale of Sir John Harvey's goods. Probably little in the way of restitution had been accomplished when Berkeley and Kemp were appointed governor and secretary. Panton at once presented a petition to the House of Commons, which delayed their departure for a time; and a subsequent petition to the Lords stopped their vessels in the Downs. Panton, in his petitions, prayed that Harvey, Kemp, and Captain Wormeley, a member of the council, who had acted with them, might be brought to justice for their "many arbitrary and illegal proceedings in judgment, tyranny, extortion, and most cruel oppressions, which have extended to unjust whippings, cutting of ears, fining, and confiscation of honest men's goods, degrading of honest commissioners, converting fines to their own private use, favoring and supporting popery and many other wrongs."[1] As to Berkeley's commission, Panton said that it had been obtained surreptitiously. Berkeley, Kemp, and Wormeley retorted that Panton was a turbulent person and were permitted to sail for Virginia.

The commission to the new governor and council was sealed on August 9, 1641.[2] This document and the accompanying instructions are the earliest detailed papers of their kind which are now accessible. It will be well, therefore, to examine them with some degree of care. In the first place, it should be said that a royal commission and a royal charter were both letters patent under the great

[1] These petitions, etc., are calendared in the Royal Historical Manuscripts Commission's *Reports*, iv, 104. The orders are in *Commons Journals*, ii, 283, *Lords Journals*, iv, 411, 421, 424.

[2] *Virginia Magazine of History*, ii, 281; *Harvard Historical Studies*, vi, 219. A note in Royal Historical Manuscripts Commission's *Reports* (iv, Appendix, 237) states that Wyat's instructions were word for word like those of Berkeley. Wyat's commission of 1638 is calendared in the same volume, p. 22.

seal, and had the same authority, the principal difference between them being that a charter was generally granted to a number of persons sharing equally in its benefits, and was usually unlimited in point of time. In the second place, it may be noticed that the commission contains a large grant of power which is limited by the much more lengthy and detailed instructions. In the third place, besides the grant of powers more or less closely specified, Sir William Berkeley and the council are directed to perform all other things concerning the plantation "as fully as any other governor and council resident there within three years, had" performed them. This clause is also contained in such of the earlier commissions as have come down to us, and probably was in those which are no longer known. Granting that this was so, it appears that Berkeley and his council, in interpreting their powers, went back to the precedents which had been established in the days of the last governors under the charter, for we find a similar clause in the commission to the first royal governor after the dissolution of the company. Presumably, therefore, it is correct to say that after 1624 the Virginians enjoyed the constitutional rights which had been given to them by Smythe, Sandys, and those who worked with them, although there is no record of the holding of an assembly in the earlier years of the royal rule.[1]

To take up Berkeley's commission in detail, he and his council, which included such ill-assorted persons as John West, Richard Kemp, and Samuel Mathews, were given full power to direct and govern, correct and punish, the colonists, and order all affairs of peace and war within the colony. In performing these functions, they were to obey

[1] Unless we may follow Alexander Brown (*First Republic*, 647) in regarding the phrase, "The Governor, Council, and colony of Virginia assembled together," as forming such a record.

such orders as the Lord Commissioners and Committees for the Plantations from time to time should give them. In case of the death or enforced absence of the governor, the council should choose one of their number to perform the governor's functions, and new councilors should be appointed by the king upon the joint nomination of the governor and council. The instructions contain thirty-one articles. They require that Almighty God be daily and duly served according to the form of religion established in the Church of England, and that no innovation in matters of religion be suffered. The Oaths of Allegiance and Supremacy were to be taken by all the planters and by such mariners and merchants as the governor and council thought necessary; all who refused should be shipped to England. Yearly, or oftener, a general assembly should be held to make laws which were to be "as near as may be to the laws of England." The governor possessed a negative voice, but the laws were not required to be sent to England for confirmation. The governor and council exercised the appointing power. They also were expected to act as a higher judicial court, but the assembly, including the burgesses, speedily assumed the rôle of a court of appeals. The commission and instructions, in short, contemplated that the governor should be merely the first among equals and that the council, which included the secretary, should exercise very considerable power. Sir William Berkeley was a masterful man. As time went on he became more and more absolute, especially after 1662, when he was authorized to suspend councilors, to appoint members of the council temporarily, and to perform many functions without consulting the council at all. In this way that body became largely ornamental.

Besides these constitutional provisions, the instructions

provided that all tobacco must be shipped to England, and that no vessels other than those of English subjects should be permitted to trade in the colony, save "upon some unexpected occasions," and then only after bond had been given to land all goods laden in the colony in the port of London. The instructions also contain the usual Utopian provisions, with which the student of Virginia history becomes very familiar. Every owner of five hundred acres of land, for example, is required to build a house of brick with a cellar, the house to be at least twenty-four feet by sixteen. Moreover, the planters were to limit the production of tobacco, not build slight cottages, nor move from plantation to plantation as the need of new fields for tobacco demanded.

Sir William Berkeley in religion was a follower of William Laud; in Virginia he found a congenial atmosphere. From the beginning the colony on the James River had been religiously regular, but the first Church Act of importance was passed in 1623.[1] This enacted that places of worship and suitable burying grounds should be provided on every plantation and that the service should be according to the canons, both in substance and in circumstance. Each absence from service entailed a fine of one pound of tobacco, and continuous absence could be satisfied only by the payment of fifty pounds of tobacco, while he who disparaged a minister and could not prove his assertion, paid five hundred pounds of tobacco. Apparently there was sometimes justification for disparaging remarks, as an act made in 1631[2] declared that ministers must not give themselves to excessive drinking or riot, spending their time idly day or night, playing at dice or cards. In January, 1641–42, while

[1] Hening's *Statutes*, i, 122. [2] *Ibid.*, i, 158.

Sir William Berkeley was on his way[1] to Virginia, the assembly passed an act for the organization of the Church with vestries, as in England; and in 1642, soon after his arrival, it passed another act perfecting this organization, especially by making better provisions for the collection of tithes. Under these laws the parsons were nominated by the vestries and approved by the governor.[2]

Nonconformity of the New England type never flourished in Virginia, partly, no doubt, because the social organization which there obtained was unfavorable to its growth. A few Nonconformists, from time to time, appeared within the Old Dominion, and missionaries went from Boston to convert the Virginians to the New England way of religion; but they had little success, as Daniel Gookin, who removed to Massachusetts, seems to have been their only important convert. In 1645 there were not two hundred Nonconformists in the Old Dominion. Governor Berkeley seems to have used with moderation the power to expel from the colony those outside of the regular Church organization; but the administration of all penal laws in early Virginia is wrapped in obscurity, owing to the destruction of records[3] in the fire which the Union soldiers found burning in Richmond after its evacuation by the Confederates.

[1] *Virginia Magazine of History*, ix, 52.

[2] Hening's *Statutes*, i, 240, 277. On this general subject, see Latané's "Early Relations between Maryland and Virginia" (*Johns Hopkins Studies*, xiii, Nos. iii, iv) and a long and somewhat discursive review by R. S. Thomas in *Virginia Magazine of History*, iv, 348, 469; v, 106, 228.

[3] See note as to these records in the *Virginia Magazine of History*, viii, 64. The only remaining knowledge of the early court proceedings is derived from a series of notes which were prepared by Conway Robinson. These are incomplete and are useful only for purposes of illustration. Some of the entries have been printed in the *Virginia Magazine of History*, iii, v, etc. See also *Lower Norfolk Antiquarian*, No. 2, pt. 3.

NOTES

I. General Bibliography. — Winsor, in his *America,* iii, 152–166, enumerates the sources of information and the secondary works relating to the period covered in this chapter so far as they were printed prior to 1884, when that volume was published. Since that time Alexander Brown has published his *First Republic in America,* Boston, 1898, and his *English Politics in Early Virginia History,* Boston, 1901. The former of these works consists of a narrative formed of extracts and abstracts from documents, some of which have not yet seen the printed page, cemented together with expositions and comments by the author. The latter work is an amplification of the general thesis which pervades the former. This, in brief, is that hitherto the history of the Old Dominion in the time of the "Sandys Supremacy" has been written from the works of Captain John Smith and other documents which the "Court Party" allowed to see the light. Mr. Brown's mission, as he conceives it, is to rescue the history of that time from the wrong accounts which have thus influenced our conception of those eventful years. In all this he sees a sort of conspiracy on the part of the king and the enemies of the Sandys faction to stifle the truth, and looks upon Captain John Smith as the tool of these conspirators. That James, Sir Thomas Smythe, Warwick, Sir Nathaniel Rich, and their friends, were hostile to Sandys and Southampton cannot be denied, but the origin of this hostility had little to do with what is sought to be conveyed in the use of the words "court" and "patriot." Captain John Smith doubtless disliked the Sandys faction, who had dismissed his claim for compensation somewhat cavalierly; but his account of these years seems to be very near the truth. Mr. Brown, by his intemperate and ruthless onslaught on Captain John Smith, has done much to arouse a sentiment in favor of that inimitable writer; it has also led to a perhaps unjust questioning of Mr. Brown's own statements. A savage review of Brown's *Republic* by the late W. W. Henry, with a reply by Brown and a rejoinder by Henry, will be found in the *Virginia Magazine of History* (vi). Professor Turner, in a more friendly notice of the "English Politics" in the *American Historical Review* (vii, 162), says that it is to be hoped Mr. Brown "will soon supplement *The Genesis of the United States* with volumes containing material for the later history of the company. This, rather than controversial writing, is what is now needed to make clear the early history of Virginia" — a statement in which all who have studied the complicated history of these years will most heartily join.

The *Virginia Magazine of History and Biography* and the *William and Mary Quarterly* are doing excellent work in bringing to light material on the local history of Virginia, while on the general history of the colony and its relations to England the Royal Historical Manuscripts Commission has done great service in revealing to investigators the scattered storehouses of manuscripts in England. The only student who, up to the present time, has made effective use of these new materials in any extended way, is Philip Bruce, in his *Economic History of Virginia in the Seventeenth Century.* Much of his work has a purely local interest, but the chapters on agricultural development and on systems of labor are of value to the general reader. Mr. Bruce is the safest guide on the last few years under the company.

II. Population. — In 1634, the census (Wynne and Gilman, *Colonial Records,* 91) gives the total number of people in Virginia as 4914, not including two hundred and five who arrived in that year. A few of these were negro slaves, but by far the greater part were servants. Of these, some were educated men, but the greater number were those who "guided the plow or wielded the spade, the hoe or the ax." Bruce, in the last chapter of his first volume, and in the second chapter of his second volume, gives a mass of information as to the condition and numbers of the servants. One thing that impresses the reader of his figures is the average youth of the serving class.[1] This is accounted for by the practice of sending large numbers of children to the colony. Bruce says that fourteen hundred or fifteen hundred children were sent to Virginia in 1627. Slavery was not recognized by law until 1661, when the general assembly provided that an English servant running away with a negro slave should serve for the time of the slave's absence as well as for his own. In general it may be said that the punishment meted out to servants was an additional term of service; but an incorrigible runaway was branded on the cheek and had his hair cropped.

There are numerous entries relating to convicts deported to Vir-

[1] See an interesting review of Eggleston's *Transit of Civilization,* in the *Virginia Magazine of History* (viii, 437), as to the relative proportions of free and servile immigrants.

ginia. The peculiarity of these records has attracted an undue amount of attention to them. Contemporary opinion also was unfavorable to the character of the early emigrants to Virginia, who are sometimes described as the scum of the land, jail birds, and Christian savages; see, for instance, Fuller's *Holy State*, bk. iii, ch. 16, and Aubry's *Brief Lives*, ii, 158. The recorded cases may be found in *Middlesex Records*, ii, *William and Mary Quarterly*, ii, 61, and elsewhere, Neill's *Virginia Carolorum*, and Brown's *First Republic*. An English student, Hugh E. Egerton, in his *British Colonial Policy* (39), takes a gloomy view of the character of the bulk of the early Virginia settlers; his opinion is based mainly on the entries in Sainsbury's *Calendars*. The Virginia law of 1661–62 (Hening's *Statutes*, ii, 53), which prohibited the private burial of servants, and required that three or four of the neighbors should view the corpse before the interment, has been viewed as casting an unfavorable light on the treatment of servants by the masters, and incidentally reflecting on the characters of the servants. It may have been passed, however, to protect the masters from unjust imputations.

Punishments in early Virginia were like those in contemporary England. For example, in 1624 Edward Sharples was sentenced in Virginia to the pillory, and to have his ears cut off (*Virginia Magazine of History*, vii, 135). Six years later, William Matthew, servant, was convicted of petit treason by a jury of fourteen persons, and was sentenced to be drawn and hanged (*Virginia Records*, Ms., Richmond, i, 215). Runaway servants were whipped (both men and women) and branded, and sometimes condemned to work with a shackle on the leg (see *Virginia Magazine of History*, v, 236, 237; viii, 64–73, 165). Bruce found only one record of a slave dying under the lash in all the seventeenth century — although there were probably two thousand slaves in the colony in 1670; but the records are very imperfect, and some cases may have escaped Bruce's eye.

III. The Proclamation of 1637. — "A Proclamation against the disorderly transporting His Majesties' Subjects to the Plantations within the parts of America. 30 April, 13 Charles I." In this it is stated that the king is informed "that great noumbers of his subjects have beene and are every yeare transported into those parts of America" which have been granted by patent and there settle with their families. Many of them are of "idle and refractory humours whose only or principall end is to live as much as they can without the reach of authority." It is, therefore, ordered that officers of ports are to suffer no subsidy men, or men of the value of subsidy men, to embark for the plantations without license from the commissioners of plantations, and none under the value of subsidy men without the certificate from two justices of the peace where the emigrant last dwelt, that he has taken the Oaths of Supremacy and Allegiance, together with certificate from the minister of his parish that he has conformed to the discipline of the Church of England. Said port officers to return a list every half year to the commissioners of plantations of those embarking for the plantations. This proclamation is reproduced in facsimile in the *Bulletin* of the Boston Public Library for October, 1894.

IV. Political Views of Sandys. — Two letters in the "Manchester Papers" (Royal Historical Manuscripts Commission's *Reports*, viii, pt. ii, 34, 45) have been held to reflect Sandys's later political ideas. The first of these is dated February 12, 1619–20; the writer complains that the "Governor" had introduced a translation of the Genevan form of ministering the sacraments. Probably the reference was to the governor of the Summer's Isles, and not to Sandys, as has been advanced. The second letter is dated May 16, 1623, and is to the effect that Sandys is opposed to monarchical institutions in general, had moved the Archbishop of Canterbury to give leave to Brownists and Separatists to go to Virginia, and designed to make a free popular state there with himself and his assured friends as leaders. This letter seems to be the same that Brown prints in his *First Republic* (529) and incorrectly quotes on a succeeding page (251). It purports to recite a conversation which Sir Nathaniel Rich had with Captain Bargrave. The latter is reported as saying that Sandys "carried a more malitious heart to the government of a monarchy than any man in the world." For Bargrave had heard him say that "if our God from Heaven did constitute and direct a form of government, it was that of Geneva" and that it was his intent "to erect a free state in Virginia." It is well known that Sandys befriended the Pilgrims and that he held radical views on government in Church and State; but besides this gossip of Captain John Bargrave, there is no evidence that he intended to make a free popular state in Virginia with himself as leader.

CHAPTER IX

THE FOUNDING OF MARYLAND

THE Old Dominion had its rise in the action of English merchants and other public-spirited men; Maryland owes its beginning to the desire of Sir George Calvert to found a great family estate in America. He was, perhaps, the most respectable and honest of the mediocre statesmen whom James, Charles, and Buckingham gathered about them. He was an ardent advocate of the Spanish Marriage. As Secretary of State he was cognizant of the agreement of 1623[1] that obliged the English king to give privileges to members of the proscribed faith which were in violation of his coronation oath. In the end Calvert's Spanish policy utterly failed and he was obliged to resign,[2] but, by humbling himself before Buckingham, he was allowed to sell his interest in his office to his successor. Large estates, wrung from the dispossessed Irish had already been given him, and it was natural, therefore, that his faithfulness to his royal master should be rewarded with the title of Baron Baltimore of Baltimore in the peerage of Ireland.[3] A few weeks later, on the acces-

[1] See Gardiner's *History of England*, v, 68.

[2] *Ibid.*, v, 309; Eggleston (*Beginners of a Nation*, 260) prints in full Salviati's account of Calvert's fall from power; Gardiner gives the gist of it.

[3] The Baltimore peerage has troubled many writers. E. L. Taunton, for example, speaks of the second holder of the title as "Lord Cecil Baltimore," while Mereness says that in 1634 Baltimore became a member of Parliament, although no Parliament was held between 1629 and 1640. If one had been held, however, Baltimore could not have been a member because his religion would have excluded him from the Commons, while his Irish peerage would not have admitted him to the Lords.

sion of Charles, he refused to take the oaths and retired from the Privy Council. Precisely when he became a Roman Catholic is not known; nor can it be stated whether his interest in the Spanish Marriage was due to his conversion or his conversion was the result of prolonged intimacy with the Spaniards.

Sir George Calvert had long been interested in the English colonization of America.[1] He had subscribed to two shares of Virginia stock (twenty-five pounds); he was a member of the Council for New England and attended at least one of its meetings. As Secretary of State it fell to his lot to excuse the persecution of Sir Edwin Sandys, and on the dissolution of the Virginia Company he became one of the council to administer the affairs of that plantation. His first active interest in colonization, however, was in connection with Newfoundland. There, on the peninsula of Avalon, he sought to establish a colony which was at first Protestant, and after his conversion, Roman Catholic. The attempt ended in failure, after teaching him valuable lessons and seriously diminishing his resources. After a winter's residence in Newfoundland, Sir George Calvert, now Lord Baltimore, sought a warmer clime and landed at Jamestown with his family and followers in October, 1629. But the Virginians disliked him as a Roman Catholic, and possibly suspected him of designs upon their territory. At all events, they offered him the Oaths of Allegiance and Supremacy, which he refused to take, although he expressed his willingness to take an oath of his own concocting.[2] He was, therefore, ordered out of the colony.

[1] Brown's *Genesis*, ii, 8, 41.

[2] *Maryland Archives* (Council, 1636–67), iii, 16, 17; see also letter of Mathews, Pott, Smythe, and Claiborne (Council of Virginia) to the Privy Council, Nov. 30, 1629, in *Virginia Magazine of History*, vii, 374.

Returning to England, Lord Baltimore justified the Virginians' dislike by asking the king for a piece of that colony for his own use. Upon the dissolution of the company, all ungranted lands in Virginia had come into the possession of the crown, and the king could grant them, or portions of them, to any person or persons who happened to please him. Sir Robert Heath, the Attorney-general, who had managed the legal side of the destruction of the company, also asked for a bit of the Old Dominion and, in 1629, received a grant of the southernmost part of Virginia and adjoining lands farther to the south. Lord Baltimore asked for the land between the James River and the thirty-sixth parallel, which was the northern limit of Heath's grant, but the Virginians objected so stoutly that he was obliged to content himself with the tract between the Potomac River and the fortieth parallel, which was the southern boundary of New England by the charter of 1620. The tract given to Heath the king named Carolana, for himself; that given to Baltimore he called Maryland, in honor of his wife, Henrietta Maria, — in its Latin form of *Terra Mariæ* the suggestion in the latter name fitted in happily with the desires of the Catholic founders of the colony.

The province of Maryland extended from New England, on the north, to the southern bank of the Potomac River from its source to its mouth at a place called Cinquack, and thence in an ill-defined manner to the Atlantic Ocean; the western boundary was the meridian of the source of the Potomac. Almost every mile of this indefinite frontier, at one time or another, has been a subject of dispute. The source and mouth of a river, for example, are points easily alluded to on paper, but they are very difficult to determine on the spot. In the case of Maryland the wrong branch of the Potomac was chosen, with the result that the whole western limit is erroneous. The Indian word "Cinquack" doubtless meant a precise locality to the person who advised George Calvert, but what that meaning was has never been ascertained. Moreover, the bank of a river is an unusual way of stating a boundary. Calvert probably wished to monopolize the commerce of the Potomac by naming the southern bank as a boundary; but that, in course of time, turned out to be mainly Virginian. As the authority of Virginia extended only to high-water mark, it was difficult to enforce the duties which were laid on tobacco exported and, so long as Maryland strove to regulate the commerce of the river, friction with Virginia was certain to arise. A century and a half later this dispute was turned to happy account to bring about the formation of the Federal Union. Even the fortieth parallel proved to be difficult of ascertainment and had to give place to Mason and Dixon's Line. Whatever its exact limits may have been, Maryland was a splendid estate. Its soil was fitted by nature for the easy production of tobacco and breadstuffs, and it was blessed with a more salubrious climate than that of the James River. Before the charter passed the seals, Sir George Calvert died and the patent was issued (1632) to his son, Cecil or Cecilius Calvert, second Baron Baltimore, also a Roman Catholic.

The best way to understand the provisions of the Maryland charter as to government is to compare them with the corresponding sections in the charters of Avalon (1623), Carolana (1629), and New Albion (1634). It is evident from even a cursory examination that the Carolana, Maryland, and New Albion grants are practically identical as to jurisdiction and religion. With an important modification as to the tenure of the soil, they are evidently modeled on the Avalon patent, which in its turn was based on still earlier grants. In fact the three later charters have a strong family likeness, which was quite natural because Sir Robert Heath probably drew all of them, and was himself the grantee named in the first. There is little that is novel[1] or peculiar in the Maryland patent except that it happened to be the charter of the first successful proprietary province.

The statement of powers conferred upon Baltimore in the Maryland charter is so ambiguous and contradictory that the intentions of Charles or the expectations of Calvert are not easy to discern. In one clause the king delegates to Baltimore whatever power the Bishop of Durham possesses or had ever possessed. As this warlike churchman in his diocese had been practically absolute, this clause by itself would have conferred almost absolute power.[2] But the further requirements that the laws and ordinances of Maryland should not be repugnant to the laws of England and that no interpretation of the charter should be permitted by which the allegiance due to the king should suffer any diminution destroyed about nine tenths of the force of the Bishop of Durham clause. Moreover, in Maryland the laws must receive the consent of the freemen of the province assembled either in person or by deputies. It turned out, therefore, that the proprietary's power was so circumscribed that the institutions of Maryland ultimately became the most liberal of any outside of Connecticut and Rhode Island.

[1] For example, the clause prohibiting any interpretation of the charter by which the allegiance due to the king should be diminished was in the Avalon and Carolana charters as well as in that of Maryland.

[2] See Lapsley's admirable essay on the "Palatinate of Durham" in *Harvard Historical Studies*, No. viii.

The religious aspect of the Maryland charter has aroused the most interesting speculations. Lord Baltimore was given the patronage of all churches and chapels which might be established in the province; but these were to be consecrated according to the ecclesiastical laws of England. Moreover, no interpretation of the charter should be permitted by which the "sacred things of God" (*sacro sanctæ*), or the allegiance due to the king, may suffer any diminution. Substantially the same words are used in the Avalon, the Carolana, and the New Albion patents, except that in the Avalon grant there is no clause requiring the churches to be consecrated according to the ecclesiastical laws of England, and in the other grants the phrase "true Christian religion" replaces "*sacro sanctæ*." In all of these patents the Church mentioned is clearly the Established Church of England. It will be well to examine the laws of England so far as they governed the relations of the Roman Catholics to the crown.

The Acts of Supremacy and Uniformity (1559)[1] separated the Church in England from the Roman Catholic Church, prescribed uniformity in religion for all subjects of the English crown, and directed that clergymen should acknowledge the religious headship of the monarch by taking the Oath of Supremacy. Those who remained faithful to the old religion could scarcely fail to deny the right of Elizabeth to the throne. Parliament faced this contingency by making the second denial of the queen's title treason. In 1563 Roman Catholics were excluded from the legal profession, from teaching, and from the universities, and in 1571 the penalties of treason were denounced

[1] 1 Elizabeth, c. 1 and 2. The religious laws may be found in the *Statutes of the Realm*, or in other collections of English statutes. Portions of them are given in the smaller compilations, as Gee and Hardy's *Documents relating to Church History*, or Prothero's *Select Statutes*.

against those who spoke of the queen as "a heretic, scismatic, tyrant, infidel, or usurper of the crown," or absolved English subjects from their allegiance or received such absolution. As the conflict with Spain drew nigh, it was provided that Roman Catholic priests should leave the realm under the penalty of death in case of return, and in 1593 this penalty was extended to all Roman Catholics who were not possessed of goods to a considerable amount. It was difficult to evade the former of these requirements, for any person who was suspected of being "a Jesuit, seminary, or massing priest," and refused to answer, should go to prison until he became compliant. As for well-to-do Roman Catholics, they should retire to their estates, and not go above five miles from them without license, and should pay twenty pounds each month for not attending the services of the Established Church.

Such was the law at the accession of James. He was welcomed by the Roman Catholics, but he was powerless to stem the tide of English public opinion. In 1606 and 1610 three laws dealing with the Roman Catholics were placed on the statute book. These provided, in brief, that every "Popish recusant convicted" must receive the sacrament according to the English form or pay twenty pounds the first year, forty pounds the second year, sixty pounds the third and succeeding years, in addition to the monthly assessment of twenty pounds for not attending the regular religious services; and the king might seize two thirds of the recusant's lands and hold them until he or she should conform, in place of exacting the fine. Moreover, all recusants were required to take the Oath of Allegiance, which was formulated anew in the law of 1606. If printed in full, this oath would occupy a whole page of the present volume. The person taking it acknowledged that James was the lawful king of England, that the Pope had no power to depose the king or to discharge an English subject from his allegiance, that, notwithstanding any excommunication, he would bear faith and true allegiance to the king, and defend him against any conspiracy which might arise by reason of such excommunication, that he abhorred the damnable doctrine that excommunicated princes might be murdered or deposed by their subjects; and that the Pope had no power to absolve him from this oath, which is taken without any equivocation on the faith of a Christian. After 1610 three members of the Privy Council, provided one of them was one of the four great officials, might require this oath of any noble, man or woman. Moreover, no recusant could bear office in the army, or navy, or the judicial system, act as a physician, or hold any public office. The act of 1610 was especially directed to "the reformation of married women recusants," which the lawmakers hoped to accomplish by committing all such to prison, except where a husband could and would purchase his wife's freedom by the payment of ten pounds per month. This extended to all women, those above the grade of baroness as well as those below.

If these laws had been rigorously enforced, there would have been an end of Roman Catholicism in England; but they were not rigorously enforced, partly because James had a lingering fondness for those who believed religiously as his mother had believed, and partly, perhaps, because he felt a certain catlike enjoyment in the hold which the law gave him on the property of many of his subjects, and kept the penalties, fines, and assessments suspended, Damocles-like, over their heads. The government of England, however, was so decentralized in those days and for a century thereafter, that even the good will of the monarch could not avail to protect his people, because the local magistrates sometimes, in defiance of the known wishes of the king, enforced the laws. According to the Middlesex records, it appears that in the ten years preceding 1619 eleven hundred indictments were returned for not attending the services of the Established Church. Some of those indicted were Separatists, but most of them were, probably, Roman Catholics. The Middlesex magistrates also succeeded in ferreting out a priest, John Lockwood, who was indicted for having been ordained by pretended authority derived from the see of Rome, and had remained feloniously and traitorously within the kingdom as a false traitor to the lord, the king. Lockwood was convicted and sentenced to be drawn from Newgate to Tyburn, and there be hanged, and while living be cut down and disemboweled, and then be beheaded and quartered and his head and quarters be placed where the king has been pleased to appoint. Whether Lockwood was executed is not stated.[1] Let us hope that James interfered in time to save him; but such was the fate which the laws of England in the year 1632 provided for a Roman Catholic priest, and the charter of Maryland expressly provided that the laws of that province must not be repugnant to the laws of England. Had the charter of Maryland given to the grantee any power to override the laws of England or to dispense with the taking of the oaths which the statutes provided that English subjects must take, the charter would have been null and void; and had there been no such provision in the charter as that just recited, laws of Maryland repugnant to English laws would themselves have been null and void, and would have been good ground for the overthrow of the charter. It is well for the

[1] *Middlesex County Records*, ii, 63, 80, 188–209.

student once in a while to look the facts squarely in the face and to remember that while to-day religious freedom is a corner stone of American polity, in 1632 uniformity in religion was the keynote of the policy of England.

Although he was unversed in the conduct of affairs, Cecil or Cecilius Calvert, the second Baron Baltimore,[1] soon showed himself to be an astute, capable man, and the most successful absentee landlord of his day. In the management of men he was always tactful and courageously liberal. He never saw the shores of Maryland,[2] but on at least two occasions it seemed as if he might visit America. The first of these was soon after the founding of the colony, when he suggested his own appointment as governor of Virginia,[3] with a salary of two thousand pounds, as a way out of the difficulties which had arisen between that province and Maryland. The other occasion was in 1642, when William Arundel, his wife's cousin, petitioned that a writ of *ne exeat regno* might be granted against Baltimore, who was intending to depart for Maryland; the writ was granted, but two days later Baltimore made affidavit that he had no intention of suddenly leaving the kingdom, and the writ was probably not issued. In securing the Maryland charter and in colonizing that province, the son simply carried out the wishes of the father, in whose mind the desire to found a landed estate was the leading motive. In the case of Cecilius Calvert, however, the desire to provide an asylum for his persecuted fellow Roman Catholics,

[1] Hugh E. Egerton, a recent English writer on *British Colonial Policy*, thinks that if statesmanship can be likened to walking a tight rope "no more triumphant exhibition of such statesmanship was ever given than when the Popish son of the Stuart favorite was able to plead his fidelity to the [Puritan] Commonwealth as opposed to the stubborn Royalism of Virginia." This is a harsh judgment.

[2] *Johns Hopkins University Studies in History*, xxi, 368.

[3] *Virginia Magazine of History*, x, 267

at the moment, was his most prominent motive; but, later, when he became financially distressed, material considerations exercised a very strong influence upon him.

The early history of Maryland is hard to unravel, and probably it always will be, owing to the absence of the local records, which disappeared in the troubled times of the so-called rebellions in the province; but the rescue of many most important papers from the English descendants of the founder of Maryland has done something to reveal the motives of Calvert and of those who worked with him. Among these is a letter which Charles Calvert, the son and successor of Cecilius, wrote in 1678 in answer to questions which had been propounded by the Lords of Trade.[1] In considering the value of this letter, regard should be had for the fact that English Roman Catholics were then (in 1678) under the ban of suspicion of complicity in the Popish Plot, which is connected with the names of Titus Oates and Thomas Dangerfield. There was every reason, therefore, for Lord Baltimore to make out the most favorable case, and especially to guard against seeming to favor unduly English Roman Catholics. On this account his statements should be regarded with great caution. He says that, according to the charter of Maryland, the first lord proprietor had absolute liberty to carry any persons out of England who should be willing to go, but found great difficulty in securing recruits. This statement is undoubtedly correct, as the number of English Roman Catholics who could emigrate and wished to do so must have been very limited, and Baltimore's religion would have deterred English Protestants from seeking

[1] *Maryland Archives* (Council, 1667–87), 267; Fortescue's *Calendars of State Papers*, under date March 26, 1678. The latter is merely an abstract in modern phrase.

his province. Adherents of the Established Church, who wished to better their condition by going to the New World, would find a welcome in Virginia, and nearly all varieties of Puritans could be accommodated somewhere in New England. Under these circumstances Charles Calvert says that only persons would go to Maryland "as for some reason or other could not live with ease in other places. And of these a great part were such as could not conform in all particulars to the several laws of England relating to Religion." These were willing to emigrate only on condition that all Christians should enjoy a general toleration in the new colony, "and that reproachful nicknames and reflecting upon each other's opinions . . . might be made penal." "These," he continued, "were the conditions proposed by such as were willing to go and be the first planters of this province, and, without the complying with these conditions in all probability this province had never been planted." This statement seems to refer to the act of 1649, for putting an end to religious disputation. It is interesting, however, because of the categorical declaration that toleration was suggested to the proprietor by the colonists. There was no reason why the lord proprietor should have struggled against this proposition. Under the rule of general religious liberty, Roman Catholics might enjoy the services of their own religion, if they were celebrated quietly. Under this provision Protestants might also seek the soil of Maryland, and, in time, possibly might dispossess the Roman Catholics; but that was a contingency which must be faced. Religious toleration was the groundwork of success in Maryland.

In November, 1633, two vessels — the *Ark*, of three hundred tons, and the *Dove*, of fifty tons — sailed from the Thames with the first emigrants bound for Maryland; but they were speedily turned back by order of Sir John Coke, Secretary of State, on account of some informality in their clearance papers. They were then boarded by the "Searcher," and the Oath of Allegiance was administered to one hundred and twenty-eight passengers. This being done, the ships were allowed to sail; but before finally leaving England they put in at the Isle of Wight where three Jesuit priests came aboard, and probably other persons also. In a letter to Lord Strafford, written at the time, Lord Baltimore says that about twenty gentlemen and three hundred laboring men had embarked for Maryland.[1] The three hundred in this letter is usually regarded as a mistake for two hundred, which number is more in accord with other accounts, and also with the size of the vessels. The religious convictions of these colonists is uncertain — if oaths had any efficacy in those days, one hundred and twenty-eight of them were Protestants. Another indication of the religious proportions of this first band of emigrants to Maryland is contained in the *Relatio Itineris* of Father White. He tells us that of the dozen who died on the passage to the Chesapeake two only were Roman Catholics. It can by no means be argued from this statement that five sixths of the colonists were Protestants, because, undoubtedly, most of the leaders were Roman Catholics. The bulk of the passengers, among whom most of the Protestants would be found, were laboring men and women, who must have been fearfully crowded on the narrow decks of vessels no larger than the *Ark* and the *Dove*. Among these the mortality would have been the greatest. It is probable that in the first few decades three out of every four

[1] Strafford's *Letters and Dispatches* (ed. 1739), i, 178.

persons in Maryland were not of the faith of the lord proprietor.[1]

When the preparations for the first expedition were well begun, Baltimore drew up an elaborate set of instructions for the guidance of his brother, Leonard Calvert, who was to represent him in the colony. In these instructions he gave positive directions that the services of the Roman Catholic religion should be performed "as privately as may be," and that no scandal or offense should be given to any of the Protestants.[2] These directions were "to be observed on land as well as at sea"; but Leonard Calvert and the Jesuit fathers ignored them from the start. The Jesuits, indeed, may well have rejoiced at the successful accomplishment of the first stage toward the realization of their dream of founding a Roman Catholic colony within English dominions. In other words, they hoped to do for England what Le Jeune[3] and the French Jesuits had planned to do for France and to save the souls of the natives within the English sphere of influence as the

[1] Writing in 1642, Father More, S.J., stated that in "leading the colony to Maryland by far the greater were heretics" (Foley's *Records of the English Province of the Society of Jesus*, iii, section 7, 364). In 1641 Father White said that "three parts in four at least are heretics" (Foley's *Records* as above, 362). Possibly these statements did not refer to the first colonists, as Eggleston (*Beginners*, 263) points out. Bancroft, Johnson, and other Protestant writers have generally deemed them conclusive as to the religion of the first settlers.

[2] Maryland Historical Society's *Fund Publications*, No. 28 ("Calvert Papers"), 132. "Inpri: His Lopp requires his said Gouernor & Commissioners tht. in their voyage to Mary Land they be very carefull to preserue vnity & peace amongst all the passengers on Shipp-board, and that they suffer no scandall nor offence to be giuen to any of the Protestants, whereby any iust complaint may hereafter be made, by them, in Virginea or in England, and that for that end, they cause all Acts of Romane Catholique Religion to be done as priuately as may be, and that they instruct all the Romane Catholiques to be silent vpon all occasions of discourse concerning matters of Religion; and that the said Gouernor & Commissioners treate the Protestants wth as much mildness and fauor as Justice will permitt. And this to be obserued at Land as well as at Sea."

[3] While the Maryland colonists were steering across the Atlantic, Father Le Jeune was gaining his first actual knowledge of Indian life. In 1634 the Huron Mission was established by the heroic Brebeuf. Cf. Parkman's *Jesuits in North America*, chs. iv, v, and Thwaites's admirable edition of the *Jesuit Relations*. Whether there was any connection between the two schemes is not yet known.

French missionaries desired to save those who lived in the frosty regions farther north. The plan was a noble one, but the English missionaries were hopelessly handicapped by the mere fact of their English allegiance. The mode in which they sought to accomplish their designs was in conflict with laws which had been on the English statute book for centuries. It met, therefore, with the determined opposition of the wily and able Lord Baltimore.

Full of enthusiasm, little imagining the bitter disappointment which the future had in store, Father White and his companion priests, while still in sight of the shores of England, committed the principal parts of the *Ark* "to the protection of God especially, and of His most Holy Mother and Saint Ignatius, and all the guardian angels of Maryland."[1] The mariners murmured somewhat at this, and, but for an accident, the expedition might have come to an ending before it left the Isle of Wight. As it was, however, the ships cleared the English Channel, and pursuing the tedious and roundabout southern route reached the Chesapeake with the loss of only twelve of the passengers. Arrived in the Potomac, their first care was to explore that river for a suitable site for their settlement. To every headland, island, bay, and stream, they gave a saintly name. Forgetting the injunction of Lord Baltimore to perform their services "as privately as may be" they publicly celebrated mass on St. Clement's Isle and declared that they had come to Maryland "to glorify the Blood of Our Redeemer in the salvation of barbarians, and also to raise up a kingdom for the Saviour [and] to consecrate another gift to the Immaculate Virgin, His Mother."

[1] These details are taken from Father White's *Relatio Itineris*, of which numerous editions have been printed.

The place which they finally pitched upon for their first settlement was on the borders of a small river which makes into the Potomac not far from its mouth, and which they named St. George, for England's patron saint; their first town they called St. Mary's. On the shore of this stream was an Indian village occupying what seemed to them to be the most eligible location. In return for a present of knives, hoes, axes, and English cloth — articles of inestimable value to the Indians — the natives abandoned to the newcomers one half and then all of their huts; and they even seem to have labored for the whites.

Among the more energetic Virginia colonists was William Claiborne, or Cleburn, as the name is pronounced and now generally spelled.[1] He had originally come to Jamestown as surveyor for the company; but at this time he held from the king the appointment of secretary of the province, and later on was appointed treasurer of Virginia for life. His professional duties, and the business of fur trader, which he pursued with profit, had given him an acquaintance with the outlying parts of Virginia. When Baltimore applied to the crown for a grant of land within the old chartered limits of Virginia, Claiborne had gone to England to oppose him. He had established a post on Kent Island, in the Upper Chesapeake, at least as early as 1629,[2] and probably as far back as 1625,[3] having purchased the land from the natives. In 1631, some time before the Maryland patent was issued, Claiborne had obtained from the king a document giving him the right to carry on the fur trade along the coast. In 1631 also his

[1] For his descendants, see *Virginia Magazine of History*, i, 313–324, 436–440; ii, 424–425; viii, 382. There is a valuable paper on Claiborne from the Mss. of S. F. Streeter in *New England Historical and Genealogical Register* for April, 1873, 125–135.

[2] Neill's *Terra Mariæ*, 94.

[3] Doyle's *English in America*, i, 388.

settlement had sent a burgess to the Virginia general assembly.[1] When the Maryland colonists appeared, Claiborne asked the advice of the Virginia Council, of which he was a member. In giving their answer the councilors were doubtless influenced by a letter from the Privy Council, in which it was stated that private rights would not be affected by the grant to Lord Baltimore, so Claiborne went on with his business without permission from the Maryland authorities. As he carried on his enterprise under a license from the English king, and had purchased from the Indians the island on which his station was established, he may well have thought that he came within the purview of the Privy Council's declaration. Upon the righteous treatment of him and his partners, the peaceful settlement of Maryland largely depended. Unfortunately it fell out otherwise, owing, in part, to the inexperience and incapacity of Leonard Calvert, and also, in part, to the jealousy of a rival Virginia fur trader. The latter told the Marylanders that Claiborne was inciting the Indians to attack them on the ground that they were enemies of England and friends of the Spaniards.[2] This was an atrocious calumny, for the Indians, upon being summoned before a mixed board of Virginians and Marylanders, denied that Claiborne had said anything of the kind; but Baltimore, acting on this misinformation,[3] directed his brother to arrest Claiborne and keep him prisoner and confiscate his property. Early in 1635, therefore, one of Claiborne's trading boats was seized by

[1] Hening's *Statutes*, i, 154.

[2] *Maryland Archives* (Council, 1667–87), 165–167, 187; Maryland Historical Society's *Fund Publications*, No. ix, "Streeter's Papers," 68–70.

[3] Latané (*Early Relations of Virginia and Maryland*, 14) points out that Baltimore intended to deal fairly with Claiborne, and so instructed his brother, who bungled the business. See also Bernard Steiner's "Beginnings of Maryland" (*Johns Hopkins University Studies in History*, vol. xxi). These accounts are the best that have yet appeared.

the Marylanders. Armed conflicts followed, in which Claiborne's men were defeated; some of them were killed, others were wounded, and one of them was hanged as a pirate. The mode adopted to dispose of this so-called pirate is unique in the annals of colonial jurisprudence. Captain Thomas Cornwallis commanded the party which captured him; he then sat on the jury which indicted him; was later one of his eighteen judges in the guise of a member of the Maryland assembly; as a councilor, he voted to confirm the governor's sentence of death; and as a member of the assembly voted for a bill confirming the death sentence.[1] The Maryland assembly also passed a bill attainting William Claiborne of sundry contempts, insolvencies, and seditious acts, mutinies, commanding sundry persons to commit the grievous crimes of piracy and murder, and declared his property forfeited to the lord proprietor.[2] Complicated legal proceedings in England followed. In the end Baltimore's title to Kent Island was established to the satisfaction of the lawyers; but the rightfulness of this decision is not at all clear to the historical student. As for Claiborne, he retired to Virginia and waited for his opportunity.

The Indians living at St. Mary's and in the immediate vicinity belonged to a worn-out and dying stock. They welcomed the coming of the Englishmen to protect them from the more masterful tribes of the interior and readily fell under the influence of the Jesuit missionaries. With the Susquehannas, who lived on the upper shores of the Chesapeake and in the valley of the river which still bears their name, and with the Indians of the middle Potomac,

[1] Maryland Historical Society's *Fund Publications*, No. ix, "Streeter's Papers," 42–50, 143.

[2] Maryland Historical Society's *Fund Publications*, No. ix, "Streeter's Papers," 54.

the case was very different. They attacked the whites, and the whites retaliated. In 1639, 1640, 1641, 1642, 1643, and 1644, for six consecutive years, the Maryland records give us accounts of expeditions against the Indians. In 1643 either the strong tribes had penetrated to the vicinity of St. Mary's, or the Indians who had at first been friendly had now turned against the whites, for in that year Leonard Calvert by proclamation authorized any one to shoot any Indian who was found near the settlement except those who bore visibly "a white flag or fane." The next year Giles Brent, who acted as governor in the absence of Leonard Calvert, authorized the inhabitants to "shoot them whatsoever Indians they are." Indeed, throughout the eighteenth century the Indians greatly troubled the settlers of Maryland.

The Maryland system of landholding had little fixity; it rested upon instructions which Lord Baltimore gave to his brother Leonard, the first governor, and these the proprietor felt free to alter, as he did in 1641, 1648, 1649, and at other times. The terms upon which he parted with his property varied according to the year in which a settler went out, but the prevalent idea was to give land in accordance with the number of persons whose transportation the colonist provided and always upon a rental tenure. In the beginning the proprietor clearly had it in mind to encourage the formation of large estates,[1] the grantee to enjoy manorial rights. Land was

[1] For example, Captain Thomas Cornwallis, "one of the greatest propagators and increasers" of the colony, secured land on account of seventy persons whom he transported to the province. Another large grant was to the Jesuit fathers, White and Copley, who secured land by virtue of the transportation of sixty persons.

It has been said that Cornwallis was a Protestant. This was true of the Cornwallis family in general, but the Maryland Thomas Cornwallis, writing to Baltimore, describes himself as "a real Catholic" (Maryland Historical Society's *Fund Publications*, No. 28, 172). He was also charged before the House of Lords with taking certain children to the

also granted to those who advanced money to the lord proprietor but who did not emigrate to the colony. In no long time the large grants began to be split into small parcels, and a system of small proprietors came into existence. At one time, however, it seemed as if the Jesuits were on the point of absorbing a considerable portion of the province.

Three thousand miles of blue water between Maryland and the nearest English bishop made the missionaries forgetful of the English statute book. They had come to America to found an asylum for persecuted English Roman Catholics and to convert the heathen to the Christian faith.[1] In the latter part of their plan they had good success. As they were large importers of laborers, they secured great tracts from the proprietary's agents, and then forgetful of what they owed him, they purchased other lands from the Indians. Moreover, they maintained the supremacy of the Canon Law over the legislation of Parliament, lord proprietor, and assembly, and declared that the Bull "In Cœna Domini" placed opposers under the displeasure of Almighty God. When Baltimore realized what was going on, he was greatly disturbed, for the Jesuits were acting in defiance of the Statute of Mortmain. If their purposes and doings were once understood in England, the Maryland charter would not be worth a month's purchase. Its forfeiture would cost Baltimore and his partners thousands of pounds and, more important, would destroy the only place of compara-

colony against their mother's wishes for the alleged purpose of "seducing them to popery." See *Lords Journals*, viii, index, under Foord and Cornwallis, or *Maryland Archives* (Council, 1636–67), 164 and fol.

[1] There are valuable articles on the Roman Catholic side of Maryland's history in *American Catholic Quarterly Review* and *American Catholic Historical Researches*. The matter is well summed up from the same standpoint in J. G. Shea's "The Catholic Church in Colonial Days," 28–85. (This forms volume i of *A History of the Catholic Church within the Limits of the United States*.)

tive safety for Roman Catholics within English dominions. So he sent John Lewger — a personal friend of his and a very capable man — to Maryland as his agent and also as Secretary of the Province (1637). Mr. Lewger was a recent convert to the Faith but he speedily brought matters to an issue with the missionaries. These complained to the lord proprietor that the new secretary maintained that in an English dominion the privileges of the Church depended on the temporal law. On the contrary, they asked, was not a restricter of ecclesiastical liberty liable to excommunication? To Baltimore this suggestion seemed to be "very extravagant," to use his own words. With his tactful patience, he chose his time, and in 1641 he struck the blow. In that year he drew up new regulations for the granting of land, which included the recognition of the principle of the Statute of Mortmain. He also secured from Henry More, Provincial of the Jesuits in England, a release of the property of that order in Maryland, and a declaration that the enforcement of the English laws would not bring upon himself or Mr. Lewger or his other officers in Maryland the anathema of the Bull "In Cœna Domini." Lord Baltimore evidently felt that it was desirable to justify himself for these proceedings, especially in the eyes of his brother. He therefore wrote Leonard Calvert explaining his policy. In this letter[1] he declared that the Jesuits designed his destruction and would use English or Indians to accomplish their object, all under the pretense of God's honor and the propagation of the Christian faith, which to his mind was only a mask or vizard to hide their designs. "If all things," he continued, "that clergy-

[1] Maryland Historical Society's *Fund Publications*, No. 28, "Calvert Papers," pt. i, p. 217.

men should do upon these pretenses should be accounted just and to proceed from God, laymen were the basest slaves and most wretched creatures upon the earth." Evidently he was not that kind of layman, for he went on to declare that if the greatest saint upon earth intruded himself into his house to save the souls of his family and at the same time to bring about his temporal destruction, he should expel such an enemy and provide other clergymen to perform the necessary spiritual task — "those that will be impudent must be as impudently dealt withal." Nevertheless, he permitted the Jesuit mission to continue in the colony on a modest scale and in due subordination to himself; but the days of its prosperity were over.

The subject of religion in Maryland has afforded an almost inexhaustible field for argument, and the answers to the various questions which have been raised seem to depend somewhat upon the religious convictions of the debaters. The theme has attracted the attention of eminent men, as Mr. Gladstone [1] and Cardinal Manning; [2] of patient students, as Edward Neill, Sebastian F. Streeter, and Bradley T. Johnson; and of brilliant writers, as George Bancroft and Edward Eggleston.[3] The publication of the Maryland records and of the Calvert Papers has made it possible to review the question; but some points still remain open to doubt.

In the early days of the province two religious cases came up for adjudication and were both decided against the Roman Catholics. The first of these was decided in 1638. It appears that William Lewis, a Roman Catholic overseer of Captain Cornwallis's servants, chanced upon

[1] Preface to *Rome and the Newest Fashions in Religion.*

[2] *The Vatican Decrees in their Bearing on Civil Allegiance.*

[3] Maryland also sometimes competes with Rhode Island as showing the way to religious freedom; see, for instance, *American Catholic Quarterly*, xx, 289.

two of them as they were reading aloud from a Protestant book. Possibly realizing Lewis's proximity, the reader raised his voice and recited how "the Pope was antichrist and the Jesuits antichristian ministers." At this, the overseer turned on them, asserted that what they were reading "came from the devil," that all Protestant ministers were "ministers of the devil," and forbade them to read that book any more. Thereupon, the servants set about formulating a petition to the Virginia authorities praying them to intervene, on the ground that Lewis was a traitor under the laws of England. But the Maryland rulers at once interfered to avoid the dangers to which such an appeal would have exposed the enterprise. They fined Lewis five hundred pounds of tobacco and placed him under bonds of three thousand pounds of tobacco to refrain from "incautious and unnecessary arguments in matters of religion . . . ignominious words, or speeches, touching the books or ministers authorized by the Church of England."[1]

The second case is more difficult to understand and had to do with one of the important men of the colony, Mr. Thomas Gerrard. Having taken away the key of "the chapel" and carried off certain books, he was ordered to restore key and books and pay a fine of five hundred pounds of tobacco. It is not unlikely that this dispute was partly in the nature of a family affair, since Mrs. Gerrard was a "Protestant Catholic," which term is sometimes used in the Maryland records to describe adherents of the Established Church. The details of the conflict, however, are unimportant, for it is perfectly clear from

[1] This case is to be found in *Maryland Archives* (Provincial Court, 1637–50), p. 35 and fol. It has naturally attracted the attention of Roman Catholic writers, see *American Catholic Historical Researches*, xi, 53.

what we know of these cases that the Roman Catholic government of Maryland was determined to give no offense to Protestants, and it is equally clear that this policy was distasteful to some of the early Roman Catholic colonists.

The fifteen years before 1660 were full of trouble and anxiety for Lord Baltimore. He had undertaken a task which proved to be far beyond his financial means, and he was living in comparative poverty. Whatever part material considerations may have played in the inception of the Maryland design, there can be little doubt that Baltimore was forced by his necessities to look well to the possibility of gaining money from the colony. Up to this time settlers had been attracted to Maryland in small numbers. There is no accessible information as to the size of the population or of the numbers of immigrants who sought its shores; but there is no reason to suppose that these numbers were large. On the other hand, there does not seem to have been the terrible loss of life at St. Mary's that there was at Jamestown. Moreover, although Indian wars lasted for years, there was no general massacre like those which wrought disaster in Virginia. Nevertheless, the province did not prosper. For this there were several reasons. The religion of the lord proprietor and of the leading men of Maryland and the toleration of Roman Catholics in that province served to send Protestant settlers to Virginia or New England, rather than to Maryland. Furthermore, the enforcement of the contracts under which land was granted and the firm grasp which Lord Baltimore strove to keep on the governmental organization made immigrants prefer colonies where more liberal conditions prevailed. As to the second of the deterrent influences just enumerated, it is true that quit-rents were exacted in Virginia; but they were collected with difficulty, and for long periods of time were scarcely collected at all. At one time, indeed, Lord Baltimore suggested to the crown that if he were placed in command in Virginia he could increase the royal revenue derived from that province by some eight thousand pounds sterling. In Maryland the land office was well managed; but the comparison of the methods pursued on either side of the Potomac was likely to induce settlers to seek Virginia and not Maryland. Above all, the constitutional arrangements of early Maryland were not altogether to the liking of the colonists.

The Maryland charter gave extensive legislative rights to the lord proprietor, guaranteed the rights of Englishmen to the settlers, and secured to the crown the undiminished allegiance of Baltimore and of his colonists. Legislative power in the province was exercised by the proprietor with the consent of the freemen of the province, assembled in person or by deputy, in such manner and form as should seem best to the proprietor. To him also was given the power to make ordinances; but both laws and ordinances must not be contrary to the laws of England. Furthermore, the ordinances could not "extend to oblige, bind, charge, or take away the goods or chattels, or interest of any person or persons, of, or in member, life, freehold, goods or chattels." Upon the interpretation and application of these conflicting and ambiguous phrases the growth of the province of Maryland and the freedom of its people depended.

In the beginning Baltimore acted as if the charter authorized him to formulate statutes to which the settlers should give their assent or dissent; but the colonists insisted on taking unto themselves the right of initiative and circumstances compelled Baltimore to yield. He then tried to reduce the power of the colonists to the lowest possible point by manipulation of the franchise and the apportionment. These, as stated in the charter, depended entirely upon the action of the lord proprietor, except so far as the freemen were able to force him to comply with their desires, which proved to be a long and arduous task. The earliest assemblies seem to have included all the freeholders of the province. The phrase used in the charter was "liberorum hominum," which is translated freemen; but in the charters which have practically the same provisions as the Maryland grant the word is freeholder, and as a matter of fact "liberorum hominum" was so interpreted in Maryland; but as practically every person who was not a servant was a freeholder, the words "freeman" and "freeholder" were really synonymous. These general meetings were found to be inconvenient as soon as the colonists began to plant at any distance from St. Mary's. A curious custom then grew up of allowing such freemen as could not be present to send their proxies to those who were to attend the meeting. Frequently the governor and secretary — both of whom were appointed by Baltimore — held enough proxies from absent freemen to outvote all those present; but sometimes two or even one of the leading men held enough proxies to outvote both governor and secretary. In 1641, for instance, Giles Brent, with seventy-three proxies, formed a standing majority of the assembly. Then the freeholders began to depute one or more of their number to represent them in the assembly; but there were curious variations in the working of this institution. For example, we find that John Longford voted for Robert Philpot as delegate from the Island of Kent.[1] He then repented his vote, attended the assembly

[1] *Maryland Archives* (Assembly, 1637–64), 6.

in person, "revoked his voice," and was allowed to sit and vote alongside of the delegate who represented the other freemen of the Island — all of which may be regarded as a somewhat unusual mode of minority representation. As time went on these irregularities were remedied. The larger estates were subdivided; servants became freemen entitled each to fifty acres of land and a vote. In this way the suffrage in Maryland came to be enjoyed by as large a proportion of the population as in Virginia, perhaps even by a larger proportion.

The phrase "liberorum hominum" did not carry its usual connotation to a certain spinster who is described in the records as "Mistress Margaret Brent." She was a woman of ability and resolution, as her appointment to administer the property of the lately deceased Leonard Calvert shows. In this capacity she demanded a seat and voice in the assembly and was refused; whereupon "the s'd Mrs. Brent protested against all proceedings in this present Assembly unless she may be present and have a vote as aforesaid." In the reigns of Elizabeth and James, women sometimes voted in town and parish meeting in England, and there are instances of their holding office. It is not improbable that Mistress Margaret Brent regarded the government of Maryland as analogous to that of an English public corporation and, therefore, held that her action was not in the nature of demanding political rights.

In no long course of time Maryland lost much of its early aristocratic character and became a colony of small landed proprietors. In general, the cultivation of the soil of a state or colony by numerous freeholders is regarded as the most favorable form of social organization. In the case of Maryland, however, it proved to be otherwise, for the products of Maryland in the early times, like those of

Virginia, demanded cultivation on a large scale. It fell out in this way, therefore, that the liberal provisions which had been made for the reward of servants really retarded the prosperity of the proprietary province north of the Potomac in comparison with the royal province which lay south of that river.

NOTES

I. Bibliography. — The Maryland Historical Society, "by authority of the State," has published many volumes of records under the general title of *Archives of Maryland.* The volumes have no consecutive numbering, and are usually cited by some contraction of the long title, as "Council, 1687–93." These volumes are exceedingly valuable to any one who wishes to gain an insight into Maryland institutions. Another helpful collection of original matter is the "Calvert Papers," which the Maryland Historical Society is printing in its *Fund Publications.* The great value of some of the papers printed, and the promise held out by the "Calendar" prefixed to the first selection, prompts the wish that the society will see its way clear to printing more of the documents in full. Foley's *Records of the English Province of the Society of Jesus* (vol. iii) has some interesting matter dealing with Maryland; but E. L. Taunton (*Jesuits in England,* p. viii) states that "Foley's value consists almost as much in his omissions as in his admissions. And I am bound to remark," he goes on to say, "that I have found him, at a critical point, quietly leaving out, without any signs of omission, an essential part of a document which was adverse to his case."

John Leeds Bozman studied the manuscript records of Maryland to good purpose. His *History of Maryland* is still a serviceable book, although it was first published in 1811, — the best edition is that of 1837. The second volume covers the years 1633–60. He did not have access to the "Calvert Papers" or to the Jesuit records; much of what he says on religious topics, therefore, needs revision. Bernard Steiner's "Beginnings of Maryland" in the *Johns Hopkins Studies* (vol. xxi) is the best concise account of Maryland's founding that has yet appeared; it is especially good on the Claiborne episode. McMahon's *Historical View* (vol. i, all ever published) is oftentimes instructive, although printed in 1831, and Mereness's *Maryland as a Proprietary Province* is a useful compilation on the institutional side. Kilty's *Landholder's Assistant* contains many documents which are of use to the student of the constitutional history of the province.

II. Northey's Opinion. — In this connection the opinion of Attorney-general Northey, given in 1705, is of interest: "As to the said clause in the grant of the province of Maryland to the Lord Baltimore, relating to ecclesiastical power, I am of opinion the same doth not give him any power to do anything contrary to the ecclesiastical laws of England, but he hath only the advowsons of, and power to erect and consecrate churches, and such power as the Bishop of Durham had, as each palatine, in his county palatine, who was subject to the laws of England; and the consecration of chapels ought to be by orthodox ministers only." See the opinion in full in Chalmers's *Opinions of Eminent Lawyers,* i, 2, or p. 42 of the American reprint, or Forsyth's *Cases,* 31.

CHAPTER X

THE BEGINNINGS OF NEW ENGLAND

SEVENTEENTH-CENTURY Puritanism was an attitude of mind[1] rather than a system of theology, — it was idealism applied to the solution of contemporary problems. In religion it took the form of a demand for preaching ministers and for carrying to its logical ending the reformation in the ecclesiastical fabric which Elizabeth had begun and had stopped halfway. In society it assumed the shape of a desire to elevate private morals, which were shockingly low. In politics it stood for a new movement in national life which required the extirpation of the relics of feudalism and the recognition of the people as a power in the State. In short, Puritanism marked the beginning of the rising tide of human aspiration for something better than the world had yet known. If this definition is vague, Puritanism itself was vague. In the reign of James I the word "Puritan" was regarded as a term of reproach. For instance, in 1620 a member of the House of Commons, using the word in debate, was "staid by command," and, later, railing against Puritans, was expelled.[2] There was no organized Puritan party with a platform or statement of principles. If one had inquired of the men who are now

[1] E. L. Taunton, in his interesting book on the *Jesuits in England*, says that Puritanism was "not so much a religious as a mental attitude." Acting on this definition, he stigmatizes Father Parsons, S.J., as a Puritan!

[2] Royal Historical Manuscripts Commission's *Reports*, xiv, pt. 2, p. 13; *Debates of 1620–21*, i, 45. Sir Edward Coke, in the course of this debate, declared that "whatsoever hindereth the observation of the sanctification of the Sabbath is against the Scriptures."

designated as Puritans what their wishes were, he would have met with nearly as many answers as there were men of whom he made the inquiry. Between the Nonconformists, who regularly attended the services of the Established Church, and the Brownists, who held that the "establishment" was sinful and refused to attend its ministrations, there was a gulf much wider and deeper than that which separated a conservative Nonconformist from those who adhered strictly to the service book.[1] In the course of their religious conflicts the Puritans found themselves in alliance with all the forces of unrest in the State, until their party, if such a word may be used, comprised all persons who were opposed to the government of England in Church and State as it was administered by the second Stuart.

Most numerous among the Puritans were the Nonconformists. These were clergymen and laymen who scrupled some one or more things in the church service or regulations, but continued to attend the parish churches. Some of them disliked the surplice, others thought that the use of the ring in the marriage ceremony was a relic of pre-Christian days, practically all of them desired a preaching ministry. In 1603 the Nonconformists did not object to the bishops, but as the conflict assumed, more and more, the form of a contest with the hierarchy, they demanded that the laity should be represented in the

[1] The word "Puritan" is often used inaccurately by writers on American history to denote only the people of Massachusetts Bay. To these authors the Massachusetts people seem to be apart from the rest of the world, and to be alone entitled to the distinction of being classed with Cromwell, Milton, Hampden, and other great Puritans. Some New England writers seek to separate Bradford and the early settlers at Plymouth from the Puritans and call them Pilgrims. Any such use of the word "Puritan" is historically inaccurate and therefore undesirable. Roger Williams, William Coddington, William Bradford, William Brewster, John Winthrop, John Endicott, John Haynes, Thomas Hooker, Theophilus Eaton, and John Davenport were all Puritans.

church organization; in the end the great mass of them favored Presbyterianism. As their name implies, the Nonconformists belonged to the national Church. They proposed to stay in it, to gain control of it, and to mold it to their will. They had no desire of toleration for themselves, and they had no intention of tolerating any one else. In truth, in this respect at least, "New presbyter was old priest writ large," to use Milton's phrase: the one was as intolerant as the other. Next in importance among those who came to be called Puritans were the Independents. These cut loose from the Established Church, or, perhaps it would be better to say, were turned out of that body. They set up for themselves, each little congregation managing its own religious affairs. The Independents had little interest in the religious beliefs of others, and were willing, for the most part, to tolerate almost any one, even Roman Catholics and Jews; in return they demanded toleration for themselves. At the extreme end of the Puritan line were a few earnest persons who adhered to the ideas of Robert Browne, and may fairly be called Brownists. These regarded the existing Established Church as contrary to the Gospel. They separated themselves from that organization and would probably, had the chance come to them, have put an end to the establishment.

On James's southward journey in 1603 a deputation of Nonconformists intercepted him and presented a petition to which nearly one thousand clergymen of the Church of England had given their assent; for this reason it is known as the Millenary Petition. The petitioners asked (1) that the cross in baptism and the ring in marriage be omitted, (2) that the cap and surplice be not required, (3) that church songs and music be "moderated to better edification," (4) that the Lord's day be not profaned, (5) that "popish opinions" be no longer taught, (6) that none but preaching ministers be maintained, (7) that pluralities and nonresidency be abolished, (8) that ministers be compelled to subscribe only to the Articles of Religion and the royal supremacy and not be compelled to acknowledge the validity of every word in the service book, and finally (9) they requested that men be not excommunicated "for trifles and twelve penny matters." In these demands were contained all the principal points of dissatisfaction with the existing Church settlement. Many of them take us back to the early days of Elizabeth's reign and to the Convocation of 1563,[1] when the Church refused by one vote to grant them. It must be remembered, however, that the Queen's "Injunctions" of 1559 had already granted a considerable part of the demands of the earlier radicals. For instance, in that document Elizabeth had commanded that once in each month every clergyman should preach that "works devised by man's fantasies, besides Scripture, as wandering of pilgrimages, setting up of candles, praying upon beads, or such like superstition, have not only no promise of reward in Scripture, but, contrariwise, great threatenings and maledictions of God";[2] and the ministers should not extol the dignity of

[1] By 1563 the more radical men among the Protestants had come to an agreement on certain points and presented their demands to Convocation. They asked that (1) Sundays and "the principal feasts of Christ be kept holy days" and that all other holy days be abrogated; (2) that the minister should face the people and read distinctly; (3) that the cross in baptism be abandoned; (4) that kneeling be left to the discretion of the several bishops; (5) that the surplice only be used; and (6) that organs be removed. Edwin Sandys, Bishop of Worcester, and afterwards Archbishop of York, would have granted all or most of these demands. Of the members of Convocation present, forty-three voted in favor of granting them and thirty-five against. When the proxies were counted, however, the settlement was defeated by one vote, there being fifty-eight Ayes and fifty-nine Noes. The vote of one man, and he an absentee, decreed that the Established Church should never be a truly national church. See Prothero's *Statutes*, 191, from Strype's *Annals*, i, 502.

[2] Prothero's *Statutes*, 184–190. The clauses quoted in this paragraph are con-

images, relics, or miracles. Elizabeth further enjoined that all shrines, "paintings, and all other monuments" of superstition should be taken away, "so that there remain no memory of the same in walls, glass windows, or elsewhere."[1]

With our knowledge of the history of the first half of the seventeenth century, it is difficult to understand how the Nonconformists could have so thoroughly misconceived the character of James Stuart. In extenuation of their mistakes, it should be remembered that he had done everything possible to surround his religious leanings with an impenetrable cloud of doubt. The result of these tactics was that each of the three religious groups in England looked upon him somewhat in the light of a coming champion, although the bishops seem to have been less certain than either the Roman Catholics or the Nonconformists. The Roman Catholics, on their part, clung to the fact that he was the son of the murdered Mary of Scotland and had listened to the advances of emissaries of their faith and had made some general statements to

tained in sections ii, iii, and xxiii. There are over fifty sections in all.

[1] Edward VI had previously enjoined the destruction of "shrines and coverings of shrines; tables, candlesticks; trindles of wax; pictures, paintings, and all other monuments of feigned miracles, pilgrimage, idolatry and superstition." He had been taken at his word, as, for instance, at St. Michael's, in Bedwardine in Worcester (*Church-Warden's Accounts*, 20), the churchwardens paid John Davis for hewing down the seats of the images in the Church and whitewashing the walls. In 1548 the churchwardens of the same parish sold off most of the church effects as follows :—

	s	d
Ares covering which was used to the sepulter sold to Mr. Bland .	6	4
Lamp and censer	4	
Standards of brass, candlesticks, etc.	14	
A copper cross	2	
A platter		18
A holywater pot of lead and certain organ pipes of lead . .	2	10
For the "sayle and old clothes to cover saynts"	3	4
The table that stood on the high altar		12

etc.

See also Swayne's *St. Edmund and St. Thomas, Sarum* (Wilt's Record Society), and Thomas North's *Chronicles of the Church of St. Martin in Leicester.*

If other parishes were as zealous as these, there could have been "few monuments of superstition" for Elizabeth's subjects to destroy or sell, let alone Cromwell and his Ironsides.

the effect that loyal Roman Catholics would not be persecuted. His words meant absolutely nothing; but in their cruel plight and their ignorance of James's character, the English Roman Catholics may well be excused for believing that the new king meant what he seemed to say. The English Nonconformists, on their part, had not the slightest doubt of James's favorable disposition. Had he not been instructed by George Buchanan and John Knox? Only twelve years, indeed, had passed away since James had declared the Presbyterian Kirk of Scotland to be "the purest in the world"; and, on the other hand, had described the service of the Established Church of England as "an evil said mass in English." Between 1590 and 1603 a man of James's temperament might honestly have changed his mind, and it is certain that, as the end of Elizabeth's reign drew near, the advantages of the Established Church as the supporter of monarchy became more evident to him. He, therefore, caused Whitgift, Archbishop of Canterbury, to be informed that on his accession the existing arrangements would be maintained. The old archbishop, however, indulged in no overconfidence and waited with some anxiety to see how far James would forget his Presbyterian training,—and he had not long to wait.

At first it seemed as if James would yield enough to satisfy the desires of the great mass of the Nonconformists; but to every suggestion of reform Whitgift opposed obstacles, and some of his objections were undoubtedly based on sound business considerations. James then hit upon the expedient of bringing the bishops and leading Nonconformists together. This meeting, which took place at Hampton Court, is generally spoken of as the Hampton Court Conference; but in reality it was a series of meetings at which James conferred at first with one set of people, then with another, and finally with both. There were both closed sessions and open meetings. At the latter were present church dignitaries and well-known Nonconformist scholars and controversialists. Our knowledge of what took place is scanty.[1] Such as it is it gives the impression that the reformers were borne down by the ill-natured gibes of James and the indecent interruptions and browbeatings of Richard Bancroft, Bishop of London, who soon succeeded Whitgift as Primate. Toward the close of the proceedings Dr. Reynolds, one of the most eminent Nonconformist scholars of his time, happened to refer to presbyters. This word reminded James of his Scottish experiences, when Knox had "lessoned" him upon the whole duty of a king. Turning to the Nonconformists he charged them with aiming at Presbyterianism, and declared that that form of Church government agreed "as well with monarchy as God and the Devil." "If this be all they have to say," he added, as he went forth, "I shall make them conform themselves, or I will harry them out of the land, or else do worse." Here was a king after the hierarchical heart. Whitgift was heard to mutter something about the voice of God in man, and Bancroft thanked Almighty God for "his singular mercy in giving us such a king as since Christ's time the like, he thought, had not been seen,"—a phrase which carries one forward a century to Dr. Sacheverell's likening the execution of Charles I to the crucifixion of Christ, of which, he said, it was an "exact transcript and representation."

[1] See Gardiner's *History of England*, i, 152 and fol.; he gives the bibliography of the subject on p. 155. Barlow's *Summe and Substance of the Conference*, written on the Bishop's side, is almost the only original source of information in print. What appears to be the Nonconformist brief is given in a condensed form in Royal Historical Manuscripts Commission's *Report on the Beaulieu Manuscripts*, 32–40.

In the democratic latitudinarianism of the present day language like that which has just been quoted seems incomprehensible; but it should be remembered that Bancroft was fighting for what was dearest to him, and also that those were the days of Shakespeare, when speakers and writers were not bound down by the forms of college-taught rhetoric. Furthermore, it must not be supposed for one instant that the Nonconformists were behind the bishops in their power of utterance. What Reynolds and Knewstubs and their two companions said at Hampton Court we do not know, but we have Cartwright's description of the Establishment in the "Admonition to Parliament," which he and other Nonconformists drew up in 1571, and there is no reason to suppose that the power of description had diminished among them since that date. The hierarchy is described in this paper as "antichristian and devilish," while the service book is declared to be "an imperfect book, culled and picked out of that popish dunghill, the portuise and mass-book full of all abominations." The ecclesiastical courts naturally came in for objurgation; the archbishop's court they described as "the filthy quake-mire and poisoned plash of all the abominations . . . and the commissary's court, that is but a petty little stinking ditch that floweth out of that former great puddle, robbing Christ's church of lawful pastors, of watchful seniors and elders, and careful deacons." Persons using language of this kind had little right to complain of words like those uttered by Bancroft, — nor is there evidence that they made any complaints on that score.

Whitgift, as we have seen, felt reassured by the king's language, but he was too well acquainted with the strength of the Nonconformists to feel that the battle was won.

He dreaded the opening of Parliament, as well he might, for two thirds of the members of the House of Commons were Nonconformists, or were very closely allied with them. March 19, 1604, James met his first Parliament at Westminster. Instead of avoiding controversial topics, he plunged into them headlong. On coming into the kingdom, he had found three religions, — so he said. The first was the public form by law maintained. The second was "falsely called Catholic, but truly Papish"; for the laity of this religion there was some excuse,[1] but for the priests who maintained that the Pope had an imperial civil power over all kings and emperors, they could expect no mercy. The third religion comprised the Puritans or Novelists who lurked "within the bowels of this nation." These did not differ from the Established Church in doctrine, but in their "confused form of polity and parity; being ever discontented with the present government and impatient to suffer any superiority, which maketh that sect unable to be suffered in any well governed commonwealth." In some sort as an answer to this diatribe the Nonconformist majority at once took up the subject of reforms in Church and State. The chairman or reporter of the committee on religion was Sir Edwin Sandys. On his report a bill was passed and sent up to the Lords. There it was strenuously opposed by the bishops, and a conference between the two Houses was held. As the bill was finally lost, owing to a disagreement between the two branches of Parliament, it is impossible to say what the propositions of the Commons were, but the Articles of

[1] James's attitude is discernible in a note of October 24, 1608, in which the Council advises the Bishop of Chester that the king's wish is not to stop altogether his proceedings against recusants, but to have him proceed with moderation and only against obstinate persons. — *Calendars of State Papers, Domestic, 1603–1610*, 463.

Debate in the conference between the Houses have been preserved and give us an idea of the propositions which Sandys brought forward. These are in brief: (1) that ministers should be obliged to subscribe to the articles only concerning the doctrine of faith and the sacrament, that no contrary doctrine be taught, and that masters of households be also compelled to subscribe; (2) that none be admitted to the ministry except Bachelors of Art or of a higher degree in schools and having testimony of ability to preach and of good life, or else such as are approved by the testimonial of six preachers of the county; (3) that no more pluralities be permitted; (4) that better maintenance be provided for the holders of smaller livings; and (5) that faithful ministers be not "deprived, suspended, silenced, or imprisoned for not using the cross in baptism or the surplice." These proposals of Sandys seem to a student, who is far removed in time and space from the England of James, to be not unreasonable, but the bishops would have none of them. In reviewing this subject Samuel Rawson Gardiner, the historian of England in the seventeenth century,[1] says: "Little as they thought what the consequences of their acts would be, Elizabeth and Whitgift, James and Bancroft, by making a schism inevitable, were the true fathers of Protestant dissent." He goes on to declare that perhaps "a schism was sooner or later unavoidable, but, if the Commons had been allowed to carry out their views, it might have been deferred." It is not for us to regret their action, for their refusal of needed reforms led directly to the settlement of New England.

Soon after the close of the Hampton Court Conference, Bancroft became Archbishop of Canterbury. Acting in harmony with James, he set to work to compel conformity.

[1] *History of England*, i, 178, 179.

With the meeting of Parliament, Convocation also came together. Its principal work was the elaboration of a set of regulations which are known as the Canons of 1604. Most of these were in the nature of a codification of existing ecclesiastical laws; but a series of new enactments sought to deal with Nonconformity and Separatism. Their nature can easily be gathered from one or two extracts: —

"IV. Whosoever shall hereafter affirm that the form of God's worship in the Church of England, established by law and contained in the book of Common Prayer . . . containeth anything in it that is repugnant to the scriptures, let him be excommunicated *ipso facto*. . . .

"IX. Whosoever shall hereafter separate themselves from the communion of saints, as it is approved by the Apostles' rules, in the Church of England and combine themselves together in a new brotherhood . . . let them be excommunicated."[1]

These canons were never confirmed by Parliament, and were therefore not enforced by the civil courts. The punishment of excommunication as applied to laymen under the Canons of 1604, for this reason, operated usually in a modified way and did not, as a rule, cut off the excommunicated person from the protection of the law.[2] For the Nonconforming clergyman, however, they meant deprivation for himself and starvation for his family; for the Separatist, they meant little or nothing. Once in a while, however, a layman fell within the clutches of the Church authorities. For example, a certain John Turner was excommunicated in 1625 for not attending the service of

[1] Prothero's *Statutes*, 444, from Cardwell's *Synodalia*, i, 248. Also printed in Latin in *ibid.*, 164.

[2] On this subject, see Stephen's *Commentaries on the Criminal Law*, iv, 17. The civil disabilities of excommunicated persons were removed in 1813 by 53 George III, c. 127, § 3, save only six months' imprisonment.

the Established Church. The miller refused to grind his corn, and probably other men also declined to serve him. At all events the High Commission claimed Turner,[1] and having him in custody refused him bail and placed him in irons. For fifteen years he remained a prisoner in the Gate House for no other apparent reason than because he refused to take the *ex officio* oath. In common with other victims of the High Commission, he was compensated as well as he might be by the Long Parliament. Another sufferer was Thomas Brewer,[2] Brewster's co-worker. He was imprisoned for fourteen years (1626–40) for saying that the bishop's office was not properly derived. At least this was the reason stated; but his proneness to printing was, possibly, the real motive.

To return to 1604; all things being thus arranged, James by proclamation[3] admonished all persons to conform themselves to the Established Church before the first day of the ensuing November; "God requireth at our hands," he said, "that what untractable men do not perform upon admonition, they must be compelled unto by authority." In the following December Bancroft directed the bishops to deprive of their livings all of the clergy who had not conformed. About three hundred Nonconformist ministers were at once driven from their cures.[4] They were given two months to settle their affairs, and then they and their families were to leave their homes and shift for themselves as well as they could. Their future lot can hardly be said to have been uncertain, for whether the Canons of 1604 were binding on the courts of law or not, the Act of

[1] Royal Historical Manuscripts Commission's *Reports*, iv, 35. See also the case of Nathaniel Bernard in Gardiner's *History of England*, vii, 250.

[2] Arber's *Pilgrim Fathers*, 247.

[3] Cardwell's *Documentary Annals*, ii, 63; Prothero's *Statutes*, 420.

[4] Gardiner's *History of England*, i, 197.

Parliament of 1593 dealt with both clergymen and laymen who placed themselves outside the pale of the Church.

The title of the celebrated law of 1593 is "An Act to retain the Queen's subjects in obedience." It was in force in 1605, and was continued by successive statutes, at least until 1628.[1] Among its provisions, these may well be noted: any person who obstinately refuses to attend the services of the Established Church and (1) by printing, writing, express words, or speeches, should persuade other persons to abstain from attending those services, or (2) should be present at any other religious services — should be committed to prison without bail until he conformed. If, however, three months' imprisonment did not bring about conformity, the recalcitrant should abjure the realm and all other her Majesty's dominions, forever under pain of death as a felon in case of return without permission.[2] Abjuration of the realm in the cases of these persons entailed the forfeiture of goods and chattels forever and of lands during life. The law also provided a fine of ten pounds sterling per month for all persons who fed or sheltered those who obstinately refused to attend the parish church.

In ten years of James's reign, as has already been noted, eleven hundred persons were indicted in Middlesex Sessions for not attending church; probably most of them were Roman Catholics, but some of them were Separatists.[3] In 1611, for instance, three men, who are described as Brownists,[4] were convicted of attending unlawful religious assemblies, and having remained "in prison for the

[1] The last act continuing, it passed in 1627 and provided that it should remain in force until the end of the next session of Parliament. The original law is given in the *Statutes of the Realm* as 35 Elizabeth, c. i. It should be carefully distinguished from c. ii of the same statute, which relates to the Roman Catholics.

[2] Prothero's *Statutes*, 89.

[3] *Middlesex County Records*, ii, 292–306.

[4] *Middlesex County Records*, ii, 71;

space of three months after conviction and not conforming themselves" were banished out of the realm and were ordered to take shipping from London for Amsterdam in the Netherlands before the end of one month after the next Easter Day.

Another instance of the working of James's and Bancroft's resolutions has been preserved for three hundred years. Among the Nonconformist clergymen who refused to obey the orders of king and bishop were Richard Clifton of Babworth and John Robinson of Norwich. For a time they found shelter in the manor house at Scrooby, where resided William Brewster, who "held the post" at that place. There they ministered to a little band of religious enthusiasts, the best known of whom was William Bradford, then a lad of from sixteen to eighteen years of age. The members of this group began to feel insecure in their homes, and before long they were hunted and persecuted on every side. Some of them were imprisoned, others had their houses beset night and day and hardly escaped seizure, so that most of them resolved to leave their homes and means of livelihood and go to the Low Countries. This had to be done in a secret manner to avoid the loss of goods consequent on a conviction under the act of 1593.[1] How many good men and women were indicted and cast into prison and banished from the realm under threat of death as felons in case of return, how many more were worried by a sense of constant insecurity into exiling themselves, is

The way in which Roman Catholic recusants and Protestant Separatists were associated in the minds of those in authority may be seen in a letter from the Bishop of Hereford to Lord Salisbury recounting the apprehension of Roger Cadwallader, a dangerous seminary priest, and Thomas Bailies, a Brownist, *Calendars of State Papers, Domestic, 1603–1610*, p. 601.

[1] The act of Richard II prohibiting migration from the realm was repealed in 1606–07 (4 James I, c. 1, § iv). See Coke's *Third Institute*, ch. 84, and Richard Thomson's *Essay on Magna Charta*, 234. See also Note II.

not known, and probably never will be. There must have been many besides those whose experiences have been cited because in that historic band at Leyden were men and women not only from Scrooby, Austerfield, and Bawtry, but also from Canterbury and Sandwich in the southeastern corner of the island, from Chester, on the borders of Wales, from York in the northern region and Newbury in the southern-central part, and also from Norwich and Wrentham in the eastern counties. Brewster and Bradford and their companions who had gone to Leyden from all parts of England, made the first permanent settlement in New England at Plymouth.

In the exciting political struggles of James's Parliaments, the Nonconformist laymen found ample field for their exuberant energies. With the death of James, in 1625, a new page opens in English history. The old leaders of the generation of Sir Edwin Sandys give place to new men, to John Pym and Sir John Eliot. The leaders of the Nonconformists and the other opponents of the Stuart policy in the House of Commons now determined to put pressure upon the new king by refusing to open the purse except on their own terms. This they thought they would be able to do with more effect because James had left behind him debts amounting to seven hundred thousand pounds sterling. For generations, at the beginning of each monarch's reign, it had been customary to grant him for life the subsidy of tonnage and poundage, which may be roughly described as equivalent to the customs revenue. When this had once been granted, the monarch was able to raise or lower the rates at will, and in this way to increase or diminish the amount of money collected under the grant. For example, James had changed the rates, and the judges had decided that he had acted within his rights.[1] The Commons now voted to grant to Charles the subsidy of tonnage and poundage for one year only, on the plea that within the twelve months an inquiry could be made into the financial needs and organization of the government, and the necessary reforms embodied in a later grant. It fell out otherwise, however, for the Lords voted against the grant of tonnage and poundage for one year, and Charles continued to collect it without authority from Parliament, and, as a matter of fact, kept on collecting it until the final catastrophe placed the ports of the kingdom and the collection of the customs in the hands of the Long Parliament.

The conflict which started in this way seems at first sight to be about constitutional matters; but politics and religion were so inextricably commingled in that age that religion really had the greater share in bringing it about, since the only way to secure ecclesiastical reforms was to act through the king's need of money. With a half filled exchequer and this conflict impending in England, Charles undertook to wage war directly or indirectly with the greater part of Europe. One expedient after another was tried to fill the treasury. Of these the most interesting was the Forced Loan of 1626. In theory, there was no simpler way for the king to obtain money than to raise it by a forced loan. The Council made out a list of rich men and marked against the name of each an amount of money which he could easily pay, if he wished so to do. Each demand was made in a document, which was authenticated by the privy seal; and was hence known as a "privy seal." Packages of these

[1] In the well-known Bate's case, see Gardiner's *History of England*, and Prothero's *Statutes*.

"privy seals" were sent to leading men in the several counties who were supposed to be favorable to the king's cause;[1] these visited the persons named and demanded the required sum. One way to avoid payment was to outrun the collector and gain the other side of the border of the county, — this was the way in which Sir Edwin Sandys played his part. Others refused point-blank to pay a penny in an un-Parliamentary way and loudly asserted the unconstitutionality of the demand.

Among the more strenuous objectors to the forced loan was Theophilus Fynes-Clinton, Earl of Lincoln, who not only refused to pay, but procured the compilation and printing of an "Abridgment of the Laws of England" relating to the subject of taxation. He was summoned to London and shut up in the Tower for two years, until the meeting of Parliament necessitated his release. Associated with him in his resistance were his brothers-in-law, Lord Saye and Sele, and Isaac Johnson, and a former steward of his estate, Thomas Dudley. Probably the best known of those who refused to contribute to the loan were Sir Edmund Hampden, uncle of John Hampden, and his four companions. Upon being locked up, they applied for writs of habeas corpus; their case is known as the Five Knights case. The judges refused their application, and the Five Knights returned to prison, where Sir Edmund Hampden died. This was in 1627.

While Charles was thus rousing against himself the forces of English constitutional conservatism, he was also straining to the breaking point the loyalty and affection of the Nonconformists. In civil matters he acted on the advice of George Villiers, Duke of Buckingham; in reli-

[1] There is some interesting matter on this subject in Hamilton's *Quarter Sessions from Elizabeth to Anne*, 20–23.

gious affairs he followed the counsel of William Laud, who in 1628 became Bishop of London and in 1633 Archbishop of Canterbury. Like Charles and like Buckingham, William Laud was a sincere man; his career, however, gives us a striking example of the ill effects which are sometimes produced by intrusting the management of affairs to a "scholar in politics." In religion he was one of those devout and earnest men for whom uniformity, ceremonialism, and old-time doctrine have always had great charm. For half a century, at least, the doctrine of the Established Church had been Calvinistic, as any one may see by reading the Lambeth Articles[1] which Whitgift formulated. Laud, on the other hand, preferred dogmas similar to those which in Holland were associated with the name of Arminius, and he wished to restore what had been destroyed in accordance with the Injunctions of Edward and Elizabeth.

One thing must be granted to Laud and his royal master: if the Nonconformist movement was to be stayed, it was high time to set about it. All over England Church preferments were falling into Nonconformists' hands. In Boston, for example, the corporation had purchased the right of presentation to one of the churches of the town, and had acquired the vicarage and probably the impropriated tithes; in other words, this Nonconformist municipal corporation had secured the right to nominate one of the parsons of the town and to support him out of the funds of the Established Church.[2] In other places, where

[1] Strype's *Whitgift*, ii, 280; brief extracts are in Prothero's *Statutes*, 226.

[2] Professor H. D. Foster of Dartmouth called my attention to extracts from the *Boston Assembly Book*, bearing on these matters. See also Bacon's *Ipswich* and the "Great Court Records" of that town. In 1603 or 1604 Samuel Ward, brother of Nathaniel Ward, at one time minister at Ipswich, Massachusetts, was "elected public preacher for this town," his salary to be paid by the treasurer "without warrant from the bailiffs." Other entries will be found in the "Borough of Leicester Accounts."

the laymen did not possess as complete power as this, they sometimes appointed a virtuous and learned preacher "to teach the word of God and to visit and counsel the sick as need shall serve." This action was in direct contravention of James's proclamation of 1622[1] forbidding clergymen under the degree of bishop or dean "to preach in any popular auditory upon the deep points of predestination, election, reprobation, and of the universality, efficacy, resistibility, or irresistibility of God's grace." By 1625, the Nonconformists had acquired such large funds that an association was formed — comprising four citizens of London, four lawyers, and four Nonconformist clergymen — to buy up impropriated tithes, to employ preachers and lecturers, and to provide additional compensation for Nonconformist ministers and schoolmasters.

It came about in this way that in some places the Established reader of the service book and the Nonconformist preacher of God's word successively occupied the parish church on Sundays, and there was likely to be a good deal to dishearten the regular clergyman and to annoy the Nonconformist congregation. Often the greater part of the parishioners would remain outside until the prescribed service was over, and would then come trooping in to gather righteousness from the lips of their chosen sermonizer. On the one hand, the regular clergyman might well object to reading the service to empty benches and paid choir boys, while, on the other hand, the Nonconformists were strongly of the opinion that those who preached to the parishioners should be paid out of the funds devoted to religious purposes.

Charles and Laud determined to put an end to the reli-

[1] Royal Historical Manuscripts Commission's *Reports*, v, 410.

gious confusion which has just been described.[1] In December, 1629, the king issued to the bishops certain instructions which had been formulated by Laud. In the future, it was ordained that there should be no afternoon sermons at all and no lecturer or preacher should open his mouth in the morning, unless he had first "read divine service according to the Liturgy printed by authority, in his surplice." Furthermore, no lecturer should be employed unless he was willing to accept a regular appointment. The bishops were ordered to look carefully into the doings of all the lecturers and preachers in their dioceses and to "take order for any abuse accordingly." Furthermore, the king commanded that no controversial topics should be discussed in any sermon. At about this time, Laud became head of the High Commission, and before long he had silenced John Cotton, the minister at Boston, and had fined for nonconformity his leading supporters, Richard Bellingham [2] and William Coddington.

When Parliament met, in 1628, the Earl of Lincoln and Lord Saye and Sele were in their places in the House of Peers and Hampden's companions had been released. The sting of their imprisonment remained, however, not only in their own minds, but in the minds of thousands of Englishmen as well; the Commons at once voted to consider grievances before the grant of money. From this proceeded in no long time the Petition of Right, which is one of the corner stones of the English constitution. Soon afterward

[1] Samuel Ward's answers to the questions of the High Commission give a moderate Nonconformist's view of the religious situation in 1635–36. Looking to the future, he was optimistic, saying that "he was not of so melancholy a spirit, nor looked through so black spectacles as he [George Herbert] that wrote that religion stands on the tiptoe in this land looking westward." *Calendars of State Papers, Domestic, Charles I*, vol. ix (1635–36), Introduction.

[2] There is a good article on Bellingham by E. H. Goss in *Magazine of American History*, xiii, 262.

Parliament was dissolved, having voted a small sum of money, and Charles and Laud seized what seemed to them to be a favorable opportunity to issue a Declaration on Religion. In this document, which is still prefixed to the English Service Book, the king declared that the Thirty-nine Articles contained the true doctrine agreeable to God's word and that in the future no man should either print or preach to draw the Articles aside in any way, but should take them in their literal and grammatical sense. The Nonconformists gave their answer in the next session of Parliament. After six weeks, filled with contention, during which the king sought to tire out his opponents by a series of short adjournments, the crisis came. On March 2, 1629, when the Speaker rose to adjourn the House for eight days, Denzil Holles and Benjamin Valentine seized him by the arms, thrust him back into his seat, and stood in front of him. Then Sir John Eliot drew from his pocket a short declaration of the position of the majority, but the Speaker refused to allow it to be read. Thereupon, the door was locked, and a stout member, Sir Miles Hobart, put the key in his pocket. The king, learning of what was going forward, summoned his guard to force the door of the House. It was under these circumstances that Holles, with one hand on the Speaker, repeated the declaration, put it to the House, and declared it carried. The members then passed out, and for eleven years no Parliament met in England.

NOTES

I. Bibliography. — There is no good account of the rise of seventeenth-century Puritanism. The movement was largely social in its character; but hitherto all treatment of it has been mainly religious with more or less of politics thrown in. Gardiner's *History of England* is by long odds the best thing that has yet been done; but he so studiously avoids social and economic factors that some of his readers find it difficult to discover why there should have been any Puritan movement at all. The older accounts are almost entirely religious and regard seventeenth-century nonconformity as the child of Elizabethan separation — which is plainly impossible. See, however, Samuel Hopkins's *The Puritans: or The Church, Court, and Parliament of England during the reigns of Edward VI and Elizabeth* (3 vols.) which does not touch seventeenth-century nonconformity and independency at all. Palfrey's *New England* (vol. i, ch. vii.) contains what is perhaps the best account; but it is now necessarily somewhat obsolete. Other works on the theme are Dexter's *Congregationalism as seen in its Literature;* Marsden's *Puritans;* Neal's *Puritans;* Brown's *Congregationalism in Norfolk and Suffolk* and his *Pilgrims in Old and New England;* Ellis's *Puritan Age and Rule;* Strype's *Annals, Life of Whitgift, Life of Parker;* Fuller's *Worthies;* and D'Ewes's *Journal.*

II. Migration from the Realm. — *Statutes of the Realm,* ii, 18. 5 Ric. II, Stat. i, c. 2 (1381). "And the King our Lord, of his Royal Majesty, defendeth the Passage utterly of all Manner of People, as well Clerks as other, in every Port and other Town and Place upon the Coast of the Sea, upon Pain of Forfeiture of all their Goods; except only the Lords and other Great Men of the Realm, and true and notable Merchants, and the King's Soldiers; and every Person, other than is before excepted, which after Publication of this Ordinance made, shall pass out of the said Realm without the King's special license, . . . shall forfeit to the King as much as he hath in Goods."

CHAPTER XI

THE COMING OF THE PILGRIMS

RICHARD CLIFTON and John Robinson[1] were the central figures of a small group of religious enthusiasts whose fortunes must be traced with some degree of care. In the early years of James's reign, the former of these was rector of Babworth and was a Nonconformist. His sermons drew to him hearers from the neighboring villages of Scrooby and Austerfield, and when he was driven from his living he found refuge at the first of these hamlets, where he was soon joined by John Robinson, who had been driven likewise from his cure at Norwich. The two ministered to such as were willing to brave the penalties of the law in the house of William Brewster, who kept the post at that village.[2]

William Brewster, in early life, had attended the University of Cambridge. He had also served in the house of William Davidson, one of Elizabeth's principal advisers, a part of the time in company with George Cranmer, the intimate companion of Sir Edwin Sandys. Brewster's father had kept the post at Scrooby,[3] and thither the

[1] O. S. Davis's *John Robinson, the Pilgrim Pastor*, has some information not elsewhere conveniently accessible.

[2] As to Scrooby and Austerfield, see Henry M. Dexter's "Footprints of the Pilgrims" in *Sabbath at Home* and in Massachusetts Historical Society's *Proceedings* for 1871, 128, and Morton Dexter's *Story of the Pilgrims*.

[3] In 1603 James had suggested to the then Archbishop of York that he would like to acquire for the crown the manor of Scrooby, as it would be a convenient stopping place on the journeys to and from Sherwood Forest and Scotland; but nothing came of the project. See *Calendars of State Papers, Domestic, 1603–1610*, 33.

younger William repaired on his father's death, or shortly before. Scrooby was on the great northern road which was then the main line of travel between London and Edinburgh. As master of the post, it was Brewster's duty to provide horses and other essentials for the posting service. He also furnished refreshment and lodging to those belated travelers who could not push on to a larger town.[1] He lived in a house belonging to the Province of York, which Archbishop Sandys had granted on a lease of twenty-one years to his eldest son, Samuel Sandys. The relation of landlord and tenant, or, perhaps, of owner and bailiff, which existed between Sir Edwin Sandys's brother and the future Pilgrim elder proved to be of great service to the emigrants when the removal to America came to be agitated. At Leyden, Brewster pursued the trade of a printer. When he died at Plymouth in 1644, he left behind him a substantial collection of books. They numbered nearly four hundred titles, of which one quarter were printed after the sailing of the *Mayflower* — a fact which is interesting as showing us that at least one Pil-

[1] In 1605 Sir Timothy Hutton journeyed southward from York and made the following payments: —

	£	s.	d.
"Item, to the post of Scrobie ffor 11 myle, and the gyde 6*d*.	0	10	0
Item, to hym that kept the post horses, and for drising of bootes . .	0	0	6
Item, for a cawdall and supper, and breakfast	0	7	10
Item, ffor fyre	0	0	7
Item, to the chamberlain and the maid that burnt the boothowse . .	0	0	6
Item, to the powre	0	0	6"

On his return journey Sir Timothy made a shorter stop at Scrooby as his payments were only: —

	£	s.	d.
"The post of Scrobie for 7 myle, and for hymselfe	0	8	0
For burnt sack, bread, bear, and suger to wyne that was gyven . . .	0	2	0
The ostler 3*d*.; the powr 6*d*.	0	0	9"

Hunter, in his *Founders of New Plymouth*, 68, 69, first called attention to these entries in *The Correspondence of Dr. Matthew Hutton* (Surtees Society, 1843), 198, 203. See Massachusetts Historical Society's *Proceedings*, 1871, 100 note. For the general duties of "the post," see Joyce's *History of the Post Office*, and the documents printed in Arber's *Pilgrim Fathers* (p. 73) from the British Museum.

grim had funds wherewith to purchase something beyond the bare necessaries of life. Of Brewster's books, sixty-two were in Latin and ninety-two were devoted to secular subjects. Among them one notices a translation of Jean Bodin's *Six Bookes of a Commonweal*, Sir Thomas Smith's *Commonwealth of England*, Machiavelli's *Prince*, in Latin, and Ralegh's *Prerogative of Parliaments*.[1] William Brewster, therefore, was not only able to buy books, but clearly must have been able to have read good books with appreciation.

The most remarkable man who listened to Clifton and Robinson in Brewster's house at Scrooby was William Bradford, the son of a yeoman farmer of Austerfield. As a boy, Bradford showed precociousness; at the age of twelve he could read his Bible, which only about forty Englishmen in a hundred could then do at any time in their lives. Before his death he had familiarized himself with Hebrew, with Greek and Latin, with French and Dutch, without affecting an English style singularly pure, strong, and attractive. Besides being a scholar, Bradford was a born leader of men; he had great common sense and an extraordinary capacity for bringing difficult business transactions to prosperous endings. The key to his success lay in the fact that in his own character he realized the sense of his declaration that "all great undertakings must be both enterprised and overcome by answerable courages."

Fleeing from England, the fugitives from Scrooby and Austerfield first found shelter at Amsterdam. That city swarmed with religious refugees of all sorts and conditions of men and women. These filled their time with conten-

[1] See Henry M. Dexter's "Elder Brewster's Library," in the Massachusetts Historical Society's *Proceedings*, Second Series, v, 37; and see also *ibid.*, iii, 260.

tion, even to disputes as to whether or not the parson's wife should wear whalebone in her bodice. It was no place for clear-headed men like Robinson, Brewster, and Bradford. So they removed to Leyden, where there already was a church of Scottish Presbyterians. Robinson's reputation soon attracted to him many of the best of the religious exiles from England. The Leyden church became a strong congregation.

As the second decade of the seventeenth century drew toward its close, the Leyden people began to feel a new unrest. The reasons for their uneasiness are set forth by Bradford and Edward Winslow.[1] First in place, but probably not in importance, was the heartrending difficulty of making a living at Leyden. Bred to a plain country life and to the innocent trade of husbandry, the exiles were compelled to practice mechanic employments. They found it possible to keep body and soul together only by severe toil, and by compelling their children to labor until "the vigor of nature being consumed in the bud" their bodies bowed under the burdens and became decrepit in youth. The hardness of the place was so great that some of the exiles could not endure the life. These returned to England, where they lived in danger of conscience and some "preferred and chose the prisons in England rather than this liberty in Holland with these afflictions."

Moreover, the times were stormy in the Netherlands, for the people of that little country were divided into hostile factions by religious differences. A minority held

[1] The reasons for the removal from Leyden are stated by Bradford in his *Plymouth Plantation*, and by Winslow in the "Briefe Narration of the True Grounds or cause of the first Planting of New England," which is appended to his *Hypocrisie Unmasked* and is reprinted separately in Young's *Chronicles of the Pilgrims*. Arber brings the original material together in his *Pilgrim Fathers*.

to the belief of Arminius that all men could attain salvation through repentance. The majority held to the strict Calvinistic idea of predestination. This conflict led to the death of John of Barneveld, to the exile of Hugo Grotius, and to the holding of the Synod at Dort. This body pronounced the Arminians to be innovators and disturbers of religion in the Church and nation, teachers of faction, and workers of schism; as such they were deprived of their offices in Church and university until they should repent. Their leaders were banished under pain of death in case of return. This outcome occurred after Brewster and Bradford and their comrades had made up their minds to a second removal; but the constant disputations and threatenings of internecine conflicts may well have alarmed the peace-loving Pilgrims, although they were in theological sympathy with the victorious party. The renewal of the war with Spain was also imminent as the Twelve Years' Truce would come to an end in 1621, and the opening scenes of the Thirty Years' War were already being enacted not so very far away. Already many of the children of the exiles had become soldiers and sailors. The young people were intermarrying with the Dutch, and, in this way, were fast losing their language and their English manners and modes of thought and action. All the time the parents stood helplessly by, for in their poverty they could not educate their children, even as imperfectly as they themselves had been educated. In another land and in other circumstances their condition might be greatly bettered; it could hardly be made worse.[1]

[1] As early as 1593, or 1594, Separatists had contemplated a removal to the New World. See petition for leave to emigrate to the "Bay of Canyda," where the petitioners state they might worship God according to their consciences, do Her Majesty and their country good service, and greatly annoy the bloody and persecuting Spaniards about the Bay of Mexico, *Calendars of State Papers, Domestic, Elizabeth*, iii, 400; *Acts of the Privy Council*, xxvii, 5, xxviii, 153.

As they thought the matter over and talked about it among themselves, the missionary zeal which is always strong in the hearts of English people made them think that they might advance the kingdom of Christ by founding churches and a Christian state in the New World, and be as stepping-stones to others, and also might convert the natives to the true faith. Above all, however, their one great desire was to get back once more to English dominions, that they might die as they had been born — subjects of the English crown. To do this, they were willing to brave many dangers and hardships.

The objections to the enterprise, indeed, seemed to be great; new climate, new food, new beverages, new diseases which would infest their bodies with sore sicknesses. Furthermore, to their imagination, the savages appeared as cruel, barbarous men who delighted to torment their captives and to eat broiled collops of their flesh before their victims' eyes. But to these objections it was answered that, while many of these misfortunes were likely, they were not certain. Some of them might never befall, others could be patiently borne and overcome. The savages could not be more cruel than the Spaniards were certain to be if they reconquered the Dutch. For these reasons many of Robinson's congregation determined to make a second removal, this time to America.

Having come to this conclusion, there followed long and intricate negotiations with the Dutch authorities, the Virginia Company, certain London merchants, and the English government. At the present day, after an enormous amount of study has been given to the problem, the course of these negotiations is still involved in uncertainty. One thing, however, seems to be clear, the dealings with the Dutch had no serious basis, since one of the reasons for the emigration of the Pilgrims was to escape from the Dutch influence; under these circumstances it is improbable that they would have crossed the Atlantic to settle in New Netherland. Their attention was directed toward Virginia — partly by the fact that Sir Edwin Sandys[1] was now supreme in the Virginia Company and was able to procure for them a grant of land at such a distance from Jamestown that they would be able "to live as a distinct body by themselves under the general government of Virginia." They tried to gain some guarantee of liberty in religion from the king and the Church authorities; but they could not obtain such a concession, although they offered to take the Oath of Supremacy. Nevertheless, James was understood to say that he would not disturb them, if they lived peaceably. This verbal assurance seemed to some of them to be but a sandy foundation. The leaders, however, decided to go on; they reasoned that, if there was no security in the king's spoken word, there would be little safety in a written confirmation of it, "for if afterwards there should be a purpose, or desire to wrong them, though they had a seal as broad as the house floor it would not serve the turn; for there would be means enough found to recall or reverse it." Having come to this determination, the next thing to do was to procure the necessary funds, and this proved to be a difficult task. Finally, they entered into negotiations with Mr. Thomas Weston, who may possibly have been an emissary of the Council for New England.

Since the disastrous ending of the attempted coloniza-

[1] There is no reason to question Sandys's kindness toward the Pilgrims; but his intimacy with Brewster is largely conjectural. See, however, Alexander Brown's *First Republic in America* and William Elliot Griffis's *The Pilgrims in their Three Homes*.

tion at Fort St. George at the mouth of the Kennebec River in 1608, little had been attempted toward English colonization in the North. English fishermen frequented the banks off Newfoundland and the coasts of New England, once in a while a fur trader visited the harbors and dealt with the natives of that region, and occasionally an exploring vessel sailed along the northern shores. The best known of these last expeditions was that of Captain John Smith, in 1614, when he explored the coasts of what are now the states of Maine, New Hampshire, and Massachusetts and assigned to many prominent points the names which they still bear. Sir Ferdinando Gorges had been the most persistent of the old partners under the charter of 1606. The outburst of colonizing fervor that marks the last years of James's reign stirred him to renewed activity. He obtained for himself and his associates a grant of North America between the fortieth and the forty-eighth degree of north latitude, under the name of New England (1620). The governing body of this corporation was known as the Council for New England.[1] Among the members who are enumerated in the charter are several whose names have already been mentioned in tracing the history of Virginia, the Earl of Southampton, the Earl of Warwick, Sir Dudley Digges, Sir Thomas Gates, Sir Nathaniel Rich, and Sir Thomas Wroth; among those

[1] The history of this corporation has been admirably summarized by Charles Deane in the third volume of Winsor's *America*. The records, such of them as have been preserved, are in American Antiquarian Society's *Proceedings* for April, 1867, and October, 1875. Some additional information is in *American Historical Review*, iv, 678. From the printed records, Sir Ferdinando Gorges and Sir Samuel Argall seem to have been the most active members of the corporation; but we have only a small fragment of the records. See also *Commons Journals*, i, 884, 898, 904; and Royal Historical Manuscripts Commission's *Reports*, iii, 21, iv, 123. The records of fifty-six meetings are known, all of which were held in London. Two persons only attended seven meetings; there were three and no more at fourteen; the largest number in attendance at any one meeting was eight. Gorges attended fifty-three of the fifty-six, Argall twenty-seven, Mason eleven, Warwick ten, and Calvert one.

who joined it later were Sir Samuel Argall and Sir George Calvert.

The charter gave to the grantees what amounted to a monopoly, so far as Englishmen were concerned, of the fisheries of New England. For this reason a great outcry was raised by the Virginia Company and the subject was brought up in the House of Commons by Sir Edwin Sandys.[1] To the arguments which he and his friends advanced, Sir George Calvert, who was then Secretary of State, replied with the technical assertion that Virginia, New England, and Newfoundland were gotten by conquest, were governed by prerogative alone, and were, therefore, not subject to the legislation of Parliament.[2] In the end the matter was arranged between the two corporations; but Gorges asserts that the conflict frightened away capital from the new scheme.[3] With this great enterprise in mind, it may well be that Sir Ferdinando looked with eager eyes on the proposed Pilgrim migration. It is possible that Weston was his agent and that between them Captain Jones of the *Mayflower* was induced to take the Pilgrims to the coast of New England instead of that of Virginia. It works out into a pretty plot; but there is no evidence that Weston was unfaithful or that Jones was bribed. It is certain, however, that Gorges was well pleased to find the Pilgrims settled within the limits of New England.

[1] *Debates of 1620–21*, ii, 97.

[2] It was extremely fortunate that James took this position and carried his point, as the monarchy was too weak to enforce what successive kings regarded as their rights. This lack of strength gave the colonies time to grow and to develop their institutions in a direction quite opposed to royal desires. When Parliament began to exercise power which constitutionally belonged to it, rebellion and revolution resulted.

On the opposition side in the Commons it was pointed out that Parliament had legislated for Ireland before that country had been annexed to the crown, and cited an act of 11 Henry VII. Cf. *Debates of 1620–21*, i, 318–319.

[3] See Massachusetts Historical Society's *Collections*, Third Series, vi, 71, and Baxter's *Gorges*, ii, 44.

Every step in the migration from Leyden to America was full of trouble. The money was hard to get and, finally, could only be obtained on terms similar to those which had held for some years in the colonization of Virginia. The basis of the arrangement[1] was the cost of transporting one emigrant to America. This was assumed to be ten pounds, and the shares in the enterprise were given a par value of that amount. Each emigrant was rated as holding one share and each ten pounds put into the common stock was also rated as one share. For seven years the colonists were to be fed and clothed out of the common stock; for seven years the product of their labors should go to the common stock. At the end of that time there was to be a division of all the property of the association, each member, whether colonist or capitalist, receiving according to the number of his shares. Thus a colonist whose transportation was paid out of the common stock would be entitled to one share, but if he paid his own passage he would have two shares; a merchant investing one hundred pounds would have ten shares at the division. A planter would be entitled to the same number of shares provided he went in person with his wife and three children above the age of sixteen and paid the cost of transportation and provided also that all of them lived to the end of seven years. In the event of their death at an earlier time, the amount of their share would be reckoned according to the length of time they lived and labored in the colony.

To us this balancing of the life of William Bradford or

[1] The agreement is in Bradford's *Plymouth Plantation* (Deane's ed.), 45. The merchants tried to get the Pilgrims to sign a different agreement, to the effect that planters and adventurers should each take half of the common stock at the division; but they refused to do this until 1623, when the concession seemed to be the only way to avoid starvation.

Mary Chilton or Priscilla Mullins against the investment of ten pounds by a London merchant seems preposterous and even scandalous. Yet it was under this arrangement, or something similar to it, that the founders of the United States entered upon their life in the New World. In Virginia, the share was rated at twelve pounds, ten shillings; the diminished rate of the Pilgrim enterprise probably represents the lower cost at which a colonist could be landed on American soil in 1620 compared with 1609. It is certain that the supply of money seeking investment in colonial enterprises was not sufficient to pay the transportation across the Atlantic of all who wished to emigrate. As the world goes, therefore, the arrangement must be regarded as fair to both parties. The Leyden colonists had hoped for better terms and had understood that the capitalists would grant them. They had expected to have one day in the week for themselves and to retain their houses and home lots at the division. They were grievously disappointed when they found that this could not be; but they had gone too far to draw back.

A small vessel of sixty tons was bought to convey those of the Leyden congregation who proposed to emigrate to Southampton, where the *Mayflower*, a ship of thrice her size, was fitting out for Virginia. It was expected that the smaller vessel would cross the Atlantic with as many passengers and as much freight as she could carry and would remain in American waters to serve for fishing and trading. She leaked so badly, however, that she had to be left behind. Alone, the *Mayflower* crossed the Atlantic in the autumn of 1620. How many of this first band of Pilgrims came from Leyden is uncertain. A large proportion of Robinson's congregation never came to

America; those who did emigrate came at three separate times, the last being 1629. Only thirty-five of the *Mayflower's* passengers have been identified as belonging to the Leyden Company, and of these less than a dozen came from Scrooby and Austerfield.[1] Among those who did not belong to the Scrooby congregation, but who joined the Robinson people at Leyden, was Edward Winslow, a man of ability, then some twenty-five years of age.[2] Another recruit was Miles Standish, a professional soldier. Of those who came from England and had no part in the life in Holland was William Mullins[3] of Dorking, the father of Priscilla, and John Alden, who was hired as a cooper at Southampton. Others, whom it is difficult to identify with exactness, were servants who were sent out by the merchants to labor in their behalf. There were also two sailors who were engaged to remain in the colony for one year.

The *Mayflower* finally set sail from Plymouth, England, on September 6, 1620. Since the 21st of the preceding July, those of her company who came from Leyden had been on shipboard. This long delay was owing in part to the misadventures of the smaller vessel; but it also seems to have been due in some measure to the bad management of the enterprise. It certainly was unfortunate that the departure was postponed to so late a period in the year. The voyage of the *Mayflower* across the North

[1] See Morton Dexter in Massachusetts Historical Society's *Proceedings* for April, 1903, 167. Earlier and less complete enumerations are H. C. Murphy's articles in the *Historical Magazine*, iii, 261, 330, 357, and George Sumner's *Memoirs of the Pilgrims at Leyden*.

[2] There is no adequate life of Edward Winslow, owing probably to the fact that his greatest services were performed in England as agent for Massachusetts. He left New England in 1650, never to return, and died at sea while in the employ of the Protectorate.

[3] At one time it was argued that he was a Walloon and that his name was Molines. Cf. H. M. Dexter in Massachusetts Historical Society's *Proceedings*, Second Series, v, 37.

Atlantic has been told over and over again — never so effectively as by William Bradford. Even Pilgrims were not free from seasickness, — to the unsettling of the temper of one lusty able seaman, who cursed them roundly and said that he hoped to cast half of them overboard before the journey's end. It happened otherwise, for his dead body was the first to be thrown from the ship — "and it was an astonishment to all his fellows," says Bradford, "for they noted it to be the just hand of God upon them." The autumn gales which sweep the Western Ocean spared not this historic ship and her heroic band. One of them died on the way; but his place on the list was made good by the birth of a son to Master Hopkins, who was appropriately christened "Oceanus."

On November 11, 1620, a low, sandy shore greeted their eyes. It was the coast of Cape Cod and not that of the Delaware region, to which they were bound. The ship's course, therefore, was laid to the southward; but half a day's sailing brought her amongst the dangerous shoals which lie between the southern shore of Cape Cod and the island of Nantucket. The roaring of the breakers on the tide-rips and the failing wind caused the Pilgrims to retrace their course. The next day they entered Provincetown harbor and fell on their knees and blessed God for their escape from the dangerous shoals. And well they may have rejoiced. Even now, with buoys, lightships in the sea, and lighthouses on land, and steam to propel the vessel against tide and wind, the passage of Nantucket Shoals is not to be lightly undertaken by a novice in its navigation.[1]

[1] One of the most attractive allurements to divert the student of history from the narrow path of fact is the inquiry as to what might have happened had the facts been otherwise than as they were. For instance, an English writer, Mr. J. A. Doyle, informs us that "if the Plymouth settlement had never been

Landing on the shore of what is now Provincetown harbor, the Pilgrims first set foot on American soil. The neighborhood, however, did not seem to them to be a good site for a settlement. For a month and more they explored the near-by land and the coasts farther off. At length, on the sixth day of December, 1620, some ten of the Pilgrims with a party of seamen set off in a large sailboat or shallop which they had brought with them for service on the coast. It was a bitter day when they started, and the spray froze on their coats as they voyaged along. Tracing the inner shore of Cape Cod, they explored every likely spot and beat off the natives who attacked them. Friday, December 8, found them off the high land of Manomet. As they sailed northward in the growing darkness of that December afternoon, the weather grew worse with increasing wind and flurries of snow, and the sea grew constantly rougher. They were steering for Plymouth harbor, which had been so named on the map published by Captain John Smith, six years before. Suddenly the mast went overboard, broken in three pieces. They then took to the oars and by great good fortune and a strong flood tide were swept into the harbor, where they anchored under the shelter of an island which later they named Clark's Island in honor of the mate of their ship. The next day was fair with bright sunshine; they employed themselves in repairing damages as well as they could, and on Sunday they rested. On Monday morning, December 11, Old Style, or December 21, New Style, they were up betimes. The tide was high

made, the political life of New England would in all probability have taken the same form and run the same course as it did" (*Puritan Colonies*, English edition, i, 61). On the other hand, it may well be questioned if the Nonconformists would ever have emigrated had not the Pilgrim experiment been made and in a measure succeeded. But speculations of this kind have little profit except to those who enjoy controversy.

on that morning at about nine o'clock. Taking advantage of this, they sounded the harbor and found it fit for shipping[1] and also went ashore and found divers cornfields and little running brooks. The place seemed to them "very good for situation," so they returned to their ship, which was still lying at anchor in the harbor at the end of Cape Cod. On December 16, Old Style (26, New Style), 1620, a fortunate turn of the wind enabled the *Mayflower* to sail across the bay and anchor in Plymouth harbor. After several days spent in viewing the eligible sites on the mainland, they decided to make their settlement at the place where the town of Plymouth now stands. They had no sooner reached this conclusion than the weather became stormy and wet, and so continued for some days.

Bradford nowhere gives us the name of the ship which brought him to New England. To him and his companions the *Mayflower* must have seemed a woe-laden bark indeed. Of her passengers, one died before the shores of the New World rose above the horizon. Four more passed away while she lay in the harbor at the end of Cape Cod, and her anchor had not been at the bottom of Plymouth harbor many days before another death occurred. Then came death upon the Pilgrims so heavily that they forebore all work and devoted themselves to nursing the sick and the dying on the ship and in the rude hut which they had built on the land. Sometimes two or three of their small number died in a day and in the time of their greatest distress, but six or seven remained in sufficient health to care for the rest. When the *Mayflower* set sail

[1] So the Pilgrims wrote; but the *United States Coast Pilot* warns modern mariners against the dangers of ice in and about Plymouth harbor in the winter season.

for home in April, 1621, scarce fifty were alive. Of the dead, none more deserve remembrance than the wives and mothers who spent their strength for their husbands and children. Eighteen married women graced the *Mayflower's* decks when her anchor went down in Cape Cod harbor; when the first summer greeted the Pilgrims at Plymouth, but four of them were alive. It is the heroism of this pathetic tragedy that gives the Pilgrim story, as typified by Plymouth Rock, its place in our annals; for, truthfully, it may be said that the *Mayflower* brought to American shores that undefinable moral quality which is sometimes called the "New England conscience."

Before leaving England the Pilgrim leaders had secured a patent from the Virginia Company, authorizing them to settle within the limits of Virginia and conferring upon them a large measure of self-government. This document was inoperative outside of Virginia. It became necessary, therefore, to make other arrangements, especially as several of their number being "not well affected to unity and concord . . . gave some appearance of faction." For this reason, a compact or association was drawn up on November 11, 1620, or it may be that articles of association which had already been formulated were made over to suit the altered circumstances. The original list of the signers of this compact has long since disappeared, but Nathaniel Morton, writing in 1669, gives forty-one names as appended to the agreement. The Mayflower Compact, to give this document its popular name, was in the general form of a Separatist church covenant. In the beginning and again in the ending is an acknowledgment of allegiance to the king of England. This was natural, for it was to place themselves within the scope of English laws and customs that the leaders had left their old homes in

Leyden. In the body of the Compact, the signers promise all due submission and obedience to "such just and equal laws, ordinances, acts, constitutions, and offices from time to time, as shall be thought most meet and convenient for the general good of the colony."[1] This Compact was not in any way the constitution of an independent state, as has sometimes been said. It was, indeed, precisely the opposite, — an agreement made by Englishmen who, finding themselves on English soil without any specified powers of government, agreed to govern themselves until the king's pleasure should be signified. There was not the slightest thought of independence, and the government thus instituted was legal as between the signers under the Common Law. How far the Compact gave its signers a legal right to govern other English subjects may well be doubted; but as to the advisability of the small minority of the *Mayflower* band obeying the behests of the officers appointed under it, there could be no question.

John Carver was the first governor. On his death in April, 1621, William Bradford was chosen in his place, and was annually reëlected until his death in 1657, with the exception of five years, when he absolutely refused to serve. As the colony grew in size assistants were appointed to relieve him of some of the care and responsibility. In 1621, the Council for New England conferred upon the men of Plymouth rights of jurisdiction; but as this document had no legal force, the government of Plymouth throughout its history as a separate colony rested upon the memorable Mayflower Compact. The

[1] See Mourt's *Relation* (Dexter's edition), 6. The Compact is also in Bradford's *Plymouth Plantation*, and in nearly every secondary work on Plymouth or New England.

signers of the Compact became the first voters of the colony exercising their rights in a general meeting. They were practically all the adult male passengers of the *Mayflower* excepting two seamen who were engaged to stay in the country for one year and one or two servants. As the years rolled by, the franchise became more restricted, until finally it resembled the system which prevailed in the neighboring colony of Massachusetts Bay.[1]

In the early years of the Pilgrim settlement, there was almost unintermitted hunger. The seas off the coast teemed with cod and other food fishes, while the forests at their back sheltered wild beasts and game of various sorts. The shores of their harbor contained shellfish, and the beds of the rivers and brooks were alive with eels. Yet, in the midst of this plenty, the Pilgrims looked to agriculture for their supply of food, and when that failed, they experienced keen distress. The reason for this is not far to seek; in those days, middle-class Englishmen knew little of sport. In England and in Holland, not one of them probably had ever gone in pursuit of a wild animal, and few, if any, had ever caught a fish. The first plan of the colony probably included fishing for the English market as a part of the enterprise, but this fishery presumably would have been carried on by the hired crew of the smaller ship which was left behind. At all events, when the Pilgrims went afishing in America, they found that their hooks were too large for the shore fish. They seldom pursued the animals in the wilderness, or the wild fowl along the shore. From time to time they eked out their scanty fare with clams and

[1] In 1638–39 a representative system had been established; it was closely modeled on that which had already been organized in Massachusetts. Cf. below, p. 346, and *Plymouth Colony Records*, xi, 31.

eels — the former they dug from the mud, the latter they trod out by their feet.[1]

Agriculture at Plymouth was long retarded by the vicious system under which the colony was founded. It will be recalled that for seven years there was to be no private ownership of land and no reward for the industrious colonist. During that time, whatever was produced went into the common stock and during that time also every one was to be fed and clothed from the common stock, regardless of his capacity or industry. The Pilgrims' experience in this "common course and condition," as Bradford terms it, clearly evinced to that great administrator's mind "the vanity of that conceit of Plato and other ancients . . . that the taking away of property and bringing in community into a commonwealth would make them happy and flourishing as if they were wiser than God." For it was found to retard employment and to breed discontent among the colonists. The younger men grew restive when they saw the fruits of their strength and activity being used for the support of other men's families, while the able men thought it injustice that they should have no more food and clothing than those who could not produce one quarter as much as they did. The aged and graver men considered it an indignity to be ranked with the younger and meaner sort; "and for men's wives to be commanded to do service for other men, as dressing their meat, washing their clothes, etc., they deemed it a kind of slavery, neither could many husbands well brook it."[2]

The picture which arises in one's mind of the life at

[1] On this general subject, see an interesting article by E. H. Goss on "The Hungry Pilgrims" in *Magazine of American History*, xiii, 477–480.

[2] Bradford's *Plymouth Plantation* (Deane's edition), 135.

Plymouth in the early days is interesting. One can imagine Governor Carver, and, after his death, Governor Bradford, summoning the men and grown-up boys about him, and going to the field to prepare the soil or care for the growing corn. Probably the world has never seen a more disinterested and law-abiding set of men than those who followed Bradford in the summer of 1621; there were not two black sheep among them, but, with all his care, they could not grow food enough to fill the hungry mouths in the settlement. This was not because they had to clear the land, for they had happened upon abandoned Indian cornfields; it was not that they planted the wrong thing or planted it in the wrong way, for the Indians showed them how to grow Indian corn, and the seed they had taken from an Indian storehouse for which they compensated the natives. The cause of their distress was almost entirely that "common course and condition"[1] of which Bradford speaks so contemptuously. At length their exigencies became so pressing that it was absolutely necessary to make other arrangements unless the settlement were to be abandoned, and the whole amount of human lives and suffering as well as money of their friends in England be absolutely unproductive. In 1623, therefore, a parcel of land was assigned to each family for present use only. This had good success as it made all hands exceedingly industrious. Now the women went willingly into the fields and took their little ones with them to help set the corn, "whom to have compelled would have been thought great tyranny." At one time

[1] It is a mistake to call this "communism," as that word has a very different connotation from the system which prevailed at Plymouth or at Jamestown. These were joint-stock enterprises, limited in point of time; communism is a scheme for equalizing the social conditions of life. Doyle (*Puritan Colonies*, English edition, i, 72), however, refers to the Plymouth system as communism.

it seemed as if even this expedient would be of no avail. For the dry summer and the hot sun caused the corn to wither and turn brown. In this time of awful expectation, they set apart a day of humiliation "to seek the Lord by humble and fervent prayer." The answer was a soaking rain which caused the corn to revive, and in the end there was a liberal harvest — "for which mercy (in time convenient) they also set apart a day of thanksgiving."[1]

In the summer of 1623, before the harvest was gathered, two vessels, the *Anne* and the *Little James*, came into the harbor. They brought more than sixty passengers, among whom were the wives and children of some of those who were already in the colony. The desolateness of the settlement and the poverty of the settlers daunted and dismayed the newcomers. The colonists were ragged, some were almost half naked; they had nothing better to give their friends than a lobster, or a piece of fish without any bread, and only a cup of fair spring water to wash it down.[2] But the scanty fare, such as it was, throve with the settlers, for there was not a case of sickness in the colony.

It is easy to cast blame on Bradford and the other principal men at Plymouth for modifying the agreement with the London merchants and to say that what they did was to break their contract. In reality, they did the only thing which could have been done to save the enterprise from failure. Bradford must be regarded as the managing partner on the spot and, as such, clothed with a measure of discretion. In the end what saved the Pilgrim colony from extinction and gave the settlers a chance to repay the London merchants for their advances was a well-managed

[1] Bradford's *Plymouth Plantation* (Deane's edition), 96, 142 note.

[2] There is a most interesting letter from Bradford and Isaac Allerton describing the condition of the colony at this time in *American Historical Review*, viii, 294.

fur trade along the coast to the eastward and also to the southward.

When the Pilgrims decided upon the Plymouth hillsides as the site of their new homes they chanced upon a spot from which the natives had been swept by mortal disease, to use the picturesque phrase of Cotton Mather, "the woods had been cleared of those pernicious creatures to make room for a sounder growth." The plague, as the early colonists called it, or the smallpox, as one medically trained historian of the present diagnoses it,[1] or perchance measles, had sent the Indians to a happy hunting ground with the exception of one only, Squanto or Tisquantum by name. He was brought to the settlement by a more forward savage named Samoset, who had lived for some time with Englishmen. The Pilgrims took Tisquantum into their settlement and cared for him tenderly, according to their lights. He gave them in return many useful lessons, without which they would probably have starved; he also acted as guide and interpreter. In the spring of 1621 appeared a royal visitor, Massasoit, war chief of the Wampanoags, who lived at some distance from Plymouth — to the southward. Him the Pilgrims received as best they might with *aqua vitæ*, of which "he drank a great draught that made him sweat all the while after." "They then," so Winslow tells us, "treated of peace," and it was agreed that neither the red men nor the white should injure the other, and if any offense should be committed the offender should be punished. This treaty was in reality a defensive alliance, the Pilgrims assuring Massasoit that if he kept his word, King James would esteem him

[1] See S. A. Green's "Centennial Address" before the Massachusetts Medical Society, p. 12. Hutchinson (*History of Massachusetts*, i, 34 note) is authority for the tradition that the "bubonic plague" was the disease. He states that the smallpox swept off large numbers of the natives in 1633.

as a friend and ally, — the agreement in all its parts was kept by both white men and red men for more than half a century,[1] until Massasoit and Bradford and Winslow had long been in their graves. Winslow's description of the natives is interesting; the chieftain's face, he tells us, was painted a sad red-like murrey with his head and face so carefully oiled "that he looked greasily." His followers also were painted as to their faces, some black, some red, some yellow, and some white, with crosses and curious devices. The alliance with this important tribe of Indians was cemented, not long afterward, by Winslow's bringing Massasoit back to life from a state of coma. Assured of the aid of these Indians, there was little danger of trouble with the natives living to the south and east of Plymouth; but with those living to the north and to the west, matters did not proceed so smoothly.

While these events were transacting at Plymouth, the Council for New England had been granting land in the New World with a lavish hand. Among other grants was one to Thomas Weston, who had negotiated the agreement with the Pilgrims. In 1622 he sent out a colony to the shores of what is now called Boston harbor, but which in those days was known as Massachusetts Bay. There, on the southern side of the harbor or bay in what is now the town of Weymouth, his men built a few huts and began to trade with the Indians. Weston had been grievously disappointed at the outcome of the Plymouth settlement, which, for the first three years, was a losing venture to all concerned. To his colony, therefore, there came no women, old persons, or children, but only strong lusty men. Starvation, nevertheless, early befell them. They begged from

[1] See, for example, entries in the "Court Records" under date of 1641 in *Plymouth Colony Records*, ii, 20, etc.

the Indians, they stole from the Indians; they made themselves such a nuisance that the natives decided to kill them. To make a clean job of it, these Indians tried to stir up the savages along the coast to do away with the Plymouth people also. It turned out otherwise than the natives had expected, for the Weston colonists were forewarned and sent one of their number, through the snows which blocked the wilderness in the early spring, to Plymouth. This appeal for aid the Pilgrims at once answered, for the lives of Englishmen were at stake. Captain Miles Standish, with such men as could be spared, sailed in the shallop for Massachusetts Bay. Arriving at the settlement, he found everything in confusion; the men scattered about, some of them even living with the Indians. His first work was to collect the scattered colonists and get them to a place of safety. Then he turned on the Indians and did his work so thoroughly that ten years later, when the natives found a wandering white man in the wilderness, half crazed with starvation and hardships, they surrounded him and sent to Plymouth to ask Governor Bradford as to what they should do. As for Weston's men, they were removed to Plymouth whence most of them returned to England.

The next colony to come to the shore of Massachusetts Bay was led by Robert Gorges, son of the persistent Sir Ferdinando. The younger Gorges had with him several men of means and ability and also two clergymen, one a Church-of-England man, William Morrell, who was to act as religious superintendent of New England; the other of doubtful religious views whose name was variously spelled from Blaxtun to Blackstone. In place of settling on the northwest corner of Massachusetts Bay, or Boston harbor, where his patent was, Robert Gorges found shelter in the abandoned huts at Wessagusset (1623). The history of this attempt is a story of misfortune. Sir Ferdinando Gorges, in sending out this colony, had undertaken an enterprise beyond his financial ability. At all events it was soon given up, although some of his men remained. In 1628 there were eight plantations along the New England coast, stretching from Dover and Portsmouth on the north, southward to Plymouth. Of these Plymouth and Portsmouth were the largest. A few of the Gorges' colonists who remained on the shores of Massachusetts Bay were men of substance for the most part. The most picturesque of these early settlers was Thomas Morton; whose career will be treated in a later chapter. All these were forerunners of the Great Emigration to Massachusetts, which was the most successful colonizing enterprise of the first half of the seventeenth century.

NOTES

I. Bibliography. — The sources of early Plymouth history are William Bradford's *History of Plymouth Plantation*, the earlier account which Bradford and Winslow wrote at the time and sent to England by the returning *Mayflower* (this is usually called "Mourt's Relation," from the name signed to the prefatory note), the *Plymouth Colony Records*, and a few shorter pieces by Winslow, Bradford, and others. Of these "Mourt's Relation," being written at the time by the actors themselves, is of the first authority for the events that it relates. Bradford (*Plymouth Plantation*, Deane's ed., p. 6) tells us that he began his great work in 1630, — years after the most interesting events in the Pilgrim story had become matters of history. Furthermore, it should be remembered that Bradford, who was born in 1589, was not one of the leaders in the migration from England; his knowledge of the motives which actuated the leaders of that time must have been gathered from conversation and then written down from memory years later. Winslow's *Hypocrisy Unmasked* was written after 1640. Under these circumstances it is truly unfortunate that the early leaves of the Plymouth records are, for the most part, illegible or destroyed.

For three quarters of a century the manuscript of Bradford's great work was lost to sight. Portions of it were known through extracts which had been made before its disappearance. It was found in 1855 in the muniment room of the Bishop of London at Fulham. A transcript was procured by Mr. Charles Deane, and under his editorship was printed as a volume of the *Collections* of the Massachusetts Historical Society.[1] The manuscript has recently come into the possession of the state of Massachusetts and may now be inspected at the State House at Boston. A facsimile edition has been printed by an English publishing firm and a verbatim edition has been published by the state of Massachusetts; but Deane's edition is the most useful for the student.

Morton Dexter's *Story of the Pilgrims* was written for young people, but it is the best account of the settlement of Plymouth yet

[1] See Winsor's paper in Massachusetts Historical Society's *Proceedings*, xix, 106, and Deane's own account of the finding in *ibid.*, April, 1855, vol. iii, p. 19. The circumstances under which the manuscript returned to America are recounted in G. F. Hoar's *Return of the Manuscript of Bradford's History*.

printed. Arber's *Story of the Pilgrim Fathers* is made up of excerpts from the leading Pilgrim sources, with some comment by the editor. John Brown's *Pilgrim Fathers of New England* is an interesting book from an English pen. The account of the Plymouth settlement in Doyle's *Puritan Colonies* is an appreciative and discriminating treatment of this part of the subject. Probably the best statement in brief compass is Franklin B. Dexter's chapter in Winsor's *America*, iii. The accompanying notes give ample bibliographical detail.

II. The "Mayflower." — The hawthorn (*Cratœgus oxyacantha*) is one of the commonest and thorniest shrubs to be seen in England, where it is extensively used for hedges. Its flower is called "the may," or sometimes "mayflower." The latter was a favorite name for ships. For instance, a *Mayflower* belonging to King's Lynn served against the Spanish Armada in 1588. In 1600 a committee of those interested in a voyage to the East Indies viewed several vessels, among others a *May Flower*, and in 1659 a *May Flower* belonging to the East India Company foundered in the Bay of Bengal. A *Mayflower* also brought passengers to Massachusetts in 1630. With the propensity to attach to known objects information as to things which are not known, it has been suggested that these references, excepting the first of them, relate to the ship which brought the first settlers to Plymouth; but this is pure conjecture. The entries as to the East India Company's ship are in Henry Stevens's *Dawn of British Trade to the East Indies*, pp. xi and 13. The *Mayflower* is nowhere mentioned by name by Bradford or Winslow. There can be no doubt but that the ship of 1620 bore that name, because, in the list of vessels and passengers going to Virginia in 1620, the *Mayflower* is mentioned with about the number of passengers that the Pilgrim ship carried, and her return is noted at about the time the Pilgrim ship probably reached England. Moreover, in the allotment of land at Plymouth, the assignments were made according to the date of the recipient's arrival, and this was stated by grouping them under the names of the three vessels which brought colonists to Plymouth in the early years. We know when the other ships arrived, and therefore the unplaced ship must have been the bearer of the first Pilgrims, and her name is given as the *May Flouer*. Those who are grouped under this name are also known to be the survivors of the 1620 voyage. Putting these facts together there can be no reason to doubt that the name of the famous

Pilgrim ship was *Mayflower.* See Manchester Papers in Royal Historical Manuscripts Commission's *Reports,* viii, pt. ii, p. 37. The same entry is given in Brown's *First Republic.* The land records are in *Plymouth Colony Records,* xii, 4, in Hazard's *State Papers,* i, 100, and in Arber's *Pilgrim Fathers,* 382. R. G. Marsden, in *English Historical Review,* xix, 669, gives details of many *Mayflowers* and shows with some degree of probability that the captain of the Pilgrim ship was Christopher Jones instead of Thomas Jones, as has been supposed, in which case all arguments based on the supposed bad character of the latter would fall to the ground.

III. The Landing on Plymouth Rock.—It is difficult to treat a subject like this historically, because the matter is one of sentiment rather than of fact. We rightly celebrate the coming to America of the ideals typified in some of the Pilgrims. Harking back to the characteristics of our remote ancestors, like them we associate events with trees and with stones. It is to be hoped that Plymouth Rock may long continue to form the theme of annual after-dinner discourses, and of more formidable set orations. From the historian's workshop, however, the outlook is necessarily somewhat different. He sees that there never was a "landing" on Plymouth Rock or elsewhere, as described in oration or shown in painting and engraving. Pilgrim foot first pressed the soil of the New World on the shores of Provincetown harbor. The Pilgrims first went on shore on the mainland inside of Plymouth harbor, on December 11–21, 1620, having three days previously entered the harbor, and having for two days been encamped on Clark's Island. The *Mayflower* was then at anchor at the end of Cape Cod, twenty-five miles or more away, and did not reach Plymouth harbor until December 16–26. During the winter she served as refuge and hospital, and it was not until the end of March, 1621, that the last of her passengers left her for the shore. On the day (December 12–22, 1620) we commemorate as "forefathers' day," we have absolutely no knowledge of the doings of the forefathers. The mistake as to date arose in transferring old-style dates to those of modern times and is entirely excusable. The tradition of Plymouth Rock being used as a landing place goes back to Elder Faunce who, in 1741, at the age of ninety-one, undertook to repeat what he had heard years before from the original settlers. See Palfrey's *New England,* i, 171, note 3.

There is a considerable literature on this general theme. The passages in "Mourt's Relation" are easily found under the date.

The account in Bradford's *Plymouth Plantation* was written at least ten years after the event, and adds little to our knowledge. Of modern discussions may be noted brief articles by Professor Goodwin and the present writer in Massachusetts Historical Society's *Proceedings* for 1903. See also the *Nation* for July 20 and August 24, 1882, and *Magazine of American History*, vols. viii and ix.

CHAPTER XII

THE GREAT EMIGRATION

THE Massachusetts Bay Company owed its existence to a grant of land in America which had come from the crown through the Council for New England. It was in March, 1627–28, that Robert Rich, Earl of Warwick, acting as president of the Council for New England, signed a patent giving to John Endicott and five associates lands extending from the Atlantic to the Pacific between the parallels of two points situated respectively three miles south of the head of the Charles River and three miles north of the source of the Merrimac.[1] The plan of those who received the grant of this imperial area seems to have been to secure a profitable return from fishing in the ocean, trading in furs with the Indians, and such agriculture as might seem desirable. The plantations were to be cultivated largely by tenants and servants as was the case in Virginia at the moment. In the beginning, therefore, the scheme was designed to be a commercial venture. A year later, these associates and others, who had meantime joined them, procured from Charles I a confirmation of this grant with extensive rights of jurisdiction. The new corporation sent out expeditions to take possession of their domain. The representative on the New England coast was John Endicott, one of the original grantees. Up to this point, the enterprise does not seem to have been reli-

[1] Cf. S. A. Green's "Northern Boundary of Massachusetts" in American Antiquarian Society's *Proceedings*, vii, 11.

gious in any way.[1] The greater part of the associates were Nonconformists or Separatists, but some of them were conforming members of the Established Church. In the summer of 1629 a change took place in the control of the company which placed it in the hands of Nonconformists who were determined to seek new habitations and to found another Canaan on the western side of the Atlantic. To understand this movement aright, it will be necessary to glance briefly at some portions of the history of England in the years following 1625.

William Laud was now Bishop of London, but, owing to his influence with the king, he was the practical ruler of the Established Church, as well as chief minister in civil affairs. He was very active in the Star Chamber and in the High Commission and may be said to have dominated the Council. The closing of Parliament in March, 1629, and the imprisonment of Sir John Eliot which followed, gave plain warning to all who might oppose the government that no halfway measures would be pursued. It is one of the most serious mistakes which students of history make to regard William Laud, Oliver Cromwell, and John Winthrop as intolerant. Toleration had nothing to do with the problems which they were seeking to settle. Laud and Winthrop were believers in an ecclesiastical establishment in every state. Their craving for uniformity in religion was not peculiar to them. It was due, in part at least, to a consciousness that the only way to preserve the national religion from alien control was to maintain the state Church at the cost of the freedom of human thought, nay of humanity itself. They should be regarded in the light

[1] On the early history of the Massachusetts Bay Company, see an article by S. F. Haven in *Archæologia Americana* ("Transactions of the American Antiquarian Society"), iii, pp. ix–cxxxviii.

of combatants engaged in a life-and-death struggle for something which they thought was worth living and dying for. It is as reasonable to think of the Union soldier with arms in his hands tolerating an armed Confederate clothed in his garb of gray as it is to think of William Laud tolerating John Winthrop or of John Winthrop tolerating William Laud. In times of stern religious enthusiasm toleration has no place. It is when religion has a weak hold on a people that toleration prevails, — except sometimes when it is used as a cloak under which shelter may be found.[1]

Whether the considerations just mentioned are true or false, the case of Alexander Leighton was full of meaning to those who disagreed with William Laud. Leighton was a stiff-necked Scot, a graduate of St. Andrew's who had studied medicine at Leyden in Holland, and had in both places absorbed religious fervor. Coming to London, he was refused permission either to preach religion or to practice medicine; but he did both and also wrote books. The first of these to attract attention was entitled "An Appeal to Parliament, or Sion's Plea Against Prelacy." It was circulated in manuscript as early as 1628, and was afterward printed, when its author was exercising his office of the ministry in the Netherlands. Incautiously venturing to London, he was seized and brought before Laud and the Council in the Star Chamber. According to Leighton, the only remedy for the present condition of woe in Sion was the extirpation of the prelates — those "knobs and wens and bunchy popish flesh" who were further described as "Athaliah's Arminianized and Jesuitical crew." The result for Leighton was a fine of ten thousand pounds, the equivalent of two hundred thousand dollars in our day and money. Besides this, the condemned

[1] See on this topic Traill's *Social England*, iii, 433.

author was sentenced to stand in the pillory at Westminster, be whipped, have one of his ears cut off, his nose slit, and be branded in the face with the letters S. S., and, at some later time, stand in the pillory at Cheapside, again be whipped, lose his other ear, and be imprisoned for life. The fine, of course, he could not pay, but the first round of torture and mutilation was inflicted; Charles forgave Leighton the second whipping and one ear, and the Long Parliament set him at liberty after ten years' imprisonment, with such compensation for his sufferings as the estate of William Laud might afford. Four days after the High Commission pronounced this sentence, John Winthrop approached the coast of New England.

Of good old English stock, John Winthrop was born in the Armada year, 1588, some months before William Bradford first saw the light of day. He attended the University of Cambridge, but did not receive a degree. At an early age he married and began to manage his own or his father's landed estate. Later on he read law and acted as an attorney in the Court of Wards. Winthrop regarded this position in the light of an "office," but what its duties and obligations may have been seems to be difficult of ascertainment. He had no connection with the formation of the Massachusetts Bay Company, unless reliance can be placed on his statement that "with great difficulty we got . . . abscinded" certain requirements in the original form of the Massachusetts Charter. The sentence in which these words occur was written many years after the sealing of the charter and when Winthrop had long been the most prominent member of the corporation. He may well have forgotten the exact course of events in that earlier time and have used the word "we" where "they" would have been more accurate.

Moreover, Winthrop does not seem to have taken part in the opposition to the Forced Loan of 1626, and other early unconstitutional measures of Charles I. Indeed, his son, John Winthrop, Jr., joined the expedition for the relief of La Rochelle, which, taken by itself, would imply that the Winthrops stood well with the court. Whatever their position may have been in the earliest years of Charles's reign, the contest over the Petition of Right, the subsequent stormy scenes in the House of Commons, and the imprisonment of Sir John Eliot found Winthrop acting with the opposition. He soon lost his office and began to look about for new avenues of usefulness.

From an early age Winthrop had been given to religious introspection. In 1606 he began a series of notes or "Experienta," which have been preserved and throw a flood of light upon his religious condition, which must have been similar to that of many another Nonconformist. In one of the early entries in this journal of religious impressions Winthrop notes that in 1606 he covenanted with the Lord to reform "these sins by his grace, pride, covetousness, love of this world, vanity of mind, unthankfulness, sloth, both in his service and in my calling. . . . God give me grace to perform my promise, and I doubt not but he will perform his. God make it fruitful. Amen."[1] In worldly matters Winthrop possessed a cool, calculating temperament which gave him great advantage in dealing with the men of that day, most of whom were not in any respect passionless. Before taking any action, he carefully went over the pros and cons and sometimes set them down upon paper. It was natural, therefore, when about to take the great step of leaving England and embarking for the New World, that he should reason the

[1] Winthrop's *New England*, i, 65.

matter out both as regards the undertaking and himself. It seems in every way probable that the paper of reasons which is attributed to him by the filial editor of his *Life and Letters* came from his pen.[1] In this paper the carrying the gospel into America and erecting a "bulwark against the kingdom of anti-Christ which the Jesuits labor to rear up in those parts" is given as the foremost motive. This was doubtless suggested by the Catholic reaction which seemed to be overtaking the Protestant states and churches of Europe. Economic and social reasons are then adverted to, such as the overpopulation of England, which is so great that man, "the most precious of all creatures, is here more vile and base than the earth we tread upon . . . and thus it is come to pass, that children, servants, and neighbors, especially if they be poor, are counted the greatest burdens, which if things were right would be the chiefest earthly blessing." On the western side of the Atlantic the Lord had provided a whole continent for the use of man; why should it longer "lie waste without any improvement?" Furthermore, luxury in England had grown to such a "height of intemperance in all excess of riot, as no man's estate almost will suffice to keep sail with his equals." The present enterprise seemed to be the work of God to save his chosen English people from the general ruin: "What can be a better work and more honorable and worthy a Christian," he asks, "than to help raise and support a particular church?" To these favorable arguments several doubts were raised as, for example, the ill-success of other plantations. The answer to this objection was

[1] Cf. Massachusetts Historical Society's *Proceedings*, 1863–64, p. 340. The *Reasons* is printed at greatest length in R. C. Winthrop's *Life and Letters of John Winthrop*, i, 309. In briefer form it is given in Hutchinson's *Collection of Papers*, 27, and in Young's *Chronicles of Massachusetts*, 269.

that none of the earlier planters had sustained any great damage except those of Virginia, "which happened through their own sloth and security." Moreover, there were great and fundamental errors in that enterprise which would be avoided in this, as, for instance, "1. their main end was carnal and not religious;" "2. they used unfit instruments, a multitude of rude & misgoverned persons, the very scum of the land." So objections and answers follow one after the other. Ambition also played a leading part in determining Winthrop's action, as did the desire to better their condition play some part in inducing many another to leave England. As things were in the home land, Winthrop saw no chance of employment in public affairs; if he did not embrace this opportunity, he feared "that talent which God hath bestowed upon him for public service were like to be buried." Farseeing as he was, Winthrop grievously miscalculated in this. Had he stayed in England, his great ability in the management of men and his calm self-poise would have placed him high among the leaders of the Commonwealth and the Protectorate, and might even have contributed to fend off the Restoration for many a year. Every American, however, must rejoice at Winthrop's choice, since it was the Restoration which led directly to the American Revolution and the separation from England.

The Great Emigration was in many respects singularly like that earlier fleeing of the Israelites into the wilderness. In both cases the religious motive was at the bottom, and the exiles forsook the fleshpots of their earlier home, which was, to use Winthrop's words, "some pinch to them at first." As the Israelites clave to their God and to the religion which he gave to them, so the Massachusetts leaders left the land of their birth to establish a "particular church" in the American wilderness and to nourish and watch over it in its infancy. They had not the remotest thought of founding in New England an asylum for the religiously persecuted of the earth. What they came here to do was to secure the freedom of their own consciences. They departed from their country, kindred, and fathers' houses that they might enjoy divine worship without offense either to God, man, or their own consciences; or, as Winthrop expressed it, "to live under a due form of government, both civil and ecclesiastical." They came to establish a Bible Commonwealth in which they should play the principal parts and bend others to their will.

On July 28, 1629, nearly five months since Sir John Eliot's resolutions were voted by the House of Commons, Matthew Cradock, governor of the Massachusetts Bay Company, read to the assembled shareholders in that enterprise certain propositions which had been conceived by himself, so the secretary stated in the records.[1] These propositions were that the government and control of the company should be transferred to those who were to emigrate to the colony. Mr. Cradock requested the stockholders to regard this suggestion as confidential and to think it over carefully. The actual impulse to the Great Emigration came four weeks later, when a dozen gentlemen of substance met at Cambridge [2] and signed an agreement (1629) pledging themselves to be ready with their families to depart for New England by the first of March next, to inhabit and continue there, provided that before the last day of the ensuing September (1629) the charter of the Massachusetts Bay Company and the whole government "be first, by an order of court, legally transferred

[1] *Massachusetts Colony Records*, i, 49.

[2] The "Cambridge Agreement" is printed in many places, as, for instance, in Hutchinson's *Collection of Documents*, 25; Winthrop's *Life and Letters*, i, 344; Young's *Chronicles of Massachusetts*, 281.

and established to remain with us and others which shall inhabit upon the said plantation." Everything fell out as the signers of this Cambridge Agreement planned. It was found that the charter could be legally transferred,[1] and the government was turned over to those who proposed to emigrate, Winthrop being elected governor. On Easter Monday, March 29, 1630, the new governor began his *History of New England* on the flagship, which was then at anchor near the Isle of Wight. This vessel had been appropriately renamed for Lady Arabella Johnson,[2] who with her husband, Isaac Johnson, Thomas Dudley, and William Coddington accompanied Winthrop to New England, where in a few years they were joined by Richard Bellingham and John Cotton. After a prosperous voyage, on Saturday, June 12, 1630, the fleet of eleven ships anchored off the mouth of Salem harbor.

At Salem was a colony composed of those who were termed the "Old Planters," who had come to America before 1628, and of settlers who had been sent over before the change in the management and character of the Massachusetts Bay Company. Above eighty of the Salem colonists had died in the preceding winter; many of the survivors were ill; and there was so little food

[1] See Note III.

[2] See Note II. Winthrop, in his *History of New England*, spells this name "Arbella," from which it has been inferred that Isaac Johnson's wife's first name was "Arbella," as the ship's name was changed from *Eagle* in her honor. This form was frequently used at the time as a contraction for Arabella. For instance, see the "Montagu Manuscripts," i, 139 (Royal Historical Manuscripts Commission's *Reports*), where Arabella Stuart is called by a correspondent of Sir Ralph Montagu "Lady Arbella." It would be as correct to say that Montagu's name was "Raphe," because it was often so spelled in letters and journals, or to say that Lane's name was Rafe because it is so given on the title-page of Hariot's "Brief and True Report," as it is to say that Arabella Stuart's name was "Arbella" because Montagu's correspondent chose so to write it. Isaac Johnson's wife, it may be added, is called Lady Arabella by an early settler of Massachusetts named Pond in a letter to his father (Massachusetts Historical Society's *Proceedings*, Second Series, viii, 472).

on hand that Winthrop found it necessary to release from their contracts those who were left of the servants whom the company had sent over to labor for its benefit. The outlook was so dispiriting that no less than two hundred passengers returned to England on the vessels which had brought Winthrop and his companions to New England. Affairs at Salem were so gloomy, indeed, that Winthrop sought another site for his settlement and after some exploration pitched upon the shores of Massachusetts Bay or Boston harbor as the most eligible place. The vessels were unloaded and such preparations made for the winter as the strength of the settlers permitted. Some of the newcomers provided themselves with huts, but others were obliged to live in tents. At best there was much hardship for men and women, who were weakened by the voyage and who had but scanty fare. Before December two hundred of the immigrants had died. Roger Clap, one of the first settlers of the neighboring town of Dorchester, gives us a picture of the hard conditions of the first winter. He relates that frost-fish, mussels, and clams were a relief to many. Occasionally the Indians brought small quantities of corn to exchange for clothes and knives; once Clap secured a peck of it in exchange for a little puppy dog. Up to the end of December the winter had held off, as is not infrequently the case in New England. Suddenly, on the 24th of that month, a blizzard struck the infant settlement. The cold came on with violence. Such a Christmas Eve the newcomers had never seen before. That any of them were alive when the warm weather came again in the spring of 1631 was due to the foresight of Winthrop in dispatching the ship *Lyon* for England immediately after their arrival, to go to the nearest port for provisions and return with all speed. She reached the colony in the middle of February, 1631, with Roger Williams and other passengers and about two hundred tons of goods. Following the *Lyon* came other vessels, especially one from Virginia with corn. The supply of food for some years hardly equaled the demand. We find, for instance, Nathaniel Ward, one of the most prominent men in the colony, writing to Winthrop as late as 1635 that he was nearly destitute, having only six bushels of corn remaining for himself and those dependent upon him; but there was no famine in Massachusetts comparable to that which harassed the early comers to Virginia.

Few colonists came to Massachusetts in the years 1631–32,[1] as the hardships reported by the first settlers and the stern discipline maintained in the colony deterred many from emigrating who would otherwise have done so. With 1633, however, the tide of immigration again set in, and continued until the physical contest with Charles I required the presence in England of every available Nonconformist and Independent. Then, for some years, the ships carried more passengers eastward than they brought westward. In May, 1634, Winthrop estimated the population of Massachusetts at four thousand.[2] It is sometimes said that the authorities in England connived at the departure of those who were hostile to the Established Church.[3] Of the truth of this surmise, however, there

[1] Among other documents relating to this time may be noted the following letters: Thomas Dudley to the Countess of Lincoln, in Young's *Chronicles of Massachusetts;* John Masters to Lady Barrington, in Royal Historical Manuscripts Commission's *Reports*, vii, 547; and Richard Saltonstall to Emanuell Downing, in *ibid.*, xii, Appendix, pt. i, 449, and in full in Massachusetts Historical Society's *Proceedings*, Second Series, viii, 208.

[2] Winthrop to Sir Nathaniel Rich, in Massachusetts Historical Society's *Proceedings*, xx, 43.

[3] Egerton (*British Colonial Policy*, 46, 47) appears to believe that Charles had some well-thought-out plan of using "the colonies as a safety valve for dissent, and as instruments for English

seems to be little evidence. On the other hand, there is evidence that the home authorities were alarmed at the size of the outgoing throng. They might well have tried to stop it, because the removal of large numbers of persons from certain districts threatened to upset the social fabric. For example, one conforming minister reported to Laud that he had not carried out his orders, because if he had done so all his parishioners would have gone in a body to New England.[1] In 1634 the matter came to a head in consequence of a communication to Laud from Henry Dade, Commissioner of Suffolk, that two hundred and forty persons were already embarked for Massachusetts and that about six hundred more were making preparations to leave. "Suffering such swarms to go out of England will overthrow trade," Dade asserted, all on account of a dislike of the Book of Common Prayer, which aversion the commissioner termed "giddiness." The archbishop appealed to the Privy Council, and eleven vessels were stayed for a few weeks. But the passengers, being good Nonconformists, said their prayers regularly, took the Oath of Allegiance, and were eventually permitted to sail.[2] At about the same time, the king appointed a Commission for the overseeing of the colo-

shipping and trade." His authority for this statement is an extract from Winthrop's *New England* (i, 103) which in a court of law would be regarded as hearsay evidence, as Winthrop prefaced his statement with the information that his correspondent was "assured from some of the council." This statement was made at the time of Sir Christopher Gardiner's return to England. He laid sundry information before the Council; but the decision was in favor of Massachusetts. Cf. Prince's *Annals* (ed. 1826), 430. At all events the king soon gave his assent to an entirely different policy, which was plainly set forth by the attacks on Massachusetts, the appointment of Sir Ferdinando Gorges as governor-general, and the commissioning of Laud and others favorable to Laud's policy to exercise full authority over the colonies. See the commission in abstract in *Virginia Magazine of History*, viii, 156.

[1] See *Calendars of State Papers, Domestic*, Charles I, v, 255.

[2] *Calendars of State Papers, America and West Indies*, 1554–1660, p. 174. The same letter is calendared in greater detail in *State Papers, Domestic*, Charles I, vi, 450.

nies.[1] This body comprised William Laud, now Archbishop of Canterbury, Richard Neile, Archbishop of York, Lord Keeper Coventry, and nine other officers of state. The commissioners were authorized to make laws and orders for the government of English colonies in foreign parts, to impose penalties for offenses in religious matters, to remove governors, to appoint judges, and to hear and determine all manner of complaints from the colonies, with power to revoke charters and patents which had been surreptitiously or unduly obtained. This commission in effect was intended to make Archbishop Laud the ruler of the colonies. It turned out otherwise, however, for the contest over ship money,[2] the troubles with Scotland, and the ever continuing lack of funds made it impossible to compel the New Englanders to respect the authority of archbishop, commission, or king, — "the disorders of the mother country were the safeguard of the infant liberty of New England," and Massachusetts soon outgrew all the colonies which had been established before that time.[3]

In the year 1630 seventeen vessels with two thousand colonists reached the shores of Massachusetts, among them the *Mayflower*. In the summer of 1633, when the movement was at its height, ten or a dozen ships came in each month; in twelve years' time, nearly two hundred vessels discharged their human cargoes into New England ports. Jeremiah Dummer[4] informs us that this great

[1] *Virginia Magazine of History*, viii, 156.

[2] The ship-money conflict also drove many persons to New England. See for example, *Calendars of State Papers, Domestic*, Charles I, xii, 88, 356.

[3] On the early attacks on the Massachusetts government, see Charles Deane in the *Memorial History of Boston*, i, 329–383. Egerton (*British Colonial Policy*, 52, 53) has a few words on the subject.

[4] *Defence of the Charters*, 13, and Hutchinson's *Massachusetts*, i, 91. In 1634 "Tom" Verney, a younger son of Sir Edmund, was fitted out for Virginia at an expense of £117 12*s.* 6*d.* (*Verney Memoirs*, i, 136). This sum multiplied

enterprise cost no less than two hundred thousand pounds sterling, the equivalent of about four million dollars in our money. He apportions the expenses as follows: passage money, ninety-five thousand pounds; freight of cattle, twelve thousand; materials, eighteen thousand; arms and ammunition, twenty-two thousand; food brought over, forty-five thousand. This expenditure was in addition to the personal disbursements of private individuals, which must have reached a large figure. In 1643 the population of Massachusetts Bay was over sixteen thousand,[1] more than all the rest of British America put together.

The first settlements in Massachusetts were at Salem, at Cape Ann, and on the shores of Massachusetts Bay. These antedated the formation of the Massachusetts Bay Company, but they were eliminated as social and political factors by the coming of the Great Emigration. Salem survived and, after a few years, became a populous town. With this exception, the most important settlements were Boston, Charlestown, Dorchester, Roxbury, and Watertown; the last of these was situated some miles up the Charles River. Between Watertown and Charlestown and Boston was founded the Newtowne which was intended to be the capital city, and to be surrounded by defensive works. This plan fell through, but Newtowne became the site of the first college in English America. One family in forty of those who came to New England in the earliest years had some member who was a college graduate. Three-fourths of these graduates came from

by twenty will give a very rough idea of the cost of fitting out one of "the better sort" for the colonies at the height of the first great movement. Lady Verney employed an "emigration agent," which doubtless increased the total cost. The fact that such people existed at such an early date, however, has an interest in itself.

[1] These figures are based on Dexter's *Estimates of Population* (American Antiquarian Society's *Proceedings*, October, 1887).

the older Cambridge. The name of the Newtowne, therefore, was appropriately changed to Cambridge.

The title to the soil of Massachusetts[1] was derived from the king of England indirectly through the Council for New England. That monarch based his right to the soil upon the original discovery by John Cabot in 1497 and the formal "taking possession" by Sir Humphrey Gilbert some eighty years later.[2] Title by discovery holds good ordinarily for a more limited time; but as no other nation had occupied the country in the interval between Cabot's and Gilbert's voyages, the title of the English king by right of discovery was certainly as good as that of any other European potentate, except so far as such title might be affected by the action of Pope Alexander and by the fact that Cabot, so far as we know, did not see the coast of New England. As to the first of these points, the action of Pope Alexander must be considered as relating to Spain and to Portugal; it is not probable that he intended to debar other Christian powers from making discoveries in the unknown parts of the world, — it must be remembered that this action was taken before the Protestant Reformation. At the time of the grant by James I an English king would not have thought himself in any way bound by papal bulls. As to the second point, it is extremely doubtful what land Cabot saw; it certainly was some part of the continental system of North America. In later times, when the unoccupied parts of the earth's surface have come to be very much smaller than they were in James's reign, it would be preposterous to assert that seeing a cape or a small section of coast line

[1] See Charles Deane's luminous article in Massachusetts Historical Society's *Proceedings* for 1873, pp. 341–358, with abundant references.

[2] See especially Marshall's opinion in the case of Johnson and Graham, lessees, *vs.* McIntosh, Wheaton's *Reports*, viii, 543. An abstract is given in Note IV.

conferred rights to a whole continent; but the claim was no more absurd when put forward by James than when advanced by others. One more thing should be borne in mind: when these claims were first made, it was not generally thought that America was three thousand miles wide, so that the grant to the Council for New England stretching from the Atlantic to the Pacific did not appear extravagant. At that time no questions as to the extent inland of title by discovery had arisen; the "hinterland" was open to the first comer. At a later day, the idea began to prevail that the possession of the mouth of a river conferred exclusive rights to inland territory drained by the main stream and its tributaries. But no such refinements existed in the first part of the seventeenth century. The Massachusetts title, therefore, as coming from the English king was as good, if not better, than that of French and Dutch colonists. It was held at the time that the title to the soil was in the king, who might bestow it on his subjects on such terms as he saw fit.[1] This grant was limited by the adverse possession of subjects of other Christian princes and also by the occupancy of the natives. In the New England charter it was stated that the aboriginal inhabitants of portions of the land therein conveyed had been removed by the plague; as to the survivors, it was clearly the business of the grantees to extinguish their claims. The Massachusetts Bay Company recognized this obligation. In 1629 they instructed Endicott, their agent in New England, to search out Indian claimants and satisfy their reasonable demands "that we may avoid the least scruple of intrusion."[2] Those who received allotments of lands from the company were also

[1] See Note V, on conditions of the New England grant.

[2] *Massachusetts Colony Records*, i, 394, 400.

expected to satisfy the Indians, and they seem to have done this. The early records are lost for the most part — including the original Indian deeds; but there is no dearth of later deeds, two, for example, from the Squaw Sachem and Webcomet,[1] of lands now included in Cambridge, Charlestown, and Somerville. Except for land obtained by conquest from the Pequots not a foot of the soil of Massachusetts or New Plymouth was held in derogation of Indian rights. So thoroughly, indeed, did Massachusetts perform this work of extinguishing the Indian title by purchase that the enemies of the colony pointed to this fact as evidence that the Massachusetts people were prepared to maintain their rights to the soil entirely apart from the title conferred in the patent of 1629.[2] The Massachusetts people were also extremely anxious for the Indian's education and salvation. John Eliot, the "Apostle to the Indians," was only the greatest and most successful of numerous missionaries. A building especially intended for the Indians was erected in connection with Harvard College, and Caleb Cheeshahteaumuck, an Indian, actually attained the bachelor's degree.

It was inevitable that intercourse with the natives should prove disastrous to the weaker race. The Indians absorbed the vices and diseases of the whites without acquiring their virtues. In 1633 the smallpox carried off many of the neighboring tribes who had been untouched by the former plague, or, as Winthrop phrased it, "the Lord hath cleared our title."[3] The aborigines also

[1] *Massachusetts Colony Records*, i, 43, 201; Frothingham's *Charlestown*, 66 note.

[2] As a further protection for the natives the General Court enacted (1633–34) that no private person should purchase Indian lands without permission from the authorities (*Massachusetts Colony Records*, i, 112).

[3] Winthrop to Sir Nathaniel Rich, in Massachusetts Historical Society's *Proceedings*, xx, 44.

acquired a fondness for the alcoholic drink of the white men, which wrought especial havoc with them. The equality and cordiality with which Newport and Bradford greeted the sachems of Virginia and Plymouth have already been described. Winthrop was even kinder. In March, 1631, he entertained John Sagamore and James his brother and divers sannops; and, a little later, Chickatawbut, another sachem, dined with him and stayed all night; the Indian chief wore English clothes, sat at the governor's table, and behaved as soberly as an Englishman. On his departure, the governor gave him cheese, a mug, and other small things. In the following September one of the settlers who had stolen corn from the natives was ordered to restore it twofold, pay five pounds, and be degraded from his title of "Mr.," while his two servants who had acted with him in this theft should be whipped. At a later date, when the ill effects of the consumption of strong liquors by the Indians became evident, all persons were forbidden to sell, truck, barter, or give to any Indian, directly or indirectly, any strong liquors, from rum and brandy to cider and perry under penalty of forty shillings for each pint, except in cases of sickness or sudden extremities, when one dram might be given to relieve a native.[1] For more than a generation Massachusetts lived at peace with the natives within her borders. Occasionally she afforded aid to the inhabitants

[1] George Bancroft (*History of the United States*, ii, 100) thinks that "in the springtime of English colonization" there were some 180,000 Indians in the United States east of the Mississippi, and that in 1883 there were in the mainland of the United States, excluding Alaska, some few thousand less. These figures do not agree with the report of the Board of Indian Commissioners that in 1876 there were 266,000 Indians in the United States, of whom 104,000 wore citizens' dress. In 1880 the census takers reported that 66,000 Indians paid taxes, and there are reasons for believing that the Indian population has been increasing, within recent years at least. See Garrick Mallery in *Proceedings* of the American Association for the Advancement of Science for 1877.

of other colonies, as in the case of the Pequot War and the Narragansett War; but she sometimes refused to follow the other colonies in attacks on the natives. The troubles which culminated in King Philip's War seem to have been part of a spirit of unrest which prevailed throughout the settled portions of North America, in Virginia and Maryland as well as in New England. In later times the attacks of the French Canadians and their savage allies made life in the frontier New England towns extremely insecure, but the Indian policy of the English colonies had nothing whatever to do with inciting those invasions.

The political problem which confronted the fathers of Massachusetts when they began to take account of stock, so to speak, was extremely difficult of solution. They had brought to Massachusetts two thousand colonists, and there were then in the colony not more than twelve members of the Massachusetts Bay Company — including all its officers. The governor, assistants, and freemen of the company possessed by grant from the king power to correct, govern, punish, pardon, and rule all the king's subjects within the limits of their patent; in other words, not more than twelve gentlemen, with Winthrop at their head, possessed the legal right to govern two thousand of their fellow-subjects. They proceeded at once to the discharge of their new duties and before leaving the flagship voted that each one of the assistants should exercise the functions of an English justice of the peace, or magistrate.[1] It is true that there were no laws in existence for him to administer, but that difficulty was easily overcome by his executing upon all delinquents the English common law or the laws of Moses, in both cases accord-

[1] *Massachusetts Colony Records*, i, 74.

ing to his interpretation thereof. Most of these gentlemen had at one time or another exercised the office of magistracy in England, and what they proposed to do was to act in Massachusetts precisely as they would have acted in England, subject to the additional influence of the laws of Moses, on the one hand, and the American wilderness, on the other. The latter exception speedily proved to be very potent. In October of the year of landing one hundred and nine persons applied to the Great and General Court, as the supreme governing body was called, for admission to the freedom of the corporation.[1] The case was a difficult one to deal with, because if these persons were not admitted there might be a second exodus, this time toward the north, where Captain John Mason[2] and Sir Ferdinando Gorges possessed hundreds of square miles of ground clamoring for colonists, or to the south, where thousands of acres of New Plymouth Colony were bare of settlers. The great mass of the Massachusetts men had come to the colony because some leading person had migrated from their vicinity, or because they expected in the New World to better their worldly conditions. Winthrop and the principal men had crossed the ocean to found a state on the lines of the Old Testament, where the conduct of men and women should be regulated by the laws of God, and in which they should play the parts of Moses and Aaron. If they admitted ten times their own number to the Massachusetts Bay Company, that ideal would be endangered; on the other hand, if they refused admission to strong, able men, these, with their followers, would desert Massachusetts for New Hampshire

[1] October 19, 1630, *Massachusetts Colony Records*, i, 79.

[2] For Mason, see J. W. Dean's "Captain John Mason" in Prince Society's *Publications*.

or Maine or New Plymouth. In these circumstances they endeavored to steer a middle course, and, while admitting the claimants, to deprive them of power to do evil. This they hoped to accomplish by restricting the rights of the freemen merely to the election of the assistants and by keeping the number of the latter so small that it would include only the foremost men among them.[1] In doing this, they acted in plain violation of the charter; but they would probably have justified their action on the ground that the freemen of the corporation for the purposes for which the corporation was established might exercise some discretion as to details. In fact, at a later day Winthrop referred to this and other extra-legal acts as "details," giving one the impression that in his opinion the main provisions of the charter had been observed.

At the time that these new members were admitted, it was provided that in the future no persons should be admitted freemen who were not members of some of the churches within the colony,[2] in other words, who were not religiously in harmony with the existing members of the corporation. This remained the basis of the franchise in Massachusetts until after the Restoration. If the project of establishing a Bible Commonwealth was permissible, this was the best means which could be devised to carry out the scheme, since it placed the government of the colony in the hands of those who were especially interested in the welfare of "the particular church" which they had come over to nourish.

At first the assistants performed legislative functions

[1] See *Massachusetts Colony Records*, October 19, 1630, May 18, 1631.

[2] Vote of May 18, 1631. On March 3, 1635-36 it was further provided that no member of "any church which shall hereafter be gathered without the approbation of the magistrates, and the greater part of the said [existing] churches, shall be admitted to the freedom of this commonwealth."

without much regard to the requirements of the charter. There was a certain justification for so doing, because in the Great and General Court the consent of the governor or deputy governor and six assistants was necessary to the legal transaction of business, whereas in the Court of Assistants seven formed a quorum, and matters could be determined by majority vote.[1] As there were only seven or eight assistants on this side of the water, it would be necessary for them all to attend the meetings of the Great and General Court and vote with practical unanimity. Moreover, there were few freemen of the Massachusetts Bay Company in the colony who were not also assistants. The assistants passed laws and levied taxes, and, after the admission of the great mass of freemen in May, 1631, continued so to do. At a later time, an Attorney-general of England stated as his opinion that the Massachusetts Bay Company, by its charter, had no legal right to lay taxes on persons who were not members of the corporation.[2] In the early days, however, not only the Great and General Court, but only one portion of it, undertook to tax every one in the colony,[3] according to his ability for the support of both civil and religious organizations.[4] The first important protest against this policy came from Watertown, which had been settled by Sir Richard Saltonstall, George Phillips, a minister, and their companions. These gentlemen seem to have held religio-political views somewhat unlike those of most of the other settlers.

[1] See vote of March 8, 1630–31, in *Massachusetts Colony Records*, i, 84.

[2] Doyle's *Puritan Colonies*, ii, 278, from "Colonial Papers," Ms. 1681, May 30.

[3] See votes of assistants in *Massachusetts Colony Records*, under date of November 30, 1630, July 5, 1631, October 1, 1633 (possibly a General Court, although only the names of seven persons are given in the record as being present).

[4] In this connection it is well to bear in mind that in England and Virginia, as well as in Massachusetts, religion was supported by assessments, in the payment of which there was nothing voluntary.

Saltonstall soon returned to England, leaving members of his family behind. He later wrote to Winthrop, advocating toleration somewhat after the Independent mode. Phillips appears to have been an out and out Independent, and was charged by those who did not like him with having the temerity to suggest that even Roman Catholics might have some justification for their beliefs. In 1632 he thought that the time had come to protest against the action of the assistants. So he assembled his parishioners and secured the passage of a vote that "it was not safe to pay money after that sort for fear of bringing themselves and their posterity into bondage." Winthrop summoned the protestors before him and informed them that the board of assistants was after the nature of a parliament; he added that the freemen of the corporation in their general meeting might object to acts of the assistants without fear of being called in question for so doing. The Watertown men apologized and departed, and were probably glad to get off so easily.[1]

There were two copies of the charter in Massachusetts: one of these was the original document with the great seal affixed; the other was an exemplification, or attested copy, which had been given to Endicott for his information. Nevertheless, it is certain that, up to this time, the great body of freemen and the other colonists knew little or nothing of its provisions. In April, 1634, a committee of two freemen from each town waited upon the assistants and said that they would like to see the patent.[2] This request was inconvenient, but it was difficult to deny it. So the committee scanned the charter carefully and discovered that supreme power was lodged in the Great and

[1] Winthrop's *New England*, i, 70 (February 17, 1632).

[2] Winthrop's *New England*, i, 128.

General Court, and not in the assistants.[1] The provision in this regard was somewhat peculiar, as it conferred powers of legislation and also of judicial and executive action upon the freemen, together with seven members of the board of assistants, of whom either the governor or the deputy governor must be one. In the charter the number of the assistants is given as eighteen in addition to the two executive officers. The intention of the framers of the patent evidently was to give to a minority of the assistants the power to veto the action of the freemen. The matter worked out very differently, however, because not more than twelve assistants were chosen in the early years. This provision, therefore, meant that the action of the freemen must receive the consent of a majority of the assistants, which was quite a different thing. Furthermore, the charter provided that four meetings of the Great and General Court should be held in each year. These various provisions, of course, were designed to meet the needs of a business corporation whose officers and stockholders lived in England and held their meetings in the city of London, although no such technical requirement is in the charter. Its omission was probably due to the fact that those who drew up the patent took the New England charter of 1620 as their model and omitted the statement of residence. The latter charter provided for a "Council established at Plymouth in the County of Devon for the planting, ruling, and ordering of New England in America"; the Massachusetts grant provided for the establishment of a corporation by the name of the "Governor and Company of the Massachusetts Bay in New England."[2] There is otherwise little that is peculiar

[1] See these provisions of the charter in *Massachusetts Colony Records*, i, 11.

[2] In the reign of Charles II two chief justices gave as their opinion that this

in the Massachusetts charter. The Virginia charter of 1609 and the New England patent of 1620, for example, authorize the grantees through the proper officers "to correct, punish, pardon, govern, and rule" English subjects who shall inhabit in the colony and also on the voyage thither; almost precisely the same words are used in the Massachusetts patent. In a similar way, each of these charters authorizes the grantees under it, through the proper officials, to "encounter, expulse, repel, and resist by force of arms, as well by sea as by land and all ways and means whatsoever" those who should attempt the destruction, invasion, detriment, or annoyance of the said colony or colonists. Finally, each charter guaranteed to those inhabiting within the limits therein granted and to their posterity the liberties, franchises, and immunities of subjects of the English crown to all intents and purposes as if they had been born within the realm. Considering these likenesses, it is not going too far to suppose that the requirement of residence was omitted through inadvertence.[1]

The freemen of the corporation,[2] having discovered their power, proceeded to exercise it. This they did by evolving a representative system. As long as the freemen attended the court in a body, those living in and near Boston possessed great advantages. To give the freemen in general their rightful share of power, those living in the several towns deputed certain of their number to attend the General Court and represent them. Of course, these deputies were more in number than the assistants, and thus it was not necessary that the freemen should all

phraseology actually required the official residence of the corporation to be in New England. Chalmers's *Annals*, 173; Osgood's *Colonies*, i, 143.

[1] See Note III.

[2] There is an excellent article on "Representation and Suffrage in Massachusetts" by G. H. Haynes in *Johns Hopkins University Studies*, xii, Nos. 8, 9.

attend to outvote the officials.[1] At first the deputies seem to have conferred together outside of the General Court, in a species of convention or caucus, and then to have voted in the General Court as a body. Ultimately, however, these preliminary meetings were given up, and, as a regular thing, matters were debated freely in the General Court. In the beginning of such a system there was naturally a good deal of confusion, as, for example, the choosing of non-freemen[2] as deputies or a town sending more deputies than its size or importance entitled it to. These matters were remedied as they arose by means of fines. Soon the system was recognized by act of the General Court. One of the first things which the new deputies accomplished was to repeal the votes by which the power of the General Court had been restricted; but the process by which the consent of the assistants to their loss of power was obtained is nowhere stated. From that time on, the constitutional history of Massachusetts is, to a great extent, a story of the defensive tactics adopted by the assistants to save what remained of their power. From being ruled by an oligarchy, Massachusetts came to be an aristocratic republic[3] substantially independent of England. For many years, the franchise was restricted to those members of approved churches whom the existing freemen were willing to admit to a share in their privileges. This was a somewhat peculiar mode of regulating the suffrage, for it must be remembered that only the freemen could vote for the governor, deputy governor, and assistants. It should also be said that the number of

[1] On this general theme, see *Massachusetts Colony Records*, i, 95, 116, 118, and Winthrop's *New England*, i, 76.

[2] *Massachusetts Colony Records*, i, 174.

[3] *Massachusetts Colony Records*, ii, 95: "Our government is not a pure aristocracy, but mixed of an aristocracy and democracy in respect to the General Court."

freemen was not large, or, in other words, that the franchise in Massachusetts was confined to a comparatively small number of persons. Nevertheless, it may well be doubted if in any other way so thoroughly representative a body of voters could have been secured. The church members were, as a matter of fact, almost invariably the best men in their respective towns. The freemen of the Massachusetts Bay Company were the better men among the church members, and these sent to the General Court the more important of their number. Seldom in history has a more able representative body had so long a measure of life as the Massachusetts General Court.

In studying this period, it must be borne in mind that the government of the Bay Colony was, as stated above, an aristocratic republic, that is to say a republic in which the franchise was strictly limited to the upper classes. John Winthrop was in no sense a popular man or one who had any confidence in what would nowadays be regarded as liberal government. He brought over to America the ideas of an English gentleman of that time, and his ideas changed very slowly after his arrival in America. We find him, for instance, speaking of the "commons," the "meaner sort," and the "people." In 1638 he wrote to Thomas Hooker[1] of "the unwarrantableness . . . of referring matters of counsel or judicature to the body of the people, *quia* the best part is always the least, and of that best part the wiser part is always the lesser." In 1644 occurred one of the small revolutions which were not infrequent in early Massachusetts. Winthrop was deposed for a time and was charged, among other things, with desiring the establishment of an arbitrary government and with having acted despotically.

[1] *Life and Letters of John Winthrop*, ii, 237.

He defended himself successfully on the second charge and composed a treatise to show that the government of Massachusetts was not an arbitrary government. This paper shows that he had a dread of a "meer democracy" but highly approved of "a mixt aristocracy." This latter was a form of government in which the people ruled through elected officers, who, being once chosen, were practically irresponsible, so long as they acted upon good motives. He contrasted the case of a magistrate and that of a carpenter; the latter agreed to provide skill and faithfulness, while the magistrate agreed to provide only faithfulness and such ability as he might happen to possess.[1]

According to the charter, the officials were to be chosen by the freemen in the meetings of the General Court.[2] Once a year, therefore, in Massachusetts was held what was termed a Court of Elections, at which, after 1634, the voting was by papers. At first the freemen attended this meeting in a body; but this was soon found to be inconvenient, especially for those who lived in the frontier towns and were obliged to leave their families and friends to the mercy of the Indians, to abandon their daily tasks, and to journey to Boston, which was then a dangerous and time-consuming operation. The first step away from this system was to authorize the freemen of far-off towns to give their proxies to the deputies of their town.[3] From this beginning the system of proxy voting spread; and from this again was evolved a true voting system, by which the freemen cast their votes in their respective towns, which were carried to Boston by the deputies and there counted.

[1] See Winthrop's "Little Speech" delivered in 1645 in Winthrop's *New England*, ii, 228.

[2] The "freemen" had resumed their right of election as to the governor and deputy governor in May, 1632. Winthrop's *New England*, i, 75.

[3] See vote of March 3, 1635–36, in *Massachusetts Colony Records*, i, 166.

The change from proxy voting to the modern system necessitated some kind of nominating machinery, so that the freemen of the several towns should exercise their choice as between certain persons, instead of voting without any guidance whatsoever, and thus often throwing away their votes on persons who could not by any possibility be elected.[1] After many experiments, what might be called a legislative caucus was evolved, by which the deputies from one General Court carried down to their towns the names of the persons to be voted for by the freemen, and then carried back the votes to the next General Court. With the development of proxy voting, there went hand in hand the extension of the secret ballot. It was in 1634 that the governor was voted for "by papers" for the first time. When the system of the freemen voting in the town for the general officers was adopted, those votes also came to be given by papers; and finally, the deputies themselves were balloted for.

From what has already been said, it is clear that the Massachusetts Bay authorities were constantly violating the provisions of the charter under which they held their lands and exercised jurisdiction; many of the laws which they passed were directly contrary to English laws, although the charter required that their legislation be "not contrary or repugnant" to the laws and statutes of England.[2] Furthermore, the magistrate administered the law and executed justice in many cases in a different way from that in which magistrates in England acted. The authorities must have known that by doing these things they were violating the charter, since Winthrop and

[1] See Trumbull's edition of Lechford's *Plain Dealing*, 58, for a description of an election.

[2] *Massachusetts Colony Records*, i, 12.

Ludlow and others also had received legal educations. It was to this, probably, that many a high-handed deed was due. The rulers knew that their proceedings would not bear inspection in England. They either locked up or placed under bonds those who seemed likely to appeal from their decision to the courts of the mother country. When these expedients were unnecessary or undesirable, they banished from their midst those whom they regarded as unfit members of their "Bible Commonwealth."

NOTES

I. Bibliography. — *The Records of the Governor and Company of the Massachusetts Bay in New England* (often cited as the "Colony Records") and John Winthrop's *History of New England* together form a singularly complete official and semi-official history of the colony after its settlement. As to the genesis of the enterprise, these records are disappointing; Winthrop's *History* begins abruptly with the voyage, and the early entries in the "Records" do not convey much information on this theme. Robert C. Winthrop's two volumes entitled, *Life and Letters of John Winthrop,* throw some light on the motives which actuated the first governor. The *Collections* and the *Proceedings* of the Massachusetts Historical Society contain a vast quantity of material on Massachusetts history. Among the mass of records and papers relating to the early history of Massachusetts the following deserve especial mention: the *Reports* of the Boston Record Commission, Hutchinson's *History of Massachusetts* and the accompanying volume of documents, Young's *Chronicles of Massachusetts;* the Cambridge *Records,* the Watertown *Records,* and Roger Clap's *Memoirs* of the settlement of Dorchester are among the principal sources for the history of a community whose official and unofficial records have been published more completely than those of any other people of equal importance.

Of the secondary books, Palfrey's *New England* still holds the first place. Winsor's *Memorial History of Boston* is practically a history of Massachusetts, which is inadequately treated in his *America;* the two in combination give very complete bibliographical information. Ellis's *Puritan Age and Rule in the Colony of Massachusetts Bay* contains the results of long-sustained research, but is very hard reading. C. F. Adams's *Three Episodes of Massachusetts History* is the result of prolonged study and is also interesting. The volume containing the course of "Lowell Lectures"[1] which were delivered under the auspices of the Massachusetts Historical Society contains several admirable studies.

II. The Families of Clinton and Gorges. — The family of Clinton is said to take its rise from Renebaldus, who came to England in the

[1] *Lectures delivered in a Course before the Lowell Institute, in Boston, by Members of the Massachusetts Historical Society, on Subjects relating to the Early History of Massachusetts:* Boston, published by the Society, 1869.

time of William the Conqueror. The children of Thomas Clinton, Earl of Lincoln, who died in 1618, were closely associated with the settlement of New England: —

Thomas Clinton, Earl of Lincoln

Theophilus Fynes-Clinton, Earl of Lincoln, m. (1) daughter of Lord Saye and Sele, one of the most noted Puritans and warmly	**Frances, m. John Gorges, son of Sir Ferdinando Gorges**	**Arabella, m. Isaac Johnson**	**Susan, m. John Humphrey**
		Assistants of the Massachussets Bay Co.	

interested in the settlement of New England, whose son, Nathaniel Fiennes, brother of the Countess of Lincoln, played a prominent part on the Parliamentary side; (2) Elizabeth, daughter of Sir Arthur Gorges and widow of Sir Robert Stanley.

— J. Edmondson's *Baronagium Genealogicum*, p. 100.

III. Transfer of the Charter. — There has been abundant disputation over the transfer of the government of the company from England to the colony. Enemies of Massachusetts have stigmatized it as an act of bad faith; it has been defended on the ground that such was the intention of the original grantees. This latter contention rests on the following passage in Winthrop's "Essay on Government": —

"The last clause is for the Governinge of the Inhabitants within the Plantation. For it beinge the manner for such as procured Patents for Virginia, Bermudas & the Weste Indies, to keepe the chiefe Governm^{t} in the hands of the Company residinge in England (& so this was intended & with much difficulty we gott it abscinded) this clause is inserted in this & all other Patents wherby the Company in England might establish a Governm^{t} & Officers here in any forme vsed in England, as Govr & Counsell, Iustices of Peace, Maior, Baylyfs &c, & accordingly Mr. Endicott & others with him, were established a Govr & Councell heer, before the Governm^{t} was transferred hither." [1]

Doyle asserts that Winthrop, in this statement, was referring to the lack of any requirement as to the residence of the company. Judge Mellen Chamberlain,[2] on the other hand, contends that the statement refers to the subordinate governments which the charter designed to be established in Massachusetts Bay. For learned discussions of the subject, see Joel Parker, in Massachusetts Historical Society's volume entitled "Lowell Lectures" (also printed separately as "The First Charter and the Early Religious Legislation of Mas-

[1] *Life and Letters of John Winthrop*, ii, 442.

[2] Massachusetts Historical Society's *Proceedings*, Second Series, viii, 109.

sachusetts"); Charles Deane's "Forms used in Issuing Letters-Patents" in the same society's *Proceedings*, xi, 166; and Judge Parker's reply in the last-named volume, p. 188. In the footnotes to these articles are copious references to the older authorities. See also Osgood's *American Colonies*, i, 143.

IV. Title by Discovery and Indian Rights. — Chief Justice John Marshall gave the opinion of the Supreme Court of the United States in the case of Johnson and Graham's Lessee *vs.* William McIntosh, in which the plaintiff's title was based on purchase from the Indians, the defendant's on a patent from the United States. To avoid conflicting settlements and consequent wars with each other, it was necessary, so Marshall declared, to establish a principle, which all colonizing nations should acknowledge as the law by which the right of acquisition, which they all asserted, should be regulated as between themselves. "This principle," says Marshall, "was that discovery gave title to the government by whose subjects, or by whose authority, it was made, against all other European governments, which title might be consummated by possession. . . ." The original inhabitants "were admitted to be the rightful occupants of the soil, with a legal as well as just claim to retain possession of it, and to use it according to their own discretion; but their rights to complete sovereignty as independent nations were necessarily diminished, and their power to dispose of the soil at their own will, to whomsoever they pleased, was denied by the original fundamental principle that discovery gave exclusive title to those who made it."

Marshall then makes a long historical examination of the practice of European nations, concluding with the purchase by the United States of Louisiana — a country almost entirely occupied by numerous tribes of Indians, who are in fact independent. He continues: "The United States, then, have unequivocally acceded to that great and broad rule by which its civilized inhabitants now hold this country. . . . They maintain, as all others have maintained, that discovery gave an exclusive right to extinguish the Indian title of occupancy either by purchase or by conquest. . . . All our institutions recognize the absolute title of the crown [in colonial days,] subject only to the Indian right of occupancy, and recognize the absolute title of the crown to extinguish that right. This is incompatible with an absolute and complete title in the Indians." See Wheaton's *Reports*, viii, 543. In a briefer form, the case may be found in Curtis's *Decisions*, v, 503.

V. Terms of the Massachusetts Patent. — The Massachusetts Bay Company held its land of the crown in free and common socage as of the manor of East Greenwich in the County of Kent, paying one fifth of the ores of gold and silver found within the limits of their grant. The fact that they held their land as of the manor of East Greenwich means that they were entitled to free alienation of the soil, to devise it by will, and in case of intestate succession, to have it descend equally to the sons, and, if there were none, to the daughters, — as primogeniture did not prevail in that county. See article by Joel Parker in Massachusetts Historical Society's *Proceedings*, xiii, p. 114, and G. F. Hoar's paper on the "Obligations of New England to the County of Kent" in American Antiquarian Society's *Proceedings*, April, 1885.

CHAPTER XIII

DISSENTERS AND EXILES

AMONG the host of immigrants who sought the shores of New England, there were many persons who did not approve of the doings of those in high station at Plymouth and Boston, and also many persons whose opinions the magistrates of New Plymouth Colony and of Massachusetts Bay severely reprobated. In each case, the ultimate question at issue was whether the ideas of the dissentient minority or those of the representatives of the majority should prevail, for it must constantly be borne in mind that the magistrates, both at Plymouth and at Boston, represented the public opinion of their respective settlements, or they could not have maintained themselves in power in those frontier villages. There was no middle ground which men could occupy in the seventeenth century; it was a time of strong opinions, tenaciously held: either Thomas Morton must be permitted to furnish the Indians with firearms, or he must seek another sphere of activity; either Anne Hutchinson must be permitted to stigmatize the ministers, or she must leave the colony. In each and every case the victory was with those leaders under whose guidance the colonies had been founded. It was the natural outcome, for law and might were on the side of the constituted authorities. At great expense of treasure and cruel loss of life the beginnings of these colonies had been successfully made; but the difficulties were still great and the outcome was still dubious.

Under the circumstances, it was imperative that the leaders should be supported. In studying a controversial matter like the present, it is well to remember that the men of Plymouth and Massachusetts, the leaders as well as the plain people, were seventeenth-century English men and women, possessing the same prejudices and the same failings as their brothers and sisters whom they had left behind in the old land. They possessed, not merely the great qualities which marked the race in the days of Shakespeare and Milton, of Sir Philip Sidney and Oliver Cromwell, they also possessed the defects of that race and age.

The earliest exclusions and cases of religious discipline in New England occurred at Plymouth, possibly because that colony was the first New England settlement in which "religious persecution" could arise. It was on Christmas morning, in the year 1621, that Governor Bradford summoned the workers about him and prepared to go forth to the day's labor as usual. Of those who had recently come over in the *Fortune*, several held back, saying that their consciences would not permit them to labor on that day. So Bradford left them and went his way. Returning at noon, he found the conscience-stricken workingmen playing at bowls. He took the balls from them and sternly ordered them to seek their habitations because his conscience forbade his permitting games on that day, for to him Christmas was not a holiday. The consciences of the New England rulers, indeed, have been too little regarded, and the consciences of their victims too much respected. In the case of William Bradford, his ideas of right and wrong compelled him to regulate the conduct of Christmas revelers, and also to incur the wrath of John Lyford and Roger Williams.

John Lyford had been sent across the Atlantic by his friends, either to get rid of him, or, perchance, in the futile hope that life in the western wilderness might instill into him a modicum of virtue and a grain of self-respect. Arriving at Plymouth, he cringed before Bradford, shed tears, and joined the Pilgrim church, — after making due acknowledgment of his former irregular religious walking. Presently, however, he became a center of disaffection, and Bradford relates that, at length, "it grew to this issue that Lyford with his complices . . . withdrew themselves and set up a public meeting apart on the Lord's day," where Lyford ministered the sacraments according to the rites of the Church of England. Suspecting that Lyford was sending information to the home authorities, Bradford boarded a ship which was sailing for England, read the letters written by Lyford and his friends, and sent on copies of them, carrying the originals ashore. So Lyford was banished from Plymouth. For a time he lived at Nantasket and later at Cape Ann, and lastly in Virginia, where he speedily died.

The man who gave most trouble to the early governors was Thomas Morton, Gent.,[1] as he wrote himself, or, as his enemies dubbed him, that "pettifogger of Lincoln's, sometimes Clifford's, Inn." He was a man of some learning, of equal wit, and of an exceedingly jovial disposition. The wilderness appealed strongly to him, and he doubtless saw a chance of profit in the fur trade. Coming to New England in 1625, he soon cut loose from respectability. He set up a maypole on Merrymount as he called it, or Mount Dagon as Bradford termed it, which is now known as Mount Wollaston, in the present town of Quincy. At this place he gathered around him "all the scum of the

[1] On the Morton incident, see Adams's *Three Episodes*, i, 198–208.

country," to use the Pilgrim Governor Bradford's phrase, and acted the part of "Mine Host," with beer and brandy, to all who would come, — all of which doings were alien to the general atmosphere of the New English Canaan, as the Merrymount "Lord of Misrule" christened the Puritan settlements. The Pilgrims disliked rival fur traders who interfered with their own dealings with the Indians, and usually paid more than was necessary for the furs. But it was not until Morton's establishment became the center of a lively traffic with the natives in gunpowder and fire-arms that the Pilgrims did more than remonstrate. Then they reminded him of a royal proclamation against selling European weapons to the Indians. The "pettifogger of Lincoln's Inn" answered that the king's proclamation was not law, and advised the Plymouth people to look well to themselves, if they came to molest him. The further conduct of the business was intrusted to Captain Standish, who was an adept in the art of looking out for himself, — but the episode ended less bloodily than most of that valorous person's exploits. After some preliminaries, in which Morton outwitted Standish, the Pilgrim leader seized his prey by the coat collar, marched him to the water's side, and took him to Plymouth. The Pilgrims banished him to England; but before long he was back again at Merrymount with more beer and brandy, the same jovial temper, and the same lack of discretion.

Merrymount and its neighborhood now passed into the hands of the Massachusetts Bay Company. Soon John Endicott, its agent on the coast, visited Merrymount, hewed down the maypole, and advised the remnant of Morton's men "to look well that there be better walking." This well-meant and sage advice fell on deaf ears, and Morton, on his return, not merely resumed his old habits but refused to respect the fur-trading regulations of the Massachusetts Bay Company. Thereupon Endicott again visited Merrymount. This time he went armed with an attested copy of the Massachusetts charter, which was carried in a long tin box. Morton avers that he thought the box contained some musical instrument. He fled to the woods, and Endicott returned empty-handed home.

By August, 1630, the Massachusetts Bay Company was sufficiently well established in the colony to deal with interlopers and undesirable persons — under both of which descriptions was Thomas Morton. He was captured, set in the bilboes, his goods were confiscated, and he, himself, was deported to England. Obdurate to the ship's side, he had to be hoisted aboard with a tackle. As he passed down the harbor, the torch was applied to his beloved hut at Merrymount, — possibly as an argument against another return.

In England, Morton carried his complaints to Sir Ferdinando Gorges and William Laud. From the latter he secured a promise as to "the cropping of Mr. Winthrop's ears,"[1] which statement came under the eyes of that gentleman. He also published a book entitled *The New English Canaan.* This work gives us the first gleam of that peculiar humor which now seems indigenous to the American soil. The humor was not so apparent to "King Winthrop" or to John Endicott, who is described as "the great swelling fellow of Littleworth." Years afterward Thomas Morton, an impotent old man, revisited the scenes of his early hilarity; but he was so poor that "he was content to drink water." He of Littleworth sat in the governor's seat. After a year's imprisonment, Morton was fined one hundred pounds and set at liberty to seek the

[1] Morton to Jeffreys in Hutchinson's *Massachusetts*, i, 31 note.

wherewithal to satisfy the demands of Massachusetts justice. Two years later, "old and crazy," he died at York, Maine.

The most picturesque of the early exiles from Massachusetts Bay was Sir Christopher Gardiner, Knight of the Holy Sepulchre or of the Order of the Golden Melice, — which, is not certain. It is clear, however, that he was a knight of one kind or another; but who he was, or whence he came, no one knows. He suddenly appeared in New England, led an exciting existence for a few months, and then dropped out of sight.[1] He reached Massachusetts Bay a few weeks before John Winthrop and on the banks of the Neponset River built him a hut. There he resided with two servants and a "comely young woman," who was said to be his cousin. Suddenly there came inquiries from a woman whom Sir Christopher had abandoned in Paris and from another whom he had deserted in London; each claiming to be his wedded wife. Whatever the truth of the matter was, Sir Christopher Gardiner was clearly an undesirable inhabitant of a Bible Commonwealth. He eluded arrest and escaped to the woods. The comely young woman, however, was easily captured and the authorities meditated sending her "to the two wives in Old England," but her good looks saved her. In 1631 she married a settler of Maine, where she died quietly in 1656.

The Indians came upon Sir Christopher as he was slowly working his way toward the Dutch settlements in New Netherland and bore the Knight of the Holy Sepulchre in triumph to Plymouth, whence he was taken to Boston. Soon letters arrived addressed to Sir Christopher Gardiner in care of Governor Winthrop. The Massachu-

[1] Charles Francis Adams has treated this chapter of Massachusetts history very fully and fairly in the Massachusetts Historical Society's *Proceedings*, xx, 60, and in his *Three Episodes*, i, 250.

setts magistrate opened the letters and discovered that the much-married knight was an agent of Sir Ferdinando Gorges. He was later allowed to sail for England and departed, professing himself to be under "much engagement for the great courtesy" which he had received in Massachusetts. When he reached England, however, he gave to Gorges and Laud valuable evidence as to the irregular, not to say illegal, proceedings of the Massachusetts authorities. In point of fact, one of the few blunders which those astute magistrates committed was the neglect to secure Sir Christopher's personal attendance in the colony.

Of the exiles from Massachusetts in the first ten years of her history, three stand forth as peculiarly interesting: Roger Williams, Anne Hutchinson, and Robert Child. The first of these [1] was a youthful parson of engaging manners and conversation whose religious convictions prevented preferment in England.[2] Winthrop noted his coming as that of "a godly minister." John Wilson, the pastor of the Boston church, was about to return to England on the first of several attempts to induce Mrs. Wilson to brave the terrors of the Atlantic voyage. It was proposed that Williams should occupy the vacant pulpit in Wilson's absence; but this invitation Williams refused because in his own words he "durst not officiate to an unseparated people."[3] In this declaration may be seen the fundamental difference which divided Williams from the settlers of the Bay Colony; he was a Separatist who

[1] See Note I.

[2] On Williams's parentage and early career, see Henry F. Waters in *New England Historical and Genealogical Register*, xliii, 291–301. Two curious letters from Williams in 1629 are calendared in Royal Historical Manuscripts Commission's *Reports*, vii, Appendix, 546 *a*, and in full in *New England Historical and Genealogical Register*, xliii, 315. These letters show that Williams was as unsettled in love as Bradford says he was in judgment; and that he was as disrespectful to a lady much older than himself as he was to the Plymouth governor.

[3] Narragansett Club's *Publications*, ii, Preface, 2; Massachusetts Historical Society's *Proceedings*, 1871, 338.

believed the Established Church to be sinful; to his mind the Establishment was an anomaly; the state had no right to say to a man, "Go to the religious services provided by the state or be punished." The founders of Massachusetts, on the other hand, were Nonconformists. On sailing from England they had issued a farewell address to their "brethren in and of the Church of England,"[1] in which they termed it "their dear mother." From this position they very slowly drifted toward Presbyterianism tempered with Independency. When, for instance, they formed the first church in Boston, Winthrop says that they used the imposition of hands only as a sign and not with any intent that Mr. Wilson should renounce the ministry he had received in England. It was their persistence in what he deemed to be an error that made it impossible for Roger Williams to work in harmony with the Massachusetts founders, for he held that "a man ought not to pray with the unregenerate even though it be with his own wife or child."

Ere long Roger Williams shook the dust of Massachusetts from his shoes and sought a more fertile field at Plymouth. The Pilgrims, it will be remembered, were Independents who saw little that was sinful in the Church Establishment, but who were, on the other hand, outside its pale. At Plymouth, Williams earned his living by labor and trade and sometimes assisted the Pilgrim elders in a spiritual way. Bradford thought that he had "many precious parts, but [was] very unsettled in judgment." In no long time, however, the Plymouth governor tells us that Williams "began to fall into strange opinions, and from opinion to practice, which roused some controversy

[1] On this subject there is a good paper by Robert C. Winthrop in the Massachusetts Historical Society's *Proceedings*, xviii, 289.

between the church and him and in the end some discontent on his part, by occasion whereof he left them somewhat abruptly." Before his sudden departure, however, Williams found time to administer sharp admonitions and reproofs to Bradford, which the Pilgrim chronicler thought were somewhat lacking in truthfulness. Bradford's nature, however, bore little malice, and he wrote that Williams "is to be pitied and prayed for, and so I shall leave the matter, and desire the Lord to show him his errors, and reduce him into the way of truth, and give him a settled judgment and constancy in the same; for I hope he belongs to the Lord,"[1] which, nevertheless, seemed still uncertain to Bradford, the "sharpest admonitions," perchance, even then rankling in his soul.

Returning to Massachusetts, Williams ministered to the Salem church, which was more radical than the other churches in the new colony. Soon it began to be whispered about that in his spare moments at Plymouth he had written a treatise on land titles. In this essay he was said to have charged King James with telling "a solemn public lie" and to have been guilty of blasphemy, while Charles I was described in even worse phrase, for to him Williams said certain passages in Revelation[2] were applicable. As for the colonists of New England, they lived "under a sin of usurpation of others' [the natives'] possessions."[3] This extraordinary language alarmed and angered the magistrates, especially as the people of Plymouth and Massachusetts had taken every care to compensate the aboriginal occupiers of the land. They called

[1] Deane's *Bradford*, 310.

[2] These passages were xvi, 13–14; xvii, 12–13; and xviii, 9, or perhaps 19, which the reader can peruse for himself, if he so chooses.

[3] Williams's position is carefully examined by Charles Deane in Massachusetts Historical Society's *Proceedings* for 1873, pp. 341–358.

Williams to them, and after some correspondence "he appeared penitently and gave satisfaction of his intention and loyalty. So it was left and nothing done in it."[1] Soon after Williams acknowledged the righteousness of the colony's title by purchasing for himself land and a house at Salem.

From this inauspicious beginning matters went from bad to worse. It is surmised, but not proved, that Williams incited Endicott to deface the red cross of St. George in the ensign under which the trained band of Salem paraded, because it savored of idolatry.[2] This action troubled the other colonists, because it seemed to imply that the Salem people were more sensitive against idolatry than were the rest of the settlers. In December, 1634, Winthrop writes that Williams had "broken his promise to us, in teaching publicly against the king's patent, and our great sin in claiming right thereby to this country, &c. and for usually terming the churches of England anti-Christian. We granted a summons to him for his appearance at the next court."[3] Events now marched rapidly on.

The success of the Massachusetts settlement had attracted to that colony men of all sorts and conditions. Some persons came because wages were high; others crossed the Atlantic to seek the "mines" which were supposed to dot the American soil; and not a few, perhaps, like the Rev. George Burdet,[4] mistook Massachusetts for that promised land where "there was little law and less

[1] Winthrop's *New England*, i, 122.

[2] In a letter in *Calendars of State Papers, America and West Indies*, 1574–1660, p. 194, J. Cudworth states that "'the people of Salem have cut out the cross in the flag or antient that they carry before them.' Capt. Endicott their captain utterly abandons it." As the flag was a white banner with a red cross in the middle, it is hard to see what was left except a white sheet after they had cut out the cross.

[3] Winthrop's *New England*, i, 151.

[4] Adams's *Three Episodes*, i, 310.

conscience and not too much of either." To sift the goats from the sheep, the magistrates prepared an oath of fidelity which might be tendered to any person in the colony.[1] Williams now interfered. He had not been able to commune with the Boston people because they were unrepentant; in a similar way, it was sinful for a magistrate, who was presumably regenerate, by offering the oath of fidelity to commune with a stray settler who was unregenerate, — for to Williams's mind to offer an oath was an action of God's worship and it was blasphemy to commune with those who were not regenerate.[2] His protests aroused so much excitement that the magistrates were obliged to withdraw the oath. Another point which Williams made was that "the magistrate ought not to punish for the breach of the first table except when the civil peace should be endangered." The first table included idolatry, perjury, blasphemy, and sabbath-breaking;[3] but probably Williams meant only that the civil authorities could not compel attendance at the prescribed religious services. With his Separatist proclivities, he naturally objected to any state enforcement of religious observances, although the obligation to attend public service was then the rule in England and Virginia as well as in Massachusetts. Williams may have had in mind Robert Browne's definition of the magistrates' authority that it concerned the outward provision of the Church and outward justice, "but to compel religion, to plant churches by power, and to force a submission to ecclesiastical government by laws and penalties belongeth not to them."[4] For the present, however, the General Court forebore to take action, desiring with Bradford, perhaps, that "the Lord [would] show

[1] *Massachusetts Colony Records*, i, 115, 117.

[2] Winthrop's *New England*, i, 158.

[3] Palfrey's *New England*, i, 407.

[4] Works of Robert Browne quoted in Dexter's *Congregationalism*, 101, 105.

him [Williams] his errors and reduce him into the way of truth." It fell out quite otherwise.

In disposing of its great domain the Massachusetts Bay Company granted lands to bodies of settlers who founded towns and churches in harmony with the religious aspirations of the rulers. At about this time the people of Salem, which had been settled before the Great Emigration, asked for an enlargement of the bounds of their town. Under ordinary circumstances, the General Court would have acceded to this request; but the support which the Salem people had given to Mr. Williams, in view of his opposition to the action of the constituted authorities caused them to pause. This hesitation made it evident that Williams's congregation must choose between him and the Massachusetts Bay Company; they, very naturally, abandoned Williams. Upon this he resigned his pastorate in a passionate and disrespectful letter in which he termed the Massachusetts churches "ulcered and gangrened" and their ministers "false and hirelings." The issue was now joined, — either Williams must go or the founders of Massachusetts must abandon their experiment. As they were the stronger, it was Williams who went. In these disputes, for the most part, Williams held to the ideas of the more radical Independents; he believed in the absolute separation of church and state. The Massachusetts leaders, on the other hand, believed that religion should guide and control all human affairs. Despite the incompatibility of ideas, however, Williams would probably have been allowed to remain had he not enforced his opinions with so much vigor and persistency.[1]

[1] Personal animosity had little if any share in bringing about Williams's removal, which is the more remarkable because he had denounced the Massachusetts churches "as full of anti-Christian pollution" (see Savage's *Winthrop*, i, 171; Knowles's *Roger Williams*, 78; Dexter's *As to Roger Williams*, 50).

It was the autumn of 1635, when this decision to send Williams away was reached. He was given six weeks in which to set his affairs in order, and this period of respite was lengthened into months on account of his illness. Winthrop understood that, in return for this accommodation, Williams would refrain from attacking the magistrates; but it was not in him to keep silent. So they decided to ship him off to England. He eluded arrest, and, taking to the woods, passed the winter with his Indian friends. In the spring of 1636 he appeared within the limits of New Plymouth Colony and was requested to move on. The most noticeable thing about Williams's going is the smallness of his following; he seems to have made no steadfast friends at Salem. Far otherwise was it with Mistress Anne Hutchinson; her departure deprived Boston of a large part of its most earnest and substantial inhabitants.

"Of a haughty and fierce carriage, of a nimble wit and active spirit, and a very voluble tongue," Mrs. Hutchinson, according to John Winthrop, was "more bold than a man, though in understanding and judgment inferior to many women."[1] Her husband, on the other hand, commended himself to the generally genial governor as a "peaceable man of good estate." John Winthrop hated Anne Hutch-

John Haynes, soon to become one of the founders of Connecticut, was governor at the time and pronounced the sentence of banishment. Professor Diman's exposition of the reasons for Williams's expulsion is remarkably clear (Preface to Narragansett Club's *Publications*, vol. ii). Williams always maintained friendly relations with John Winthrop and his son, for many years governor of Connecticut. In 1636 or 1637 (Dorr's *Providence Proprietors*, 4) Williams asked the elder Winthrop "whether I may not lawfully desire this of my neighbors, that as I freely subject myself to common consent, and shall not bring in any person into the town without their consent, so also that without my consent, no person be violently brought in and received." This setting himself on one side and the remainder of the community on the other was typical of Williams; it led to his banishment from Massachusetts and it gave rise to bitter controversies in Providence.

[1] Winthrop in "Welde's Short Story" in Adams's *Antinomianism*, 158.

inson as he hated no other person who comes to us through his pages; his description of her, therefore, savors of prejudice; but she was a dangerous person to be at large in a Bible Commonwealth. Living nowadays, she would easily find a niche among the women radicals of the day; she would found another Brook Farm on original lines; or she would start a woman's club to discuss the religion of the Hindoos. As the case stood at Boston in her time, the only thing which she could do was to discuss topics more or less closely connected with theology. No morning paper then brought to the villager the scandals of the neighborhood; no theater stimulated his barren existence; no telegraph or cable connected that frontier hamlet with other towns or lands. There was nothing to live for, save love, work, and religion; apart from the actual bread-getting and love-making, everything assumed a religious aspect. Politics and religion were then so closely interwoven that neither the participants nor ourselves can disentangle them; while the ministers' utterances and the gossip of chance visitors took the place of the modern novel, theater, and newspaper.[1]

The Hutchinsons belonged to the social upper rank and lived in a large and commodious house nearly opposite that occupied by Mr. Winthrop. Mrs. Hutchinson speedily became popular; she nursed the women in their illnesses and sympathized with them in their distresses. They fell into the habit of assembling in her house to listen to her repetition of the minister's sermons and to share the good things which she set before them. From repeating, she went on to explaining; from explaining, she proceeded to criticising, and her comments were in no long time con-

[1] Henry M. Dexter (*As to Roger Williams*, 106–108) gives an admirable comparison.

veyed to the ears of those whom she criticised. The Boston church at that time rejoiced in two ministers: John Wilson and John Cotton. Cotton was the older of the two and the greater man; but his tardy migration to the colony found the first place occupied by Wilson. That worthy speedily recognized in Anne Hutchinson a dangerous visionary; on her part, she regarded Wilson as a coarse-grained, narrow man. He became so distasteful to her that she habitually left her pew and walked out of the meeting-house when he began to preach. At about this time John Wheelwright[1] landed at Boston. It was suggested that he should be invited to join Wilson and Cotton as a third minister. Winthrop said, however, that as they had just rid themselves of one firebrand in the person of Roger Williams, they would better wait awhile and see what sort of a man Wheelwright was before they gave him permanent employment. It is possible that Winthrop may have been cognizant of the fact that Wheelwright had been dismissed from the Church of England for the ecclesiastical crime of simony; but he did not make any such allegation at the time.

Two other persons now became prominent in the colony: Henry Vane[2] and Hugh Peters.[3] The latter was a popular preacher of the militant type and later became chaplain to General Sir Thomas Fairfax. At a later time Henry Vane was described by Milton as "young in years, in sage counsel, old." The sage counsel had not yet come to him when he landed in Massachusetts, and he always possessed

[1] On Wheelwright, see an article by E. M. Wheelwright in Colonial Society's *Transactions*, i, 271.

[2] See Hosmer's *Sir Henry Vane* and the article in the *Dictionary of National Biography*.

[3] On Hugh Peter, or Peters, see C. H. Firth in *Dictionary of National Biography*; Felt's *Memoir and Defence*; Massachusetts Historical Society's *Collections*, Fourth Series, vi and vii; Essex Institute's *Collections*, xxxviii; Royal Historical Manuscripts Commission's *Reports*, vii, 115. Further references are given in Boase and Courtney's *Bibliotheca Cornubiensis*, i, 465, and iii, 1310.

a certain sophomoric freshness which would have been ludicrous had it not been pitiable. Anxious to show honor to Vane's father, who was a Secretary of State, the Massachusetts freemen elected the young man governor, with Winthrop as a sort of balance wheel, in the guise of deputy governor. Vane's mind ran to politics and was as untrammeled by authority and precedent in its sphere as Mrs. Hutchinson's was in religious matters. The two radical reformers felt a natural affinity for one another and joined in an eager and fierce attack on the established order of things. They soon converted to their side most of the members of the Boston church; Winthrop and Wilson stood almost alone.

Mrs. Hutchinson meanwhile had evolved a religious system of her own. Possibly she understood it, but certainly few modern students comprehend it in its entirety. Winthrop, indeed, wrote that there was little difference between her doctrines and those generally accepted in the colony. Two things, however, were perfectly clear then and are perfectly clear now. The first of these was that Mistress Anne Hutchinson became convinced that she was enlightened from above. She was equally clear that John Cotton and John Wheelwright were of the elect; they labored under a covenant of grace and were certain of eternal salvation. As to the other ministers, she was doubtful at first, but ultimately reached the conclusion that they labored under a covenant of works; the light had gone from them — if they had ever enjoyed it. Now it happened that no idea was more abhorrent to English Nonconformists than the notion of self-illumination; to them the word of God as contained in the Scripture was the final record of the divine message to man. The conception that any man — much less any woman — should pretend to be inspired by the Almighty was not to be held for one instant. Moreover, the ministers of the colony could scarcely be expected to agree with this seventeenth-century transcendentalist as to their own spiritual condition. Winthrop and Wilson, Peters and Shepard — the last the minister at Cambridge — were not the men to stand idly by in such an emergency. They lost no opportunity to cast a reproach on Mrs. Hutchinson and her followers.[1] What they said and what they did can only be surmised, but the result of their efforts is fully recorded.

In the spring of 1637 the Court of Elections was held at Newtowne, which was soon to be called Cambridge. It was the end of May, the day was bright and warm, and the meeting was held in the open air. Climbing into a convenient oak, Wilson harangued the freemen with vigor and eloquence. The old leaders were triumphant; Winthrop was chosen governor with Thomas Dudley as deputy, and the Hutchinsonians were left out of the magistracy altogether. To guard against future dangers from unrestricted immigration, the General Court at its next meeting provided that no town or person should entertain any stranger above three weeks or assign land to a newcomer, except with the license of one or more of the magistrates.[2] Similar regulations are sometimes found in the records of English towns and parishes, and the statute law of England operated to prevent change of residence. In Massachusetts, the towns acted as agents of the company in the distribution of land. It did not seem unreasonable to the owners of the undivided tract that the consent of one of the chosen directors of the company should give

[1] Abner C. Goodell (Colonial Society's *Transactions*, i, 133) states that the rock of Anne Hutchinson's offending was "the heresy that sanctification was no evidence of justification."

[2] *Massachusetts Colony Records*, i, 196.

the corporation's assent to any allotment of land or to the acceptance of any newcomer within the limits of the patent. These proceedings greatly angered Harry Vane; in August, 1637, he sailed for England, to prove as prickly a thorn in the flesh of Oliver Cromwell as he had been in that of John Winthrop. His departure greatly facilitated the casting out of Mrs. Hutchinson and such of her followers as did not repent in time. Among the first to recover from the spell of her wit and volubility was John Cotton, upon whose brow the Hutchinsonian crown of grace had not rested easily. He and John Davenport, then on his way to the founding of New Haven, dominated at a synod which was held at Newtowne in September of that year, at which ninety-one opinions or expressions were denounced as blasphemous or unwholesome.[1] Throughout the summer there had been great excitement and much discussion, and the anti-Hutchinson party proved to be in the ascendant in the General Court which met in November. Mrs. Hutchinson and her friends refused to yield, and it was determined to send away some of the more prominent of them.

Among those to be dealt with was Mrs. Hutchinson. The way in which this was done shows at once the peculiar organization of the colony, and the closeness with which Winthrop followed English precedents in conducting judicial proceedings. The Great and General Court of Massachusetts was the highest authority in the colony, not merely in legislative matters, but in judicial affairs as well. At this time the deputies and the assistants still sat together as one body, presided over by the governor. It was this body, with Winthrop at its head, which came together to consider what should be done with Mrs.

[1] Adams's *Antinomianism*, 95–130.

Hutchinson. The proceedings which followed have been misnamed a trial; they were, rather, in the nature of a public examination to exhibit to the deputies the reasons for the condemnation of Mrs. Hutchinson. The General Court, therefore, was in somewhat the same position, as regarded that person, as was the Privy Council in England in some of the most noted inquiries which have also been miscalled trials. At these proceedings, the person under examination had no counsel to aid him, while the government was often represented by two, and sometimes by more, of the most famous lawyers in the land. The prisoners frequently had no idea of what was charged against them; and the confessions of other persons, unsworn to, and sometimes only in unattested copies, were used as evidence, and the right of cross-examination was denied to the prisoner. In one case the accused asked in vain to have the statute defining treason read to the jury, for this was a trial in the court of King's Bench; and when the jury returned a verdict of not guilty, they were imprisoned and fined. The language used toward the prisoners under examination was often most outrageous; Sir Edward Coke, for example, had called Ralegh to his face "the most vile and execrable traitor that ever lived" and had declared that there "never lived a viler viper upon the face of the earth." The demeanor of John Winthrop and his principal assistants in Cambridge would have distressed, by its mildness, Sir Edward Coke or Sir Francis Bacon.

The examination of Mrs. Hutchinson proceeded with slowness, and the case against her seemed to be on the point of breaking down, when her "voluble tongue" came to the magistrates' aid. She gave to the assembly a long history of her spiritual growth, which was due, so she said, to revelations from God.[1] "How do you know that it is God that did reveal these things to you, and not Satan?" inquired crafty Elder Nowell. "How did Abraham know that it was God that bid him offer his son?" demanded Mrs. Hutchinson. "By an immediate voice," said Thomas Dudley, the deputy governor. "So to me by an immediate revelation," declared the seventeenth-century prophetess. Now the deputies were plainly satisfied. The proceedings ran rapidly to their finish, which is thus recorded:—

"GOVERNOR WINTHROP. The Court hath already declared themselves satisfied concerning the things you hear, and concerning the troublesomeness of her spirit, and the danger of her course amongst us, which is not to be suffered. Therefore if it be the mind of the Court that Mrs. Hutchinson, for these things that appear before us, is unfit for our society,—and if it be the mind of the Court that she shall be banished out of our liberties and imprisoned till she be sent away, let them hold up their hands.

"All but three held up their hands.

"Those that are contrary minded hold up yours.

"Mr. Coddington and Mr. Colburn only.

"MR. JENNISON. I cannot hold up my hand one way or the other, and I shall give my reason if the Court require it.

"GOVERNOR WINTHROP. Mrs. Hutchinson, you hear the sentence of the Court. It is that you are banished from out our jurisdiction as being a woman not fit for our society. And you are to be imprisoned till the Court send you away.

"MRS. HUTCHINSON. I desire to know wherefore I am banished.

"GOVERNOR WINTHROP. Say no more. The Court knows wherefore, and is satisfied."

A few days later Mrs. Hutchinson's followers were dealt with. Six were fined, others were disfranchised, and some were disarmed.

One thing was still left to do, and that was to deal

[1] Adams gives an eclectic speech of Mrs. Hutchinson in his *Three Episodes*, i, 499–502.

with Mrs. Hutchinson in "a church way" or, in plain language, to excommunicate her. Ample time was given her for reflection and for conference with the ministers. Finally (March, 1638) she was brought before the Boston church — her own church. Wilson presided at the meeting, and he was ably seconded by John Davenport and Thomas Shepard. Weary and ill, Mrs. Hutchinson gave herself out as converted from the error of her ways. She recanted her "gross and fundamental errors," saying that they had arisen from "the height and pride of her spirit." That should have been the end; but Mrs. Hutchinson's love of talking and hazardous way of using words again made clear the path of her enemies. Up rose "the holy, heavenly, sweet-affecting, and soul-ravishing Mr. Shepard" and charged her with having lied. It was in vain that she asserted Shepard had misunderstood her. He called her "a notorious imposter"; Hugh Peters declared she should have been a husband rather than a wife: and John Eliot, who was later to win immortality as missionary to the Indians, asserted that "she hath carried on all her errors by lies." Finally, John Cotton burst forth upon her; "But now for one not to drop a lie, but to make a lie and to maintain a lie;" and so he left her to her fate, which was thus pronounced by John Wilson, no one gainsaying: —

"Forasmuch as you, Mrs. Hutchinson, have highly transgressed and offended and forasmuch as you have so many ways troubled the Church with your errors and have drawn away many a poor soul, and have upheld your revelations; and forasmuch as you have made a lie, etc. Therefore in the name of our Lord Jesus Christ and in the name of the Church I do not only pronounce you worthy to be cast out, but I do cast you out and in the name of Christ I do deliver you up to Satan, that you may learn no more to blaspheme, to seduce and to lie, and I do account you from this time forth to be a Heathen and a Publican and so to be held of all the brethren and sisters of this congregation and of others; therefore I command you in the name of Christ Jesus and of his Church as a Leper to withdraw yourself out of the Congregation; that as formerly you have despised and contemned the Holy Ordinances of God, and turned your back on them, so you may now have no part in them nor benefit by them."

And, so cast out by Church and Commonwealth, Mrs. Hutchinson sought other scenes of activity.

Of the three distinguished persons — Roger Williams, Anne Hutchinson, and Robert Child — whose reforming tendencies brought them into collision with the Massachusetts magistrates, only the last-named remains to be considered. The Massachusetts people on leaving England had proclaimed their connection with the Established Church, but on arriving in America had found themselves obliged to set up a modified form of church government, in which there were elements of Presbyterianism and elements of Independency. It stood midway between Independency, on the one hand, and Presbyterianism on the other, and was described at the time as the New England Way. It was this moderation in change, or, perhaps, the stubborn way in which the Massachusetts leaders adhered to it, that brought upon them the wrath of Roger Williams, who was a good deal of a Brownist, of Anne Hutchinson, who was a radical in matters of doctrine, and of Robert Child,[1] who stood for Presbyterianism. In 1646, within twelve months of the battle of Naseby, Dr. Robert Child and six others presented a "Remonstrance and Petition" to the General Court of Massachusetts.[2] This paper was framed with great skill and

[1] Dr. Child was interested in mining, see letter of Rich: Leader to John Winthrop, Jr., 21 August, 1648, in Massachusetts Historical Society's *Proceedings*, Second Series, iii, 192.

[2] The petition is printed at length in

with the evident expectation that it would carry conviction to the Presbyterian majority of the Long Parliament, even though the Massachusetts rulers might not appreciate it. The petitioners described the government of the Bay Colony as an "ill compacted vessel," and desired the substitution of Presbyterianism for the existing ecclesiastical polity. If they could not have the religious establishment which they desired, they asked for the recognition of religious discipline "according to the best reformations of England and Scotland," — in other words, that Presbyterianism might be tolerated. The fact was that Robert Child and other Presbyterians were excluded from the franchise on the ground that they were not members of approved churches. This exclusion they regarded as unwarranted and arbitrary and as depriving them of rights which belonged to freeborn Englishmen.

There was so much truth in the last assertion that Winthrop, with Dudley and Bellingham, felt it necessary to defend themselves and the system under which they governed. This they did in a document comparing the "fundamentals of the Massachusetts" with the institutions of England.[1] Instead of stating boldly that the representative system of England was absurd in its working, they averred that in England representatives were chosen "for all the people, but not by all the people; but only by certain freeholders and free burghers in shires and corporations"; while in Massachusetts the deputies are chosen "for all the people, but not by all the people, but only by the company of freemen according to our charter." They summoned Child and the other

Hutchinson's *Collection of Papers*, 188. The substance of it is given in Winthrop's *New England* (Savage's edition), i, 285. The "Declaration of the General Court concerning A Remonstrance, etc.," is in Hutchinson's *Collection*, 198.

[1] Hutchinson's *Collection*, 201; *American History Leaflets*, No. 25.

petitioners before them and placed them under bonds to appear when called upon. The petitioners, persisting obstinately and proudly in what Winthrop termed their "evil practice," were fined from ten to fifty pounds apiece and advised to "study to be quiet and to meddle with your [their] own business." Instead of so doing, they appealed to Parliament, which was now in the hands of the Covenanting majority. Their appeal took the shape of a petition[1] in which the Presbyterians asked that religion might be established in Massachusetts according to the Reformation of England; that the laws of England might be established in the colony; and that arbitrary power might be taken away. With this was another petition which pretended "to be in the name, and upon the sighs and tears of many thousands" and prayed for liberty of conscience and a general governor. With these two petitions were twenty-three queries chiefly about the validity of the patent and the legality of the doings of the Massachusetts rulers, both civil and ecclesiastical. The magistrates, getting hold of these documents, summoned Dr. Child, who, coming before them, "fell into a great passion and gave big words" until he was threatened with committal to the common prison unless he would behave as a gentleman and a scholar. Ultimately he gained his liberty and made the best of his way to London.

Meantime, Dr. Child's brother in England, who was major of a regiment in Kent, with the aid of William Vassall, at one time an assistant, but now in opposition to the magistrates, prepared and printed a pamphlet entitled "New England's Jonas Cast up in London." At this time Edward Winslow was in England, representing

[1] Winthrop's *New England*, ii, 293.

the interests of Massachusetts and New Plymouth. He answered this publication with another which he named the "Salamander," pointing therein at Mr. Vassall, who was never quiet but when he was in the fire of contention. Upon his arrival in London, Dr. Child presented a petition reciting the misdeeds of Massachusetts; but "God met with them all" according to Governor Winthrop. It fell out that Robert Child's seventeenth-century temper got the better of him and induced him, being upon the Exchange, to box the ears of Francis Willoughby, a resident of Charlestown in Massachusetts, whose father was a person of influence in the city of London. Child was arrested and, to secure his freedom, promised in writing never to speak evil of New England again or to occasion any trouble to the country or to any of its people. "Besides," added Winthrop in concluding his account of these occurrences, "God had so blasted his estate, as he was quite broken, etc." With this "etc." Dr. Robert Child passes out of the ken of history. The Independents, with Oliver Cromwell at their head and the New Model Army at their back, were now supreme. Pride's Purge removed Child's friends from the House of Commons. For the present, at least, no Presbyterians were likely to trouble Massachusetts, for, as Roger Williams exultingly wrote, there came upon England "a wonderful calm and liberty, and all violent hands, though not tongues, [were] held in by the army."

NOTES

I. The Antinomians. — C. F. Adams has included in his *Antinomianism in Massachusetts Bay* (Prince Society *Publications*) the important material having to do peculiarly with Mrs. Hutchinson and her beliefs. Documents are also to be found in Hutchinson's *Collection*, beginning with p. 63. Mr. Adams, in his *Three Episodes of Massachusetts History*, gives by far the best account that has yet appeared of Thomas Morton, Sir Christopher Gardiner,[1] and Mrs. Hutchinson, although his mode of historical treatment has not always commended itself to students of Massachusetts history.[2] Williston Walker, in his *Creeds and Platforms of Congregationalism*, also deals with Antinomianism as well as other outlying sects, while Palfrey and Ellis give the traditional Massachusetts view.

II. Roger Williams. — The biographies of Williams are noted by C. S. Brigham in his "Bibliography of Rhode Island History" (Field's *Rhode Island*, iii, Appendix), and are all controversial in tone. Thomas Seccombe's article in the *Dictionary of National Biography* is an excellent notice from a fresh point of view. Professor Diman's "Preface" to the second volume of the Narragansett Club's edition of Williams's writings is the most scholarly account of the career of the founder of Providence. The case against him is vehemently stated by Henry M. Dexter in his *As to Roger Williams*. Every history of Rhode Island or of Providence necessarily has to do with Williams's career, as Arnold's *Rhode Island*, Richman's *Rhode Island*, Brigham's article in Field's *Rhode Island*, and Rider's "Soul Liberty" in *Rhode Island Historical Tracts*, Second Series. W. H. Whitsett, in *A Question in Baptist History*, and H. M. King's *Baptism of Roger Williams*, contain some interesting matter as to whether Roger Williams was baptized by sprinkling or by immersion. A contemporary hostile opinion of Williams is given by George Fox in his *A New England Firebrand Quenched* (London, 1649). Williams in return gives his testimony of what he termed "the unclean spirit of the Quakers"[3] in *George Fox digged out of his Burrowes* (Boston, 1676).

[1] Mr. Adams has treated the career of Sir Christopher Gardiner in Massachusetts in a scholarly manner in Massachusetts Historical Society's *Proceedings*, xx, 60–88.

[2] See, for example, Robert C. Winthrop, Jr., in Massachusetts Historical Society's *Proceedings*, Second Series, viii, 370, 402, 486.

[3] Massachusetts Historical Society's *Proceedings*, Second Series, iii, 258.

CHAPTER XIV

THE SOUTHERN NEW ENGLAND COLONIES

In the years 1635–38 four groups of plantations, which later developed into the states of Connecticut and Rhode Island, were settled south of Massachusetts. Some of these settlements were made by persons whose longer stay in Massachusetts was distasteful to the rulers of that colony; the others were made by persons to whom further residence in Massachusetts was uncongenial. It was in the winter of 1635–36 that Roger Williams,[1] to avoid deportation to England, sought the wilderness and, after some vicissitudes, began a settlement on a river which flows into the northern end of Narragansett Bay. To the little hamlet he gave the name of Providence. Exactly what his plans were, if, indeed, he had thought out any definite scheme of action, is difficult to determine. Possibly he only intended to found a trading station where he and his family with a few friends could live in quiet; but the thought that he might do something to rescue the Indians from the heathen's doom may have had something to do with his determination. Certainly he does not seem to have had in contemplation the founding of a state. One evidence of this is the fact that he secured from the Indians a small tract of land in his own name and not in

[1] There has been some discussion as to the date of Williams's banishment. See Rhode Island Historical Society's *Proceedings*, 1888, p. 52.

that of himself and associates; it is reasonable to suppose that, if he had looked upon himself as acting for his associates, he would have procured the grant in their united names.[1] The omission to do this gave rise to serious trouble between Williams and his neighbors. Ultimately he was obliged to yield to their wishes and to part with most of his proprietary rights; but he seems to the end to have regarded his fellow-townsmen as guilty of ingratitude, and some of them looked upon him as seeking to deprive them of their rights. At all events they seem to have been much more concerned in securing good home lots and farms than they were in problems of government, whether in Church or State.[2]

In obtaining his lands directly from the Indians, Roger Williams no doubt felt that he was securing a valid title; but the accuracy of his view may well be questioned, and the transaction also gives rise to interesting speculations from the point of view of English legal theory and of the

[1] "The land was mine own as truly as any man's coat upon his back," he said at a later time. It does not do, however, to base an argument upon any one statement of Roger Williams. He was a man of many words and of changeable ideas. At one time he declared that in going to Providence he had it in mind to found a refuge for the "most Jewish, Pagan, and anti-Christian consciences"—so Mr. Richman says. At another time Williams averred that his "soul's desire was to do the natives good."—Rider's *Rhode Island Tracts*, No. 14, p. 53.

[2] See "Plea of the Petuxet Purchasers," Rhode Island Historical Society's *Publications*, New Series, i, No. 3; H. C. Dorr's "Proprietors of Providence and their Controversies with the Freeholders," in *ibid.*, iii, 143–230; Williams's letters of 1678, in *ibid.*, viii, 156. The settlers looked upon themselves as feudal proprietors. The law of petty treason (1647), for example, provides that a man condemned for this crime shall be "drawn and hanged; the woman to be burned alive, . . . the lands to go by escheat to the Lord of the Fee. 25 Edw. III, 2; only we do declare touching this matter, that each town is, of good right, the Lord of the Fee, in respect of all the lands contained within its bounds, from whom every man hath received his lands, which Lords being all here present in this General Assembly, and conceiving the wives and children ought not to bear the iniquities of the husbands and parents, at least as the case stands with us, do therefore jointly agree, so far as in us lies, to allow the privilege of rent throughout the whole colony, and propagate that country proverb in Providence Plantations, 'the Father to the bough and the Son to the plow,' he having first defrayed the charges about the delinquent."—*Rhode Island Colony Records*, i, 162.

institutions of the North American Indians. According to English law, the title to the soil of North America, at least to that part of it upon which Providence stands, was in the English king. By charter, James I had granted this land to the Council for New England, and the Council for New England, in its turn and after its manner, had granted this soil to more than one set of grantees. Legally speaking, the men of Providence had no right whatever to their farms except such as long-continued occupancy could give them, — a title derived solely from the natives had no standing in the courts of England.[1] Moreover, regardless of its legal position, a title resting solely on an Indian grant could have little value. The Indians held land in common as a tribe, and no one person could divest the tribe of its rights; an Indian sachem was a chosen chief rather than a hereditary patriarch, as Canonicus, for instance, has so often been pictured. Furthermore, the aborigines had no conception of private ownership of land, and therefore could not have understood the meaning of an English deed, no matter how carefully and conscientiously it might have been explained to them. The chiefs, when they affixed their marks to the paper which Williams had prepared, doubtless had in mind nothing more than giving to their friend permission to occupy and use a portion of the tribal domain. In later times, the Indian sachems came to Williams's trading house and helped themselves to his goods, somewhat to his dismay, but in strict conformity to their institutional ideas which require additional compensation for the continued occupancy of the tribal lands. In brief, the people of Providence, and those of Aquidneck also, having no title from

[1] See on this subject, Henry C. Dorr, in Rhode Island Historical Society's *Publications*, New Series, iii, 146, and Marshall's decision as above, p. 354.

the English sovereign, were merely squatters, until time and the king made good their right.

In an institutional way, also, the position of the men of Providence was peculiar. They had no license from the king to govern themselves, and did not obtain such permission until 1663. In the interval they acted upon the same principle as that which obtained at Plymouth, namely, the right of English subjects finding themselves outside of any governmental organization to take care of their concerns until the sovereign should make some provision for their government. The men of Providence therefore established a government, or semblance of a government would be more truthful, which was the purest democracy that up to that time had ever developed in an English-speaking community. In the new colony there was a good measure of equality in both civil and religious affairs. Williams argued for equality in religion; some of his fellows were disposed to extend this to civil affairs also, and to proceed on the theory that a man must act according to his conscience in civil as well as in ecclesiastical matters. There was no Church establishment in the Providence settlement; no man was obliged to support religion, or to attend divine service, although Williams ministered to those who came to listen to him. Nevertheless, the first religious case which arose at Providence is worth recalling, because it shows how difficult it was in those days for people to understand the separation of Church and State for which Williams argued, and how difficult it is for even the best of men to be consistent. Among the few adherents who followed Williams from Salem was Joshua Verin. He seems to have enjoyed his new-found liberty, and for a year did not go to church. Not only did he stay away from Mr. Williams's services, he refused to permit his wife to attend them, even going so far, if Williams may be believed, as to endanger her life with furious blows.[1] Acting possibly upon the initiative of their religious leader, the townsmen took the case under advisement and disfranchised Verin for restraining his wife's conscience, although he averred that his own conscience would not permit him to allow her to listen to Williams's exhortations. Some time afterward Verin shook the dust of Providence from his feet and returned to Salem, which seemed to those who remained at Providence to be good reason to appropriate his land.[2] At Salem he would be obliged to attend divine services several times each week, but there also he could preserve discipline in his family, and feel certain that, following the Epistle of Paul to Titus, his wife would be obedient to her husband, "that the word of God be not blasphemed."[3] What Joshua Verin's scruples were, if they were truly of a conscientious cast, cannot be stated, but in view of the instability of Roger Williams's religious convictions, it is not impossible that he may have conscientiously objected to the precise form of doctrine which

[1] Williams's letter to Winthrop, telling his side of the story, is as follows:

"Sir, We haue bene long aflicted by a young man, boysterous & desperate, Philip Verins sonn of Salem, who, as he hath refused to heare the word with vs (which we molested him not for) this twelue month, so because he could not draw his wife, a gracious & modest woman, to the same vngodlines with him, he hath troden her vnder foote tyranically & brutishly: which she & we long bearing, though with his furious blows she went in danger of life, at the last the maior vote of vs discard him from our civill freedome, or disfranchize, &c: he will haue justice (as he clamours) at other Courts: I wish he might, for a fowle & slanderous & brutish cariage, which God hath deliuered him vp vnto; he will hale his wife with ropes to Salem, where she must needes be troubled & troublesome as differences yet stand. She is willing to stay & live with him or else where, where she may not offend, &c. I shall humbly request that this item be accepted, & he no way countenanced, vntil (if need be) I further trouble you: So with due respects to Mrs. Wintrop, Mr. Deputie, Mr. Belingham, &c. I rest,

"Your worship's vnfaigned
"Roger Williams."

— Massachusetts Historical Society's *Collections*, Fourth Series, vi, 245.

[2] *Rhode Island Colony Records*, i, 17 and note. Winthrop's *New England*, i, 283. *Early Records of Providence*, i, 4.

[3] Titus, ch. ii, 5.

Williams was inculcating at the moment. At any rate, it was not long after Verin's disfranchisement that Williams became a Baptist, and so remained for three or four months, when he left that fold. For the remainder of his life he was one of that small band of persons "who professed to be seeking the true church, ministry, and sacraments," and were hence called "Seekers."

In 1640, the householders of Providence came together and drew up an agreement which served them as a fundamental law for the next few years. By this instrument, five men, who were called the disposers, should be chosen four times in each year to have charge of the disposal of the land, the management of the common stock, and the admission of inhabitants. As to the last, however, the Providence lawmakers went beyond the so-called Massachusetts Alien Act of 1636, by providing that the objection of any one resident should be sufficient to bar out a newcomer, although the disposers might be ready to admit him. In point of fact, Providence seems to have been painfully exclusive, so far, at all events, as giving outsiders the right to share in the colony's lands.[1] The freeholders further reserved the right, in general meetings, to ratify or to disavow the doings of the disposers and, in all things, to exercise supreme power. Ordinarily disputes between man and man were to be referred to arbitration, but disagreements between the disposers and one or more of the inhabitants were to be settled at a general meeting. This agreement continued for five years, when it was superseded by another, which opened the franchise to poorer men. There was no one at Providence who wielded authority similar to that which William Bradford exercised at

[1] "Item that none sell his field or his lot granted in our liberties to any person but to an inhabitant, without consent of the town." — *Early Records of Providence*, i, 3.

Plymouth, for Williams and Harris, the ablest of the early settlers, for one reason or another were in opposition to each other and to the inhabitants generally. As the case stood, this constitution had no sanction except force, which sometimes led to riot and bloodshed. Indeed, as Williams once wrote, the peace of Providence was "like the peace of a man who has a tertian ague." Two years before this constitution was formulated, Mistress Anne Hutchinson and many of her followers found refuge on a large island which divides Narragansett Bay into two unequal parts, and is known by the name of Rhode Island.[1]

The Hutchinsonians had no sympathy whatsoever with the doctrine of "soul liberty," nor were the leaders among them tolerant of democratic ideas; but they and Roger Williams had this in common, that the rulers of Massachusetts thought their room better than their company. The most important man among them was William Coddington, who in Boston had been accounted one of the richest of its inhabitants, and had served the Massachusetts Bay Company as assistant, and at one time as treasurer. At first the newcomers settled on the northern end of the island of Rhode Island, or Aquidneck, as the natives called it; their village they named Portsmouth. On the "seventh day of the first month," 1637–38, while at Providence on the way to their new home, the Hutchinsonians formed themselves into a body politic by signing a document, which closely resembles the Church covenants of that time: —

"We, whose names are under written, do here solemnly, in the presence of Jehovah, incorporate ourselves into a Bodie Politick, and

[1] On the origin of this name, see Brigham's *Rhode Island*, 50 note; Richman's *Rhode Island*, i, 242; J. G. Kohl in *Magazine of American History*, ix, 81.

as he shall help, will submit our persons lives and estates unto our Lord Jesus Christ, the King of Kings and Lord of Lords, and to all those perfect and most absolute laws of his given us in his holy word of truth, to be guided and judged thereby."

As justifying this action they referred to certain specified passages in Exodus, Chronicles, and Kings. They elected Mr. Coddington to be "judge" amongst them and promised to yield to him all due honor according to the laws of God; he, on his part, covenanted to do justice and to maintain their fundamental rights, whenever these should be ascertained in public meeting. The earliest government at Portsmouth, therefore, was a "Bible Commonwealth," in which the will of God was ascertained, from time to time, by the freeholders in general meeting assembled. Like the Providence people, they equalled the Massachusetts Bay Company in exclusiveness by providing that no newcomer should be received except by consent of the "Body," and then only upon his submission to the existing government.[1] From this time on, for the next few years, there were rapid and radical changes in the institutions of the islanders, but the history of this time is difficult to get at, and even more difficult to narrate with clearness and brevity. The Hutchinsonians, like their prophetess, were restless. In 1639 Coddington and his personal friends abandoned Portsmouth and made a settlement near the southern end of the island, which they called Newport. Most of the Hutchinsonians lived and died on Rhode Island; but the changeful spirit of Mrs. Hutchinson could not long be content in any one place. In 1642, on the death of her husband, she removed from the shores of Narragansett Bay, and settled at the western end of Long

[1] *Rhode Island Colony Records*, i, 53.

Island Sound, within the limits of what is now Westchester County, New York. There she lived with her children, her grandchildren, and her servants, untroubled by any superior authority, for about a year, when she and her whole household, to the number of sixteen persons, were murdered by the Indians. "God's hand," wrote Winthrop, "is the more apparently seen therein, to pick out this woful woman to make her and those belonging to her, an unheard of heavy example of their [the Indians] cruelty," which is the most regrettable sentence that the first governor of Massachusetts ever penned.

The fourth colony to be settled within the limits of the present state of Rhode Island had for its founder one of the most interesting characters in New England history. His name was Samuel Gorton, and in earlier life he had lived in London as a clothier. In 1636 or 1637 he appeared at Boston. He made no long stay at that place, possibly because his opinion that "heaven and hell had no actual existence" was in opposition to that of the men of Massachusetts. Removing to Plymouth, he lived there for some time without giving offense, but at length found himself summoned before the magistrates and finally before the Great and General Court. How far he had gone in formulating his beliefs at that time cannot be discovered; but it was not long after this that we find him declaring that the Scriptures were no more than "tales";[1] that oath-taking in court was opposed to the commandment, and that baptism by the sign of the cross or by water was of no efficacy. It is likely that he had already begun the promulgation of these doctrines; but he was at the moment before the magistrates because he had had the temerity to defend a serving woman whose actions did

[1] Winslow's *Hypocrisy Unmasked,* 50.

not please the authorities. The governor being fatigued, one of the assistants stated Gorton's offense to the General Court, when the accused, "stretching out his hand toward his face, said with a loud voice, 'If Satan will accuse the brethren, let him come down from Jehoshua his right hand and stand here.'"[1] As a result of this bearding of the Plymouth magistrate, Gorton soon found himself outside the limits of that colony. His next field of activity was Portsmouth, where William Coddington was still exercising the chief magistracy. In that place, also, Gorton's religious proclivities seem to have been borne with, but there again he undertook to defend a maid-servant, possibly the same one, and again lost his temper, calling the presiding judge "a just ass" and swinging his arms about. So Mr. Coddington sentenced him to be whipped and saw to it that the punishment was inflicted. As Coddington turned away, Gorton broke from the whipping post and ran to him, "drawing a chain after one of his legs, the upper part of his body being still naked," and told him that one of these days he should have the chain again.[2] Next Gorton betook himself to Providence, where Williams soon described him as "bewitching and bemadding poor Providence both with his unclean and foul censures of all the ministers of this country . . . and also denying all visible and external audiences in depth of familisme, against which I have a little disputed and written, and shall (the most High assenting) to death. As Paul said of Asia, I of Providence (almost) all suck in his poison, as at first they did at Aquidneck. Some few and myself withstood his inhabitation and town privileges." Williams and those who acted with him were successful in banishing the intruder. So Gorton

[1] Winslow's *Hypocrisy Unmasked*, 67.

[2] *Ibid.*, 53.

once more went into exile. He "bought land" of the natives and began a little settlement at Shawomet, some miles south of Providence on the western side of Narragansett Bay.

Up to this time the authorities of the Bay had kept their hands off of Gorton; but now some of the Providence people appealed to Massachusetts for aid against the Gortonites.[1] The Massachusetts leaders expressed themselves as averse to meddling in the matter, and answered that they could do nothing. They advised the men of Providence to place themselves under the government of Massachusetts or of Plymouth, which some of them later did. Gorton himself had also aroused the suspicions of the Massachusetts people by his dealings with Miantonomo, the chief of the Narragansetts, whom they justly suspected of plotting to exterminate the settlers. To the remonstrances of the Massachusetts magistrates, Gorton replied in lengthy epistles. One of these was directed to "The Great and Honored Idol General now set up in Massachusetts." In this letter he informed the Massachusetts magistrates that they were a "generation of vipers" and, as at Plymouth and Portsmouth, suggested that they should come down and fight the matter out. Whatever may have been the failings of the Massachusetts leaders, hesitancy to accept a challenge was not one of them. Forty men sought Shawomet, captured Gorton and nine or ten companions, and bore them to Boston in triumph, leaving their families behind. When they had Gorton safe and sound at the capital, they knew not what to do with him. Eventually they convicted him of blasphemy, of which he was being constantly

[1] Massachusetts Historical Society's *Collections*, Third Series, i, 2; Winthrop's *New England*, ii, 59.

guilty, according to Massachusetts ideas. In the end, he departed for England where he engaged in a paper warfare with Edward Winslow. Gorton's pamphlet was entitled *Simplicity's Defence against Seven-headed Policy*,[1] and Winslow's was called *Hypocrisy Unmasked.* Gorton obtained from the Earl of Warwick, Chairman of the Commissioners of Trade and Plantations, an order directing Massachusetts to permit him to live in peace at Shawomet; but Winslow secured from the Commissioners a second order, considerably modifying the first. As for Gorton, he returned to Shawomet, which he appropriately christened Warwick, and lived reasonably happy ever after.

The four colonies of Providence, Portsmouth, Newport, and Warwick[2] were now well settled, but as yet they had no confirmation of the title to their land, which still rested on occupancy and on purchase from the natives. Any day Edward Winslow, on behalf of Massachusetts, Plymouth, and Connecticut, might secure a grant of their lands from the Long Parliament or from the king. To ward off this danger, Roger Williams went to England and procured from the Commissioners of the Long Parliament (1643) a patent of incorporation. The meaning and legal standing of this document is exceedingly vague. It begins with a recital of the appointment of the Commissioners and the settlement of the plantations of Providence, Portsmouth, and Newport.[3] It then proceeds to authorize the inhabitants of those towns to rule themselves and such others as shall hereafter inhabit within certain limits by such a form

[1] Reprinted in Force's *Tracts* and in Rhode Island Historical Society's *Collections*, ii.

[2] Those portions which deal with Gorton are reprinted in *New England Historical and Genealogical Register*, iv, 212. An excellent "Notice of Samuel Gorton," by Charles Deane, precedes this reprint. Williams's letter is in *ibid.*, 216.

[3] W. E. Foster has pointed out that these settlements "were scarcely less than little 'states.'" — *Life of Stephen Hopkins*, i, 158.

of civil government as the greater part of them should find most suitable to their condition, but their laws and punishments must be as near as may be to the laws of England. This latter proviso is found in many colonial documents, and meant much or little as the existing government in England was interested or not in colonial matters and was able to make its will respected. A further proviso in this instrument reserved to the Commissioners and their successors the right to dispose of the general government of the plantation as they should conceive most conducive to the general good of the plantations in America, the honor of his Majesty, and the service of the State. This brief statement of some provisions of the patent shows clearly enough its institutional indefiniteness; its legal standing is even less certain. It was issued by the Earl of Warwick and other persons who had received their authority from the Long Parliament, which professed to act in the name of the king. It was issued before the battle of Naseby and while affairs in England were in an extremely critical condition, and when it would be absurd to regard Parliament as exercising sovereign authority. It was, possibly, on account of this uncertainty that Williams and the Narragansett settlers made no use of this license until Cromwell's victories over the king had determined in some measure the question of sovereignty in England.[1]

The patent bears the date of 1643, but it was not until three years and more had passed away (1647) that the major part of the voters of Providence, Newport, and Portsmouth met at the last-named place and proceeded to act under its provisions.[2] One of the first things which they did was to admit the Warwick colonists to a share in their rights

[1] The patent was confirmed by Cromwell as Protector in 1655. *Rhode Island Colony Records*, i, 317.

[2] See *Rhode Island Colony Records*, i, 147 and fol.

under the patent, and to provide that all voters should set their hands to an engagement to uphold the new government. They also established a general organization for the four colonies or settlements. This had only a brief existence but it is interesting as showing what some seventeenth-century Englishmen regarded as a desirable framework for a political society. For a legislative body, they instituted a general court in which the voters of the several settlements should be represented by committees, and their executive officers were a president and four assistants, one from each settlement. In all this they merely reproduced in its essential features the government which had been instituted by the Connecticut colonists; but with the democratic instincts which pervaded the Narragansett settlers, they forecasted the future and attempted to establish what would now be called a joint system of initiative and referendum. According to this plan, the voters of each settlement might propose legislation, which should be ratified or rejected by the next legislature; or that body might propose regulations, which should be confirmed or voted down by the people of the several settlements. Eight years later, in 1655, there were only forty-two voters in Providence, seventy-one in Portsmouth, ninety-four in Newport, and thirty-eight in Warwick — in all two hundred and forty-five.[1] Having in mind these figures, this arrangement would seem to be somewhat overponderous, even when the individual voters were as stiff in their opinions as were the settlers of Rhode Island and Providence Plantations. The new fundamental law was constantly amended and the voters themselves do not seem to have regarded the constitution of their embryonic republic with any degree of affection or respect, if we may regard the practice of

[1] *Rhode Island Colony Records*, i, 299.

illegal voting or ballot stuffing as evidence of lack of appreciation. It was in 1649 that the General Assembly ordered "for the prevention of corruption of votes for the future, that . . . none shall bring any votes, but such as they receive from the voters hands." Such as it was, the joint government or federation continued for only three years. In 1651 William Coddington returned from a visit to England with a commission from the Council of State of the Commonwealth which authorized him to govern Rhode Island during his lifetime, with the aid of a council of six persons to be appointed by the people.[1] This arrangement was not at all to the liking of the Rhode Islanders. They sent one of their number to England, who was soon followed by Roger Williams. Eventually, the authorities of the Commonwealth annulled Coddington's commission and directed the inhabitants of the four settlements to proceed under the patent of 1643. From this time until the Restoration, in 1660, and even for three years longer, the federation preserved a somewhat feeble existence.

The general liberty which existed in Rhode Island and Providence Plantations attracted to those settlements persons who were out of sympathy with settled government anywhere and asserted that it was against the rule of the gospel to execute judgment upon transgressors against the private or public welfare.[2] Their declaration induced those in authority to enact two laws, providing that no newcomer should be received as a freeman in any town except by the consent of the assembly, and that any one

[1] On this episode, see Henry E. Turner's "William Coddington in Rhode Island Colonial Affairs" (*Rhode Island Historical Tracts*, No. 4).

[2] Sir Henry Vane in 1654 declared that "the noise [of the tumults at Providence] echoes into the ears of all, as well friends as enemies. . . . Are there no wise men amongst you? No public self-denying spirits?" — *Rhode Island Colony Records*, i, 285.

making slanderous speeches could be sued in any town. Roger Williams was stimulated to action by the threatened anarchy and wrote an admirable letter defining the line between liberty and license: —

"There goes many a ship to sea, with many hundred souls in one ship, whose weal and woe is common, and is a true picture of a commonwealth. . . . It hath fallen out sometimes that both Papists and Protestants, Jews and Turks, may be embarked in one ship; upon which supposal I affirm, that all the liberty of conscience, that ever I pleaded for, turns upon these two hinges: that none of the Papists, Protestants, Jews, or Turks be forced to come to the ship's prayers or worship, nor compelled from their own particular prayers or worship, if they practise any. I further add, that I never denied, that notwithstanding this liberty, the commander of this ship ought to command the ship's course. . . . If any of the seamen refuse to perform their service or passengers to pay their freight; if any refuse to help, in person or purse, towards the common charges or defence; if any refuse to obey the common laws and orders of the ship, . . .; if any shall mutiny and rise up against their commanders and officers; if any should preach or write that there ought to be no commanders nor officers, because all are equal in Christ, therefore no masters nor officers, no laws nor orders, nor corrections nor punishments; I say, I never denied, but in such cases, whatever is pretended, the commander or commanders may judge, resist, compel, and punish such transgressors, according to their deserts and merits."[1]

This brief survey of the settlements of the towns on or near Narragansett Bay gives one an insight into the peculiarities which have marked off the State of Rhode Island and Providence Plantations from the other States of the Union. Foremost among these peculiarities may be mentioned a spirit of intense local patriotism which has no parallel elsewhere; the people of each town seem to be zealous for their local rights and distinctions, and the people of all the towns of the State seem to combine

[1] *Narragansett Club Publications*, vi, 278.

together only in opposition to other colonies and States. In Rhode Island, individualism has always had its highest development; in colonial days there was no capital in which the people of all the settlements were on a footing of equality. The General Assembly had no fixed place of meeting, but convened successively in different parts of the colony. There were no rules in Rhode Island by which affairs should be carried on; what one found on the island of Aquidneck he might be reasonably certain he would not find in Providence or in Warwick. There was one great exception to this general statement: everywhere in the colony men held strong opinions, and everywhere there was extreme toleration for the ideas of others. In such a community, men of power and independence were likely to arise who would profoundly influence the thoughts, lives, souls, and doings of others; and such men have been Rhode Island's chiefest contribution to American nationality.

The Massachusetts Bay Company expelled Roger Williams and William Coddington from their corporate limits because they did not like the opinions which these gentlemen held and promulgated; John Haynes and Thomas Hooker, Theophilus Eaton and John Davenport, sought the Connecticut Valley and the shores of Long Island Sound of their own free will and against the wishes of the rulers of the colony on the Bay. Precisely why Haynes and Hooker and their companions deserted Massachusetts for the Connecticut Valley is one of the unsolved problems of New England history. Haynes and Roger Ludlow,[1] the third important settler of Connecticut, had

[1] John M. Taylor in his *Roger Ludlow* suggests that disappointed ambition led Ludlow to the banks of the Connecticut. At all events he did not remain there long, as he soon removed to Fairfield and in 1654 returned to England.

borne prominent parts in Massachusetts. The former, as governor, had pronounced the sentence of banishment against Roger Williams, and in the Church no minister had been more highly regarded than Hooker. Probably they and their companions were actuated by a variety of motives. Hooker, for instance, disliked the close connection between Church and State which obtained in Massachusetts, and preferred a broader franchise than one which rested on Church membership.[1] All three of the Connecticut leaders probably felt themselves overshadowed by Winthrop, Dudley, and Endicott, by John Cotton and John Wilson. A third consideration possibly had more potency than either of these with the ordinary emigrants: this was the belief that the fertile Connecticut Valley offered a better chance for worldly advancement than the gravelly and rocky hills of eastern Massachusetts; in point of fact the new migration may be regarded as a part of that incessant search for cheaply acquired fertile lands which has been one of the mainsprings of the growth of the United States.[2] With the whole continent at their backs, it seems a little singular that any one should have felt straitened for room in Massachusetts; but the peculiar town system of that colony, which demanded concentration of settlement, had much to do with this feeling. When Hooker and his Newtowne flock first became discontented and complained of the scantiness of their bounds, the General Court granted them more land on the opposite side of the Charles River; but this new land was inconvenient of access, and its possession did not

[1] G. L. Walker's "Thomas Hooker" (*Makers of America Series*) repeats the traditional view of Connecticut's rise.

[2] Many of the original settlers of Connecticut had that restless pioneer spirit which became so well known in later years. For example, the town of Wethersfield had scarcely been founded ere many of its inhabitants made another migration and founded the town of Milford in New Haven Colony.

remove their discontentment. In 1635 one of the greatest of the Nonconformist ministers, Thomas Shepard, arrived at Boston with a strong band of followers. These offered to buy out the Newtowne (Cambridge) people, and this circumstance led the General Court to consent to their departure. So overland they went (1636) through the forests, with their wives and their children, their cattle and their household goods, Mrs. Hooker riding in a horse litter, making the first of those pilgrimages toward the setting sun which later became a marked characteristic of American life. Preceding or following them went other settlers from Dorchester, Watertown, and Roxbury, — those from the last-named town settling at Springfield, which later was found to be within the limits of Massachusetts.

Before this time Dutch and Plymouth fur traders had sought the banks of the Connecticut and had established trading stations on the sites of the modern Hartford and Wethersfield. The newcomers built their houses and cultivated the soil about these posts with slight regard for the rights of the earlier occupants.[1] Some of them also settled higher up the river, at Windsor. While these colonists were slowly gathering on the upper reaches of the river, other settlers were taking possession of the mouth of the stream. These were the advance guard of a colony which Lord Brooke and Lord Saye and Sele designed to plant in the Connecticut Valley. These Puritan noblemen had secured from the Earl of Warwick the title to an enormous tract of land, which he had received from the Council of New England, of which he was at one time president. The leader in this new venture was John Win-

[1] For instance, cattle belonging to the Dutchmen were "impounded for trespassing on the Englishmen's corn." — *Colonial Records of Connecticut*, i, 51.

throp, Jr.,[1] but the expedition which actually took possession of the mouth of the river was a forlorn hope which had been hastily sent from Boston to forestall the Dutch. The Englishmen came in good time and managed to mount two guns on shore before the Dutch appeared, looked upon them, and sailed back to New Amsterdam. The Dutch fur traders at Hartford were not so accommodating, but with the phlegmatic obstinacy which marks their race they held on to the post for many a year, although constantly harassed and insulted by their English neighbors.

The land history of Connecticut is very complicated and hard to unravel. The title to the soil rests on a deed or grant which bears the signature of the Earl of Warwick, but whether it was given as president of the Council for New England or was merely a transfer of private rights cannot be discovered. At all events, in 1631 Lord Saye and Sele, Lord Brooke, John Hampden, John Pym, and their associates, among whom were Sir Richard Saltonstall and Herbert Pelham, received some kind of a grant of land from Warwick in which the bounds were stated with more than usually exasperating indefiniteness. South of Massachusetts the new colony extended from the Narragansett River one hundred and twenty miles along the seashore and so due west to the South Sea. The settlements higher up the river were made without any arrangements with the associates and possibly against their wishes;[2] but the relations between the Saybrook colonists and the settlers farther up the stream were usually harmo-

[1] Winthrop's early connection with Connecticut has been somewhat exaggerated. It was 1649 before he ceased to be a Massachusetts magistrate, and 1650 before he transplanted his family to the scene of his later years. See Massachusetts Historical Society's *Proceedings*, Second Series, iii, 197. The more important facts in the life of the younger Winthrop are summed up in the American Antiquarian Society's *Proceedings*, 1898, p. 295.

[2] See a letter printed in Winthrop's *New England*, i, 397.

nious. The first Connecticut colonists were squatters; they held their lands by virtue of continued occupancy, conquest of the Pequots, and purchase from the River Indians and the Saybrook grantees.[1] They made good their title by long-continued possession and by procuring a confirmation of it from Charles II (1662). The boundary history of Connecticut is in many respects of great interest and importance; but it will be convenient to consider the more significant of the controversies which arose in other connections.

The Indian title to the soil of Connecticut was uncertain. The Mohegans held the western and central part of the area which is now comprised in the State of Connecticut. To the east, the Narragansetts inhabited the greater part of the mainland of what is now the State of Rhode Island. Between these two strong Indian tribes lived the Pequots and sundry smaller tribes which were nominally tributary to them. At one time, the Connecticut River Indians requested the English to come and settle on their tribal lands, probably in the hope that the whites would defend them against their more powerful enemies. The Connecticut settlers soon found themselves involved in difficulties with the Pequots and their tributary tribes. As has so often happened in the course of colonizing enterprises, the continued prestige of the whites depended upon, or seemed to depend upon, the punishment of the natives, — and the Pequot tribe was swept from the face of the earth. The New England colonists undoubtedly did their best to deal fairly with the Indians; but native intrigues and policies were too involved for their simple English understandings.

[1] See Trumbull's *History*, i, and Appendix i; *Colonial Records of Connecticut*, i, 568; Andrews's "River Towns of Connecticut" (*Johns Hopkins University Studies*, vii, No. 7).

Connecticut and Massachusetts combined in this mission. The military forces were led by Captain John Mason of Connecticut and by the redoubtable Captain John Underhill, at that moment of Massachusetts; with them was associated as a spiritual guide the Rev. Mr. Stone of Hartford. Embarking the allied troops, Mason and Underhill sailed eastwardly from Saybrook, passing within sight of the Pequots, who had assembled at Stonington. The savages, seeing the ships going by, supposed that the whites were retiring from the Connecticut Valley; they were inexperienced in the military capacity of Captains Mason and Underhill and the Rev. Mr. Stone of Hartford. Before starting out, these had held a council of war, at which two plans had been suggested. As the military men could reach no conclusion, they requested Mr. Stone to pray. He spent most of that night in prayer. The next morning he sought Captain Mason and assured him that he was entirely satisfied with the plan of approaching the Pequots' stronghold from the direction of Narragansett Bay. Mason and Underhill took from the Connecticut River, besides the white soldiers, a band of Mohegan warriors. In the Narragansett country they procured the services of a more numerous body of Narragansett braves. Approaching the Pequots' stronghold, just before the break of day, the white soldiers advanced to the attack while their red allies waited in the rear to pick off any escaping Pequots. The surprise was complete, but the whites soon became scattered among the wigwams, inside the fort. Disaster seemed impending, when it occurred to them to set fire to the village. The Pequots perished by the hundreds in the flames or at the hands of the whites or their savage allies; seven were captured and seven escaped. The war begun in this way was vigorously prosecuted, until the

Pequots as a nation ceased to exist. As a rule, Indian warfare is barren of valuable lessons, but this episode in New England history is characteristic of the thoroughness with which the New Englanders of that day performed their tasks. The curious reader who wishes to note the doings of the New England counterpart of Cromwell's Ironsides will do well to read the extremely interesting accounts written by the commanders in the campaign.[1]

The Pequot War and the necessary labor in providing houses and clearing the fields put off for years the settling of the constitution. In the early days of the movement to the Connecticut Valley the Massachusetts government had appointed a constable to preserve order in the new settlement. When the increasing size of the Connecticut towns made more complicated machinery necessary Massachusetts authorized the leaders of the migration to exercise powers of government until further order should be made. This commission, of course, had no validity outside the limits of Massachusetts, but where those limits were no one then knew, and doubtless the majority of the colonists cared little about its legal status. At all events Ludlow and the magistrates carried on the government for some time under this commission with the sanction of public opinion. In January, 1638–39, the "inhabitants and residents" of Windsor, Wethersfield, and Hartford met at the last-named place and adopted eleven orders, which enjoy the distinction of being the first written political constitution in which the functions of government are formulated in detail. The earlier Pilgrim compact and the fundamental laws of the Rhode Island towns were rather in the nature of social compacts and

[1] Captain John Mason's "Brief History of the Pequot War" is in Massachusetts Historical Society's *Collections*, Second Series, viii, 120–153; Captain John Underhill's "News from America" is in *ibid.*, Third Series, vi, 1–28.

followed closely the phraseology of the Church covenants of that time. The Connecticut orders, on the other hand, are phrased like the later constitutions and have their rise in legal and not in ecclesiastical precedents.

By this constitution, the "inhabitants and residents" of the three towns, well knowing that the word of God requireth that "there should be an orderly and decent government established according to God," entered into a combination together "to maintain and preserve the liberty and purity of the gospel of our Lord Jesus, which we now profess, as also the discipline of the Churches, which, according to the truth of said gospel is now practiced amongst us."[1] In their civil affairs they were to be guided and governed according to the orders which were then formulated. These provided that two General Courts should be held in each year, at one of which the public officers should be chosen by those who had "been admitted inhabitants by the major part of the town where they live, or the major part of such as shall be then present" and have also taken the oath of fidelity.[2] By this section the qualification for voters was the election by those who already enjoyed the franchise. In 1658–59 this arrangement was modified so as to require personal estate to the value of thirty pounds. In 1662 the money require-

[1] Church and State were always intimately connected in Connecticut. In 1644 the General Court provided that any person who refused to contribute a "meet proportion" for the support of the ministry might be rated by authority and compelled by the civil power to pay the assessment. Attendance at the town religious service was compulsory. In point of fact in these matters, as in others, the General Assembly of Connecticut adopted the laws of Massachusetts — even using the same phraseology. Compare, for example, the Connecticut Code of 1650, titles "Ecclesiastical" and "Ministers Meintenance," with the earlier Massachusetts enactments in Whitmore's *Laws of 1660*.

[2] In 1656–57 the General Court voted that "those that shall hereafter be made free, shall have an affirmative certificate under the hands of all or the major part of the deputies in their several towns, of their peaceable and honest conversation, and those and only those of them which the General Court shall approve shall be made freemen." — *Colonial Records of Connecticut*, i, 290.

ment was reduced one third, but a certificate of honest and peaceable conversation from the major part of the townsmen was required, and even then the candidate might be refused admission to the franchise by the General Court. There is no religious qualification set forth in so many words, but having in mind the preamble which has been partly quoted above, it seems improbable that persons who were not prepared to maintain and preserve the purity of the gospel and the discipline of the churches then in existence, would have had much chance of securing the votes of the major part of the inhabitants of his town or of those who were present at the Court of Election; or to put it in another way, it is altogether unlikely that a Baptist, or an Episcopalian, or a Roman Catholic, or even an Antinomian could have secured the right to vote in Connecticut in the year 1640, or for many years thereafter. The election of officers was to be by papers, as was then the case in Massachusetts, and there was to be a previous nomination to office, as was also the case in the Bay Colony. The governor must be a member of some approved congregation "and formerly of the magistracy within this jurisdiction," and all the magistrates and deputies must be freemen. The apportionment of representation was on the town basis; the three original towns were to send four deputies each, and later towns to have as many as the General Court from time to time might determine. The General Court should consist of the governor, and at least four magistrates, and the major part of the deputies, except in such cases where the governor had refused to summon it, in which exigency the deputies could legislate by themselves. The General Court, however convened, should exercise "the supreme power of the commonwealth, and they only shall have power to make laws or repeal them, to grant levies, to admit freemen, to dispose of lands undisposed of," to question magistrates, and, in general, to deal in any matter that concerns the good of the commonwealth except only the election of magistrates, which shall be done by the whole body of freemen. Such, in brief, was this celebrated constitution which, in effect, did little more than to formulate on paper the existing government of Massachusetts Bay. It will be noticed that in one part of the constitution the suffrage might be conferred by the inhabitants of the several towns, while in another part this right is reserved to the General Court. In the early days the power to admit inhabitants and thereby to confer the franchise was exercised by the several towns, but this right was later restricted by action of the General Court.[1] In 1639 the Connecticut General Court adopted, almost in its entirety, the town system of Massachusetts as it had been developed up to the date of the emigration. Curiously enough, in the course of time, it fell out that Massachusetts grew away from its early institutional arrangements in town and commonwealth, while Connecticut held fast to those that had been established at the outset. No state, indeed, has more steadfastly and consistently held to the ideas of the fathers than has Connecticut.

The colony of New Haven had its rise in the action of two strong and influential men, John Davenport and Theophilus Eaton. They had been friends since they attended the same school at Coventry, and in London had sustained the relation of pastor and principal parishioner. For years Eaton had been interested in plans of colonization, and had ventured many score pounds sterling in the Massachusetts Bay Company. It was not, however, until

[1] See Note III.

Archbishop Laud had driven Davenport from his cure that the plan of founding a colony in New England was taken up in earnest. In 1637 two vessels sailed into Boston harbor, bringing to the New World these men, and a strong group of immigrants who had determined to abide with them. Disembarking at Boston, the newcomers found lodgings and employment in the thriving Bay Colony during the autumn, winter, and spring of 1637–38, while the leaders searched for a suitable site for their settlement. The Massachusetts men were anxious to retain Davenport and Eaton in the midst, and the people of Newbury went so far as to offer to abandon their houses and cleared lands to these orthodox sojourners. Davenport and Eaton declined these offers. They wished to work out their salvation in their own way, and may also have thought that at New Haven their doings would be unknown to Archbishop Laud, and therefore would not be interfered with. Possibly reasons of a material kind may have exercised a determining influence.[1] It cannot be said, however, that Davenport idled away his time in Massachusetts Bay, as he was one of the most ardent of the assessors who aided Wilson and Shepard in their contest with Mrs. Anne Hutchinson.

It was the spring of 1638 when Davenport and his flock sailed from Boston for Quinnipiac, or Quillipiac as the word was often spelled in those days. Like the Rhode Island and Connecticut settlers, they were "squatters" on the land in that they seem to have had no patent from the king, either directly or indirectly, and they did not

[1] See, for example, Davenport and Eaton to the Massachusetts authorities, "12th day of the first moneth, 1638," in Massachusetts Historical Society's *Collections*, Third Series, iii, 165. The same letter is reprinted in Winthrop's *New England*, i, 404, and again, from the same original, in *Bulletin of the New York Public Library*, iii, 393.

even purchase their lands of the Indians. They simply settled at New Haven and trusted to the future—which proved to be unfortunate. They chose the site of their new home with the intention of making it the commercial center of the New World. They built substantial houses and embarked on commercial ventures, but were not successful. The natural center of commerce of that region was Manhattan Island, and it was too near New Haven for the latter to develop independent trade. At length (1646) they built a "great ship," freighted her with wheat, hides, beaver, and plate to the total value of five thousand pounds, and dispatched her for London, where the treasure was to be turned into trading goods by means of which reluctant commerce might once more be wooed. The "great ship" sailed away and has never been heard from since. Once her ghostly shape appeared, with masts, and tackling trim, sailing into the harbor, and then faded away before the watcher's eyes.[1]

From an institutional point of view, the history of New Haven is interesting as showing a Bible Commonwealth of the extremest type in process of formation. On June, 1639, the "free planters" of New Haven assembled in Mr. Newman's barn. Mr. Davenport addressed them and laid before them certain propositions, which he had formulated in advance and to which they now agreed. These propositions were briefly as follows: (1) that the Scriptures are a sufficient guide in all affairs of life; (2) that the assembled free planters agree to be bound thereby; (3) that they all wish to be admitted members of a church; (4) that they feel obliged to establish such order as should conduce to the best good of the church; (5) that

[1] Winthrop's *New England*, ii, 328. Atwater, in his *History of New Haven* (Appendix iii), has brought together several versions of the appearance of this phantom ship.

only church members should be free burgesses or freemen, in other words, that the franchise should be confined to church members. So far these propositions would probably have been accepted by most New Englanders of that time outside of Rhode Island. It is in the sixth that the Brahminical caste of New Haven's institutions appears. This was, in effect, that the free planters should choose out of their number twelve men, who should select from themselves seven to be the first church members and, therefore, the first free burgesses. In order to understand the oligarchical nature of New Haven's constitution, it should be borne in mind that only the "free planters" were assembled in Mr. Newman's barn, although the precise meaning of the phrase "free planters" is not certain. It is well ascertained, however, that there were many servants, and even persons who were not servants, in New Haven who would not be comprised in any such description. Be that as it may, all power in Church and State was now in the hands of seven persons, who could pick and choose from the other free planters those whom they thought worthy of admission to the Church and government of the State. There was only one church in the colony. The only way in which the colony could grow, therefore, was by the establishment of other churches and their combination with the New Haven Church and State in a federal union.

The government which was formed in this way was unique in New England, because in Massachusetts Bay, except for a few years, the principal inhabitants in each town voted in town meeting, whether they were freemen of the corporation or not, although only such as were also freemen could vote for the members of the general government.

Other churches and towns were soon established in the vicinity of New Haven, and for some years this federative ecclesiastical republic led a vigorous and on the whole profitable existence, although disputes with the Dutch and commercial failures were not infrequent. The New Havenites did not succeed in securing a charter from the king, or even a patent from the Earl of Warwick. The consequence of this was that, when Connecticut obtained her charter from Charles II, New Haven was absorbed within the bounds of the larger colony. In these ways it came about that from the numerous isolated settlements which were made south of Massachusetts, only two colonies had a legal existence in 1663. These were Connecticut and the colony of Rhode Island and Providence Plantations.

NOTES

I. Bibliography of Rhode Island. — Clarence S. Brigham's "Bibliography of Rhode Island History" (Appendix to the third volume of Field's *Rhode Island*) is well arranged and includes titles as late as 1901. The "Records" of Rhode Island, Providence Plantations, and Warwick were edited by Mr. Bartlett and in some cases possibly revised by him. The "Court Records" were not included in this publication; they have never been printed and have seldom been studied. The local records of Providence have been printed in great detail, and the records of Portsmouth have been published under the editorship of Mr. Brigham.

There is no adequate history of Rhode Island, all of the books so far produced being full of prejudice against Massachusetts. Arnold's *Rhode Island* (N.Y. 1859–60) was a remarkable work in its day. Of the modern books, Clarence S. Brigham's *Sketch*[1] is probably the best; Irving B. Richman's *Rhode Island: Its Making and Its Meaning* contains some interesting bits of information not elsewhere easily accessible.

The best account of the institutional history of Providence is Henry C. Dorr's *Providence Proprietors and Freeholders*, which forms the principal justification for the existence of the third and fourth volumes of the *Publications* of the Rhode Island Historical Society, and is also printed separately as the ninth volume of the *Collections* of the same society.

II. Bibliography of Connecticut and New Haven. — Charles A. Flagg's "Reference List on Connecticut Local History" (*New York State Library Bulletin*, No. 53, December, 1900, "Bibliography, No. 23") contains also titles of bibliographies and general works. The public records of Connecticut have been edited by J. H. Trumbull and C. J. Hoadly in fifteen volumes. Of almost equal authority is Benjamin Trumbull's *History of Connecticut*,[2] which was based on much documentary evidence that is no longer accessible; unfortunately it stops with the year 1764. Hollister's *Connecticut* is more complete in point of ground covered, but is not always trustworthy. C. M. Andrews's "River Towns of Connecticut" (*Johns Hopkins*

[1] This forms the first part of vol. i of Edward Field's *State of Rhode Island and Providence Plantations at the End of the Century: A History* (Boston, 1902).

[2] Originally published in 1818 in two volumes without an index; reprinted in 1898 with an index and a different pagination.

University Studies) is the best account of the early settlements from the institutional and political point of view. Alexander Johnston's "Connecticut," in the *Commonwealth Series*, is a keen study of a political phenomenon and sometimes betrays a curious lack of knowledge of American history in the colonial period.

Connecticut is rich in local history. New Haven,[1] with a natural pride in its separate settlement, has its own *Colonial Records* and Historical Society. Atwater's *History of the Colony of New Haven* and C. H. Levermore's *Republic of New Haven* are among the best books of their class. Other notable local histories which in some sort supply the defect of more formal general works, are Bernard C. Steiner's *Guilford and Madison*, Frances M. Caulkins's *New London*, and Ellen D. Larned's *Windham County* and *Historic Gleanings in Windham County*.

III. Suffrage in Early Connecticut. — Professor C. M. Andrews, in his valuable and stimulating monograph on the *River Towns of Connecticut* (p. 85) gives one to understand that "universal suffrage" prevailed in Connecticut. This was possibly the case at first, owing, in part at least, to the fact that the population of that colony in the early days was singularly homogeneous; when, however, alien elements became threatening, the assembly thought it necessary to hedge about the franchise with restrictions. Moreover, as stated in the text, there appears to have been always a religious qualification in the background. The problems of government in Massachusetts, with the great stream of immigration constantly pouring in from England, were very different from those which prevailed in the slow-growing settlements in Connecticut. Professor Andrews has fallen into the habit of Connecticut writers of calling the Massachusetts people Puritans, as though the settlers of Connecticut and New Haven were any less entitled to that honorable designation than were those of Massachusetts.

[1] On the absorption of New Haven by Connecticut, see B. C. Steiner in American Historical Association's *Papers* for 1891, p. 209. There is a valuable article on John Davenport by Franklin B. Dexter in New Haven Historical Society's *Papers*, ii, 205.

CHAPTER XV

NEW ENGLAND IN 1649

BESIDES the settlements whose history has just been traced in some detail, the States of New Hampshire and Maine had their beginnings in the first half of the seventeenth century. The origin of New Hampshire is found in a grant from the Council for New England to Captain John Mason,[1] follower and friend of the Duke of Buckingham, — it was in his house at Portsmouth, England, that Buckingham was stabbed to death by John Felton. Mason was also a friend of Sir Ferdinando Gorges, and he and Gorges obtained other grants under which the first settlements were made on the coast of Maine. Later, following the example of the Massachusetts patentees, both of these men secured charters from the crown, confirming them in their lands and giving them authority to govern those subjects of the king who might settle within their limits. The Pilgrims had a trading post on the Kennebec River, and there were other settlements on the coast and possibly even inland. Some of the early colonists of New Hampshire and of Maine came direct from England, others drifted northward from the settlements in what we now call Massachusetts. The number of persons living in New Hampshire and Maine in 1649 was not large, and Massachusetts at one time or another took them under her government, usually with the consent of the majority of

[1] This Captain John Mason should be carefully distinguished from the Connecticut colonist.

the inhabitants. In this way their institutions developed without presenting any peculiar features of very great interest to the student of this first half century of New England history.

In 1643 the colonies of Massachusetts Bay, New Plymouth, Connecticut, and New Haven entered into a federal union which is known in history as the United Colonies of New England or as the New England Confederation. The reasons why Maine and Rhode Island were not admitted to this federation are stated by John Winthrop and Elder Brewster. As to Maine, Winthrop says, "Those of Sir Ferdinando Gorge his province, beyond Pascataquack, were not received nor called into the confederation, because they ran a different course from us both in their ministry and civil administration; for they had lately made Acomenticus (a poor village) a corporation, and had made a tailor their mayor, and had entertained one Hull, an excommunicated person and very contentious, for their minister." Plainly colonists who elected tailors for the chief officers of their corporation were out of place as allies of a state of which John Winthrop was the leading man, nor did the rulers of Massachusetts desire contentious persons as companions. As to the people of Rhode Island, the Pilgrim leader wrote, "Concerning the Islanders we have no conversing with them, nor desire to have, further than necessity or humanity may require."[1] At a later time, indeed, certain of the foremost men of Massachusetts more than once referred to Rhode Island as "that sink" or "sewer." It will be recalled that it was in this year, 1643, that Roger Williams went to England to secure from the Puritan authorities there protection for Rhode Island against the members of the New England Confederation.

[1] Deane's *Bradford*, 388.

The reasons for the formation of this federal bond are stated at length in the preamble of the Articles of Confederation, and may be summarized as follows: (1) the contracting parties all came to America with one and the same end and aim, — to advance the Christian religion and "to enjoy the liberties of the gospel in purity with peace," in other words to worship God as they saw fit; (2) the dispersed condition of the plantations which prevented the formation of one government; (3) the possibility of war with the French on the north, with the Dutch on the west, or with the Indians in their midst. The formation of this confederation had been long in contemplation; the reason for the consummation of the plan at this time is given us by Winthrop, when he writes that doubts had arisen about the advisability of the magistrates taking an oath to "bear true faith and allegiance to our sovereign Lord, King Charles, seeing that he had violated the privilege of Parliament and had lost much of his kingdom and many of his subjects." "Whereupon," adds Winthrop, "it was thought fit to omit that part of it for the present." The meaning of this is tolerably clear; the king was in so much trouble at home that the colonists in America could do as they pleased without fear of the courts at Westminster or the council chamber at Whitehall.

Affairs being thus ripe for the formation of a federal constitution, commissioners came to Boston from Plymouth, New Haven, and Connecticut, including Saybrook. These, with the committee appointed by the General Court of Massachusetts, consulted together, and after having "encountered some difficulties" yielded each to the other and formulated the Articles of Confederation. The Plymouth delegates had no power to sign as had the delegates from the other colonies; but the federal pact was ratified by the General Court of New Plymouth Colony at its next meeting. By these articles the United Colonies entered into a firm and perpetual league of friendship for offense and defense, for propagating the truth and liberties of the gospel, and for their own mutual safety and welfare. Each colony was to retain its "peculiar jurisdiction," with which the general government of the confederation was on no account to intermeddle. The carrying on of the business of the new government was intrusted to eight commissioners who should be chosen annually, two from each colony, and any six of whom should have power to act. Probably the arrangement of this part of the constitution gave rise to the "difficulties" referred to on the preceding page, for Massachusetts, although having as large a population and possessing more wealth than the other three colonies put together, was not only to have the same number of commissioners as the smallest colony, but was to be bound by what the commissioners from the other three colonies should agree to. It is indeed extraordinary that the authorities of Massachusetts Bay were willing to enter into such a one-sided arrangement. One concession was made to her in the provision which gave to Boston two meetings of the commissioners out of every five; otherwise, the meetings should be held in the several colonies in succession, unless some "middle place" be found which should be commodious for them all. As a matter of fact, no "middle place" was discovered; and, remembering the sturdy character of the early New England colonists, it is doubtful if the pressure of public opinion at Boston or the generous hospitality of residents of the most important town of New England affected in any marked degree the action of the commissioners from the other jurisdictions. Nevertheless, the fact that the framers of the articles had in mind the establishment of a federal capital is interesting as showing that they contemplated the founding of a stronger and more permanent organization than that which actually came into being.

The grant of authority contained in the articles was very large and included full power to determine affairs of war or peace, division of spoils, reception of new confederates, "and all things of like nature, which are the proper concomitants or consequents of such a confederation for amity, offense, and defense." The commissioners were all of them to be church members and at their meetings should choose one of their number to act as president. This officer was simply to serve as moderator and was to have no power to hinder the progress of business "or any way cast the scales otherwise than in the precedent is agreed." Besides having the right to decide certain matters, as has already been stated, the commissioners were further to endeavor to frame agreements, in general cases, of a civil nature, for preserving the peace among the confederates, for securing the speedy passage of justice in every jurisdiction to all the members of the confederation, and for the management of Indian affairs. It was under this clause in the articles that the commissioners in 1650 advised the several jurisdictions to pass identical laws for securing the support of the ministry, and to use the power of the State to compel payment of taxes for this purpose. The article which contains the grant of power which has just been described also has the celebrated provision for the rendition of fugitive servants and criminals which has been regarded as the prototype of the fugitive slave laws of a later time.

The consent of six of the eight commissioners was ordinarily required for the carrying out of the purposes of the confederation. The geographical distribution of the four colonies, however, made it necessary to provide that, in the case of sudden invasion, the commissioners of two jurisdictions might order out the military forces nearest at hand and send for aid to the other members of the confederation; but in the final determination of the justice of the war and the defraying of the expenses, six commissioners must agree.

The makers of the articles realized that, after all, the New England Puritans were human beings, which some later writers appear not to have done. They provided, therefore, that in case any of the confederates should act contrary to the articles or should injure the people of one or the other of the jurisdictions, the commissioners of those colonies which were not parties to the dispute should act as a court of arbitration. Considering the lack of experience which the framers of this federal pact necessarily had in the drawing up of a constitution, this document is a remarkable production. It did not put a final ending to disputes between the four colonies, and it sometimes proved to be unsuited to the exigencies of the time. Nevertheless, the articles continued without amendment for forty years; they carried New England successfully through the fiercest Indian war of the seventeenth century. Had the Confederation been in existence in the next century, it is very possible that the northern colonies might have been saved much of the misery of the French and Indian Wars.

The inequality of the equal representation in the board of commissioners was certain to cause trouble; in no long time it led Massachusetts to refuse to obey the mandate of the constituted authorities of the Confederation. It was in May, 1653, that the commissioners, on account of approaching war with the Dutch, voted that five hundred soldiers should be raised,[1] and apportioned them among the colonies in such a way that Massachusetts should provide two thirds of them, although in the board she possessed only one quarter of the votes and was the least exposed to attack or loss. Massachusetts also felt doubts as to the justice of the war, in view of the fact that the charge of ill faith brought against the Dutch authorities rested largely on the testimony of Indians. The Massachusetts General Court refused to pass the necessary votes to raise and equip these men. It declared that, under the Articles of Confederation, the General Courts of the several jurisdictions were at liberty to act in every case according to their consciences, which was a seventeenth-century way of asserting what came to be called later the doctrine of nullification. After a somewhat acrimonious correspondence, in which the representatives of the smaller colonies plainly advanced the idea of delegated sovereignty, the Massachusetts authorities informed the commissioners that they saw no reason to protract a fruitless and needless discussion and committed the matter to God. From this time Massachusetts judged for herself whether the acts of the commissioners were "just and according to God"[2] or the reverse, and obeyed or disobeyed accordingly.

[1] *Plymouth Colony Records*, x, 33.

[2] *Plymouth Colony Records*, x, 74–88. Two other episodes are worth noting: the first a discussion as to whether Connecticut was justified in taxing Massachusetts people at Springfield for the defense of the mouth of the river. The six commissioners of the smaller colonies thought that she was; Massachusetts thought otherwise and threatened to tax all the commerce between herself and the smaller colonies unless Connecticut drew back. In another case, Massachusetts refused to levy war against a too active Indian chief named Ninegret, on the ground that there did not seem to be sufficient reason for so doing. These cases are easily found in the volume last mentioned; reference should also be made to the second volume of the *Massachusetts Colony Records*.

New England history not only furnishes the precedent for later schemes of federal government; it is also of great interest from the standpoint of the development of local institutions. The English colonization of America came at a time when the popular local administrative bodies in England retained a good measure of vitality. In the reigns of Elizabeth, James, and Charles, the political struggle was for the mastery of the central government. The opposition party comprised those political leaders who were hostile to the policies of the reigning monarchs in both Church and State. These men were powerful in the counties, the towns, and the parishes; they imposed upon Virginia representative institutions and in New England worked out the problem of local self-government. In America the conditions made for true representative government and the development of a large measure of local liberty. It fell out, therefore, that colonial institutions reproduced popular forms which were dying out in the home land and from this beginning developed on lines radically unlike those which prevailed in England. The early Stuarts and the Puritan rulers of England were so fully occupied with English politics that they had no time to interfere with this growth and, indeed, were probably unconscious of it. Fifty years of freedom gave the English-American colonists their opportunities.

In Elizabeth's time the central government, to a very great extent, ruled by the influence which the queen and the councilors, either singly or collectively, exercised over the local magistrates and the local governing bodies. The manorial system had ceased to have much vitality; the power was now centered in the lords lieutenants, the county justices, the cities, towns corporate, unincorporated towns and parishes, all of these last being generally described as towns. The Reformation and the accompanying dissolution of the monasteries threw new burdens upon the local governing bodies and made their control, financially and politically, worth while. For this reason the Church contended vigorously and with a measure of success for the leading part in the local administrative bodies. New England happened to be settled very largely by colonists from those portions of England where popular control still continued. It was in Ipswich, for example, that the churchwardens were dismissed from office and fined for speaking disrespectfully of the people; it was at Boston, England, that efforts were made to limit the secularization of the Lord's day by providing that no tradesman or butcher should sell on that day, especially during divine service, under penalty of ten shillings.[1]

The most interesting of the local organizations was the common law parish. Originally it was an ecclesiastical division, coextensive in boundaries with the civil administrative unit. The decay of feudalism and the transference of the headship of the Church from the Pope to the king had transformed the parish. The monarch no longer summoned his feudal vassals only; now he also wrote to the towns and parishes for their quotas of armed men. The crossbow, the longbow, and the brown bill were used as late as the Civil Wars of the seventeenth century, and the foot soldiers of Miles Standish's day in both England and America, while on the march, were weighted down with iron breasts and backs and headpieces or "pots," as they were commonly termed. In the colonies, however, the agility of the savages made it necessary to provide a lighter equipment, and it was soon found that a quilted coat, instead of an iron cuirass, sufficed to turn an Indian

[1] "Boston Assembly Book," Ms.

arrow. With the weapons of the Middle Ages there lingered also some of its traditions; at Edgehill, for example, William le Néve, Clarencieux Herald, officially summoned the Parliamentary army to surrender, "and did it with great marks of fear, having a feeling sense of danger." In the battle itself a Royalist, Sir John Southcote, captured a Parliamentary captain; he released him upon receiving, as ransom, a fine horse and suit of armor, — much to the displeasure of the king.

The "church armor," as the parish military equipment was termed, in peaceful days hung on the walls of the parish church, save when it was taken down to be cleaned or "dighted." From time to time the church wardens replaced wornout parts and purchased new daggers, pikes, and swords; the imminence of war might be calculated with surprising accuracy by tabulating the entries in the churchwarden's account books for the purchase of military supplies. The parish was not only obliged to find the soldier and equip him, but also had to pay his expenses to the meeting place and sometimes to pay another man to go with the soldier to show him the way or to see that he did not desert. When the war was over there were sick, wounded, and maimed soldiers and sailors to be maintained by the parish, for these local bodies were obliged to care for them as well as for those civilians who could no longer maintain themselves.

In the older time, before the Reformation, indigent and impotent persons were cared for by the church authorities, or by private charity, or were licensed to beg. With the dissolution of the monasteries and the confiscation of church funds, many of these sources of relief dried up, and at about the same time beggars and vagabonds began to be dealt with more strictly. The government sought to place the burden of caring for the poor upon the local administrative units, but did not hand over to the parishes and towns those portions of the ecclesiastical funds which had been used to alleviate suffering. At first no general compulsory law was passed, but an effort was made to raise the necessary money by means of more or less voluntary contributions; but those who were backward in giving were to be reasoned with by the various church authorities from the parson and churchwardens of the parish to the bishop of the diocese. If one remained obstinate, the justices of the peace or the mayor of the city should charitably and gently move the "said obstinate person to extend his charity toward the relief of the poor of the parish where he dwelleth," and if he still remained obstinate, he should pay such sum as the magistrates thought reasonable or go to jail. This means of supply proved precarious, probably because the obstinate persons who had money and the magistrates whose business it was to coerce them belonged to the same class of society. After many experiments, in 1598 Parliament placed the responsibility of the care of the poor upon the parishes or towns, and in case they failed to raise such sums as seemed reasonable to the county court, the justices could themselves rate the parishioners or, at their discretion, join a poor parish with a rich one, or a parish which had been overcome by some calamity with a parish which had been more fortunate, thereby equalizing the burden. The result of this poor law, which was made permanent in 1601, was to make the town and parish organization vastly more important than it had been before. Furthermore, it compelled the towns and parishes to guard themselves jealously against incoming strangers, so that members of the laboring classes became practically tied to the locality where they happened to come into the world.

The parishes discharged their obligations by a separate tax levy, which was known as the poor rate. In some places, however, gifts of money or of land were held in trust for the relief of the poor, sometimes being invested in a flock of sheep. Persistent attempts were also made to compel the poor to become self-supporting, by spinning flax or working up other raw material, which was provided at public charge; in Boston in 1595, twenty boys and maidens were so employed. At Northampton another course was taken. There the poor children were turned over to Roger Williams, pin maker, who paid the parish twelvepence per week for each child, and in return was permitted to work them from seven in the morning until six or eight in the evening. Whatever plan was tried, some other scheme was certain to seem preferable in no long time. The burden was unquestionably heavy. Strangers were carefully looked after. In Boston, for instance, it was provided that an inquiry should be made every fortnight as to all newcomers, and those who were likely to become chargeable be removed from the town; and no householder was permitted to let a dwelling to any "foreigner" unless he first obtained a license.[1] The communal spirit rapidly strengthened, and we find that at Ipswich no one could sell a house to a stranger without permission of the authorities, and at one time, indeed, no inhabitant of Northampton was permitted to sell corn to any outsider. Moreover, in years of threatened scarcity, the towns sometimes purchased food stuffs in quantity, and doled them out at cost price to the inhabitants of the town.

[1] See also *Pittington Records*, 1622, and *Houghton Records*, 1658.

In each parish there was one ecclesiastical edifice which was taken care of at the expense of the parishioners, and in which every man, woman, and child in the town was obliged to attend divine service, or incur certain penalties ascertained by law. This requirement applied to all persons, whether they were Conformists, Nonconformists, Independents, or Roman Catholics. Every one was expected to attend the religious service provided by the State.[1] The affairs of the parish were managed by the churchwardens and vestrymen, aided and guided by the parson. The tendency was to increase the amount of hierarchical control, but at the time of the settlement of Massachusetts the secular element was still powerful. It is especially worthy of note in this connection that in the management of local affairs in New England the parson had no official recognition, as he had in England, and exercised only such power in town affairs as his personal influence gave him. It was natural that it should be so because the Puritan movement was largely a revolt of the landed gentry against clerical control; Winthrop, Saltonstall, and Bellingham, were not likely to establish in America that influence which they left England to avoid.

The Massachusetts colonists brought with them to their new homes the ideas with which they had been familiar from their childhood. We may suppose that William Coddington and Richard Bellingham in the Massachusetts town meeting argued for the restrictions with which they had been familiar in the older Boston. So too did those who came from Ipswich and Dorchester, England, to Ipswich and Dorchester, Massachusetts. Sometimes a whole parish, parson and all, removed to Massachusetts,

[1] For a detailed discussion of the religious laws, see above, p. 246.

thereby upsetting all the social and ecclesiastical arrangements of that part of the country.

The religious edifice of the New England town was known locally as the meetinghouse. As in England, it was the center of local life in Church and State. In it were held the town meetings, as the parish meetings were held in the parish churches of England, and to it on the Lord's day came every dweller in the village unless prevented by some serious illness. It also served as a convenient place in which to store the town's stock of powder and extra military equipment; but, owing to the exigencies of frontier life, every able-bodied man in the early New England towns was obliged to have his weapons near at hand, instead of hanging them on the walls of the meetinghouses. As was the case in England, the town took care of the construction and repair of the religious edifices, and, there being no tithes, supported the minister directly by taxation, to which every one was obliged to contribute.[1] In the earlier time, the lack of tithes had been made up by voluntary contribution; but by 1660, throughout New England, except, of course, in Rhode Island, the support of the clergy formed a part of the regular business of the town.

There were few, if any, indigent and impotent poor for the towns to take care of in earliest New England; but the obligation to do so was plainly recognized from an early time. The towns, in the beginning, besides being local administrative units like the English parishes, were quasi corporations[2] endowed by the Massachusetts Bay Company with large tracts of land; in later times, bodies

[1] There is an excellent article on the "Support of Religion in Plymouth and Massachusetts," by Samuel S. Green, in American Antiquarian Society's *Proceedings* for 1886, p. 86.

[2] On the legal position of the towns, see an article by Andrew McF. Davis on "Corporations in the Days of the Colony" in Colonial Society of Massachusetts *Publications*, i, and Gray's decision in the case of Hill *vs.* City of Boston, *Massachusetts Reports*, cxxii, 129.

of proprietors exercised this function. At first, however, a very important part of each town's business was the allotment of lands among the heads of families in the town. Over this problem, as might be expected, fierce contests were often waged. In Boston, for example, the more farseeing and, possibly, the richer men felt that it was desirable to reserve a portion of the town's domain for later comers. The other townsmen wished to divide the whole land grant among those on the spot. There was something to be said on both sides of the question, because the territory of Boston was necessarily limited in geographical extent; and yet, on the other hand, to men like Winthrop, it might seem to be important to reproduce in the capital of New England some of the social and political conditions which gave London a part of its place in English institutions and history. Similar considerations did not obtain in other towns; but in all, in the years 1640–50, the feeling spread among the townsmen that they and their descendants should alone be considered in future allotments of land,[1] so that from about 1650 the towns generally ceased to exercise this function. Then, however, the question of providing for the support of the poor became one of importance. In New England, as in the mother country, the communal spirit was strong and was strengthened by the position which the religious organization occupied in the social fabric. For these four reasons: (1) the peculiarities of the land system, (2) the care of the poor, (3) the prevalent communal ideas, and (4) the peculiar religious institutions of the place, it became necessary carefully to scrutinize the qualification of each newcomer before he or she was permitted to acquire legal rights.[2] It is for

[1] See, for example, *Boston Records*, i, 88; ii, 68.

[2] For examples of the working of these forces, see *Boston Records*, i, 37,

these reasons that all the New England colonists made stringent regulations for the exclusion of undesirable persons; and when as in the case of Providence, for example, admission to the rights of inhabitancy carried with it the right to a share in the undivided land, the taking in of a newcomer might well be regarded as an act of disinterestedness deserving of praise. The American nation in the nineteenth century, however, was so liberal in its policy of giving land to every immigrant that it has come to be a habit of historical writers to look at this matter from the other point of view and to stigmatize these early regulations of the New England colonies for preserving their corporate rights as alien and sedition acts on the supposition, probably, that they bore some resemblance to the famous laws of the end of the eighteenth century.

The meetinghouse, besides serving for religious uses and for the secular needs of the inhabitants, was sometimes occupied during the week by the town school. The settlers of New England were well educated, for in the time of the early Stuarts elementary education in England was widely diffused.[1] It is, indeed, astonishing to turn over in one's mind the names of persons of learning in those days. Shakespeare and Hooker, William Bradford and John Winthrop, Captain John Smith and George Sandys, six men of different attainments and scenes of activity, probably received their first intellectual impulses in the local schools of their boyhoods' homes. Another way of showing how rapidly education was spreading in the first colonizing period is to

90, 103, 135; ii, 7, 11, 16, 44, 49, 148; other entries may be found in the index under Strangers; and the Massachusetts Colony Law of 1651, Whitmore's *Laws of 1672*, p. 143, and index under Strangers. The form used for warning an undesirable person out of town may be seen in *Early Records of Lancaster* (Massachusetts), 89.

[1] See Note II.

note the increasing number of convicted felons who escaped the gallows by the process known as "benefit of clergy."[1] Complete statistics on this point of course are unavailable; but the Middlesex County Records contain statistics which may fairly be regarded as typical. These show that in the reign of Edward VI only eight and one-half per cent of convicted felons "read like a clerk"; in Mary's reign the percentage rose slightly; in Elizabeth's time no less than thirty-one out of every hundred successfully called for the "Book"; and in James's reign thirty-nine per cent escaped the felon's doom by reading the "neck verse."[2]

This education was confined to men, although the reigning monarch was a woman, and at about this time a woman acted as churchwarden of Tavistock, England. As a rule the girls grew up in ignorance of learning, with the result that their letters are very instructive as examples of phonetic spelling, and as showing us how English was pronounced in the days of Spenser and Milton. For instance, Lady Sussex exhibited an ingenuity which was credible enough in a woman who outlived three husbands including in the number that Puritan nobleman, Robert Rich, Earl of Warwick, who is so often mentioned in this volume. Yorkshire, this good lady turned into "Oyskessher," while Lincoln's-Inn-Fields becomes "Lingeslindsfilds," and "a maisismee" stands in her interesting letters for "amazes me."

By the end of James's reign there were at least five hundred endowed schools in England besides many more which were supported entirely by public contributions. These schools were scattered broadcast over the land: in Lancashire there were forty, in Yorkshire sixty, in

[1] See above, p. 186.

[2] *Middlesex County Records*, ii, xxxix.

Lincolnshire twenty, in Devonshire ten, and in Dorsetshire ten. Many of these were based on old foundations which had come down from pre-Reformation days or were reëndowments which had been made to satisfy the conscience of some religiously minded person; but the vitality of the system in early Stuart time was the outcome of the Renaissance and the Reformation. The local records contain many entries of money payments for educational purposes. At Ipswich, for instance, Mr. Eaton was employed as grammar schoolmaster at an annual salary of thirty pounds, and in 1608, Mr. George Downing was engaged to teach the children to cipher, to cast accounts, and to recite the elements of grammar. In what would now be called the primary grades the instruction was largely by catechizing, which consisted in an oral give and take between teacher and pupil. The early schoolbooks contain a medley of A B C D'isms, religious instructions, and moral precepts; for example, in the A B C of 1538, the first page of which is reproduced in Mr. Littlefield's *Early Schools and School Books*, is given the alphabet in "black letter," and the opening lines of the Lord's Prayer in Latin and in English.

The English local records of that time contain many entries of the payment of money for school purposes; but, usually, the schools were supported partly and often wholly by endowments. At Tavistock the parish provided a "new schoolhouse" in 1576, — which phrase shows that there had been an older schoolhouse in that parish. The new edifice must have been a building of some pretensions as it had glass windows which were still uncommon. The small boy of that time and place, however, resembled the small boy of all times and places, and in 1588 the churchwardens found it advisable to protect the glass windows with wire netting. Within the building there was, at least, one dictionary which was chained to the desk.

The New England settlers numbered among them a good proportion of university men; their religion demanded a knowledge of the Bible; and the form of their local government shows that they assumed that the voters could read and write. The men of Massachusetts had scarcely settled themselves in the New World before they began the establishment of a school system on practically the English model.[1] Many of the early schools were supported in part by the income of lands which were devoted to that purpose by the town or by the General Court, or were given by some private individual. In almost every case, however, these gifts proved insufficient and the deficit was made good, either by public subscription or by vote of the town. These schools were public only in the sense that they were open to the children of all the inhabitants of a town, but it was generally expected that those who could afford it would pay something for their children's tuition, but neither poverty nor lack of social rank in the parents excluded a boy from the benefit of primary education.

The school system having been evolved by custom, as was so frequently the case, was recognized by the colonial government and made the basis of a general educational system by the passage of the well-known law of 1649, as

[1] The early Virginia settlers, who were drawn from the same social strata as the New Englanders, were equally solicitous about education. The *Virginia Magazine of History*, the *William and Mary Quarterly*, Hening's *Statutes*, and the records of the Virginia Company contain numerous entries of gifts and bequests for educational purposes; but trifling results, if any, flowed from these benefactions before 1660. In his famous report to the Privy Council, Governor Sir William Berkeley states (Hening's *Statutes*, ii, 517) that "the same course" is taken as "in England out of towns, every man according to his ability instructing his children." In other words the lack of communal life made a duplication of the English town school system an impossibility in the Old Dominion.

soon as the increasing number of remote settlements made it likely that some of the newer immigrants would neglect this part of their duty to the Commonwealth. The preamble of this act is worth reprinting as showing the combined religious and æsthetic motives which actuated the founders:—

"It being one chief project of Sathan to keep men from the knowledge of the Scripture, as in the former times, keeping them in unknown Tongues, so in these latter times, by perswading from the use of Tongues, that so at least the true sense and meaning of the Original might be clouded and corrupted with false glosses of Deceivers; to the end that Learning may not be buried in the Graves of our fore Fathers, in Church and Common-wealth, the Lord assisting our endeavours."

According to this act every township of fifty householders or more should appoint one to teach "all such children as shall resort to him to read and write." Furthermore, when any town should increase to the number of one hundred families, they should set up a grammar school wherein youths "may be fitted for the University." It is interesting to note in this connection that the smaller towns were only obliged to have "writing schools," but they might combine with neighboring towns so that their brighter boys could receive secondary education. This general educational system of Massachusetts was adopted by Connecticut and New Haven and, at a considerably later period, by Plymouth. At the time of the Revolution, Rhode Island, alone of the New England colonies, lacked a public school system, although one of the earliest public schools had been opened at Newport in 1640.

Six years after the beginning of the Great Emigration, the General Court of Massachusetts appropriated a large proportion of the public revenue for the beginning of an institution of learning at Newtowne, which name was later changed to Cambridge to commemorate the Alma Mater of three college men out of every four in the colony. Two years later, a young clergyman, dying at Charlestown, left half of his property and all of his books to the new institution, which was appropriately named Harvard College in grateful recognition of John Harvard, its first private benefactor. Its first class graduated four years later in 1642. From this beginning its reputation for piety and learning rapidly spread.[1] Other New England colonies contributed to its support, and to it came students from other parts of New England, from New Netherland and even from old England. Its curriculum would seem appalling to a modern college student, and its discipline savored of the English public school where the belief still prevailed that sparing the rod spoiled the child.[2] In the day when most learned men were clergymen and when the thought of the time centered in religion, it was natural that the principal interest of the new establishment should be ecclesiastical. As early as 1647, however, Giles Firmin lectured upon anatomy; and in the same year, possibly as an encouragement to the earliest medical lecturer in America, the General Court voted that it conceived it to be very necessary that such as study physic or chirurgery should have liberty to anatomize once in four years some malefactor, in case there be such. It is to be hoped that this instruction in physic and chirurgery proved to be possible since those were the

[1] December 27, 1645, Thomas Shepard of Cambridge in New England wrote to Hugh Peters, suggesting, among other things, that he should send some of Laud's books to Harvard College. Whether anything came of the proposal is not known; it certainly would have been an interesting sight to see a fledgling Massachusetts minister perusing the Archbishop's books. See *American Historical Review*, iv, 105.

[2] See Quincy's *Harvard University*. Interesting old college laws are printed in Massachusetts Historical Society's *Proceedings* for 1875, p. 207, and *ibid.*, Second Series, xi, 200.

days when pharmaceutical knowledge relied for its efficacy largely on the terror which the name of a medicine inspired. In 1643, for example, Governor Winthrop received a paper from his friend, Dr. Stafford of England, containing a list of what were then regarded as valuable prescriptions. One of these consisted of the ashes of toads cremated in the month of March. This medicine was to be taken internally and might well have frightened one into health or the grave. In concluding his list, Dr. Stafford declared that "no man can with a good conscience take a fee or reward before the party receive benefit apparent: and then he is not to demand anything, but what God shall put into the heart of the party to give him."[1] This learned gentleman would have received the sympathy of the Maryland magistrate who put a chirurgeon of that colony under bonds to prosecute to its fulfillment a cure for which he had received compensation before there was any "benefit apparent."

The first generation of New England Puritans resembled closely in their modes of thought and in their personal habits the Puritans of the older England which they had left behind. We find the elder Winthrop taking his family and friends down Boston harbor for a day's outing, and the birds and flowers of the New World interested him and the other first comers. The more learned among them were careful students of one of the greatest of modern books, John Calvin's *Institutes of the Christian Religion* and, no doubt, agreed with that great man that the enjoyment of the gifts of God is not wrongful since he has created them for our benefit. "In herbs, trees, and fruits, beside their various uses, his design has been to gratify us by graceful

[1] See an interesting article on "Medicine in Early Massachusetts," by Dr. Oliver Wendell Holmes in Massachusetts Historical Society's *Proceedings*, v, 379. See also *ibid.*, Second Series, i, 46; Johnson's *Wonder-working Providence*, 165. The vote of the General Court noted above was passed on October 27, 1647.

forms and pleasant odors." "Shall the Lord," asks Calvin, "have endued flowers with such beauty, to present itself to our eyes, with such sweetness of smell, to impress our sense of smelling; and shall it be unlawful for our eyes to be affected with the beautiful sight, or our olfactory nerves with the agreeable odor?"[1] So, too, the Creator in providing clothing has had in view not merely man's necessity, but propriety and decency as well. Nevertheless, he asks, "Where is gratitude towards God for clothing, if, on account of our sumptuous apparel, we admire ourselves and despise others?" John Calvin was one of the greatest of men and recognized that one form of religion would not be adapted to all ages and therefore declared that one church should not despise another on account of a variety of discipline. "The Lord gave not that law by the hand of Moses to be promulgated among all nations, and to be universally binding; . . . he had a special regard to their [the Jews] peculiar circumstances."[2] The difficulty of keeping body and soul together in early New England, however, brought out the sterner and severer qualities of the early New Englanders, so that by the time the second generation of native born appeared in public life the race had lost much of the geniality which has usually marked the users of the English speech; but this was due to a variety of causes, among which their religion should be reckoned as only one. The Puritan creed only slowly assumed the sternness of aspect which made intellectual excitation save for religious purposes an impossibility.[3]

[1] *Institutes*, bk iii, ch. x, §§ 2 and 3. It was not until the first half of the seventeenth century that much attention was given to the cultivation of flowers (*Verney Memoirs*, i, 9).

[2] *Institutes*, bk. iv, ch. xx, § 16.

[3] See an interesting paper by Barrett Wendell on the "Characteristics of the Puritans" in American Historical Association's *Reports* for 1891, p. 245.

NOTES

I. The Confederation. — The Records of the commissioners are in *Plymouth Colony Records*, vols. ix and x, and in *Connecticut Colony Records*, iii, 473–514. The Articles of Confederation are in the above and also in Bradford's *Plymouth*, Brigham's *Plymouth Laws*, and *American History Leaflets*, No. 7. Winthrop's *New England* and Hutchinson's *Massachusetts* are important in dealing with this time. See also Charles C. Smith in *Memorial History of Boston*, i, 295 and fol., J. Q. Adams in Massachusetts Historical Society's *Collections*, Third Series, ix, 187, and Frothingham's *Rise of the Republic*.

II. Education in England. — The English *Sessional Papers* contain two remarkable reports having to do with education: the "Schools Enquiry Commission Report" (1868) in some twenty parts, and the "Charity Commissioners' Report" for 1837. The most useful single volume on the subject is Nicholas Carlisle's *Endowed Grammar Schools*. On the antiquity of endowments, see A. F. Leach's *English Schools at the Reformation* and "Early Yorkshire Schools" (Yorkshire Archæological Society's *Record Series*, 1899).

Instances of English schools which trained New England settlers are given in Martin's *Evolution of the Massachusetts Public School System*. The leading sources of information are concisely summed up by J. Schaffer in "The Origin of the System of Land Grants for Education" (*Bulletins of the University of Wisconsin*, No. 63). An interesting article on this general theme is in Massachusetts Historical Society's *Proceedings* for 1871, p. 387.

III. Local Government in England. — The account in the text is based on the works enumerated in the footnotes to Channing's "Town and County Government" in the *Johns Hopkins Studies in History and Political Science* and the following, most of which have been published since 1884: *Tavistock Churchwardens' Accounts*, *Accounts of the Churchwardens of St. Michael in Bedwardine in Worcester*, *Pittington Records*, *Houghton Records*, North Riding Records Society's *Quarter Sessions Records*, *Plymouth Municipal Records*, Bacon's *Annals of Ipswich*, etc. Professor Herbert D. Foster also kindly placed at my disposal his notes from the following records which are still unprinted: *Boston Assembly Book*, *Yarmouth Town Records*, *Borough of Leicester Accounts*, *Northampton Town Record Book*.

CHAPTER XVI

THE DUTCH MIGRATION

THE Dutch influence on American history came in three ways. In the first place, refugees from the despotism of the Burgundian and Spanish rulers of the Netherlands and from the religious tyranny of their own people sought shelter in England; they helped to modify the institutions of their adopted home, and some of their children and grandchildren were among the early settlers of New England. In the second place, Englishmen, fleeing from the persecution of English ecclesiastics, found refuge in the Low Countries, where they learned many things besides the Dutch speech, and some of them brought these lessons to Plymouth and to the other colonies of New England. In the third place, the commercial metropolis of America was founded by Dutchmen whose posterity has powerfully affected the development of the thirteen colonies and of the United States. Few things are harder to unravel or more easy to exaggerate than the interplay of institutional factors, and it is not easy to disentangle the institutions of one people from those of another. This is especially true in the case under consideration, because Dutch and English political ideas come largely from the same source, and the two races under similar environments would ordinarily reach the same conclusion. Until some scientific investigator, expert in early English and American history, shall make a thorough analysis of the institutions of the original thirteen states, it will be impossible to speak with authority on this subject.

For centuries Englishmen and Dutchmen had been close friends. This was due to their racial affinity, to their commercial harmony, and to their similar religious inclinations. No friendship, however long, outlasts divergencies of commercial interest. England and Holland became competitors in manufacturing and in carrying the commerce of the seas; they became rivals in the race for the spoils of the Far East. In 1623, the Dutch captured a few Englishmen who were engaged in trafficking for cloves on the island of Amboyna. The Dutch tortured them, until in the extremity of their agony they confessed to the existence of a fabulous plot to capture the fort on the island. Then they were massacred, and other Englishmen were driven away. More than a dozen years before this an Englishman, Henry Hudson, sailing in the service of Dutch merchants, had introduced to the notice of the European world the river which still bears his name. He was not the first to visit the Great River of the Mountains; Giovanni da Verrazano, nearly a century before, had anchored within Sandy Hook, and French traders may have frequented the river and perhaps built a trading post not far from the site of the modern Albany;[1] but the recorded history of the river begins with Hudson's voyage of 1609.

Henry Hudson comes into the historian's notice in 1607, and he disappears in the ice and mist of Hudson Bay in 1611. In this brief period he gained a "farther north" than any other man for many a long year and made two memorable voyages which are commemorated in the names Hudson River and Hudson Bay. His antecedents are un-

[1] These possibilities and others also are good-naturedly summed up by John Fiske in his *Dutch and Quaker Colonies*, i, 58–80. Cf. De Costa's *Sailing Directions of Henry Hudson.*

known, though conjectures have not been wanting;[1] nor is there any certain information as to the reasons for his voyaging in the service of the Dutch East India Company. Unquestionably he was an Englishman, and as certainly he sailed, in 1609, in search of a new waterway to India and Cathay. His vessel was named the *Half-Moon;* she was a "fly-boat," or fast sailing vessel whose speed was secured by making her long in proportion to her beam; she carried eighteen or twenty men. The *Half-Moon's* crew was ill assorted of Englishmen and Dutchmen and was soon discouraged by ice and storms. Hudson, therefore, abandoned his northward course through Arctic seas and steered westward for America, to which he was drawn by the knowledge of Weymouth's voyage and of the discoveries of the Virginia explorers.[2] It is not unlikely that this following up of the English explorations was in the minds of Hudson and his Dutch employers before he sailed from the Texel.

In her westward course across the Atlantic, the *Half-Moon* encountered gale after gale. In one of these her foremast was injured, but on she kept under such sail as she could carry. Off Newfoundland, Hudson sighted some French fishing vessels, and stopped long enough for his men to catch "one hundred and eighteen great coddes." On the 17th of July, in the heat and fog of a

[1] J. R. Read (*Historical Inquiry concerning Henry Hudson*) gives many facts about sundry Hudsons who lived in the reigns of Elizabeth and James; but the links connecting these persons with the navigator are still lacking. The sources are given in the original and in translation in Asher's *Henry Hudson the Navigator* (Hakluyt Society Publications, 1860). H. C. Murphy, to whom students of New York history are largely indebted, printed the contract between the Dutch East India Company and Hudson in his *Henry Hudson in Holland. An Inquiry into the Origin and Objects of the Voyage which led to the Discovery of the Hudson River*, — and, for some inscrutable reason, refused Asher a sight of the brochure, which was designed for private distribution.

[2] Murphy's *Hudson*, 47, 63, and Asher's *Hudson*, 148. The former is in many ways to be preferred.

Maine summer, he anchored in the vicinity of Penobscot Bay. While lying at his moorings the natives came to the ship in two "French shallops." "On the morning of the five-and-twentieth," so the chronicler of the expedition informs us, "we manned our scute with four muskets and sixe men and tooke one of their shallops and brought it aboard. Then we manned our boat and scute with twelve men and muskets and two stone pieces or murderers, and drave the savages from their houses, and tooke the spoyle of them, as they would have done of us," — which was quite likely after the unprovoked seizure of their boat.

Once again ataunt, the *Half-Moon* steered to the south and, rounding Cape Cod, made the Virginia coast. After coasting southward for a time, Hudson turned to the north again and possibly entered Chesapeake Bay.[1] He certainly sailed into Delaware Bay and, not liking the looks of the shoal water, soon ran out again, and, steering northward, anchored inside of Sandy Hook. On the 4th of August, 1609, a party went on shore, — tradition says on Coney Island, but the landing might have been at almost any other point. Carefully exploring the Narrows, Hudson navigated the *Half-Moon* into the upper bay, and then into the mouth of the river which now bears his name. The water was salt, and the tide ebbed and flowed with great force. Here, at last, seemed to be the long-looked-for passage to the Pacific Ocean. For eleven days, therefore, the *Half-Moon* drifted and sailed northwardly. The wonderful scenery of the Hudson — the Palisades, the Donderberg, West Point, and the Catskills — impressed the explorers. Above the site of the modern Albany the water became too shoal for the ship, but a boat party proceeded eight

[1] Asher's *Hudson*, 73 note.

or nine leagues farther on.[1] While the *Half-Moon* was at anchor in one of the northern reaches, Hudson invited a party of Indians into the cabin and "gave them much wine and aqua-vitæ, that they were all merrie. In the ende one of them was drunke." As a requital for this hospitality, the Indians the next day presented Hudson with tobacco, wampum, and venison. These natives were Iroquois of the Mohawk tribe. A traditional account of a scene of revelry at the first coming of the whites was preserved among them until the American Revolution; it is generally regarded as descriptive of the coming of Hudson and his crew, but it may possibly refer to earlier French explorers. Two things, however, seem to be reasonably certain. The first is that the Iroquois appreciated the attentions of the early Dutch navigators and fur traders, who supplied them with fire water and firearms.[2] The other assured fact is that these Indians had had slight intercourse with white men, or they would not have been so friendly. The natives of the lower Hudson showed their familiarity with the whites by attacking the *Half-Moon* at every good opportunity.

The future careers of the *Half-Moon* and her gallant captain were not fortunate; putting into Dartmouth, England, Henry Hudson was forbidden to remain longer in the service of the Dutch, and in April, 1610, he sailed from the Thames on his last voyage in quest of the Northwest Passage. Fourteen months later he was set adrift in a shallop in Hudson Bay by a panic-stricken and mutinous crew, and no trace of him has since been found. As to the *Half-Moon*, she gained a Holland port early in 1611,

[1] Brodhead, in his *New York* (i, 31), identifies localities.

[2] See New York Historical Society's *Collections*, New Series, i, 71, and Asher's *Hudson*, 173.

and four years later was wrecked on the shore of the island of Mauritius.

The Dutch East India Company had no interest in the scenery and fur trade of the Great River of the Mountains, and, indeed, had no right to explore or to trade in that region; they also had full use for their capital in the profitable exploitation of the commerce of the Spice Islands. Other Dutch merchants and some of the members of the East India Company, however, saw prospect of profitable business in the inexhaustible supply of furs in this region. From 1610 onwards Dutch fur traders frequented the river, which they named the Mauritius, for the stadtholder of the Netherlands. The fur trade soon gathered about Manhattan Island, at the mouth of the river, and in the vicinity of the present Albany, which stands at the head of navigation by seagoing vessels.

Among the fur traders who made their headquarters at Manhattan Island was Adriaen Block, whose ship, the *Tiger*, was burned in 1613. Setting to work, he built a small vessel which was launched in the spring of 1614 and christened the *Onrust* or *Restless*. In her he passed through Helle-gat River, which he so called, probably, because it reminded him of a similarly named Dutch river. Sailing eastwardly through Long Island Sound, he came to a stream whose waters were fresh at no great distance from the Sound. He named it the Fresh River or the Fresh Water River, but its English settlers called it by its Indian name of Connetticock or Long River. Block ascended the stream to a point above the site of the present Hartford. Returning to the mouth of the river he sailed eastwardly to Block Island, which still bears his name, and explored Narragansett Bay. Thence he sailed to the southward of Texel (Martha's Vineyard), Vlieland (Nantucket), coasted the outer shore of Cape Cod, and crossed Massachusetts Bay to the vicinity of Nahant, which he named Pye Bay from the variegated color of the water, rocks, and soil.[1]

While Block was still away the States-general of the United Netherlands offered to grant to the first finder of new land the exclusive trade thereof for four voyages. Upon Block's return to Holland the owners of the *Tiger* received, for three years, exclusive rights in North America between the fortieth and the forty-fifth parallels. This grant was made on the ground that Block was the first to visit seas which had been repeatedly navigated by French and English seamen, from Verrazano to Champlain and Martin Pring. Moreover, it is probable, although not susceptible of definite proof, that Samuel Argall had visited Manhattan Island in the preceding year and had compelled the Dutch traders there to recognize the authority of the English king.

There seems to be some doubt as to who was the first Dutch explorer of the Delaware. O'Callaghan thinks that Cornelis May, in 1614, discovered the cape which bears his name, but Brodhead gives the credit of the detailed exploration of the bay to Cornelis Hendricksen and leaves May altogether out of the account. The origin of the name Henlopen is also doubtful. O'Callaghan says that it was so called from a town of Friesland, but Brodhead says that it was named after Thymen Jacobsen Hinlopen of Amsterdam and that it also came to be called Inloopen because it seemed to vanish on approach. The last name would seem to have been well bestowed, for this sandy point marched up and down the map to suit the convenience of successive claimants to the soil of Delaware. Notwithstanding their

[1] For the localities mentioned in Block's voyage, see the account in De Laet, translated in New York Historical Society's *Collections*, New Series, v, 291.

numerous voyages for exploration and trade the Dutch, in 1619, had slight hold on the South Bay and River, as they termed the Delaware, or on the North and East rivers, as those on either side of Manhattan Island came to be called. In this year the English Captain Dermer, sailing from Monhegan to Virginia, passed through Hell-gate and the East River and out by Sandy Hook without having seen or spoken with a Dutchman. On his return voyage in the next year he came across some Dutch traders, exactly where is not known, and warned them not to trespass on English territory. This warning the Pilgrims soon repeated on no less than three occasions.

The year 1621 begins a new page in the history of the Dutch in America, for in that year the West India Company was chartered by the States-general. The principal object of the new corporation was the acquisition of wealth through the spoiling of the Spaniards; but a subsidiary part of the scheme was a profitable commerce. The second clause of the charter authorizes the company to make alliances with the natives, build forts, appoint and discharge officers, and "advance the peopling of those fruitful and unsettled parts."[1] Both coasts of America, the west coast of Africa, and the islands of the Atlantic were thus placed under the monopoly of the United Company of the United Netherlands, but it is more often called the Dutch West India Company. New Netherland is not mentioned in this instrument and, indeed, it had no existence at that time.[2]

[1] The charter is in O'Callaghan's *New Netherland*, i, Appendix A, and Hazard's *State Papers*.

[2] In 1621 Sir Dudley Carleton, then English minister at The Hague, by order of Sir George Calvert, Secretary of State, complained to the Dutch government of the presence of the settlers on the Hudson and the Delaware. In reply he was informed that "there was no plantation or settlement to impeach the English right." He was later ordered to require the Dutch "to discontinue the plantation"; but they replied that only

The first settlers came to Manhattan Island in 1623. They were, for the most part, Protestants from the southern Netherlands, or Walloons. In looking over the history of the founding of New Netherland, it is surprising to note how many of its promoters were not of what can strictly be called Dutch origin, but came from the country which is now called Belgium; as, for instance, William Usselincx, the founder of the West India Company, Samuel Godyn, Van Meteren, John de Laet, Gerad Mercator, Peter Plancius, Henry Hondius, and Isaac Le Maire, to mention no other names. The immigrants who came to New Netherland in 1623 were few in number, but they spread far and wide, some of them settling in Delaware, others in Connecticut, others in the vicinity of Fort Orange near the present Albany, others on Manhattan Island, on the western end of Long Island, and on Staten Island. Before long, however, it was found necessary to bring them nearer together on or near Manhattan Island, — the women and children were withdrawn even from Fort Orange.

The first governor or director of New Netherland who exercised much influence on its development was Peter Minuit (or Minnewit to spell his name phonetically), who was born in the Duchy of Cleves. To him and his council of five was confided the whole government of the province. Partly subordinate and partly coördinate were the schout-fiscal who arrested and prosecuted offenders, and the koopman or factor who also acted as secretary. These two officials reported directly to the government of the company in the Netherlands, and were consequently

fur traders were on the Hudson River. He again protested in 1622. In 1632 the Council for New England endeavored to arouse the government to take measures against the Dutch intruders. See *Calendars of State Papers, America and West Indies*, 1574–1660, p. 27.

nearly always at swords' points with the director. All officials were appointed and removed by the company, but the director was obliged to swear allegiance to the United Netherlands. In all this the settlers were not consulted in the slightest degree, nor had they any local self-government. For sixteen years now, Dutchmen had been living in this region, but as yet they had no settled clergyman, and nothing had been done for the education of their children; the keynote of this period of New Netherland history was the acquisition of wealth. Minuit secured some sort of title to Manhattan Island by purchase from the natives, — giving them goods to the value of twenty-four dollars. He also began the erection of a fort, a mill, and several houses. In each of the next few years, furs were exported from the colony to the value of sixty thousand guilders,[1] but this insignificant peltry trade had little interest for the governors of the West India Company which in one year gained sixty million guilders from the loot of the Spaniards. They determined to shift the burden of the colonial enterprise to private shoulders by extending to the colony the feudal system of land-holding which obtained in the Netherlands. This was done by the Charter of Privileges to Patroons which was issued in 1629.[2] This instrument provided that any member of the company who should within four years at his own expense transport fifty families to New Netherland should be entitled to an extensive tract of land in the colony, for which, however, he must extinguish the native right of occupancy. This grantee was

[1] These figures are from De Laet's "History of the West India Company," in New York Historical Society's *Collections*, New Series, i, 385.

[2] On the patroonships, see American Historical Association's *Report* for 1896, 140. The charter in English is in New York Historical Society's *Collections*, Second Series, i, 370; O'Callaghan's *New Netherland*, i, 112.

termed a patroon, and within his holding possessed jurisdiction in civil and criminal cases, with an appeal in cases involving over fifty guilders to the company's representative at Fort Amsterdam. No colonist living in a patroonship could make woolen, linen, or cotton cloth, or weave any other stuffs on pain of banishment. There were stipulations as to trade which were probably intended to restrict the patroons in such a way as to give a monopoly to the company; but these were so ill drawn that they were constantly evaded and gave rise to conflicts which continued as long as the colony remained in Dutch hands. The company, moreover, undertook to provide the patroons with negro slaves as far as it was convenient. The expectation probably was that great landed estates would come into being which should be cultivated by tenants, who would be assisted in their labors by slaves, the profitable fur trade with the natives being retained by the company and by those residing within the company's reservation at Manhattan.

The scheme was no sooner decided on than the leading men of the company notified their agents in the colony, who vied with one another to secure the best lands before the ordinary stockholders should have any knowledge of what was going on. Manhattan Island was reserved to the company, but Michael Pauw secured Staten Island and the mainland on the opposite side of the North River from Manhattan. This spot was of great value because the natives of the lower river were accustomed to congregate there to traffic with the company's agents. In 1637 the corporation bought out the rights which the enterprising Michael Pauw had secured, for twenty-six thousand guilders. Two other directors, Samuel Godyn and Samuel Blommaert, appropriated what is now the state of Delaware. A fourth director was the luckiest of all. His name was Kiliaean van Rensselaer, and for his share he took lands which inclosed the company's station at Fort Orange. When it was known at Amsterdam how successfully these directors had been served by their agents, there was confusion in the company which was ended only when these most enterprising men admitted others to a share in their prospective prosperity.

The South Bay enterprise was unfortunate from the beginning; Godyn and Blommaert, who had associated De Vries with them, were taken with the idea of prosecuting the whale fishery in those shallow waters. They sent out colonists who settled near the site of the present Lewiston, naming it Swannendael. Whales proved to be scarce on the Delaware shoals and the settlement languished. In 1632 De Vries himself came out with recruits and provisions. Anchoring off Swannendael, he found the houses destroyed, most of the palisades burned, and the ground bestrewn with the skulls and bones of the settlers. The Indians were naturally anxious to keep out of the power of the whites; but De Vries finally prevailed upon one of them to remain on his vessel over night. The Indian was understood to say that the settlers "emptied a pillow, to which was attached a piece of tin upon which was figured the emblem of Holland." One of the chiefs used this for a tobacco pipe, and thereupon the whites demanded that the savage who had taken the tin should be executed, probably with the idea that he had committed treason. The family and friends of the unfortunate chief, according to Indian usage, revenged themselves on the whites. For some inscrutable reason, instead of waging war on these murderous savages, De Vries sought to placate them with gifts of cloth, bullets, axes, and "Nuremberg trinkets," and that was the end of the first European settlement on Delaware Bay.[1]

Peter Minuit remained until 1632. A year later Wouter van Twiller, the husband of Van Rensselaer's niece, became governor or director. Van Twiller is one of the most interesting characters in our colonial history. De Vries, who hated him, lost no opportunity of speaking evil of him, especially dwelling upon his cowardice and love of drink. He represents himself as giving Van Twiller great quantities of unasked advice and as making extremely unsuitable remarks about the United Company to its representative at Fort Amsterdam. He also relates many stories, one of which has to do with the sailing of an English ship by the fort in open defiance of Wouter van Twiller, whereupon, according to De Vries, the governor ordered a barrel of wine to be brought, and, having taken a glass, called out, "Those who love the Prince of Orange and me, emulate me in this, and assist me in repelling the violence committed by that Englishman." The latter, however, was far away up the river, but the people finished the barrel of wine and would have mastered six casks of it — if there had been that number. There seems to have been a good deal of friction between De Vries and the authorities over the payment of duties on the furs which he had secured from the natives; possibly this insistence upon the rights of the company may have influenced the patroon's writings against the director.[2] These stories, dressed up by the matchless genius of Washington Irving, furnished the substance for the wonderful figure of Walter, the

[1] De Vries in New York Historical Society's *Collections*, Second Series, i, 251.

[2] New York Historical Society's *Collections*, Second Series, i, 255 and fol.

Doubter, of the Knickerbocker History[1] at the cost of the good name of an estimable man.

As a matter of fact, Wouter van Twiller was a plain, seventeenth-century Dutchman whose business ability and marriage connections had given him a position of great difficulty. There is little question that the office of director of New Netherland was the most difficult position to be found anywhere in the colonies: on the one hand, the United Company expected to receive returns from the colonists directly and from the fur trade indirectly; on the other hand, the members of the company made returns impossible by securing for themselves the greater part of the profit of the commerce with the natives. Moreover the States-general of the Netherlands expected that the company would undertake the settlement of the colony; but the company had no money to put into an unprofitable venture and tried to make colonization pay for itself. Finally, every colonist who went to New Netherland wished to trade on his own account, and it was the business of the director to restrict their enterprise. Besides having these unpopular functions to discharge, the director was burdened with a schout fiscal and a koopmann, each prying into his doings and reporting directly to the home authorities. Well might the director of New Netherland have been a doubter; but, as a matter of fact and justice, it does not appear that he was anything of the sort.

Wouter van Twiller came to New Netherland in 1633. He soon found that his position was far from being a bed of roses. Virginia was now well settled; the Virginians were beginning to look away from the immediate vicinity

[1] From which John Fiske makes large quotations in his *Dutch and Quaker Colonies*, i, 144.

of the James River, and Governor Harvey informed the Dutchmen that they had no right whatever to the Delaware region. To the east the New Englanders were becoming active. They denied the right of the Dutch to the Connecticut Valley; they settled New Haven hard by New Amsterdam; they demanded the right to trade on the Hudson River. At the moment the English and the Dutch were allies in Europe; the position of an English trading vessel in the Dutch colony was, to say the least, very doubtful. There is small cause for wonder that Wouter van Twiller hesitated before firing on the English ship mentioned by De Vries; when his mind was made up, he acted with vigor. He sent a sufficient force of armed men in pursuit of the defiant vessel, seized the furs that had been collected aboard of her, and escorted her out of the river. When the Pilgrims sailed up the Connecticut River in 1633, they found a Dutch trading station named Fort Good Hope on the site of the modern Hartford. It was garrisoned by Dutchmen who threatened to shoot at the interloping Englishmen, but shot not. Soon followed the great emigration from Massachusetts to the Connecticut Valley, the settlement of the river towns, and the founding of Saybrook. In the face of this rising flood of Englishmen, the only thing that Wouter van Twiller could do, with the small force at his command, was to maintain a stout appearance. As long as he remained in control of affairs at Manhattan Island, Fort Good Hope was inhabited by Dutchmen, although it stood surrounded by English farms; and all attempts on the part of the Virginians or New Englanders to gain a foothold on Delaware Bay were frustrated.

Besides his activity against the neighbors of New Netherland on the east and on the south, Van Twiller began to build a fortified town at the southern end of Manhattan Island. Like other early governors of New Netherland, he used his office to secure valuable tracts of land. He also made many enemies besides De Vries. Among these was Dominie Bogardus, the first clergyman in the colony, who is said to have called Wouter van Twiller "the child of the devil." Another enemy was the schout fiscal, Lubbertus van Dincklagen, who reported vigorously against Van Twiller and lacked three years' salary when that despotic person dismissed him. De Vries and Van Dincklagen ultimately drove Van Twiller from office; he retired to his uncle-in-law's patroonship of Rensselaerswick, where doubtless he enjoyed the perplexities of his successors.

The first of the two picturesque administrators to succeed Van Twiller was William Kieft. De Vries and Bogardus had disliked Van Twiller; they soon came to hate William Kieft. Inasmuch as a large part of our knowledge of this portion of New Netherland history is derived from the writings of De Vries and Bogardus, it may well be that Kieft was not as bad as he is generally depicted. Winthrop gives him faint praise, but praise, nevertheless, when he says that he was more discreet and sober than his predecessor.[1] The government of New Netherland from beginning to end was a despotism; this was eminently the case in Kieft's time, as he was hampered by only one councilor, a Huguenot named La Montagne. Kieft reached the colony in 1638 and at once forbade rebellion, theft, perjury, and "all other immoralities." The sale of guns and powder to the natives was prohibited under pain of death, and illicit trading was forbidden. Kieft also laid a tax on tobacco and endeavored to limit

[1] Winthrop's *New England*, ii, 316.

the use of spirituous liquors by providing that those only who sold wine at a moderate rate should be permitted to retail the stronger liquor. "Criminal prosecutions and executions for homicide and mutiny were unhappily too frequent;[1]" but the new director's vigor soon brought good results in the shape of an influx of a small number of colonists and a general rehabilitation of the company's property at Fort Amsterdam. The French missionary, Father Jogues, who visited Manhattan Island in 1643, reported that there were then four hundred men living there, speaking eighteen different languages.[2]

The student of early American history can make one generalization with some degree of confidence: so long as the white invaders were fur traders and missionaries, there was peace on the frontier; but when the newcomers were farmers or planters, Indian war broke out before very long. In other words, while their hunting grounds were preserved to the Indians, they looked upon the whites as the benevolent dispensers of useful utensils, pots of iron, articles of personal adornment, fire water, and sometimes firearms; but when the whites began to plow the soil and to build houses, they seriously interfered with the Indians' food supply and with the only article of barter for which the white traders would give the Indian those things which he desired. In Virginia and Maryland there was almost incessant Indian war as long as the Indians could fight; New Plymouth and Massachusetts were saved from the same fate by the rapidity with which the measles and smallpox sheared off the aboriginal population. As soon, however, as the New England settlements outran the infectious diseases of the whites, there was conflict with the natives. Purchase of land from Indian chiefs, fair trading,

[1] Brodhead's *New York*, i, 278. [2] *Ibid.*, i, 374.

and the impartial administration of English law made no difference. Deprived of his land the Indian must fight or starve. So it was in New Netherland: as long as the Dutchmen came as fur traders there was peace; as soon as there was colonization there was war. No doubt the crisis was hastened by the narrow-minded petulance of William Kieft, but it would not have been long deferred in any event.

Into the details of the genesis of the murderous Indian conflict which devastated New Netherland, it is not necessary to enter here. There were murders by the whites and the redskins, which were due in part to drink and in part to a desire for revenge. By August, 1641, the position of affairs was so precarious that Kieft summoned the leading men and the heads of families to meet at Fort Amsterdam. These promptly chose twelve of their number to inquire into the circumstances and to advise the director as to what should be done. De Vries, who was now resident in the colony, was chosen president of the Twelve Men, and it is on his account of the affair that we have mainly to rely. He tells us that the Twelve Men advised the director that the Indians should be punished, but that God and opportunity "should be considered"; in other words, that the enterprise should be well matured and vigorously executed. A few weeks later Kieft consulted the Twelve Men each one by himself; their voices were still for delay. In January, 1642, he again summoned the Twelve Men in a body. After some persuasion, they assented to an expedition against the Indians, but coupled this with the condition that Kieft should lead the army in person, probably because they doubted his courage and thought this was the easiest way to postpone the conflict. At the same time they seized the occasion to demand reforms in the administration of the government, greater freedom for trade, and protection against the importation of English cattle and sheep. Kieft agreed to exclude English live stock and also to permit commerce with the New England colonies upon payment of certain duties. He then dismissed the Twelve Men and sent out an expedition, which returned without having seen an Indian.

The next step in this melancholy tragedy was the massacre of the "River Indians," who had gathered at Pavonia and at Corlaer's Hook opposite Manhattan to escape the Iroquois. These fugitives were set upon in the dead of night by Dutch soldiers acting on the orders of the director. One hundred and ten of the unsuspecting victims of this treachery were killed outright. Owing to the lack of other evidence we are forced to rely on the narrative of De Vries,[1] who may have exaggerated consciously or unconsciously. He describes how babes were hacked to pieces or thrown living into the river, and says of the adults "some came running to us from the country having their hands cut off; some lost both arms and legs; some were supporting their entrails with their hands, while others were mangled in other horrid ways, too horrid to be conceived." Speedily followed war with the near-by Indians; in a few weeks the white survivors of their sudden attacks found themselves confined to the southern end of Manhattan Island in and around Fort Amsterdam. For years the conflict which began in this way went on, broken only by such periods of time as enabled the Indians to gather their crops of corn. In all this time there was but one warlike exploit which struck terror into the hearts of the savages and in some measure raised the

[1] Translated in O'Callaghan's *New Netherland*, i, 268.

spirits of the whites. Tired of the unequal contest, the settlers called to their aid a body of English soldiers of fortune of varying degrees of virtue or of the lack of it, but, for the most part, good fighters. The leader of these men was Captain John Underhill. He was a frontiersman of excessive combativeness; who, like many great soldiers, had certain peculiarities of a moral sort which had caused grave solicitude to the leaders at Boston where he had first settled. Moments of gayety were followed by hours of repentance and then by further lapses from virtue, which in their turn gave way to the hearkening to the voice of conscience. In the Pequot War, he had borne a part second only to that of Captain John Mason, and his sterling military qualities alone had made him endurable to the men of Massachusetts. His frontier instincts led him away from the settled regions on the Bay to the debatable land between New Haven and New Netherland; but whether he should loan his talents to Theophilus Eaton or to William Kieft was doubtful until the certain prospect of a fight induced him to enter the service of the latter. At the head of one hundred and fifty men, after a brilliant flank movement and a toilsome march through the snow which lay deep on the slopes of the steep rocky hills, Underhill and his men in the middle of a moonlight winter's night came to a palisaded Indian village. Eight Indians are supposed to have escaped, five hundred in round numbers are stated to have been shot or burned alive in the conflagration which marked this victory as well as the earlier capture of the Pequot stronghold on the Mystic. The Dutch were grateful for Underhill's assistance, but even gratitude could not withstand the obstreperousness[1] of his conduct, and he found it wise

[1] See J. H. Innes's *New Amsterdam and Its People*, 180.

to seek shelter at Newport in Rhode Island. Underhill's moonlight massacre on Strickland's Plains brought peace with several Indian tribes, but the desire for vengeance still rankled in the hearts of the natives in the immediate vicinity of Fort Amsterdam.

To protect the pastures and cornfields of the fugitives on Manhattan Island a stout fence was built near the line of the present Wall Street, but the prowling savages sometimes crossed this defense and killed the settlers in the huts around the fort. The West India Company was now bankrupt, and could give little assistance to the colonists; a few soldiers from Curaçoa added to the number of mouths to be filled without doing anything in return. In October, 1644, the surviving colonists, as represented by a committee, the Eight Men, as it was called, addressed a memorial to the company, which gives a striking picture of New Netherland at this time. "Our fields," the memorialists assert, "lie fallow and waste, our dwellings and other buildings are burnt . . . the crops which God permitted to come forth during the past summer remain in the fields standing and rotting."[1] All this misery they attribute to William Kieft, who had never in six or seven years been farther from Fort Amsterdam than the middle of Manhattan Island. Unless there was a speedy change, the surviving colonists would be obliged to return to the Netherlands with their wives and children, and such property as they could carry with them. The colony, the memorialists finally declare, will never be prosperous until a different system is introduced, until free local institutions are provided, and representative government is established.

In the spring of 1646 peace was finally made between

[1] Brodhead's *New York*, i, 398.

the exhausted Indians and the no less exhausted whites. It did not come in time to save Director General Kieft from dismissal, although his successor, Peter Stuyvesant, did not reach the colony until May, 1647. The intervening months formed the darkest period in Kieft's life. He was denounced on the street as a traitor, liar, and villain. The clergyman and schoolmaster of the colony, Dominie Bogardus, was not the most backward of the director's assailants; he scrupled not to vituperate the civil head of the colony from the pulpit of the barnlike structure which still served the settlers as a church. According to Kieft, the head ecclesiastic was a drunkard, and it was said that some of his doings were "unbecoming a heathen, much less a Christian, letting alone a preacher of the Gospel"; while the chief magistrate, according to Everadus Bogardus, was a vessel of wrath and fountain of woe and trouble. Kieft, naturally, declined to go to church and encouraged the playing of games and the beating of drums in the vicinity of the holy edifice while Bogardus was berating him. Friends interposed, and for a time the two chief men of New Netherland consented to live together under what might be termed an armed truce. Together they sailed for home in the good ship *Princess* to lay their plaints before the authorities there. The navigator of their vessel mistook the Irish for the English Channel, and together the director and the dominie went to the other world in a shipwreck off the coast of Wales.

NOTE

Bibliography. — Ulmann's *Landmark History of New York* (pp. 267–279) contains a good selected bibliography of New York history, both of the state and city. Detailed lists will be found in *New York State Library Bulletin*, No. 56, "Bibliography 24," pp. 287–560, and *Bulletin of the New York Public Library*, iv, v.

The sources upon which the history of New Netherland rests are printed for the most part in the set of volumes entitled *Records relative to the Colonial History of the State of New York*, and in the New York Historical Society's *Collections*, Second Series, vols. i, ii, and iii. These are enumerated at length in Winsor's *America*, iv. O'Callaghan's *Laws and Ordinances of New Netherland*, 1638–1674, contains the official documents in full. Notwithstanding this wealth of original matter, the history of New Netherland remains unwritten, possibly because there is hardly a scrap of evidence that is not highly controversial.

The two leading historians of New Netherland are Edmund Burke O'Callaghan and John Romeyn Brodhead,[1] the former an Irishman, the latter of mixed Dutch and English extraction. Both of them had their prejudices, and neither was a trained historical student. John Fiske's *Dutch and Quaker Colonies* appears to be based mainly on O'Callaghan's book with reference to Irving's *Knickerbocker History*, which is a literary landmark and exceedingly unjust toward the people and officials of New Netherland. Thomas A. Janvier's *Dutch Founding of New York* is a fair rendering of the facts contained in Brodhead's first volume. It is to be regretted that so talented a writer should have descended to historical scurrility; as in describing the highly respectable secretary of Rhode Island, William Dyer, husband of the ill-fated Mary Dyer, as "a loose fish of thievish proclivities."

[1] Brodhead's knowledge was great as to early New York history, but was weak as to the outer world; as, for example (vol. i, p. 261), where he states that the settlement of Springfield on the Connecticut River "brought the English within a few miles of the Dutch post at Fort Orange [Albany]."

CHAPTER XVII

THE MISRULE OF PETER STUYVESANT

PETER STUYVESANT was a crusty, hot-tempered official who had lost a leg in the service of the Dutch West India Company.[1] As governor of Curaçoa, he had displayed great love of show and had badly bungled the only military matter in which he had held important command. He arrived at Fort Amsterdam in May, 1647, and at once declared that in the government of his new people, he should be "as a father over his children." As with Kieft in the blush of early enthusiasm, Stuyvesant proceeded to reform abuses[2] — and at Fort Amsterdam there was an abundance of abuses to be reformed. He decreed that in the future no liquor should be sold on Sundays before two o'clock, when there was no preaching, and wine not before four; but this prohibition did not apply to the entertainment of travelers "and of those who are daily customers, fetching their drinks to their own homes." He further provided that no liquor should be sold to the Indians at any time, nor to whites after the ringing of the "curfew" at nine o'clock in the evening. Ten months later he returned to the subject as these orders, "to the shame and derision" of the director general, were not observed. Existing taprooms might continue for four years, but in the mean-

[1] A "reader" of the *Magazine of American History* (xxiii, 506) asked for "a contemporary reference to the fact that Stuyvesant used a false leg" and asked in vain, — if the indexes of later volumes can be relied on. The statement in the text is allowed to stand, however, in the hope that tradition in this instance, as in many others, is correct.

[2] *Records of New Amsterdam*, i, 1; O'Callaghan's *Ordinances*, 60 and fol.

time the owners were to engage in "some other honest business." They should report daily whether anybody had been hurt or wounded at their houses and must not sell or give brandy, wine, beer, or strong waters to the Indians, directly or by intermediaries. Despite these regulations, the director general continued to observe drunken Indians running about, and he added a threat of corporal punishment to the pecuniary fine. These regulations seem to have been needed, as the little village which clustered around the ramparts of Fort Amsterdam was hardly more than a collection of gin shops and taverns. Drunken Indians and sailors were an everyday sight. Street fighting was also common and was also to come to a speedy end. One hundred guilders, or six months in prison on bread and water, was Stuyvesant's cure for drawing a knife in the street and three times the penalty for inflicting a wound. Smuggling and illegal trading were forbidden, and speculators in land on Manhattan Island were to improve their lots at once or forfeit them. William Kieft, who had begun his term of office in an equally virtuous way, had embarked for home, the possessor, it was said, of sixty thousand guilders. The more stringent the regulations, of course, the larger was the fee required for dispensing with them; before long Stuyvesant began buying farms or boweries — to give them their Dutch name. Speedily also the Manhattanese began to dislike the parental quality of the new director's care of them.

Peter Stuyvesant, like his predecessor, was a despot. He justified Kieft's despotic deeds. He persecuted those who questioned his or his predecessor's acts. He threatened to hang on the highest tree in New Netherland any man who appealed from his decisions to their High Mightinesses in Europe. The "rights of man," he once said, were nothing to him; he was the servant of the West India Company. It must be said in Stuyvesant's justification that his task was no light one. On Manhattan Island the fort must be rebuilt, the stone church completed; in the colony the patroons must be forced to respect the rights of the company and of the States-general; on the Delaware the Swedes who were now colonizing that region must be looked to; and in the East the on-coming flood of New Englanders must be held back. The successful management of these difficult tasks required tact, good judgment, and money, — none of which commodities was possessed by Peter Stuyvesant. The treasury was bare, but money and a good deal of it was absolutely necessary; the consent of the people to taxation had therefore to be obtained or, at all events, asked, or they would certainly rebel. So Stuyvesant directed the inhabitants of Manhattan, Brooklyn, Pavonia, and neighboring places to choose eighteen persons, from which number he and his leading advisers would select Nine Men to advise him when need should arise.[1] After the first election, the Nine Men and the government would fill vacancies in the board. Except in the beginning, therefore, this organization was not an elected body; but it may be said to have been fairly representative, as its members were the leading men in the community outside of the director general and his council. The Nine Men and their constituents were, above all, desirous to monopolize the fur trade of the Hudson River. Stuyvesant at once fell in with the popular wish and issued a proclamation which restricted all trading in New Netherland to old residents who were actually living in the province and to newcomers who should take the oath of allegiance, be possessed of considerable property

[1] Brodhead's *New York*, i, 475.

and state an intention of becoming permanent residents in the colony. These provisions were modified from time to time by action of the company in the Netherlands and of the authorities in the colony. As the matter finally developed, any one could secure the right to trade who should keep an open store at New Amsterdam and obtain a "burgher right," which he could do by petitioning and paying certain fees. Stuyvesant further restricted all trade of New Netherland to those who had a pass from himself, which doubtless turned out to be a fruitful source of personal revenue.

These stringent regulations as to the fur trade, which were designed in some sort to placate the colonists, were combined with the imposition of a custom's duty of about thirty per cent ad valorem. The new director general made an honest but ill-timed effort to collect the moneys which were due to the company; he also tried to stop the illicit trade in firearms with the natives, not so much for the sake of putting an end to that dangerous traffic as of securing its profits for his masters. The result of these regulations and taxes was that New Amsterdam soon became a place to be avoided by shipmasters and coast traders, who said they could not afford to go to New Netherland and run the risk of loss of ship and cargo. Stuyvesant asserted that these oppressive measures were due to orders from the company. The Nine Men, thereupon, proposed to petition the home authorities. The director general fell in with this plan provided the petition should be drawn according to his ideas, — and that was the end of the scheme for the time being.

The enforcement of the new system brought Stuyvesant at once into conflict with the New Englanders. They contended that, as New Netherland vessels were allowed freely to pass in and out of New England ports, New England vessels should likewise be permitted freely to trade in New Netherland. Stuyvesant answered that the idea was absurd, because wherever vessels went they found new laws. In the end the commissioners of the United Colonies informed Stuyvesant that the Indian trade of New England in the future would be confined entirely to New Englanders. Complete commercial stagnation fell upon Fort Amsterdam, and the calm in commerce was accompanied by, or, rather, was the leading cause of, a storm in politics. Adriaen van der Donck was one of the most interesting of the Dutch emigrants to New Netherland. He came to the colony in the employ of Van Rensselaer, but after telling that worthy patroon's superintendent that he was a liar, he found it convenient to leave Rensselaerswyck for the even stormier Manhattan. He married the daughter of Francis Doughty, an English Presbyterian clergyman, who had been driven from Taunton in New Plymouth Colony on account of his ideas as to infant baptism.[1] Doughty soon fled from the persecution of Stuyvesant and found refuge in Maryland. Van der Donck became president of the Nine Men. Under his energetic leadership the project of an appeal to the home authorities was once more taken up and this time pushed with energy. The Nine Men asked Stuyvesant's permission to consult the people; upon his refusal they made a house-to-house canvass. When Stuyvesant realized what was going on, he seized their papers and expelled Van der Donck from the board. Van der Donck and the Nine Men past and present thereupon drew up a memorial to the States-general, 1649. In this paper the memorialists prayed

[1] Lechford's *Plaine Dealing*, Trumbull's ed., pp. xxvii, 92. Doughty's sister charged him with defrauding her of her marriage portion. "Winthrop Papers" in Massachusetts Historical Society's *Collections*, Fifth Series, i, 308.

the Netherland government to take the province under its immediate care, to establish local self-government there, to encourage trade and the fisheries, and to settle the boundaries of the colony. With the memorial went also a remonstrance or "Vertoogh van Niew Nederlandt,"[1] which was drawn by Adriaen van der Donck himself and was a severe indictment of Stuyvesant and his employers. The remonstrance is especially bitter when it describes the lack of interest displayed by the authorities in religion and education. Dominie Backerus, the successor of Everadus Bogardus, had endured Stuyvesant as long as he could and was going home; his departure would leave the colonists without a minister. As to education, the remonstrants say: "There should be a public school . . . so that first of all in so wild a country where there are many loose people, the youth be well taught and brought up, not only in reading and writing, but also in the knowledge and fear of the Lord. As it is now, the school is kept very irregularly; one and another keeping it according to his pleasure, and as long as he thinks proper." Probably the remonstrants had in mind the scandal monger Roelantsen, who taught school off and on and also took in washing. The remonstrants ask for the appointment of a governor who is not too indigent and not too covetous, for "a covetous governor makes poor subjects, . . . for nobody is unmolested or secure in his property longer than the Director pleases, who is generally strongly inclined to confiscating." Van der Donck and two of the Nine Men, armed with the Memorial and the Remonstrance, sailed for Holland. With them went Backerus, whose orthodoxy

[1] It was printed at The Hague in 1649, and is translated with notes by H. C. Murphy in the New York Historical Society's *Collections*, Second Series, ii, 253. The quoted matter is on p. 319.

was not of Stuyvesant's kind, and Cornelis Melyn, who enjoyed the costly distinction of speaking his mind openly to both William Kieft and Peter Stuyvesant. Wouter van Twiller and the Van Rensselaer family joined their efforts to those of Van der Donck, Backerus, and Melyn; but it does not appear that much was immediately accomplished by this formidable band. The company went on in the old way, and Peter Stuyvesant continued to be as covetous and as arbitrary as ever.

By 1652, however, the continued representations of Van der Donck began to bear fruit.[1] The directors of the company consented that municipal privileges should be given the little town which had slowly grown up on the southern end of Manhattan Island under the name of New Amsterdam. It is said that the company intended to leave the selection of the schout, the schepens, and the burgomasters to the burghers; but it is a matter of record that Stuyvesant appointed them himself. It seems inconceivable that he should have done this without orders from home. The company also agreed that a school might be established in the "city tavern" if Stuyvesant saw no objection. Probably the director general saw objections to this use of the building, for there seems to be no evidence that the children were ever taught there, although in 1656 the schoolmaster of that time asked for its use on the ground that the children needed a schoolroom which could be warmed in winter.

In New Netherland it made slight difference whether representatives were appointed by their constituents or by the director general; they were no sooner in office than they opposed the governor and his wishes. In 1654 the war between England and the Netherlands came to a sudden

[1] Brodhead's *New York*, i, 537.

ending just in time to save the Dutch colony from an attack by a formidable expedition under General Robert Sedgwick which Cromwell had set on foot. The danger and the inconvenience had been sufficiently great to arouse the New Netherlanders, both English and Dutch, to a lively sense of the insufficiency of the West India Company's government. With Stuyvesant's permission, delegates from the several towns and villages met at New Amsterdam in December, 1653, in a convention or landtag.[1] Among the delegates was George Baxter, an aggressive English settler of Gravesend, who had accompanied Captain Underhill to the battle on Strickland's Plains. Under his vigorous leadership, the convention drifted away from the consideration of protection against attack from without to protection against tyranny from within. They drew up a Remonstrance and Petition in which they declared that they had transformed, "with immense labor and at their own expense, a wilderness of woods into a few small villages and cultivated farms." They asked that their requests might be "received and construed favorably and without misinterpretation,"—which was a somewhat optimistic view to take. They went on to state the fears and alarms which for some time had broken their spirit and discouraged them in their labors. To lessen the danger of misinterpretation on the part of the director general and the States-general, they summarized their "fears and alarms" under six heads as follows: (1) the arbitrary government; (2) the inefficiency of the Indian policy; (3) the appointment of officers and magistrates "without the consent or nomination of the people whom it most concerns"; (4) the uncertainty of the laws made by the director and council "without the approbation of the country";

[1] O'Callaghan's *New Netherland*, ii, 243.

(5) the injustice in withholding promised grants of land; and (6) the granting of large tracts to favored individuals for their private profit. Such was this great Remonstrance and Petition which representatives of the English and Dutch people of New Netherland presented to the despotic Stuyvesant at the risk of their lives and property. The times were so stormy, however, that that great personage only fumed and wrote a lengthy defense of his conduct. To this paper the Convention replied in a document which refers to the "laws of nature," a phrase which carries us forward a century. In answering their rejoinder, Stuyvesant sought to sow discord between the Dutch and the English. Their suggestion that the magistrates should be chosen by popular vote seemed to Stuyvesant to be the height of absurdity. "If the nomination and election of magistrates were to be left to the populace, who were the most interested," he declared, "then each would vote for one of his own stamp — the thief for a thief; the rogue, the tippler, the smuggler, for a brother in iniquity, that he might enjoy greater latitude in his vices and frauds." In this somewhat airy way, Peter Stuyvesant set aside the aspirations of those whom he called his subjects for a freer and more liberal government. It is true that in 1658 Stuyvesant yielded to the burgomasters and schepens of New Amsterdam the right to nominate a double number of magistrates from which the director and council should pick the actual magistrates for the year; but this concession did not amount to much in practice.[1] For ten years more the West India Company and its faithful director general did all that they could to divert the stream of immigration from the natural

[1] There is an excellent article on the local institutions of New Netherland in the Dutch régime, by A. E. McKinley, in *American Historical Review*, vi, 1–18.

center of commerce at Manhattan Island to the neighboring English colonies.

One reason for the slow growth of New Netherland was probably the use of torture which prevailed there and nowhere else on the continent, and the excessive and disgraceful punishments which were inflicted. The use of torture to extract confession was repugnant to English ideas and, indeed, was forbidden in the Massachusetts Body of Liberties, which provided that only convicted persons should be tortured. In New Netherland it was different, and the "Council Minutes" record in 1654 the case of a man charged with burglary who should be examined, and if obstinate, tortured; and in 1655 another case of a man accused of robbery who should be subjected to torture that he might confess; and in 1663, that the council denied a motion made by one of their number to subject a prisoner to torture on the ground that he had already been once tortured and twice whipped without eliciting additional information. The instrument of torture which was used in some of these cases was the rack. As for punishments inflicted, the "Council Minutes" show that a man was publicly whipped, branded, and banished for stealing hogs, while runaways had their hair clipped, were publicly whipped, had their ears pierced with a red-hot iron, and were further condemned to work with the company's negroes for a term of one year and upwards. The curious student may read other and more shocking entries for himself in O'Callaghan's "Calendar of Dutch Manuscripts."[1]

Peter Stuyvesant had a seventeenth-century dislike for toleration in religion, which was fully shared by his

[1] E. B. O'Callaghan's *Calendar of Historical Manuscripts*, pt. i, Dutch Manuscripts, 1630–54 ("Council Minutes," 61–268).

masters, the Lords Majors of the West India Company, by their High Mightinesses, the States-general of the Netherlands, and by the colonial clergyman, Johannes Backerus, who came from Curaçoa with the new director general in 1647. The condition of affairs at New Amsterdam seems to have affected unfavorably the tempers of both Stuyvesant and Backerus, for we find the latter acting with Van der Donck and the Nine Men against his former friend, and in 1649 he accompanied the embassy which went to Holland with the Remonstrance. By this time the religious system had become so far organized as to place the management of holy affairs in the colony in the Classis of Amsterdam. This body in the Dutch Reformed Church corresponded to the Presbytery in the Presbyterian organization. The religious fabric of the Dutch colonial system, therefore, was not unlike that of the English organization where the Bishop of London was supposed to have charge of religion in the colonies. On Backerus's dismission, Stuyvesant wrote to the Classis asking that "an old, experienced, and Godly minister might be sent to them"; but no person of standing in Holland could be found who was willing to go to the colony. In this emergency Dominie Johannes Megapolensis, who had been at Rensselaerswyck since 1642, was induced to exchange his place for that of minister at New Amsterdam, and he remained there until the English Conquest. He and Stuyvesant proved to be kindred spirits; to them the sight of a Lutheran was as sin. In 1654 the Lutherans, who were now numerous at New Amsterdam, desired to have a minister of their own, but this request Stuyvesant promptly refused, stating that his oath forbade him to tolerate openly any other religion than the Reformed Dutch. They then appealed to the States-general, but the influence of Megapolensis and of the Classis of Amsterdam overbore the desire of the authorities for colonists, as it was difficult to see how permission could be granted to the Lutherans and not to the Anabaptists and the English sects. The directors, therefore, wrote to Stuyvesant that no public religious service, except that of the true Dutch Reformed Church "should be permitted in New Netherland"; but Stuyvesant should use "all moderate exertions" to win Lutherans and other dissenters from their errors.

Moderation in exertion was not Peter Stuyvesant's strongest point; or, perhaps, what seemed moderation to him was not so regarded by those whom it most nearly affected. In 1656 Megapolensis and Dominie Samuel Drisius, who had been the former's colleague for some five years, complained to the director general of the increase of conventicles. Thereupon Stuyvesant issued a proclamation[1] forbidding the holding of religious meetings not in harmony with the established religion as set forth by the Synod of Dort; the penalty for the clergyman was one hundred pounds and for the attendant laymen twenty-five pounds. Private services might still be held in one's own family, but no father could have his child baptized without a statement of his belief in the doctrines held forth by that famous Synod. The proclamation was not a dead letter: William Wickendam, a cobbler from Rhode Island, baptized people in the river at Flushing. He was fined one hundred pounds and banished, but the money was never paid because he had it not. William Hallet, the sheriff of Flushing, who had encouraged Wickendam was fined fifty pounds and removed from office.

It was on the Quakers, however, that Stuyvesant's

[1] O'Callaghan's *Laws and Ordinances*, 211.

wrath fell with the greatest weight. They not only differed from him in religion, but were disrespectful in their attitude when brought before him as a magistrate. On their way to and from Massachusetts they thought New Netherland would be a convenient stopping place, for there the members of the English sects were disposed to treat them kindly. But Peter Stuyvesant, Johannes Megapolensis, and Samuel Drisius disliked them fully as much as did John Endicott and the Massachusetts ministers. It turned out, therefore, that at New Amsterdam the Quakers suffered the whole round of human torment, short of actual hanging. The worst case which has come down to us in Quaker annals is that of Robert Hodshone or Hodgson, who sought to enlighten the people of Heemstede or Hampstead. Richard Gildersleeve, the Presbyterian magistrate of that place, would have none of Hodshone's enlightenment. He arrested him, tied him to a cart's tail with his arms bound, and so conducted him by road and ferry to the presence of the director general. Two years at hard labor or a fine of six hundred guilders was the result of this first interview with Peter Stuyvesant. The Quakers always refused to do anything to aid in the carrying out of what they regarded as an unjust sentence. Hodshone, therefore, refused to work or to pay; he was chained to a wheelbarrow and beaten with a rope's end until he fell to the ground. Three days of wheelbarrow, chains, and beatings produced no compliance, and he was again taken before Stuyvesant. Demanding to know what law he had broken, he was told that he should be beaten every day until he consented to work or paid his fine. It fell out otherwise, however, for speaking when he was commanded to be silent, he was hung to the ceiling by his hands with a log of wood tied to his feet and was then beaten with rods on the bare back until his flesh was cut to pieces. Two days later he was again punished, and then at length he seems to have been willing to labor. This torture touched the hearts of the people; an Englishwoman bathed his wounds, and Stuyvesant's sister, Anna — widow of Nicholas Biard or Bayard — begged from her brother the remission of the remainder of the sentence.

Stuyvesant, although he permitted Hodshone to depart, was determined to restrain the spread of Quaker doctrine and decreed that sheltering a Quaker for one night should cost fifty pounds. It was this proclamation which drew from the townsmen of Flushing a memorable protest. They were commanded by the law, so they declared, to do good to all men. They desired not to offend one of Christ's little ones, be he Presbyterian, Independent, Baptist, or Quaker. Do unto others as you wish all men to do to you is the true law in Church and State. They should, therefore, shelter the Quakers "as God shall persuade our consciences." This remarkable remonstrance was signed by thirty-one men, whose names are worthy of remembrance.[1] Edward Hart, the town clerk, was dismissed from office, and Tobias Feake, the sheriff, was fined two hundred guilders. But all the regulations, finings, and exhortings of Director Stuyvesant and Dominies Megapolensis and Drisius were in vain, for the Quakers, Independents, and Lutherans kept on worshiping God as their consciences dictated.

[1] The signers of the Flushing Protest given by O'Callaghan, *New Netherland*, i, 351 note, are as follows: Edward Hart, clerk, Tobias Feake, William Noble, William Charles Stiger, William Thorne, Jr., Rudolf Blackford, Edward Feake, Mirabel Stevens, John Glover, Nathan Jeffs, Benjamin Hubbard, Philip ———, William Pidgeon, George Blee, Elias Doughty, Anthony Field, Richard Stortin, Edward Griffin, Nathaniel Coe, Robert Field, Sr., Robert Field, Jr., Nicholas Persells, Michael Millner, Henry Townsend, George Wright, John Ford, Lyman Bumtell, Edward Reurt, John Masline, John Townsend, Edward Farrington.

It was in the Swedish settlements on the South Bay and River that Lutheranism predominated. Gustavus Adolphus, Sweden's greatest king, was bitten with a desire for colonial expansion, and was stimulated thereto by William Usselincx, the Flemish founder of the Dutch West India Company. For years, however, constant warfare occupied his attention until he fell at the battle of Lutzen. After that unhappy day the Swedes had their hands full in conquering and plundering large portions of the continent of Europe. At length, however, a Swedish West India Company was founded, and in 1638 two Swedish vessels, the *Key of Calmar* and a tender, anchored off the site of the ill-fated Swannendael. There were fifty colonists on board, including a clergyman and some convicted bandits who were to do the rough work of the settlement. Their leader was Peter Minuit of Cleves, who had already served a colonial apprenticeship as governor of New Netherland. The English in Virginia made uncomfortable remarks as to Minuit's commerce with the natives, and the Dutch at Manhattan desired to know what he was about and protested against his doings. Neither Englishmen nor Dutchmen, however, offered effective opposition; the Thirty Years' War was still raging, and the Swedes were too good allies in Europe to be denied a bit of wild land in America, — especially as both Dutchmen and Englishmen denied the other's right to the region coveted by the newcomers.

Unmoved by these remonstrances, the Swedes went through the process of colonization; they "bought" land of the natives, built houses and forts, and exchanged the trinkets and tools of the home land for the furs of New Sweden. Near the site of the modern Wilmington was their fort, which they named Christina in honor of

Sweden's young queen, Gustavus Adolphus's daughter; in return, in 1642, she took the colony under her royal protection. Soldiers and colonists now came over in increasing numbers; they built forts above and below the Dutch trading posts, — for the Dutch tried to maintain the semblance of possession where they could not make effectual opposition. Nothing united the two nations on the Delaware save the approach of an English fur trader or colonist; then Swede and Dutchman combined to eject the invader. This intolerable condition could not long continue. In 1648 the Thirty Years' War came to an end with the treaties of Westphalia and Münster, and Spain acknowledged the independence of the United Netherlands. To this result the Swedes had contributed most powerfully; indeed, by stemming the flood of the Roman Catholic reaction, Sweden had saved continental Protestantism and the Dutch Republic from extinction. But nations, especially republics, are proverbially ungrateful; the exhausted condition of New Netherland, slowly recovering from the Indian wars, alone saved New Sweden from immediate conquest.

In 1655 everything was favorable for the successful prosecution of a Dutch campaign against the Swedish interlopers; the Indians of New Netherland were quiet and the termination of the war between England and Holland had put an end for the time being to fears of an attack from the United Colonies of New England. Stuyvesant gathered a formidable naval and military expedition. He sailed from New Amsterdam for the Delaware in command of either three hundred and fifty or seven hundred men, as one adopts the Dutch or the Swedish computation. He seized the Swedish settlements and forts without serious fighting, for Rising, the commander at Fort Christina, could muster only thirty-one men. At the lowest estimate, indeed, Stuyvesant must have had on his ships more armed men than there were white inhabitants of New Sweden, including in this computation men, women, children, and renegade Dutchmen. Never was greater homage rendered to the military prowess of the countrymen of Gustavus Adolphus. In his dealings with the powerful English colonies to the eastward, Peter Stuyvesant was not so fortunate.

The Pilgrim fathers were hardly established at Plymouth before they became conscious of the presence of the Dutch fur traders. A few years later Bradford and De Rasieres, the secretary of New Netherland, entered into a friendly correspondence; but Bradford felt obliged to warn the Dutchmen that they were trespassing on English territory. Even the visit of De Rasieres to Plymouth did not make the Pilgrims retire from this position, and a decade later this attitude of mingled friendliness and warning was assumed by Winthrop. In 1633 the Massachusetts bark *Blessing of the Bay* visited Fort Amsterdam. Her commander showed his commission to Wouter van Twiller, who was then director general, and signified to him that the Connecticut Valley was within the limits of English territory and therefore desired the Dutch not to build there. Van Twiller replied in a very respectful letter that as the States-general of Holland had also granted the same territory to his masters, the Dutch West India Company, the settlement of the matter would better be left to the authorities in Europe. In the same year, however, the Pilgrims took a further step and established a trading station on the Connecticut. As they passed up by the site of the later Hartford, the Dutch commander at Fort Good Hope shouted out to them, "Strike your colors or we shoot"; but William Holmes and his men of Plymouth sailed on, and the Dutchmen contented themselves with words. Settling somewhat higher up the river, the Plymouth people bought land of the Indian occupants and appropriated a part of the fur trade. Van Twiller protested against their conduct and ordered them to leave the river. But Holmes replied that "he was there in the name of the king of England, whose servant he was, and there he would remain,"—and there he did remain. Two and three years later strong bands of settlers came from Massachusetts, as has already been described. They built their houses with striking impartiality around the Dutch and Plymouth trading posts. In this emergency Van Twiller sent an expedition to seize and fortify a position at the mouth of the river; but the men of Saybrook were there before the Dutch, and Wouter van Twiller's men sailed back to Manhattan Island. In this way the English secured possession of the Connecticut Valley, although the Dutch continued to maintain a small garrison at Fort Good Hope. It cannot be said that the people of Hartford and their neighbors in the Dutch fort lived an altogether peaceful existence. Fugitives from justice found refuge in the fort, and the Dutchmen's cattle and hogs invaded the Englishmen's cornfields; sticks and stones were freely used and there was an interchange of vigorous language. It was not until 1654, however, that the redoubtable Captain John Underhill, on somewhat dubious authority, tacked a notice on the door of the fort saying that he had confiscated it; but eventually the Hartford townsmen appropriated the property. As for the Plymouth people, they finally received from the freeholders of Windsor compensation for the improvements they had made.[1]

The settlement of New Haven in 1638 offered a strong

[1] Trumbull's *Connecticut*, i, 65.

contrast to the history of the Dutch colony, for at the end of the first year of its existence its population numbered over two hundred souls. English settlers then pressed westward toward New Netherland; in 1639 Greenwich already contained two houses, and fifty families lived at Stratford. Englishmen also crossed the Sound and occupied the eastern end of Long Island. All attempts to found towns on the western end of that island, independent of the Dutch, failed, but English settlers predominated in several of the towns on this end. In the convention of 1653 there were as many English delegates as there were Dutch. The activity and strength of the English colonists in New Netherland proved to be politically disadvantageous to them. In 1655 the West India Company issued an order disqualifying foreigners from holding office in the colony; they could, however, be naturalized. This sometimes happened, and Englishmen not only changed their allegiance, but also their names, so that they are sometimes hard to recognize. Carel van Brugge, for instance, who signs, as secretary, the letters to the United Colonies in 1653, was an Englishman from Canterbury whose earlier name was Charles Bridges and whose wife was widow of Thomas Willett.

When Peter Stuyvesant became director general of New Netherland, he found the relations with the New England colonies in a critical condition, and he acquitted himself well of the difficult task of not yielding to the English and, at the same time, avoided war with them. Stuyvesant says that on his arrival at Fort Amsterdam there were not over three hundred men capable of bearing arms in the whole province.[1] This is probably an underestimate, but there certainly were not over two thousand

[1] *Documentary History*, i, 689.

white colonists in New Netherland in 1647, and more than one half of these were English. Plainly Stuyvesant could offer little armed opposition to the thirty odd thousand New Englanders. That New Netherland was not then wiped off the colonial map was due to the persistent refusal of Massachusetts to sanction a war, unless the justice of it was perfectly clear.

In carrying out their policy of independence from European complication, the leaders of the Bay colony would not assent to a declaration of war, except on plain proof of aggression, and Stuyvesant acted with singular moderation. He went in person to Hartford, and negotiated with the commissioners of the United Colonies. The correspondence was somewhat acrimonious, due in part to Stuyvesant's dating his first letter from Hartford in New Netherland, which he tried to explain away by saying that the epistle had been drawn up at Manhattan and merely signed at Hartford. The matters in dispute were finally referred for settlement to two delegates from each side. The commissioners appointed Simon Bradstreet of Massachusetts and Thomas Prince of Plymouth, and Stuyvesant selected Captain Thomas Willett, who seems at one time to have lived in Plymouth, and George Baxter, his English secretary and later the author of the Remonstrance and Petition of 1653. These four arbiters, all of English birth, reported (1650) that credence should be given to Stuyvesant's explanations of what had seemed to be somewhat dubious actions on his part, and, furthermore, that the Dutch should continue to hold the lands at Hartford which were then actually in their possession. These findings were distinctly favorable to the Dutch. On the other hand, however, the delegates proposed that Long Island should be divided between the two nations, and that on the mainland a line should be drawn at least ten miles from the Hudson as the eastern limit of New Netherland, and that the Dutch should build no houses within four miles of the line. This proposed arrangement was ratified in the colonies, but was not submitted to the home governments for confirmation.

In 1651 came the Navigation Ordinance, which was designed to build up English commercial and shipping interests. It is true that the ordinance restricted English imports merely to English vessels, or to vessels of such European countries as produced the goods or from which they were ordinarily shipped. Nevertheless, it operated to place the whole business in English hands, because English shipowners, having cargoes both ways, would be able to make better rates than their foreign rivals. In thus closing the trade of the English colonies to Dutch vessels, Parliament took a leaf from Dutch commercial regulations. When the Netherlanders objected to this new policy, Cromwell suggested that the matter might possibly be arranged on the basis of a mutual freedom of trade; but to this proposition the Dutch would not so much as listen. War followed in which New England and New Netherland came near being involved.

Whenever war threatened between the English and Dutch nations, the thoughts of the former at once reverted to the massacre of Amboyna and to "the mixture of force and fraud," which drove English traders from Pularoon. Samuel Rawson Gardiner, the English historian, asserts that the mercantile rulers of Holland and Zealand were "by no means scrupulous as to the means by which they attained their ends." It is not surprising, therefore, that the New Englanders gave ready ear to rumors that Stuyvesant was endeavoring to stir the Indians to massacre the scattered settlers of the New England frontier.[1] There was some truth in this report, for Stuyvesant had repeatedly expressed an intention of employing Indians against the New Englanders in case the latter joined in the war, and to this policy, indeed, he was commanded by the directors of the West India Company. At the time, however, he had committed no overt act and offered to justify himself before delegates to be appointed by the United Colonies. These were appointed and, possibly to give them added prestige, the commissioners of the United Colonies at the same time determined what proportion of men should be raised for the first expedition against New Netherland. The delegates went to Fort Amsterdam, found Stuyvesant somewhat evasive, gathered what evidence they could, mostly from Indians, and returned home somewhat precipitately. The commissioners of New Plymouth, Connecticut, and New Haven were for instant war; but the Massachusetts General Court refused point-blank its consent.[2] The evidence, the Massachusetts authorities said, was not conclusive, and therefore the war did not seem to be just. The English authorities appear to have directed the colonists to proceed against the Dutch, but it was only the Coddington government at Newport which acted on the command. Under this commission Underhill seized Fort Good Hope, and William Dyer captured a vessel or two.

Connecticut and New Haven now petitioned the Protector to remove the Dutch, who straitened and confined

[1] The *Second Part of the Amboyna Tragedy* (reprinted as Appendix G to O'Callaghan's second volume) is undoubtedly exaggerated. Brodhead (*New York*, i, 555) appears to seek to justify the action of Stuyvesant and the West India Company by saying that "the Puritans had themselves set the example of employing Indian allies in the Pequot War," as if the employment of Indians against Indians was the same thing as using them against white settlers. This is a good example of the disingenuousness which seriously mars Brodhead's work and makes it a dangerous book to place in the hands of any persons except experts.

[2] See above, p. 420.

the English. Cromwell lent a ready ear to these representations, or perhaps he had already come to a determination. In 1654 four vessels crossed the Atlantic under command of Robert Sedgwick[1] and John Leverett, both freemen of Massachusetts who had already held rank in her military service. Sedgwick was commissioned[2] by the Lord Protector to secure such aid as he could from the New England colonies, and then, if it appeared feasible, to seize the Dutch settlements. Massachusetts Bay consistently refused to proclaim the Protector, but the General Court voted that it had received his Highness's letter which was "full of grace and favorable respect to this colony," and regretted that Massachusetts was not in "such a capacity as may be apprehended to send forth such numbers of men as might vigorously assist in the undertaking."[3] Nevertheless, Sedgwick was authorized to enlist five hundred volunteers for his expedition. New Haven and Connecticut were extremely active, and Plymouth was ready to join with them. A formidable expedition, which would have been led by Robert Sedgwick, Miles Standish, and John Mason, was almost ready to take the field when news reached Boston of peace between England and the Netherlands. Sedgwick devoted his energies to the seizure of the French posts in Maine and Nova Scotia,[4] and for nine years longer Peter Stuyvesant was permitted to go on retarding the development of the superb advantages which the position of Manhattan Island offered for trade and commerce, and, incidentally, to be a thorn in the flesh of his English neighbors.

[1] There is a good article on Sedgwick in Colonial Society's *Publications*, iii, 156.

[2] Massachusetts Historical Society's *Collections*, Fourth Series, ii, 230.

[3] *Massachusetts Colony Records*, iv, pt. i, p. 195.

[4] See Hannay's *Acadia*.

NOTES

I. Printed Records of New Netherland. — Our detailed knowledge of the history of New Netherland practically begins with the administration of Peter Stuyvesant, for it is only with the middle of the century that the printed records become abundant and give us a picture of Dutch colonial life at all comparable to that of the Chesapeake colonies or of New England. For instance, only about one hundred of the four hundred pages of O'Callaghan's *Calendar of Dutch Manuscripts* in the Secretary of State's office refer to the period before 1647; only sixty pages of O'Callaghan's *Laws and Ordinances of New Netherland, 1638-1674*, deal with the earliest time; and the *Records of New Amsterdam*, as Fernow has printed them, begin with 1653. The "Council Minutes," printed in O'Callaghan's *Calendar of Historical Manuscripts in the Office of the Secretary of State* (pt. i, "Dutch Manuscripts") throw a blaze of light into the social conditions of early New York.

II. Opportunity for Research. — J. H. Innes's *New Amsterdam and its People* stands practically alone as the only work which is based on a study of the court records, printed and manuscript. There is, indeed, as much opportunity for doing good work on this part of New York's history as there is on that of the Chesapeake colonies. It will only be when much more material has been printed and carefully studied that any definite comparisons can be made between the life of early New Netherland and that of the other colonies.

CHAPTER XVIII

THE PERIOD OF THE PURITAN SUPREMACY, 1650–1660

FROM the beginning the English colonies in America had enjoyed a large measure of freedom from the control of the mother country; since the accession of Charles I they had exercised practical self-government. The second Stuart had the will to establish a system of colonial administration as thoroughgoing as that which he desired to organize in Great Britain, but he had neither the strength nor the time to inaugurate such a policy nor the money with which to secure the enforcement of any order which might seem to him to be desirable or even necessary. English history from the death of James I to the meeting of the Long Parliament, is taken up largely with the record of illegal pecuniary exactions by the crown: tonnage and poundage collected without vote of Parliament, forced loans, petty extortions of various kinds, all culminating in the demand of ship money, the resistance to which rendered the name of John Hampden forever famous. The modern liberty of Englishmen was largely won in the contests over these matters between the king and his subjects, and every honor is due to those who risked life and purse in the cause of liberty. Nevertheless, these exactions, with the exception of tonnage and poundage, brought scanty sums of money into the exchequer. It was this royal poverty which enabled Massachusetts Bay to bid defiance to Whitehall, — "The Lord frustrated their design."[1] The activity of the religious and political opponents of Charles and Laud prevented force being used against the men of Massachusetts.

In 1640 the Long Parliament met; by 1642 it had acquired so much strength that Charles abandoned his capital and sought to overthrow Parliament by force of arms. For three years the outcome was doubtful, until the genius of Oliver Cromwell overturned the royal cause, first at Marston Moor and secondly at Naseby. From that time until 1660 republican or quasi-republican ideas were paramount in England. The establishment of the power of the Long Parliament gave vigor to all branches of government. Charles I, at the highest point of his personal administration, had commissioned Archbishop Laud and other friends of the crown to oversee colonial affairs,[2] but the commission had been a dead letter almost from the outset. In 1643 the Long Parliament took the matter in hand, and by ordinance commissioned Robert Rich, Earl of Warwick, "Governour in chiefe, and Lord High Admirall of all those Islands and other Plantations, inhabited, planted, or belonging to any His Majesties, the King of Englands Subjects, within the bounds, and upon the Coasts of America." Seventeen members of Parliament, among whom were the Earl of Manchester, Lord Saye and Sele, Sir Henry Vane, Jr., Oliver Cromwell, and William Vassall, were appointed commissioners to aid and assist him to "dispose all things which they shall from

[1] Winthrop's *New England*, i, 161.

[2] There is an historical summary of these commissions, etc., in Kaye's "Colonial Executive," 53-62 (*Johns Hopkins University Studies*, xviii, Nos. 5, 6). The proof-reading of this article is not good: Hening is printed as Henning, Gorton as Gordon, Cotton as Colton. These slips are easily recognized by those familiar with the subject and in themselves are of slight importance. Nevertheless there are so many of them that they raise doubts in one's mind as to the accuracy of the facts stated in the paper.

time to time find most fit and advantageous to the well governing, securing, strengthening, and preserving of the said Plantations," especially the advancement of the true Protestant religion. In executing these important functions, the chief governor and any four commissioners might act.[1] This board was further authorized to fill vacancies in its number, to appoint and remove "such subordinate governors, councillors, commanders, officers, and agents as they shall judge to be best affected and most fit and serviceable," and to "assign, ratify, and confirm so much of their aforementioned authority and power and in such manner and to such persons as they shall judge to be fit for the better governing and preserving of the said Plantations and Islands from open violence, and private disturbance and distraction." Such was the famous commission which established the Board of Trade and Plantations. This action of Parliament seems to have been taken in consequence of the humble petition of divers merchants trading to the Island of Barbados, and of divers inhabitants there which was presented to the House of Commons in October, 1643.[2] The petition was referred to a committee which had colonial matters in charge. Roger Williams had been in London since the middle of the preceding summer; his representations concerning the condition of the settlements on Narragansett Bay doubtless had great weight with the members of the House of Commons, but there is no mention in the record of any petition or memorial presented by him. The power enjoyed by Warwick, who was also exercising at this time the office of Lord High Admiral of England,

[1] In December, 1647, this was changed so that any five members of the board might act provided that one of them was a peer and at least two others were members of the House of Commons.

[2] *Commons Journals*, iii, 283.

was very great; but the affairs of the navy so engrossed his attention that beyond giving the patent of Incorporation of Providence Plantations and doing what was necessary in regard to the West Indies, neither Warwick nor the commissioners seem to have taken much interest in colonial affairs.

From 1643 on there are occasional references to the affairs of what were then termed the Foreign[1] Plantations, but beyond confirming this ordinance, nothing important was done until January, 1646–47. In the preceding October a "Letter from the Grand Assembly in Virginia, of 17 Martii, 1645," had been presented to the House of Commons and this was probably the foundation for the ordinance of January 23, 1646–47, which provided that goods might be transported to the plantations without paying duties for the space of three years, and also that servants might be transported, on condition that no force be used to take up any such servant or children except with the express consent of their parents. In consideration of this freedom from customs the plantations were expected to confine their commerce to English vessels, and any plantation that did not comply with this condition should be excluded from its benefits and should "pay custome as other Merchants do to France, Spain, Holland, and other foreign parts."[2]

The American colonists for the most part refused to side with the Commons in the contest with the king or sympathized openly with him. Many settlers from New England returned to the mother country, where they bore more or less prominent parts in the Civil Wars and occu-

[1] This use of the word "foreign" to denote plantations outside of England and Ireland was common in the seventeenth century.

[2] Scobell's *Ordinances*, pt. i, 113.

pied important positions under the Commonwealth and the Protectorate; but the colonists who remained in New England seem to have regarded themselves as quite outside of the scope of Parliamentary power.[1] The best example of this, perhaps, was the action of Massachusetts. In 1642 the Commons ordered that all goods exported from England to New England should be free from customs.[2] For this favor the Massachusetts General Court ordered a humble and thankful acknowledgment to be entered on their records. Nevertheless, when, at about the same time, friends of Massachusetts in the House of Commons wrote to Winthrop suggesting that they could secure the passage by Parliament of any legislation which Massachusetts might desire, he courteously declined the offer "lest in . . . after times . . . hostile forces might be in control, and meantime a precedent would have been established."[3] Later when Parliament (October 3, 1650) forbade commerce with Barbados and Virginia, the Massachusetts General Court deemed it necessary to direct that no trade should be had with those places.[4]

Warwick and the commissioners soon after their appointment sent agents to Virginia to offer the colonists there self-government and freedom from taxation by England; but Sir William Berkeley, acting under directions from the king, was able to defeat these efforts to bring Virginia into harmony with Parliament. The Virginians paid no

[1] There is an interesting article on the "Political Ideal of the English Commonwealth" by J. G. Dow in the *English Historical Review*, vi, 306.

[2] Winthrop's *New England*, ii, 98.

[3] *Ibid.*, ii, 25.

[4] *Massachusetts Colony Records*, iv, pt. i, p. 40. Another instance of the independent feeling of this colony is the vote of the General Court of Massachusetts directing the "Capt. of the Castle" "till the state of England shall alter the same, which we much desire, we being of the same nation . . . shall presently advance the aforesaid colors of England upon the Castle, upon all necessary occasion." *Massachusetts Colony Records*, iv, pt. i, p. 41. On its side the House of Commons in the vote of 1642, referred to above, speaks of New England as "that kingdom."

attention to the orders of Parliament, but it was not until 1650 that the Puritan authorities were able to do anything in the matter. In that year, however, an ordinance was passed declaring that Virginia, Bermudas, and Antego "are and ought to be subordinate to and dependent on England; and hath ever since the planting thereof been and ought to be subject to such laws . . . as are or shall be made by Parliament."[1] For the future, therefore, Parliament forbade all ships of any foreign nations whatsoever to trade with any of these plantations without license first had and obtained from the Parliament or the Council of the State, and ordered the seizure and confiscation of all vessels in these plantations or on the way thither in contravention of this law. In August, 1649, Parliament had appointed Vane and fourteen others a commission to examine the whole question of trade and commerce, including the fisheries and the Plantations in America and elsewhere, "how they may be best managed and made useful for this Commonwealth; how the commodities thereof may be so multiplied and improved, as those Plantations alone may supply the Commonwealth with what it necessarily wants." In October, 1651, partly, no doubt, as a result of this inquiry, the famous Navigation Ordinance was passed.

It has been often said that this legislation was the result of a sudden jealousy of the prosperity of Dutch commerce. In reality, however, it seems to have been one step in a series of acts all having for their aim the restricting of English and colonial trade to English and colonial vessels. The earliest of these measures goes back

[1] Scobell's *Ordinances*, pt. ii, 132, Hazard's *State Papers*, i, 559. A previous ordinance (*Commons Journals*, vi, 307) provided that colonial governors and deputies should take an engagement to the Commonwealth.

to the time of Richard II, when it was enacted "that none of the King's liege people do from henceforth ship any merchandise in going out or coming within the Realm of England, but only in ships of the King's ligeance."[1] This act was modified by many subsequent laws.[2] The policy of commercial restriction had been a favorite one with Sir Edwin Sandys and the reformers of James's time. In 1621 a bill had been brought into the House of Commons, providing that goods could be brought into England only from the places of production, except in English ships, and forbidding English merchants to import any goods whatsoever except in English vessels. This bill failed to pass, and during the reigns of James and Charles the navigation laws had remained as they were at Elizabeth's death, except that the decision in Bate's case gave the king a somewhat freer hand in the regulation of commerce by prerogative.[3] In 1645 the Long Parliament reverted to the policy of building up the English marine by confining the importation of whale oil, and gills, commonly called whalebone, to vessels fitted out from England by English subjects. Three years later the importation of French wool, silk, and wine into England, Ireland, and the Dominions thereof was strictly prohibited; on the other hand, all salt not made within the Commonwealth of England or the Dominions was ad-

[1] 5 Richard II, Stat. 1, Cap. 3, *Statutes of the Realm*, ii, 18.

[2] For instance, see 6 Richard II, Stat. 1, Cap. 8; 14 Richard II, Cap. 6; 4 Henry VII, Cap. 10; 7 Henry VIII, Cap. 2; 23 Henry VIII, Cap. 7; 32 Henry VIII, Cap. 14; 5 and 6 Edward VI, Cap. 18; 1 Elizabeth, Cap. 13; 13 Elizabeth, Cap. 11; 23 Elizabeth, Cap. 7; 27 Elizabeth, Cap. 15; 39 Elizabeth, Cap. 10. H. E. Egerton in his *British Colonial Policy* (p. 61) briefly reviews the early history of the subject.

[3] The king by proclamation forbade the importation or exportation of certain commodities; he also raised or lowered the rates sometimes in the direction of protection of "infant industries." The colonial charters, also, often contained clauses exempting the grantees and their colonists from the payment of duties. The instructions of 1641 to Berkeley provided that only English vessels should trade to Virginia; see above, p. 235.

judged to be foreign salt and to be taxed. Then came the laws of 1650 which have already been mentioned. This brief statement will serve to show that the Ordinance of 1651 was not so much the inauguration of a new policy as the restatement of a policy already several centuries old. What was new in it was the fact that now, for the first time, the rulers of England had the power and the will to carry it into effect to a greater extent, at any rate, than had been the case heretofore.

The title of the Ordinance of 1651 is an "Act for the Increase of Shipping and Encouragement of the Navigation of this Nation." It provides that no goods whatsoever of the growth, production, or manufacture of Asia, Africa, or America, as well of the English plantations as of others, should be transported to England or to any territory subject to the Commonwealth in any ship whatsoever, except such as belong to "the people of this Commonwealth or the Plantations thereof, and whereof the master and mariners are also for the most part of them of the people of this Commonwealth." No European goods could be imported into England or English dominions except in English ships or in vessels belonging to the people of the country where the goods are produced or first shipped, and then only from the ports whence the goods are usually shipped, and the coastwise trade was closed to foreigners. Furthermore, no salted fish, or any oil, or whale fins or whalebones shall be imported into England or English dominions, "except such as are caught in vessels belonging to the people of this nation," and no salted fish or oil shall be exported except in English vessels. The language of the act is not precise, but the intention of its makers was undoubtedly to confine the shipping trade almost entirely to English-speaking people, although the phrases "belong only to the people of this Commonwealth and the Plantations thereof," "people of this Commonwealth," and "people of this nation" would seem to imply that colonial ships might engage in the trade from Asia, Africa, and America, provided they were manned in part by residents of England, but that on the other hand European trade and the business of supplying England with fish, oil, and whalebone should be closed to vessels owned in the colonies.

Whether the Ordinance of 1651 was aimed at colonial shipping or was intended to include colonial ship owners in the beneficial operation of the law, may perhaps be questionable, but it is certain that Parliament in other respects intended to encourage the people of the plantations. For example, in 1642, the people of New England were given permission to export goods out of England to New England without paying any duty either inward or outward, "either in this kingdom or New England," until the House of Commons shall take further order. In passing, it is worth noting that, in this instance, the House of Commons undertook of its own authority to dispense, not merely with the laws and regulations of England, but with colonial laws as well. The justification for this order is stated to be the propagation of the gospel in New England, which was greatly advanced by the prosperity of the colonies there.[1] In 1647 the House of Commons ordered a committee to prepare and bring in an ordinance for the encouragement of piety and learning in New England. Some time elapsed, however, before this business could be taken up. In 1649 a bill was considered which provided for the maintaining of the University of Cambridge in New England and other schools and nurseries of

[1] Husband's *Ordinances*, p. 6.

learning there, and also for the preaching and propagating of the gospel among the natives. As the debate progressed, some jealousy appears to have developed against Harvard College. This was due, probably, to the fact that Massachusetts, as has already been stated, in its religious organization stood midway between the Presbyterian discipline and Independency; the "New England Way" had no friends among the two powerful elements which were then contending for mastery in the House of Commons. It fell out, therefore, that the act as passed contained no reference to the University at Cambridge which educated persons for the ministry in accordance with New England ideas, and simply provided for the formation of a Society for the Propagating of the Gospel among the Natives of that region.[1]

By the middle of the seventeenth century tobacco must have been grown in considerable quantities in Connecticut and also in New Netherland.[2] A profitable trade in this commodity had sprung up between New England and the mother country; but of course some part of this traffic was in Virginia and Maryland tobacco. In 1649, Parliament taxed all tobacco imported into England from New England as well as from the Chesapeake colonies and from

[1] There is an interesting letter from Edward Winslow to the Commissioners of the United Colonies, dated London, April 17, 1651 (Hutchinson's *Collection*, 228–232). The letter relates to the procuring of supplies for the Indian mission. In their reply the Commissioners suggest that "according to the intent of the act of Parliament, an eye may be had in the distributions to the enlarging of the College at Cambridge"—but the intent of the act would seem to be precisely the opposite. Nevertheless the "house of brick," which was known as the "Indian College," was built with the funds of the Society for Propagating the Gospel among the Natives."

[2] An act of the Connecticut Assembly in 1640 (*Records*, i, 53) provided "that what person or persons within this jurisdiction shall, after September, 1641, drink any other tobacco but such as is or shall be planted within these liberties, shall forfeit for every pound so spent five shillings except they have license from the court." See also a letter from John Winthrop, Jr., in Massachusetts Historical Society's *Collections*, Fifth Series, viii, 65, and Brodhead's *New York*, i, 277.

foreign parts. At about the same time, however, the old prohibition of tobacco planting in England was revived and made more stringent. From the bills and acts which have been noted in the preceding paragraph, it may be stated with some confidence that the English Parliament in the time of the Puritan supremacy regarded itself as competent to legislate for the colonies, and framed its legislation with a view to control colonial trade and also to confer benefits of one kind or another upon the English plantations. The attention of the Long Parliament, of the Council of State of the Commonwealth, and of the Lord Protector was so fully occupied with home affairs, however, that they had little time and few resources to devote to the enforcement of this policy so far as it was restrictive. On the other hand, the Puritan rulers of England seem to have regarded the colonists in the light of brother Englishmen ; while demanding acknowledgment of the revolutionary authorities in England and obedience to trade regulations, they were otherwise disposed to permit the colonists to govern themselves and, in general, to work out their own salvation. In a few instances, however, where English authority was openly defied, energetic measures were taken to compel satisfactory recognition of the *de facto* government at home.

In Barbados, Bermuda, some of the smaller West India islands, and Virginia there was hostility to the new rulers at Whitehall. This seems to have been due to the presence in those places of a few royalist refugees and of officials who remained faithful to the royal cause. It is quite likely, also, that the conditions of life in the planting colonies made the leaders susceptible to aristocratic ideas; but, on the other hand, the interests of the planters were so manifestly involved in the profitable cultivation of the soil which in turn required access to the English market, that no strong opposition was organized anywhere. In Virginia the General Assembly, soon after the receipt of the news of the execution of Charles I, passed an act [1] recognizing his son Charles II as rightful king, although Parliament by ordinance had prohibited the proclaiming of any person to be king, and had declared, "That the people of England and of all the Dominions and Territories thereunto belonging are, and shall be, and are hereby constituted . . . to be a Commonwealth and Free-State; And shall from henceforth be governed as a Commonwealth and Free-State; by the Supreme authority of this Nation." [2] At least one of the Virginia counties also took upon itself to proclaim Charles II and to require all his Majesty's liege people "to pray God to bless Charles the Second, King of England, Scotland, France, and Ireland, Virginia, New England, and the Caribda Islands." [3] The Barbadians also displayed some energy in proclamations with the result that in October, 1650, an expedition was set on foot for the conquest of those islands, which was effected without any trouble. The Puritan leader among the planters there was Colonel Modyford; in 1652 he made the suggestion that Barbados should be allowed representation in the Imperial Parliament,[4] and this proposition was approved by the committee on foreign affairs of that body, but nothing further was done in the matter. As to Virginia, it was 1651 before the English authorities were ready to act. Then they dispatched an expedition to the James River, and the Virginians surrendered without striking a blow March 12–22, 1651–52. There are indications that some of the voters were dissatisfied with the

[1] Hening's *Statutes*, i, 359.
[2] Scobell's *Ordinances*, pt. ii, 30.
[3] *William and Mary Quarterly*, i, 149.
[4] Egerton's *British Colonial Policy*, 60.

government as it had been administered in recent years; but how strong this discontent was does not appear.[1] The terms of the surrender[2] were probably arranged by Colonel George Ludlow, a leading planter in Virginia, who was the kinsman of General Ludlow of Cromwell's army.[3] The articles of surrender obliged the Virginians to acknowledge the authority of the Commonwealth. Otherwise, they were to have the privileges of free-born Englishmen and were to govern themselves through their assembly, wherein nothing should be done contrary to the government of the Commonwealth of England. The use of the English service book was permitted for one year, after which the act of Parliament, prohibiting its use, would take effect in the colony. Those Virginians who could not live under these conditions were to have a year in which to settle their affairs and then might transport themselves to England or to any foreign country that they might prefer. When the articles reached England, they were considered in Parliament, which confirmed some of them but referred those conferring upon Virginians the rights of free-born Englishmen to a committee which also had in charge the consideration of a charter for the colony. There the matter rested, so far as the "Journals of the House of Commons" show.[4] The provisions permitting dissatisfied Virginians to go into exile were not confirmed by Parliament,[5] and the most incorrigible of all the Vir-

[1] See, for example, "Northampton County Records for 1652" (*Virginia Magazine of History*, v. 35), where the voters protest against the levying of a poll tax because they had not been represented in the Assembly since 1647.

[2] See *Virginia Magazine of History and Biography*, xi, 32-40. "The Instructions" are on p. 38, and the report of the Commissioners dated "From aboard the Ginny Friggat in Mary-Land, Mar. 24" is on pp. 32-35. The Articles of Surrender are in Jefferson's *Notes on Virginia*, p. 201; Hening's *Statutes*, i, 363; Hazard's *State Papers*, i, 560.

[3] Ludlow's *Memoirs* (edition of 1698), i, 387; quoted in *ibid.*, p. 36.

[4] *Commons Journals*, vii, 172, 173.

[5] This statement is made on negative evidence; but see vote of the Virginia Assembly in Hening's *Statutes*, i, 384.

ginians, Governor Sir William Berkeley, remained in retirement in the colony throughout the period of the Protectorate.

The English Council of State had originally appointed five commissioners to conduct this enterprise. Of these, two perished in a shipwreck while on the way to the Chesapeake. The remaining members were Captain Edmond Curtis of the *Guinea* frigate, who commanded the expedition, William Claiborne, who had been appointed Treasurer of Virginia for life by Charles I and had been displaced by Berkeley, and Richard Bennett, son of a rich English merchant and an important planter in Virginia, who had been driven thence to Maryland by Berkeley on account of his religious affiliations. Considering the composition of this commission, the terms which were accorded appear to have been singularly liberal. This bloodless revolution naturally threw the power into the hands of the commissioners[1] and of those Virginians who were favorable to the Parliamentary cause. The Assembly elected Bennett governor and Claiborne secretary, and also appointed a council. For the next few years the Virginians governed themselves through an elected Assembly, which in turn appointed a governor and council. The three governors were Bennett, Samuel Mathews, one of the leaders in the insurrection against Harvey, and Edward Digges, son of Sir Dudley Digges, who had deserted the reform movement when to belong to it meant fine and imprisonment. Besides executing the office of governor in Virginia, Ben-

[1] The government of Virginia was never formally recognized by Cromwell; but he seems to have acquiesced in the commissioners' exercise of authority. The government of Virginia was provisional and was intended to continue only until a new charter should be granted; but Cromwell was too busy to give the matter the necessary attention. Meantime the Virginians governed themselves without yielding much obedience to the Articles. See Hening's *Statutes*, i, 369 note, 372.

nett also acted as commissioner in the reducement of Maryland, and all three represented Virginia in London in a persistent attempt to secure a new charter which would incorporate Maryland with the older colony. In 1658, on the deposition of Richard Cromwell, Sir William Berkeley emerged from retirement and again became governor of Virginia, but whether by choice of the people or by action of the Assembly or by both cannot be definitely stated.[1] At all events, he occupied the office at the accession to power of Charles II, and about four months after the latter's entry into London Berkeley ordered him to be proclaimed king in Virginia.[2]

Throughout the Puritan period Lord Baltimore had much ado to preserve his rights of jurisdiction in Maryland. Oftentimes it must have seemed to him that what had been gained by the exercise of his skill and tact would be lost through the indiscretions of his agents in the province. Once in a while, indeed, he lost his temper and issued orders which came near to overthrowing his plans altogether; but in each case he was able ultimately to secure the better of his opponents. It was probably inevitable that Maryland should be brought within the vortex of the civil wars; but the unfortunate and largely unnecessary actions of Leonard Calvert in dealing with William Claiborne and other Virginia traders brought on the crisis earlier and made it more acute than it would otherwise have been. Claiborne was no Puritan; but he espoused the Parliamentary side with a view, perhaps, to secure from the Puritans the justice which the royal tribunals had denied to him. At about the same time, a dispute arose between a ship master, Richard Ingle, who had had the

[1] See *Virginia Magazine of History*, vii, 314; Hening's *Statutes*, i, 526 note.

[2] *William and Mary Quarterly*, i, 158.

temerity to dub Prince Rupert "Prince Traitor and Prince Rogue," and the Maryland government, which, owing to the absence of Leonard Calvert, was for the moment in the hands of Giles Brent. Ingle escaped and, returning with a commission from the Long Parliament, made short work with the government at St. Mary's. He seized the "great seal of the province" and compelled the vanquished to turn over to him sundry barrels of gunpowder to replace that which he had expended in firing on them. Ingle also had disputes over business matters with Thomas Cornwallis, a leading man of the colony. The result of these difficulties in which the rulers of Maryland became involved, was a motion[1] in the House of Lords "for the settling of the Plantation of Maryland under the command of a Protestant" (December 25, 1645). The drafting of an ordinance to accomplish this purpose was confided to a committee of which the Earl of Warwick was the reporter or chairman. The ordinance passed the House of Lords nearly a year later (November 24, 1646) and was ordered to be sent to the Commons; but there is no record of its reception by that body, or of any further action in the matter. Commingled with Ingle's grievances was a charge brought by a certain Mary Ford against Cornwallis to the effect that he had stolen two of her children and had carried them to Maryland for the purpose of "seducing them to popery," in furtherance of what she described as "Lord Baltimore's poisoned purposes." The hearings on these charges and other matters relating thereto were postponed from week to week and from month to month, partly by Baltimore's skill, but more especially by the

[1] *Lords' Journals*, viii and ix. The entries may be found in the index volume under Baltimore, Ingle, and Maryland; most of them are reproduced in *Maryland Archives* (Council, 1636–67).

exigencies of the time; the cases were still on the docket when the Commons passed their famous resolution for the establishment of a commonwealth without king or House of Lords. It was under these circumstances that Baltimore appointed the Protestant Virginia planter, William Stone, his governor in Maryland (1648), and invited the Virginia Puritans to settle within his province.

Lord Baltimore, while intrusting the government of Maryland to a Protestant governor and a council equally divided between Roman Catholics and Protestants, naturally sought to bind the hands of those hostile to his religion, so far at least as to make it impossible for them to injure his fellow-Catholics. This he endeavored to do by imposing upon them an oath and by sending over to Maryland the draft of a law to which the Assembly gave its consent (1649). The following words in the governor's oath were also in the oaths which the councilors took: "I will not by myself nor any person directly nor indirectly trouble, molest, or discountenance any person whatsoever in the said province professing to believe in Jesus Christ, and in particular any Roman Catholic for or in respect of his or her religion or in his or her free exercise thereof."[1] The Act Concerning Religion was probably the joint work of Lord Baltimore and Father More, the head of the Society of Jesus in England, although it may have been somewhat amended by the Assembly in Maryland.[2] It provided that no person "professing to believe in Jesus Christ shall, from henceforth, be any ways troubled, molested, or discountenanced for, or in respect of, his or her religion, nor in the free exercise thereof within this

[1] *Maryland Archives* (Council, 1636–67), p. 209.

[2] See an interesting paper by Bradley T. Johnson on "The Foundation of Maryland and the Origin of the Act Concerning Religion" (Maryland Historical Society's *Fund Publication*, No. 18).

province, . . . nor any way compelled to the belief or exercise of any other religion against his or her consent." The act also provided the penalty of death with forfeiture of lands and goods against those who denied the divinity of Christ or the doctrine of the Trinity. Furthermore, any one who uttered "any reproachful words or speeches concerning the blessed Virgin Mary" for the first offense should pay five pounds sterling or be publicly whipped and imprisoned during pleasure, and for the second offense pay ten pounds sterling or be publicly and severely whipped and imprisoned during pleasure.[1] The authors of the act also tried to smooth over religious acrimony by providing that any one who should call or denominate another "an heretic, Schismatic, Idolater, puritan, Independent, Presbyterian, popish priest, Jesuit, Jesuited papist, Lutheran, Calvinist, Anabaptist, Brownist, Antinomian, Barrowist, Roundhead, Separatist, or any other name or term in a reproachful manner relating to matter of religion" should forfeit ten shillings for each such utterance, or be whipped and imprisoned until he or she should apologize.

The Virginia Puritans, once they were settled in Maryland at Providence, which later came to be called Annapolis in honor of Anne, Lady Baltimore, found difficulty in accepting the oath which they were expected to take on receiving grants of land. This oath obliged the taker to acknowledge Baltimore as absolute lord and to support his government and officers in Maryland. At this moment, the Puritans were supreme in England, having defeated

[1] The portion of the act which denounced the death penalty against blasphemers and imprisonment during pleasure against those who uttered reproachful words "concerning the blessed Virgin Mary" reminds one of the Long Parliament's Ordinance of 1648 which added certain Calvinistic dogmas to the first category and punishment with imprisonment for those who affirmed certain anti-Calvinistic doctrines. See Scobell's *Ordinances*, pt. i, 149.

the Royalists in the second Civil War and having cut off the king's head. Under these circumstances, it appeared to the American brethren a little incongruous and quite unnecessary to support a governor in Maryland, who had sworn not to molest any Roman Catholic in the free exercise of his or her religion. They peremptorily refused to take grants of land on these terms. For a time they even declined to acknowledge the government at St. Mary's, but were finally won over by Governor Stone.

The phrasing of the commission to Curtis, Claiborne, and Bennett, which has been described above, was somewhat peculiar in that, instead of directing them to reduce to obedience to the Commonwealth the colony of Virginia or the colonies of Virginia and Maryland, it ordered them to reduce to obedience "all the colonies within the Bay of Chesapeake." It is sometimes stated that Maryland was omitted through the efforts of Baltimore,[1] and that the words used were substituted for Virginia at the instigation of Claiborne; but there is scant evidence upon which to base either of these statements. At all events, the commissioners evidently regarded it as their duty to secure the obedience of Maryland, where, without Baltimore's knowledge, Charles II had been proclaimed by Acting Governor Thomas Greene in Stone's absence. They, therefore, proceeded to St. Mary's with the *Guinea* frigate and perhaps some other vessels. They required the Maryland authorities to conform to the laws of the Commonwealth of England and to issue writs in the name of the Keepers of the Liberties of England, and demanded that the inhab-

[1] The following account of the "reducement of Maryland" is based on Leonard Strong's *Babylon's Fall in Maryland* and John Langford's *Just and Cleere Refutation of Babylon's Fall.* Copies of these pamphlets are in the Boston Athenæum; quotations from the latter are given in Bozman's *Maryland*, ii, 434. The instructions to the Commissioners are in Thurloe's *State Papers*, i, 197.

itants should subscribe to an engagement to be true to the Commonwealth. Governor Stone refused to comply with the demand as to the writs, stating that his commission and instructions provided that these should issue in the name of the Lord Proprietary, — a requirement, by the way, which was contrary to the provision of the charter that nothing should be done in Maryland by which the allegiance due to the king should suffer any diminution. The commissioners deposed Stone and placed the government in the hands of a council of six persons, two of whom had been members of Stone's council; but later, upon Stone's promising amendment, they restored him to power.

Governor William Stone was a Virginia planter, a justice of the peace and high sheriff of his county before his appointment as chief executive of Maryland. He was a Protestant, but not of the Puritan type. He had a hasty temper, if one may judge from a single incident. It seems that on one occasion he was conversing with a gentleman about the value of an estate in which he was interested and which the other, he thought, undervalued; thereupon he thrust the hilt of his rapier toward the other's breast, and being struck in the face, seized the other man's hair and held him at arm's length until the two were separated by the onlookers. This quickness of temper may have had something to do with the unpopularity which he seems to have aroused in Maryland. At all events, in 1653 he ordered the Puritan colonists of Providence to take new oaths which they deemed to be "not agreeable to the terms on which we came hither, nor to the liberty of our consciences as Christians and free subjects of the Commonwealth of England." At nearly the same time, by direction of Baltimore, he issued an order to the effect that all writs should run in the name of the Lord Proprietary. It is sometimes stated that Baltimore took this action because he felt that the change of government in England from that of the Commonwealth to the Protectorate had undermined the authority of the Commissioners. Bennett and Claiborne did not so understand it. They proceeded to Maryland, gathered a force of those favorable to them, deposed Stone (1654), and placed the government in the hands of a council, at the head of which was a leading Puritan, William Fuller. In their instructions to Fuller and his council, they ordered him to summon an assembly in the election of which no Roman Catholic or any one who had borne arms against the Parliament should take part or should have place. The assembly chosen under these conditions was naturally in the hands of those who were opposed to Baltimore and the Roman Catholics. Among its legislative acts was a law which practically repealed the act of 1649 concerning religion and substituted for it the phraseology of the Instrument of Government under which Cromwell ruled.[1] It also provided that an assembly

[1] Article XXXVII. "That such as profess faith in God by Jesus Christ, though differing in judgment from the doctrine, worship, or discipline, publicly held forth, shall not be restrained from, but protected in, the profession of the faith and exercise of their religion; so as they abuse not this liberty to the injury of others or disturbance of the peace on their parts. Provided, such liberty be not extended to Popery or prelacy, nor to such as under the profession of Christ hold forth, and practice licentiousness." It may be noted that the idea contained in the last exception is also to be found in the charters of Rhode Island (1663) and Carolina (1665), and was doubtless devised in England to exclude from toleration the new sects which were constantly arising. In this respect, as in many others, Cromwell and the Puritans were better than their words. It was the Protector who restored the Roman Catholic Lord Baltimore and advocated the readmission of the Jews. Moreover, the persecution of the "Prelatists" has been grossly exaggerated. Lady Verney, for instance, relates that in the whole county of Bucks during the time of the Puritan supremacy only nine clergymen were dispossessed, and that in many parishes the registers show an unbroken record of baptisms, marriages, and burials (*Verney Memoirs*, iii, 100). In fact Cromwell, in place of being the hypocritical, snuffling ascetic of Sir Walter Scott's malignant fancy, was a healthy, athletic English gentleman, who loved fast horses, played cricket even when he was Protector, encouraged painting and music, wore his hair long, almost to his shoulders, and persecuted

should be held every three years, again following the Instrument of Government, and passed sundry acts concerning drunkenness, swearing, sabbath breaking, slander, etc., which will be noted later on. Finally the assembly sought to introduce the Virginia land system by which any one coming to the colony or paying the expense of another person's coming should be entitled to land.

Cromwell approved the acts of the Commissioners, although directing them to let the boundaries of the two colonies remain as they were. It was at this time that the Virginia agents in England were making every effort to secure the consolidation of Maryland with Virginia. To offset their agitation, Baltimore seems to have given in his adherence to Cromwell, although what assurances he had received of the Protector's favor are not known. At all events, he directed Stone to take possession of the government by force; this the choleric Virginian attempted to do, but was disastrously defeated in 1655 by Fuller and his men. After the surrender four of the leading men among the vanquished were executed by the order of court martial, and Stone himself narrowly escaped the same fate. As it was, he was kept a close prisoner during the remainder of the Puritan rule in Maryland. Two years later, in 1657, an agreement was signed between Bennett and Matthews and Lord Baltimore which resulted in the restoration of the Lord Proprietary on condition that no one should be punished for his part in the late contests, that those in opposition should receive suitable grants of land, and that the Act Concerning Religion of 1649 should be revived. The details of the history of this time are so

no one if it could be avoided. See Firth's *Cromwell*, 361, 454, 456–458. For an interesting account of Cromwell's family and connections see Stanley J. Weyman in *English Historical Review*, vol. vi.

little known that it is difficult to say exactly what these terms meant, or, indeed, whether we have a copy of the actual agreement; it seems almost impossible to believe that Bennett would have consented to the revival of the act of 1649 in its entirety. It is well known that Cromwell was desirous to conciliate all the different factions and parties in England; but we may be sure that if Bennett had read to him the clauses in the act of 1649, providing fine and imprisonment at pleasure for the uttering of reproachful words concerning the "blessed Virgin Mary" or for denominating another an Idolater, Presbyterian, Popish Priest, Schismatic, Roundhead, or Separatist, the province of Maryland would not have been restored to Lord Baltimore.

NOTES

I. Bibliography. — The material upon which the foregoing chapter has been based is to be found in the printed records of the several colonies and in the original papers printed at the time. For New England, we have the *Massachusetts Colony Records*, the *Plymouth Colony Records*, the *Records of Rhode Island and Providence Plantations*, the *Connecticut Colonial Records*, and the *New Haven Records*. These are supplemented by the publications of the historical societies of those states. Unfortunately, Winthrop and Bradford are no longer of assistance. Hutchinson's *History of Massachusetts* hardly makes good their loss, but Palfrey has followed the records very closely. For Maryland, we have the *Archives* in the three series of Council, Assembly, and Court Records, and also the *Fund Publications* of the Maryland Historical Society. Bozman used original matter so faithfully that his history may also be regarded in the light of a "source," especially as some of the papers which he used are not easily accessible. Hening's *Statutes* and the papers printed in the *Virginia Magazine of History*, *William and Mary Quarterly*, and other publications of like character tell the story for Virginia. The accessible records of New Netherland are noted on pp. 460, 484.

For the English side of this period, recourse must be had to the published journals of the House of Commons and of the House of Lords, and to the collections of *Ordinances* made by Husbands and by Scobell. Something, but not much, has been gleaned from the *Reports* of the Royal Historical Manuscripts Commission.

II. Authorship of the Maryland Act Concerning Religion. — The parentage of the act of 1649 has been fiercely disputed, and probably the exact truth can never be ascertained, owing to the loss of important documents and to the imperfect condition of those which remain. But the weakness of many of the arguments which have been put forward by both Protestant and Roman Catholic writers can be easily shown. For instance, stress has been laid upon the religious complexion of the Assembly of 1649; but it really makes no difference how that assembly was divided religiously, because we do not know whether it sat as one house or as two houses, or how proxies were held or used. Some Protestant writers, among whom was Mr. Gladstone, have sought to trace its genesis to an ordinance of the Long Parliament, extending toleration to some one person or some one thing; but the advocates of this thesis appear to be unaware of the fact that the Presbyterians, who formed a majority in the Long Parliament, were intolerant of all religious beliefs except their own.

Roman Catholic writers, on the other hand, seem to imply that by the act in question Roman Catholics extended toleration to English Protestants in an English colony in the year 1649. But any such theory ignores entirely the facts of English history, and the presence of the strong Protestant colony of Virginia on the other side of the Potomac River. The arguments for the Roman Catholic origin of the act, however, seem to be strong; Bradley T. Johnson surmises with a good deal of probability that Henry More, S.J., was its author. There are a few facts, however, which militate against this theory, as, for example, what seems to be hesitation on the part of Baltimore to confirm the law, the refusal of some Maryland Roman Catholics to be bound by it, and the Protestant twang of some of its provisions. In the absence of clear documentary evidence, however, the probability that the act mainly emanated from Roman Catholic sources seems to point the way to the solution of the problem. See Bradley T. Johnson's "*Foundations of Maryland and the Origin of the Act Concerning Religion of April 21, 1649,*" in Maryland Historical Society's *Peabody Fund Publications*, No. 18 (the act is given in full in the appendix of this book); Mereness's *Maryland as a Proprietary Province,* pt. ii, ch. vii; A. P. Dennis's "Lord Baltimore's Struggle with the Jesuits" in American Historical Association's *Reports* (1900, vol. i, p. 107). The chapter on the Catholic migration in Eggleston's *Beginners of a Nation* is very well done. The older books, written before the publication of the *Maryland Archives,* the "Calvert Papers" and Foley's "Records," are now obsolete; their titles can be found in Winsor's *America,* iii.

CHAPTER XIX

THE COLONIES IN 1660

In 1660 the English colonies contained between seventy-five and eighty thousand white inhabitants and New Netherland six or seven thousand more. The settlers occupied a narrow fringe of soil along the coast, the Connecticut and Hudson valleys, and a few places on the Indian trails leading westward from the shores of Massachusetts Bay. They were mainly emigrants from England or their children. In New England there were a few Scots whom Cromwell had sent there after the battles of Dunbar and Worcester, and a small band of Huguenots formed the advanced guard of the later emigration from France. In the English colonies, also, there were a few Irish laborers who had been sent over from Ireland after the reoccupation of that island by the Puritans; these were most numerous in Maryland. The Scots, the Irish, and the Huguenots were few in number and exerted little influence on the institutions of the English colonies. In New Netherland the Dutch and Swedish settlers lived side by side with an almost equal number of Englishmen; there were also in that colony settlers of other racial origins, but their presence exercised little influence on the social and legal ideas of the dwellers on the banks of the Hudson and the Delaware. The dominant element in the three colonial groups was clearly Germanic. There were a few negro slaves in each of the three sections, most numerously in the Chesapeake colonies; but their

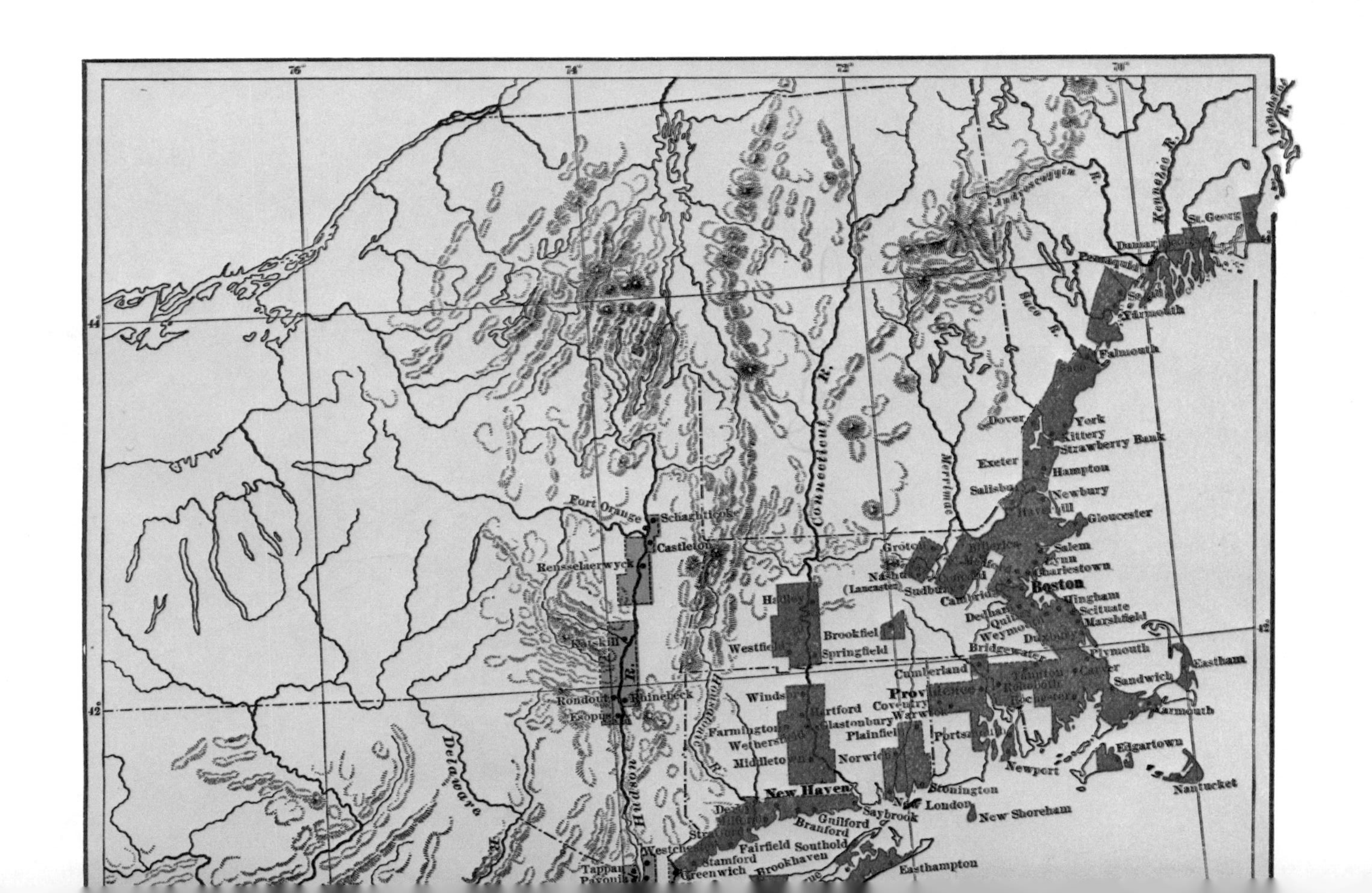
76°
74°
72°
70°
44°
42°
Penobscot R.
Kennebec R.
St. George
Pemaquid
Yarmouth
Androscoggin R.
Saco R.
Falmouth
Dover
York
Kittery
Strawberry Bank
Exeter
Hampton
Newbury
Gloucester
Merrimac
Connecticut R.
Salem
Lynn
Charlestown
Boston
(Lancaster)
Sudbury
Hingham
Scituate
Marshfield
Plymouth
Eastham
Sandwich
Yarmouth
Edgartown
Nantucket
Newport
Brookfield
Springfield
Westfield
Hadley
Bridgewater
Cumberland
Providence
Coventry
Warwick
Windsor
Hartford
Glastonbury
Plainfield
Farmington
Wethersfield
Middletown
Norwich
Stonington
New London
New Shoreham
New Haven
Saybrook
Guilford
Branford
Fairfield
Southold
Stamford
Greenwich
Brookhaven
Easthampton
Housatonic R.
Fort Orange
Schaghticoke
Castleton
Rensselaerwyck
Katskill
Rondout
Rhinebeck
Esopus
Hudson R.
Delaware R.
Tappan
Pavonia

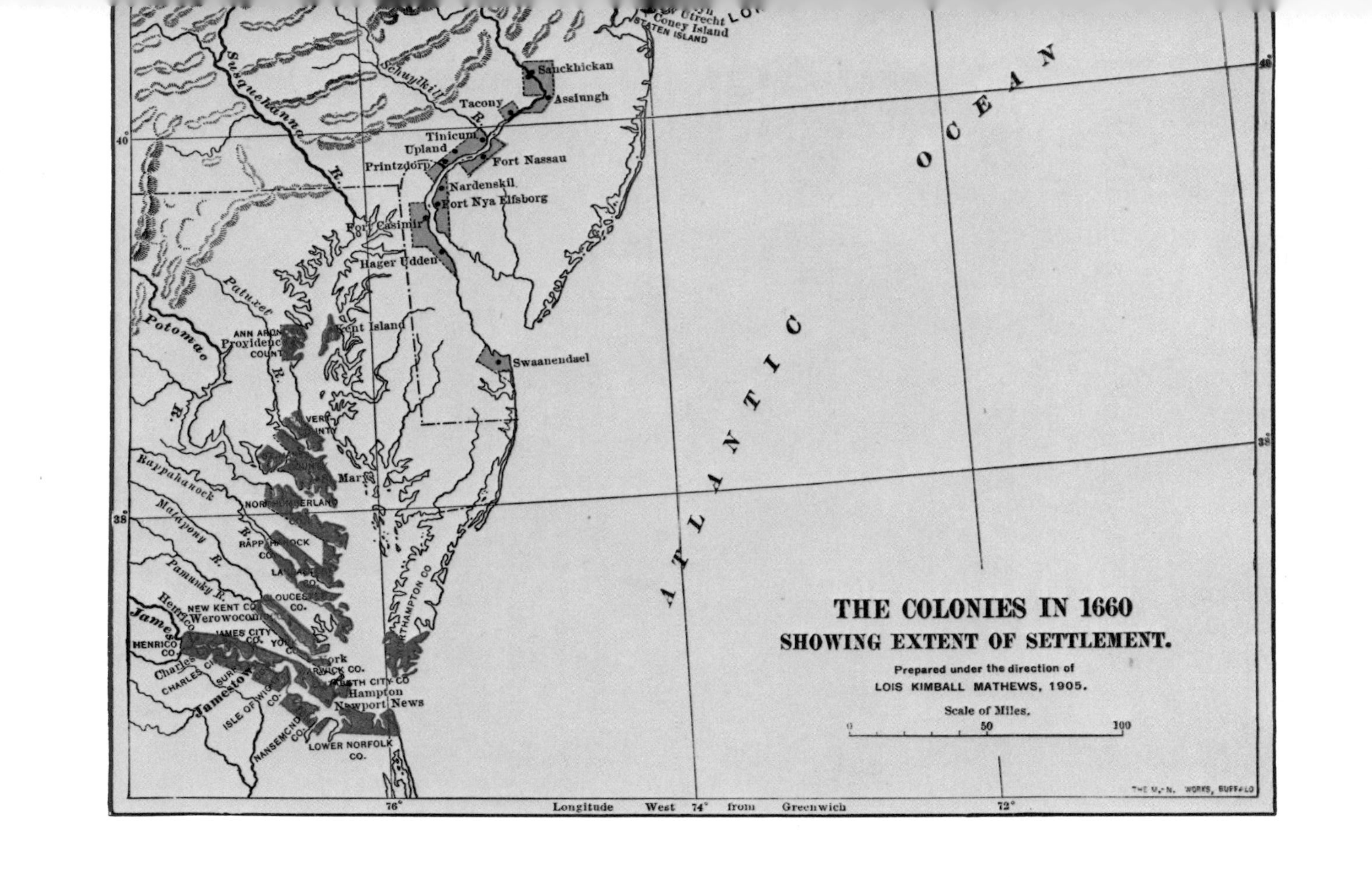
THE COLONIES IN 1660
SHOWING EXTENT OF SETTLEMENT.
Prepared under the direction of
LOIS KIMBALL MATHEWS, 1905.
Scale of Miles.
0
50
100
ATLANTIC
OCEAN
Longitude West 74° from Greenwich
76°
72°
40°
38°
Coney Island
STATEN ISLAND
Sauckhickan
Assiungh
Tacony
Schuylkill R.
Susquehanna R.
Tinicum
Upland
Printzdorp
Fort Nassau
Nardenskil
Fort Nya Elfsborg
Fort Casimir
Hager Udden
Kent Island
Swaanendael
Patuxet
Potomac R.
Providence
Rappahanock
Matapony R.
Pamunky R.
Henrico
Werowocomoco
James
Jamestown
Charles
HENRICO CO.
NEW KENT CO.
JAMES CITY CO.
CHARLES CITY
ISLE OF WIGHT CO.
LOWER NORFOLK CO.
Hampton
Newport News

numbers were too small and their arrival too recent to have affected in an appreciable manner the social and political life of the time. Had the industrial conditions in the several colonies been identical, their institutions would have developed on similar lines except as modified by religious peculiarities; but their industrial conditions were so dissimilar that the process of differentiation, which later became so marked, had already begun. It will be interesting to make a survey of the colonies at the end of this first period, to observe, on the one hand, how far this differentiation had proceeded, and to notice, on the other hand, how closely the colonists clung to the modes of actions of their kinsfolk in the old home beyond the Atlantic. In making this survey of colonial institutions as they were in the year of the Restoration the attention will be mainly directed to the English colonies, because the nature of the Dutch administration has already been pointed out, and also because it was not until after the great movement to Pennsylvania in the later years of the century that the Middle Colonies began to exert much influence on the general march of American life.

In studying institutional topics, it is necessary to note both similarities and dissimilarities. This is especially true when investigating the history of the communities which later developed into the United States. The greatest fact of American history has been the union in one federal state of peoples living in widely separated regions under very different conditions of society and industry. This union was made possible by the fact that the institutions and the political ideals of these communities had in them so much that was akin. Institutional and social peculiarities strike the student's attention with much greater force than do those things which are common to all; it is therefore necessary to be especially careful not to be unduly affected by that which is quaint or abnormal. The most marked political characteristic of the English race has always been its conservatism in adhering to that which is old for no other reason than because it is that which exists. It was this quality that made republican and democratic institutions possible in English communities. It was this spirit of conservatism that preserved in the English colonies the political and constitutional ideas which made the forces of union always more powerful than those that operated toward particularism.

The colonies had all been begun by corporations or by groups of individuals as business ventures. In New England and Maryland religious motives also had played their part, but the institutions of all had been powerfully influenced by the material considerations which actuated their founders. The governor in the early days was the business as well as the political head of the enterprise. As time went on, these financial functions became less and less important, and their places were filled more and more with political and judicial duties. In the earliest days in the English settlements, the governor was only the most important member of the council. By 1660, however, except in Connecticut, New Haven, and Rhode Island, he had become the chief executive in reality as well as in name. In all the colonies the governor with his council performed judicial functions, but in the English settlements the legislative body, including the representative branch, exercised a reviewing power.

It was not until the eighteenth century that the elective branch of the colonial legislature won the leading place in the local administration, but the beginning of this supremacy may be traced to 1660, and even earlier. Originally the governor, the councilors, and the freemen or their delegates sat together as one body. In Maryland and Virginia the governor, with or without the advice of his council, exercised the veto power. In Massachusetts the consent of the chief executive and of six assistants, as the councilors were termed in that colony, was necessary to give validity to any action of the General Court. Almost from the beginning the representative element in the colonial assemblies felt the same jealousy of the appointed branch which in England the Commons felt for the Peers. In Massachusetts the establishment of an upper house could not be prevented because the assistants possessed the "negative voice"; but in Virginia and Maryland[1] there was a disposition on the part of the elected branch to deny legislative and judicial powers to the appointed council. In Virginia[2] the General Assembly, in the New England colonies the General Courts, exercised the right to review the decisions of the judicial courts.

There is no more interesting example of the reforming influence of colonial conditions than the refusal of the colonists to reproduce the electoral system of the parent country. Representation[3] in the English House of Com-

[1] It is very difficult to make any precise statement as to when the separation into two houses took place in Maryland. In 1650 the delegates sat by themselves (*Maryland Archives*, Assembly, under date); the act of 1650 providing for the separation into two houses is in Bacon's *Laws of Maryland* (Acts of 1650, ch. i). The records of the "upper house" appear for the first time in 1659. In that year the delegates addressed a communication to the governor and council stating that they judged themselves to be "a lawful assembly without dependence on any other power in the province." This was a part of the movement which is known in Maryland history as Fendall's Rebellion; but nothing came of it. The assembly also at the same time claimed the power to review the judicial decisions of the governor and council; but it could not enforce its wishes.

[2] In 1661 the process of appeals was systematized. (See Hening's *Statutes*, ii, 65, 512.)

[3] Gneist (*Constitutional History of England*, ii, 147) has an interesting paragraph on this subject from which the figures given in the text have been taken. Absolute accuracy is unattainable in this matter; these figures, therefore, should be used only in a comparative way.

mons before the accession of James rested mainly on the will of the monarch, which was occasionally supplemented or controlled by acts of Parliament. For centuries the county franchise had been limited by law to the "forty shilling freeholders," and an attempt to change that qualification would probably have been regarded as revolutionary. The counties also came down from an historic past, and no one ever suggested an alteration of their boundaries. The borough franchise and apportionment rested on a different basis, since the king, by letters patent, could create as many boroughs as he chose and could regulate the right to vote therein. The House of Commons as it existed in the first years of James's reign was largely a Tudor creation. There were four hundred and sixty-seven members of the House of Commons which met in 1604; of these no less than one hundred and sixty-eight had been added since the death of Henry VII.[1] How far this process would have gone had the sovereigns remained unchecked is uncertain, but at the very outset of James's reign, the Commons secured the right to judge of the election of their own members,[2] and in this way to exercise a controlling influence over the constitution of their house. James created only six new constituencies, including the two universities, and in his reign also there were eight revivals.[3]

[1] Elizabeth created twenty-four new boroughs, returning forty-eight new members, and revived the rights of seven other boroughs, so that in all she added sixty-two members to the House of Commons.

[2] This is the well-known Goodwin's case, or the case of the Bucks Election. Up to this time certain royal officials had determined whether a member was duly elected or not. Possibly the Commons would not have insisted upon their rights in this instance had not James mismanaged the matter by ordering them to confer with the Peers as to the constitution of their own house. See Prothero's *Statutes*, 280, 325–333, quoting portions of *Commons Journals*, i, 149–171. For precedents see D'Ewes's *Journals*, 396–398, 438–441, 479–482, 514–516, 518.

[3] Some of these revivals were by action of the Commons. In the case of Pomfret, which had sent burgesses from Edward I to Henry VI and had then discontinued the practice owing to poverty, James granted them their former liberties and customs. In 1621 the Commons ordered (*Journals*, i, 576) that a writ should issue to Pomfret for the elec-

From this time on the apportionment remained practically stationary until the close of the eighteenth century.

The borough franchise rested upon the words of the charters, and these were oftentimes susceptible of various interpretations. The borough authorities, like the members of many other corporations, paid slight attention to the technical requirements of their letters patent. Facts as to the franchise are difficult to get, but the following, which have been extracted from the records of contested elections,[1] for the most part in the second half of the seventeenth century, give us some idea of what the electoral system was at the time of the planting of the English colonies. This material shows that twenty-four boroughs had each less than one hundred electors,[2] and that two boroughs had over one thousand apiece, while in the counties there were usually more than one thousand voters. Furthermore it appears that in many boroughs the "inhabitants"[3] were permitted or forbidden to vote, as the rulers of the borough, for the time being, were liberal or aristocratic in their sentiments.

The law at that time required that the knights of the shire should be residents of the county which they represented; but no attention was paid to this requirement. In only twenty-seven boroughs has it been possible to

tion of burgesses. In 1624 a committee reported (*Journals*, i, 697) that "a borough cannot forfeit their liberty of sending members by non-user." See also *Journals*, i, 782, and D'Ewes's *Journals*, 80.

[1] Bohun's *Collection touching the Right of electing Members of Parliament*; Carew's *Historical Account of the Rights of Elections*. These should be supplemented by the entries in the *Commons Journals*.

[2] In 1630 twelve votes only were cast at Chippenham. See *Commons Journals*, i, 684.

[3] In 1628 the Commons passed a resolution that the right of election in Boston "resteth in the commonalty and not in the Mayor, Aldermen, and Common Council." This resolution was based on the report of a committee that "the election of burgesses in all boroughs did, of common right, belong to the Commons; and that nothing could take it from them but a prescription and a constant usage beyond all memory." *Commons Journals*, i, 893; Bohun's *Collection*, 50.

reach a conclusion as to a residential qualification for the member; in sixteen of them the member was required to be a resident. In the older time residence within the borough was a qualification for the burgess. Parliament in 1571 had passed a bill [1] repealing this requirement, but it never became a law, and the residential qualification was not formally done away with until 1774. The boroughs had been responsible for the "allowance" of their members in time of Parliament; in later days it became the practice for the members to bear their own charges, but in the reign of Charles II at least one borough still paid its burgesses wages.[2] The absurdity of this representative method was patent to the reformers of that epoch; when Cromwell and the New Model took possession of the government they established a system similar to that which had meantime been evolved in the colonies, but at the Restoration the old "rotten borough" organization was brought back.

In America the qualifications for the elector and the representative rested on general laws. In 1660 every colony except Rhode Island and Maryland had a religious qualification,[3] which varied in rigor according to the religiosity of its inhabitants. In Massachusetts and New Haven the franchise was confined to church members; in

[1] D'Ewes's *Journals*, 168.

[2] Grosart's edition of Andrew Marvell's *Writings*, ii, p. xxxv.

[3] Clergymen were generally excluded from the elected representative body. In Virginia the Burgesses in 1653 suspended a minister who had been returned to that body on the ground that he was "not in a capacity of serving as a Burgess since it is unpresidential and may produce bad consequences" (Hening's *Statutes*, i, 378). In the other colonies ministers were tacitly disqualified. The settlers regarded themselves as conforming to English precedents, but the disqualification of clergymen in Parliament extended only to the House of Commons, and was due to the fact that the clergy taxed themselves in Convocation. Their disqualification rested only on a resolution which was passed in 1553 and reflected anterior usage. Lawyers also were disqualified in Massachusetts and Virginia. As late as 1658 the assembly of the latter province proposed that all lawyers should be ejected from the colony. See *Massachusetts Laws of 1660*, 224; Hening's *Statutes*, i, 302, 349, 419, 482, 495.

Virginia to users of the service book, all others having been "compelled to depart the colony with all conveniencie."[1] "Popish recusants" were disqualified from holding office in Virginia in conformity with the act of James I which is mentioned in the law.[2] In Connecticut and New Plymouth there was no formal religious qualification, but few persons exercised the right to vote in those colonies whose religious sentiments were contrary to those of the existing body of voters. There was no property qualification for the voter or representative in any colony except Connecticut, where thirty pounds of proper personal estate was required.[3] In Rhode Island, Maryland, and Virginia social and political conditions were such that probably few persons exercised the right to vote who were not possessed of property, and, indeed, of landed property. In 1654–55 the Virginia House of Burgesses had passed an act[4] confining the right to vote to the heads of families who were all land owners. In the next session, however, this act was repealed, and all "freemen" were allowed to vote on the ground that it was unjust to deprive a taxpayer of a share in the government. There was no residence qualification in any colony for either the voter or the representative. Massachusetts, indeed, by law provided that the freemen of a town might depute any freeman[5] of the Massachusetts Bay Company, no matter where he dwelt, to represent them. Nevertheless it is probable that everywhere the representative was ordinarily of the same electoral unit as those who voted for him. Throughout the colonies representatives were paid for their time and were reimbursed their expenses. This was sometimes done by the general govern-

[1] Hening's *Statutes*, i, 277.
[2] *Ibid.*, i, 268.
[3] This was reduced to twenty pounds in 1662.
[4] Hening's *Statutes*, i, 403, 411.
[5] *Massachusetts Body of Liberties*, No. 68.

ment, more often by the constituencies, but the tendency was toward payment by the colony as a whole.

The use of some kind of ballot goes back in England[1] at least to the sixteenth century. Papers, bullets, or balls were the means employed to ascertain the voter's wishes. By 1637 the system had aroused the "utter dislike" of Charles I, who prohibited the use of balloting boxes by corporations or companies. This distrust on the part of the monarch was due to what he termed "manifold inconveniences," which doubtless made it difficult for the royal officials to coerce the electors. In Massachusetts the electors were the freemen of the Massachusetts Bay Company. Like the members of corporations in England they early adopted a system of voting by ballot, using corn and black beans or "papers." In Virginia the practice varied from time to time. In the early days, the sheriff, or other returning officer, appears to have visited the plantations to collect the suffrages of the electors, but the usual practice was for the voters to meet at the county seat and express their wishes by subscription. This last word, which is used in the laws of the period, may possibly have meant a written ballot. In the later time the votes were entered on books, and the election came to resemble very closely the county elections of contemporary England.

Local government had already been profoundly influenced by religious and industrial conditions. In all the colonies the new structure was reared on the institutions of the motherland. Jamestown was expected to reproduce the pattern of an English incorporated town, and so was St.

[1] Professor Charles Gross, "The Early History of the Ballot in England" in *American Historical Review*, iii, 456. In the "Boston Assembly Book" there is an entry directing the members of the Common Council "to go by themselves to set their hands to the question and no other to inform them." This seems to foreshadow the Australian ballot system.

Mary's, the latter being provided with mayor, recorder, alderman, and common council. Baltimore directed that the houses should be built "near adjoining one to the other,"[1] and an early law provided for the erection of a "town house." James City, to give it its later name, was made sole port of entry and the official residence of the governor. The necessities of tobacco culture upset all these arrangements. James City expanded into a county, and St. Mary's became a village of thirty houses scattered along the bank of St. George's River. The county court became the local governing body in Virginia and also in Maryland. It managed the more important civil and judicial matters — religious affairs and the care of the poor were intrusted to the parish authorities.[2] The county authorities in Virginia were appointed by the governor, and were the leading men of their counties. The parishes were conducted by a close corporation which was called the vestry. Originally the vestrymen had been elected, but by 1660 the vestries had become self-perpetuating. It fell out in this way that a few leading men performed nearly all the functions of administration in the Old Dominion. In New England the concentration of settlement and the influence of the religious organization made possible an entirely different set of institutions. The Massachusetts town took the leading part in local administration, but the by-laws, or local town regulations, required the approval of the justices of the county, who were partly elected by the freemen and partly appointed by the General Court.

In the whole course of English and American constitu-

[1] See Baltimore's instructions in "Calvert Papers" in Maryland Historical Society's *Fund Publications*, No. 28, p. 138.

[2] There were few persons in Virginia in this early time who could be classed among "the poor." Such as there were seem to have been licensed to beg. See Bruce's *Economic History*, ii, 255.

tional history the control of the purse has at critical moments always been the determining factor. In England, at the time of the planting of the colonies, the king was expected "to live of his own" with such aid as tonnage and poundage, purveyance, the profits of jurisdiction, and the gains from the administration of wardships and other incidents of feudalism might afford. The crown had its landed estates which brought in funds; the expenses of the court were largely met by the exercise of the rights of purveyance. There were few salaries for officials, but royal grants of fines and forfeitures or the custody of a rich heiress, with fees and presents from the people who had business to transact with them, — these were the modes by which those who carried on the affairs of the realm were rewarded for their time and administrative ability. It was only on extraordinary occasions that Parliament was summoned for the purpose of supplying the government with extra funds. When it met and proved complacent, its beneficence took the form of a grant of a direct tax on incomes from lands and on goods, these being known as subsidies and tenths and fifteenths. The religious expenses, except the care of the parish churches, were met by the tithes; the funds needed for the care of the poor, the support of education, the reparation of the church fabric, and other local needs were met by the rates which were voted by the parishioners, or townsmen, and were assessed and collected by the local officers.

In the colonies the matter of taxation was taken up anew; but the influence of English precedents and practice was very strong. In Virginia, we find that the governor in ordinary times was almost independent of the House of Burgesses. He received many fees, for he

acted in the capacity of chancellor, exercised the office of admiral, and represented the king in authenticating grants of land; he also, as a rule, could pay himself out of such quitrents as he might be able to collect. The Burgesses provided him with a revenue of two shillings on each hogshead of tobacco exported, which may well be regarded as the Virginia counterpart of tonnage and poundage. The Secretary of the Old Dominion was also entitled to his share of fees and forfeitures. The governor and secretary between them administered nearly all the affairs of the province that were not of a strictly local nature. Except in times of scarcity or of war, the colonists had slight means of coercing the governor through pressure on the financial side. Almost the same thing may be said of Maryland, as with a permanent export tax on tobacco laid by the assembly and grants from the proprietor the governor was independent. It is for this reason in part that the Virginia and Maryland systems became so centralized in comparison with the political organizations of the other English colonies.

The settlers of New England were drawn from the Nonconformist opponents of Charles and Laud. They left the homeland at a time when their party was endeavoring to starve the king into subjection; it was altogether unlikely that they would give the executive branch of their own governments the opportunity to become independent. Moreover, in Massachusetts the deputies owed their existence to a dispute with the governor and assistants over a question of taxation. It fell out in this way, therefore, that the Massachusetts executive was never financially independent, and the case was even stronger in the colonies which were founded from Massachusetts.

The modes of raising revenue in New England and in the Chesapeake colonies show more than anything else the differentiation which dissimilar industrial conditions had already brought about. In New England the poverty of the soil and the harshness of the climate compelled the colonists to make every faculty perform its part. The legislators devised a system of taxation which levied a contribution on everything in the way of possession: lands, ships, live stock, houses, tools of trade, and even one's "ability," or income-earning power. Capital, including in that designation everything which might produce an income, was taxed, whether it was invested profitably or not. In Virginia the greater part of the revenue was raised by a poll tax which was apportioned among the planters in accordance with the number of persons on the plantation over the age of sixteen, excluding white women who did not work in the fields.[1] Each one of these persons was denominated a tithable. Each planter paid according to the number of tithables in his family. Each parish contributed to the county expenses according to the number of tithables within the parish limits; each county paid its share of the general expenses according to the number of tithables in the county. It was an extremely simple and workable system and was a tax on capital profitably employed. Land in Virginia, in 1660, was easily acquired; a man's income was in proportion to the amount of labor which he could employ on his land; in his servants and slaves was his wealth.

In the ascertainment of the annual amount of taxes to be raised the difference between Massachusetts and Virginia becomes even more apparent. In the former, at the

[1] Women servants, "working in the crop," were added to the list of tithables in 1662 (Hening's *Statutes*, ii, 170).

beginning of each year, the appropriations were made for the current financial year. The taxes were collected in money, except in times of stress, and were paid out as work was done or supplies were procured. In Virginia precisely the opposite course was pursued; the expenses were first incurred, and, at the end of the fiscal year, the debts were computed and the money raised to pay them. This arrangement was made necessary by the peculiarities of the industrial situation in the Old Dominion.

Tobacco was the most important product of Virginia in the period which we are now studying. When this crop failed or when an over-abundance reduced its value, the Virginia planters turned their attention to other commodities and experimented with silk, rice, indigo, and wheat. Under normal conditions, however, the profit from tobacco growing was so great that, except wheat, nothing else was grown for export. The planters produced enough corn and pork for their own needs; "hog and hominy" formed the diet of the laboring classes. Each planter sought to produce as much tobacco with as little expenditure of labor as possible, sometimes regardless of the future of the tobacco market. This led to a series of enactments, all having as their design the improvement of the quality of the leaf. One law prohibited the planting of tobacco after the 10th of July, because plants set out so late could not properly mature. Another law prohibited the sale of the ground leaves, which were harsh in taste. A third enactment forbade the growing of seconds, — that is, the leaves which appeared after those of the first growth had been cut. When an over-abundant crop had so lowered the price in the English market that the planters suffered loss, the only remedy which occurred to them was to bring about a cessation of planting for a year, or to regulate the amount which each planter should raise. These attempts were usually futile because the Marylanders would not join with the Virginians in limiting the production of the staple. Tobacco, besides being the most important article of export, was the medium for exchange within the colony itself, the price of everything, salaries, fees, and fines, being reckoned in so many pounds of tobacco. Of course such a bulky commodity was awkward as a medium of exchange; the Virginians, therefore, fell into the habit of running into debt with each other and with the public authorities, the balances only being discharged by the actual handing over of so many pounds of tobacco.

The land system which was evolved in Virginia was peculiar to that colony, as the very life of the settlement depended upon the importation of labor. Partly to encourage this, and partly, also, to recompense those who had invested money in the original enterprise, the company in the days of the Southampton-Sandys supremacy had provided that a person importing one laborer into the colony, or paying an amount sufficient to pay such a person's passage, should be entitled to a grant of land. In the early days of the royal government this system[1] became organized; every person emigrating to the colony or importing a laborer being entitled to fifty acres of land, in consideration of paying an annual quitrent of one shilling for each fifty acres and "seating" the grant within a reasonable time. The requirement as to seating was hard to interpret or to enforce; it meant little or nothing in 1660. This right to fifty acres of land was called a head right, and in course of time great abuses arose in the administration of the system. We read, for example, of a

[1] See Bruce's *Economic History of Virginia*, i, 411.

ship master securing head rights on account of the passengers and crew of his ship, although the crew returned to England with the vessel, and the passengers secured head rights for themselves, in case they paid their own passage money, or for the planter who paid it for them. The sailors also sometimes secured head rights on their own account. Toward the close of the century, head rights were issued on certificates of names copied from old record books which were sold by the clerks in the Secretary's office as low as one shilling apiece.[1] Under these circumstances thousands of acres were accumulated in the hands of the richer men. As early as 1636 there was at least one estate of ten thousand acres; after 1650 grants of ten and even of twenty thousand acres were not uncommon.[2] Any freeman, with a reasonable amount of diligence and success, could accumulate hundreds of acres in a comparatively short space of time. Where this was the case, one was not likely to hire land of another. Nor was there available land for rent. The fortunate possessor of a recently cleared tobacco field would ordinarily be unwilling to let it to another; on the other hand, the cultivator would be equally unwilling to hire a worn-out tobacco field. The one obligation on the part of the landowners in Virginia which might have limited the size of these estates was the condition on which they obtained their land, of paying an annual quitrent of one shilling for each fifty acres. The quitrent is sometimes described as "the latest consideration in the purchase." The title to the land was in the possessor so long as he paid the quitrent; upon default, the estate was

[1] Hartwell, Blair and Chilton, *Present State of Virginia*, 16; also given in Bruce's *Economic History of Virginia*, i, 524.

[2] Bruce (*Economic History*, ii, 254) estimates that an acre of land under cultivation was worth four shillings, the equivalent of five dollars in our time. The largest personal estate of which he has seen the inventory before 1660 was equivalent to twenty-five thousand dollars (*ibid.*, 246).

forfeited to the king. This requirement looks formidable on paper, but it proved to be easily evaded in practice. Oftentimes the quitrents were not and could not be collected, and almost always the money payment could be commuted in tobacco at two pence or even at one penny per pound. Often such poor tobacco was turned over to the collectors of quitrents that one hundred thousand pounds of it could be sold for very little money. The quitrents, however, formed a standing menace to the planter and were a continuing grievance throughout the seventeenth century.

The condition of life in New England was far removed from that which prevailed in the Old Dominion and was equally peculiar. The gravelly soil of Massachusetts and her neighbors possessed elements of endurance which were lacking in the rich lands of Virginia, but it produced with great difficulty and in small quantities. The New England farmer, by assiduous labor and the exercise of great patience and by personally overseeing the operations of his farm, was able to make it bring forth enough to feed his family and sometimes to have a little to spare for sale; but anything above the bare needs of existence had to be procured by other means than cultivation of the soil. The first settlers of the New England coast became manufacturers, fishermen, and traders in addition to being cultivators of the soil. The making of shoes began at Lynn, in Massachusetts, almost with the settlement of the town. At that place also iron works were established and conducted with profit for many years. The iron ore was procured from the mud of ponds where it had been slowly deposited by filtration from the surrounding soil. The iron produced in this way was excellent in quality, but the supply was precarious. The domestic manufacture of cloth was a part of the regular household duties of nearly every New England family, and fulling mills had been built in at least three Massachusetts towns before 1660. There were then thousands of sheep in New England, but the demand for wool was so great that it was also imported. The fishing industry of New England preceded the actual settlement and did not cease with the coming of the colonists. It furnished occupation to hundreds of men in some portions of the year and provided an important article of export to the Spanish peninsula and to the West Indies. John Winthrop had scarcely finished his dwelling house at Boston ere he began the construction of the *Blessing of the Bay*, which was the first of a long line of vessels designed for trading voyages along the coast, for fishing, and for commerce with far-off countries. By the middle of the century New England vessels plied along every American shore, and made voyages to Europe, and to the islands of the Atlantic. Life in New England was always hard and the gains were small, though constant; but there were seldom such alternations of prosperity and distress as Virginia often witnessed in the seventeenth century.

Religiously the colonies present marked divergencies; but these differences were more in the manner of their settlement than in the underlying religious beliefs of the founders. The leaders of the Great Emigration came to Massachusetts in pursuit of an ideal; the early planters of Virginia crossed the ocean solely for purposes of material gain. Beginning with 1650, however, royalist refugees flying from the pursuit of the successful Puritans settled in the Old Dominion. They were sentimentalists who had risked life and fortune in pursuit of loyalty to their king. They brought to Virginia instincts and prepossessions which had hitherto been lacking and raised the tone of life in the Old Dominion to a higher plane.[1] It is a little singular, however, that they should have sought Virginia in the period when the "Cromwellian party," led by Claiborne, Bennett, and Mathews, was in control. Although the Virginians used the English service book, they disliked the idea of hierarchical control as fully as did the New England Puritans. In both sections the local governing bodies monopolized the management of religious matters. In New England the towns and the churches, as the local religious organizations were called, hired the ministers of their choice; in Virginia the parish vestries likewise employed and paid the parsons of the several parishes.[2] Moreover, while the Virginians regarded themselves as belonging to the English Church, surplices[3] were not ordinarily used in the seventeenth century, and the communion was received in the pews. Had William Laud visited Virginia, he would have been pained at these evidences of Nonconformity, for which in England he would have silenced the parson and driven him from his parish.

The earliest code of laws which had legal force in the English colonies was the so-called Dale's Laws of Virginia. This was compiled in England; the first code to be constructed by English colonists was the Massachusetts Body of Liberties[4] of 1641. This was revised in 1649 and again in 1660. The earlier compilations formed the basis of the

[1] John Fiske points out how many of the families who made Virginia famous came to the colony after 1650 (*Virginia and her Neighbours*, ii). W. H. Whitmore's *Cavalier Dismounted* is an ill-natured criticism of Virginia pretensions.

[2] See Act of 1657-58 in Hening's *Statutes*, i, 433.

[3] L. G. Tyler's *The English in America*, 106.

[4] William H. Whitmore in *Bibliographical Sketch of the Laws of the Massachusetts Colony from 1630 to 1686* has traced the formation of this code and has reproduced it by a photographic process from the only manuscript which has come down to our time. He has also prefixed it from the same plates to his edition of *The Massachusetts Laws of 1660*. It is given in print in *American History Leaflets*, No. 25.

Connecticut code of 1650[1] and the New Haven code of 1656.[2] In 1661 the laws of Virginia[3] were brought together. The Maryland Assembly did not codify the laws of that province in these earlier years, but the student can pick out the laws from the "Assembly Records." It will be interesting to bring together in the form of a comparative study a few of the more important and more characteristic enactments to be found in these legal systems. The colonists in framing their laws and in administering them seem to have regarded themselves free to adopt so much of the Common Law as was applicable to their condition. So far as it protected them from the English government and from royal officials they looked upon it as their birthright; so far as it interfered with their development it was to be disregarded. They, therefore, either by express enactment or by omission, effected reforms which it took centuries to accomplish in England. Records and proceedings at law were in English, and the distinctions between different classes of lawyers which prevailed in England had no place in America. The colonists, indeed, disliked the legal fraternity and sought by enactments to prohibit the payment of fees to legal practitioners. Persons who were accused of crime in the colonies were permitted to have assistance, as was not the case in England; but no fee could be paid.

The condition of the criminal law in England has already been noted and may well be described as scandalous, although not so evil as it was after the Restoration. When Cromwell became undisputed ruler, he pardoned all felons then in prison who had not actually been con-

[1] *Colonial Records of Connecticut*, i, 509.

[2] *New Haven Records*, i, 559. The Connecticut and New Haven Codes are also given in Trumbull's *True-Blue Laws of Connecticut*.

[3] Hening's *Statutes*, ii, 44.

victed of murder.[1] Later, when Protector, his attention was again called to the matter by some grievous miscarriage of justice, and he addressed Parliament in 1656 in vigorous language adverting to the "wicked and abominable laws," which should be altered. "To hang a man for six and eight pence, and I know not what; to hang for a trifle, and acquit murder, — is in the ministration of the law, through the ill framing of it. I have known in my experience," he said, "abominable murders acquitted. And to see men lose their lives for petty matters; this is a thing God will reckon for." Soon afterward, a proposition was brought forward that only murder, treason, and rebellion should be punished with death; but Parliament was too busy with politics to consider the cause of humanity; the capital laws remained at the end of the Protectorate what they had been at the beginning of the session of the Long Parliament. It was in the colonies where the people had a larger measure of power and human labor was in great demand that the quickenings of mercy first translated themselves into positive enactments. Since 1620 simple theft has never been punished by death in English America. In the Body of Liberties twelve offenses only were capital. Among these were idolatry, witchcraft, blasphemy, kidnaping, and bearing false witness. To these were later added arson, cursing or smiting one's parents, and after 1652 the third offense in the case of burglary or highway robbery brought death. Blasphemy was also punished by death in Connecticut, New Haven, and in Maryland. Massachusetts, in 1647, adopted the penalty prescribed against Jesuits by the act of Elizabeth of banishment under pain of death in case of return. Toward the end

[1] Firth's *Cromwell*, 348.

of the next decade, the same penalty was denounced against Quakers in both Massachusetts and Virginia. In Virginia the law makers had as much trouble with hog-stealers as the people of the newer western states have had with cattle thieves. In 1642 the killing a tame hog, "being none of his own," was felony, the punishment of which was death. This law was repealed in 1647, and a fine of two thousand pounds of tobacco provided in its place; the bringing home an earless hog was regarded as *prima facie* evidence of theft, as the hogs were marked on the ears.[1] To run forward a few years, it may be added that in 1679 the two thousand pounds of tobacco fine was reserved for the first offense of hog stealing; for the second offense the convicted thief should stand in the pillory with both ears nailed for two hours and then have his ears cut loose from the nails; for the third offense, he should suffer death. In Maryland, besides what might be called the ordinary capital crimes, robbery and larceny were to be determined by the judge as near as may be to the laws of England, which then regarded the theft of anything over twelve pence as felony. In Maryland, also, the wilful burning or destroying of a house or stack of tobacco, corn, or hay,[2] or the plucking or cutting out another's eyes or tongue might be punished with death or with some lesser penalty, as the loss of a member, or exile, or imprisonment during life or service to the Lord Proprietor for seven years.

Religious legislation in the colonies followed very closely that of England in the same period of time. Good examples of this tendency may be found in the treatment of the Quakers and in the laws regulating the observance

[1] Hening's *Statutes*, i, 244.
[2] Burning a haystack is now (1905) a capital crime in Maryland.

of the Lord's Day. The laws as to rogues and vagabonds have been already mentioned.[1] The acts of Elizabeth and James were still in force in England in 1656. The lash, the branding iron, and the pillory with its hammer, nails, and knife,[2] to say nothing of the missiles of the populace, were the lot of those women, as well as men, who were classed under the comprehensive designation of rogues and vagabonds. When the Quakers appeared in England, New England, New Netherland,[3] and Virginia, they, with stage players and minstrels who performed in inns and ale-houses, were classed as vagabonds. Moreover, the magistrates were tempted to sentence the Quakers to the severest possible punishments under the law because they refused to give those marks of respect which were generally regarded as due to those who administered justice. Moreover, their religious scruples made them refuse to take the oath of allegiance. This brought them within the category of those whom the act of 35 Elizabeth[4] punished with banishment under pain of death in case of return. In 1656 the commissioners of the United Colonies of New England advised the members of the Confederation to banish Quakers under pain of death in case of return. Massachusetts[5] alone complied with this advice; which unfortunate action on her part led to the execution of Mary Dyer and three other Quakers.

[1] See above, pp. 210–212.

[2] Whipping, torture, and mutilation were not by any means confined to persons convicted as rogues and vagabonds. The *Maryland Archives* (Provincial Court, 1649–57, 445, 515) show that one Mary Butler, who had eloped from Virginia with Alexander King, was sentenced to receive twenty lashes upon the bare back with a whip and then be set across the Potomac and handed over to the Virginia officials; and Blanche Howell was sentenced for perjury, also in Maryland, to "stand nailed in the pillory, and lose both her ears" (*ibid.*, 1637–50, 445). "Brabling women" were ducked or sometimes towed at the stern of a boat in Virginia, while in New England men and women who scolded too much were tied to the pillory with their tongues in a cleft stick.

[3] O'Callaghan's *Laws of New Netherland*, 440.

[4] See above, p. 246.

[5] Whitmore's *Laws of 1660*, p. 156.

By 1658 the Quakers had gained a foothold in Maryland,[1] had stood covered in the presence of the magistrates, and had refused to take the engagement to the Lord Proprietor on the ground that "they were governed by God's law and the light within and not by man's law." In answer the Council directed all persons residing within the province to subscribe to the engagement or depart before a specified date "upon pain due to rebels and traitors," — namely, death. In the next year, 1659–60, the Virginia assembly grappled with the Quaker problem and provided that they should be banished under pain of being treated as felons "if they should the third time be so audacious and impudent as to return hither.[2] The master of the vessel bringing Quakers into the colony was not threatened with death, but was to be fined one hundred pounds sterling. This financial penalty seems to have been efficacious. Jefferson records that no capital executions took place in Virginia, not owing "to the moderation of the Church, or spirit of the legislature, as may be inferred from the law itself, but to historical circumstances which have not been handed down to us." [3] In 1662 the Assembly reserved the penalty of banishment for Quakers who assembled to the number of five or more and had already been twice apprehended.[4] After twelve months' absence from the regular services, however, these persons should give security for their future good behavior and prompt payment of fines or else go to prison. Furthermore, Quakers assembling for religious purposes were to pay two hundred pounds of tobacco each time they were taken; this was changed two years later to five

[1] *Maryland Archives* (Council Records, 1636–67), p. 351.

[2] Hening's *Statutes*, i, 533.

[3] Jefferson's *Notes on Virginia*, ed. of 1788, p. 167.

[4] Hening's *Statutes*, ii, 180.

hundred pounds of tobacco for the second and later offenses.[1]

The colonists looked upon the Baptists with nearly as great suspicion and fear as they regarded the Quakers. This was due in part to the fact that some persons in Germany who professed the Baptist faith had acted against social order. In 1646 the General Court of Massachusetts provided that those who condemned or opposed the baptizing of infants and continued obstinate in their opposition should be banished from the colony.[2] The Virginia Assembly in 1659 and again in 1662[3] made it penal in parents to refuse to have their children baptized.

The religious system of England contemplated the attendance of every subject of the sovereign at the services of the Established Church. Every one who failed to fulfil this requirement was fined in proportion to the persistency with which he or she refused to resort to the regular services. The Lord's Day, after the time of divine service, however, was regarded by the ecclesiastical authorities and by the royal government as designed for recreation. The average Englishman took his play seriously in those days, as well as at the present time, and was disposed to over indulgence in drink. It fell out, therefore, that Sunday afternoons and evenings often became the scenes of wild disorder. The Puritans objected to the profanation of the Lord's Day, which "precious time" (as they termed it) they thought should be given to the affairs of the soul, as the other six days of the week were devoted to material pursuits. They disliked bear-baiting, not only because it

[1] The rise of the Quakers will be treated at length in the second volume of the present work.

[2] Whitmore's *Laws of 1660*, p. 34.

[3] Hening's *Statutes*, ii, 165. The act provided a fine of two thousand pounds of tobacco for refusing to have one's child baptized by a lawful minister, of course according to the rites of the Established Church.

was torture to the beast,[1] but more especially because it ministered to the brutal instincts of the populace. Their sense of decency was outraged by the profanity about them. Coupled with the undisguised immorality which prevailed in court circles, this feeling had much to do with causing that spirit of unrest which led to the founding of New England and to the Great Rebellion.

In 1650 the Long Parliament repealed the religious laws of Elizabeth and enacted others providing that on the Lord's Day every one should resort to some public place where the service and worship of God is exercised or in some other way practice religious duty.[2] At the same time, Parliament provided suitable penalties for the desecration of the Lord's Day. In the future, for instance, any one traveling on that day, who was not engaged in some work of necessity or charity, should forfeit ten shillings, which penalty was also visited on those dancing or profanely singing in taverns, and goods which were put on sale on that day were to be forfeited.

In every colony, except Maryland and Rhode Island, the maintenance of the precise form of religion, which the civil authorities recognized, was a part of the obligation of every member of the community. In Virginia, Massachusetts, Connecticut, New Haven, and New Plymouth, every one was obliged to attend the official service on the Lord's Day under penalty of fifty pounds of tobacco for each default in Virginia and of five shillings in the New England colonies, — in this case the colonial penalty was four or five times that of England. Throughout the colonies the Lord's Day was a time of rest from labor, not only

[1] The humanity of the Puritans toward dumb animals is well set forth in the clause of the Body of Liberties, forbidding cruelty to "brute creatures which are usually kept for the use of man." *Massachusetts Laws of 1660*, 53, 144.

[2] Scobell's *Ordinances*, pt. ii, 119, 131.

in New England and Virginia, but in New Netherland as well, and in the Puritan days, at least, in Maryland. The law of New Netherland is quite exact; it was passed in 1656, and prohibited, under a suitable fine, ordinary labor on the Sabbath, hunting and fishing, and "any lower or unlawful exercise and amusement, drunkenness, frequenting taverns or tippling houses, dancing, playing ball, cards, tricktrack, tennis, cricket, or ninepins, going on pleasure parties in a boat, car, or wagon before, between, or during divine service on penalty of a double fine."[1] In Massachusetts it was felt that everything which hindered due "preparation for the Sabbath" should also be avoided, and therefore, in 1658, it was provided that on Saturday night after sundown no young people or others should take the liberty "to walk and sport themselves in the streets or fields," or frequent any house of public entertainment for the purpose of drinking under penalty of ten shillings for every such transgression or corporal punishment as the magistrate might determine; and the same rules applied to "the Lord's Day-night, after the sun is set." The appropriate officers were authorized to search taverns and houses for transgressors of this and other laws. This minute inspection was probably strict, as the fines under these laws generally went to the county. The result in the seaport towns was that would-be tipplers and other ill-disposed persons resorted to the ships at anchor in the port, which in turn made necessary further regulations. But the subject would better be left here, as the struggle between the forces of good and evil led to much legislation.

Human nature, in short, was much the same in Virginia and Massachusetts, in Maryland and Rhode Island, that it was in contemporary England. In almost any direction

[1] O'Callaghan's *Laws of New Netherland*, 211.

in which the investigator makes a comparative study, whether in the treatment of serious crime or in less grave offenses against social order and human comfort, the result is practically the same. The colonists were still Englishmen in their feelings and prejudices, in their virtues and in their vices. Contact with the wilderness and freedom from the constitutional restraints which held down Englishmen in England had not yet brought to the surface the latent elasticity of the Germanic race, had not yet resulted in making the colonists Americans. A century of exposure to colonial conditions was required to force the English in America away from the traditions and ideals of those who continued to live in the old land. The year 1660 marks an epoch in the history of the English race because the Restoration denoted the breaking down of the desire for reform in England and the intensifying of those forces which the Puritans had striven to overthrow. In colonial history it ended the first period in our annals. It saw a nation definitely planted in the New World.

INDEX